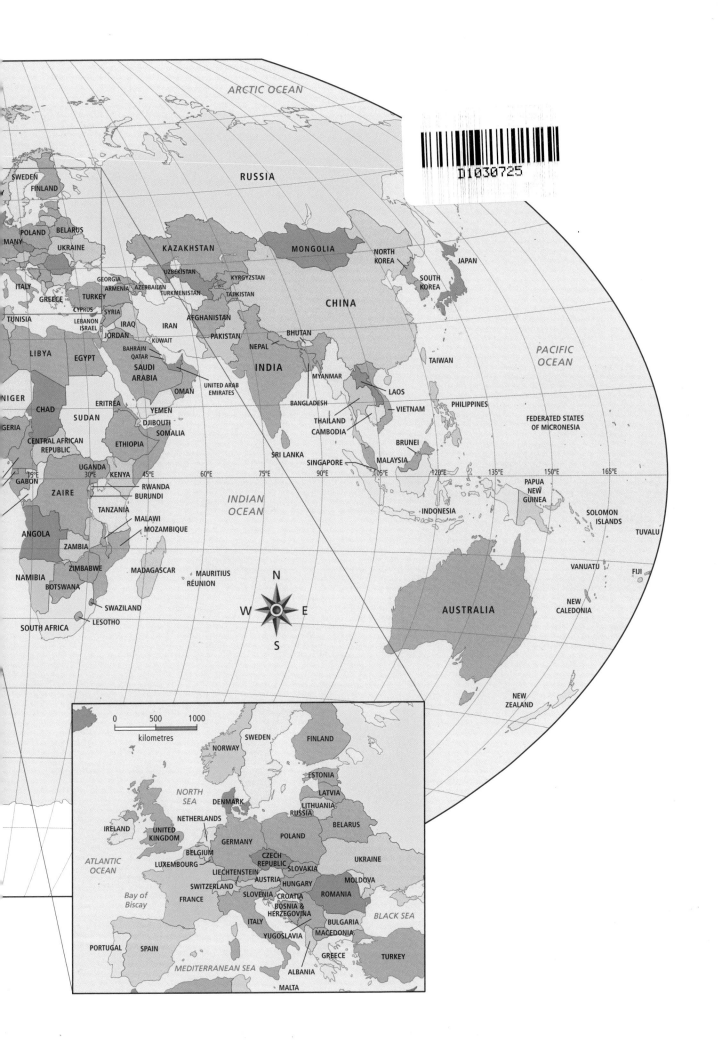

PEARSON
Human
GEOGRAPHY 8

Dennis DesRivieres

Pearson 7–8
Connected for Success

This icon appears on Pearson 7–8 classroom resources in every major discipline.
These resources incorporate skills and strategies from a common research base to
ensure a consistent approach to support ALL learners. They have embedded connections
that will save teachers time and support the improvement of content area literacy.

PEARSON

Toronto

ISBN-13 978-0-13-205381-5
ISBN-10 0-13-205381-0

Project Team
Publisher: Susan Cox
Product Manager: Aerin Guy
Managing Editor: Gaynor Fitzpatrick
Developmental Editor: Cara James
Coordinating Editor: Martha Malic
Production Editor: Ann Echlin
Proofreader: Christine Higdon
Fact Check: Christine Higdon
Editorial Support: Alisa Dewald
Index: Noeline Bridge
Production Coordinator: Sharlene Ross
Senior Manufacturing Coordinator: Jane Schell
Design: Alex Li
Composition: David Cheung
Art Coordination: Carolyn E. Sebestyen
Maps: Crowle Art Group
Technical Art: David Cheung
Illustration: Kevin Cheng, Paul Rivoche
Image Permissions: Karen Hunter
Literary Permissions: Natalie Barrington

Printed and bound in Canada
11 12 13   14 13 12

Contributing Writer
Tamar Stein

Specialist Reviewers
Dr. Ardis D. Kamra
Robert M. Leavitt
Sheila Staats / GoodMinds
Robert Morrow

Ontario Grade 8 History and Geography Reviewers
Pearson Education Canada thanks its reviewers, who
helped shape *Pearson Canadian History 8* and *Pearson
Human Geography 8* through discussions and reviews of
manuscript and proofs.

Jan Bays, Captain R. Wilson Public School, Halton
District SB

Matthew Bernstein, Cornell Village Public School,
York Region District SB

Karen Bouw, Brant Haldimand Norfolk Catholic
District SB

Tania Braganza, Coppard Glen Public School,
York Region District SB

William Branscombe, Halton District SB

Brenda Cassidy, Frontenac Public School,
Halton District SB

Marc Caterini, Mother Theresa Catholic Elementary
School, Halton Catholic District SB

Adolfo M. Diiorio, Sheridan Park School, District School
Board of Niagara

Elizabeth Ford, Lockview Public School, District School
Board of Niagara

Ryan Gibson, Queen Alexandra Middle School,
Toronto District SB

Stephen Gibson, David Leeder Middle School, Peel
District SB

Michelle Goodison, J.B. Tyrrell Sr. Public School,
Toronto District SB

Kathryn Gravill, Thornhill Woods Public School, York
Region District SB

Silvana Hoxha, Silverheights Public School, Waterloo
Region District SB

Shawna Hyland, St. Elizabeth Seton Catholic School,
Durham Catholic District SB

Lara Loseto, Walter Scott Public School, York Region
District SB

Lynn Macaulay, W.G. Davis Senior Public School,
Peel District SB

Bettina Martin, Hyland Heights Elementary School,
Upper Grand District SB

Audra Morgan, Donview Middle School,
Toronto District SB

Becky Morris, St. Matthew High School, Ottawa–Carleton
Catholic SB

Peter Nayler, Susanna Moodie E.S., Hastings and Prince
Edward District SB

Matthew A. Oldridge, Hillcrest Public School, Peel
District SB

Jette Powrie, Orchard Park Public School,
Halton District SB

Brent Reaume, A.V. Graham, Greater Essex County
District SB

Ann Marie Ricardo, Our Lady of Good Voyage Catholic
Elementary School, Dufferin–Peel Catholic District SB

Jeffrey Schaeffer, Blue Willow Public School,
York Region District SB

Barbara Stanton, St. Angela Merici, York Catholic
District SB

Caroline Thuss, St. Boniface School, Huron–Perth
Catholic District SB

Ken Venhuizen, Program Services, Learning Coordinator,
Thames Valley District SB

Brian Weigel, Williamsburg Public School, Waterloo
Region District SB

CONTENTS

UNIT 1

World Human Patterns

> How do patterns in human geography affect people around the world?

Canada's population is small compared to the size of the country. What are the advantages of this? What problems could it cause?

Some nations have large populations living in a smaller area of land. What are the benefits of a more densely concentrated population? What drawbacks can you think of?

Canada is a developed country. How does technology contribute to our standard of living?

How could standard of living be improved in countries with less advanced technology?

What's the Big Idea?

Take a look at the photographs on these pages. Human patterns set countries apart from one another. In Canada, we have no shortage of land, and many opportunities to enjoy a good standard of living. Other countries might have limited resources, or have more limited access to technology. Human patterns of population, community, development, and technology vary widely from one country to another. To help identify these patterns, geographers create maps and graphs. They also use different geographic sources to investigate and report their findings. In this unit, you will use the same methods as geographers to investigate and analyze world human patterns.

Key Terms

site, situation, rural, urbanization, developed, developing, population distribution, population density, birth rate, death rate, net migration, gross domestic product, gross national product, correlation, literacy rate, life expectancy

What You Will Learn in this Unit

- What are the main patterns of settlement and population?
- What factors affect land use?
- How can I compare population and quality of life in different places?
- How can I gather, analyze, and report information using geographic sources?
- How can I produce and interpret maps and graphs to show human patterns?
- How can I use population pyramids to predict trends in developed and developing countries?

CHAPTER 1

Recognizing Community Patterns

Rio de Janeiro, Brazil

Making Connections

List what you like about the community you live in. Create a wish list for what you think your community is missing.

Share your ideas in a small group. How might you modify your list?

WORDS MATTER

landmark a prominent object or landform, such as a hill or building, that identifies a place

Which of these two communities would you most like to visit? Rio de Janeiro, Brazil, is a huge metropolis, with a large ocean harbour, sandy beaches, and surrounding mountains. Lunenburg is a small Nova Scotia fishing town, filled with historic structures. Both communities have important **landmarks** that set them apart, making them unique.

Every community has its own distinct character, created by geography and history. Human geography is the study of the imprints people make on the face of the earth. In this chapter, you will see that places such as Rio de Janeiro and Lunenburg, although different, share important characteristics in location and land use. This will help you recognize geographic patterns in your own community. It will also support this unit's Big Idea: **How do patterns in human geography affect people around the world?**

Lunenburg, Nova Scotia

Questions to Consider as You Read this Chapter

- What are the different types of communities?

- How do site and situation influence settlement patterns?

- How can I identify different types of land use in my local community?

- What factors affect urbanization, industry, and transportation?

- How can I use maps to interpret information about patterns in human geography?

Thinking About Literacy

Identify Main Ideas to Summarize Text

In this chapter, you will read about different community patterns around the world, and the factors that influence these patterns. Identifying and recording main ideas as you read can help you find the important information in the text. Use a fishbone organizer to record the main ideas of this chapter. All of these main ideas should support the concept that "communities are different." Remember to add the details that support the main ideas. Later, you will be asked to summarize the chapter using your organizer as a guide.

How Are Communities Different?

WORDS MATTER

geography the study of the earth and people's relationship to it

rural areas sparsely settled areas

developing nation a country where most people have a lower standard of living and less access to goods and services than people in developed nations

During READING

Checkpoint

Remember to examine what you see in the picture and also question what you do not see. Consider: Who took the photo? Why? Refer to the Skills Tool Kit pages on analyzing images (pages S 12– S13).

The subject of **geography** has been around for more than two thousand years. Like geographers today, the ancient Greeks were interested in connections between people and the earth. These early geographers often compared conditions in different places and regions to gain a better understanding of the world around them. Why is making such comparisons an important theme in geography? Let's apply the focus of geography to comparing three different types of communities: rural, urban, and suburban.

Rural Settlements

Do you live in the city, in the country, or somewhere in between? **Rural areas** usually have a population of fewer than 1000 people, and include farms and small communities. There are many countries with large rural populations, particularly in the **developing nations**, where many people farm or fish to feed themselves and their families. A century ago, more than half of Canada's population was rural. The landscape was dotted with small farms, and nearby villages provided basic services. Today, Canadian farms are much larger. Many hamlets and villages have simply disappeared. Most rural people drive to the nearest large town or city to buy what they need.

Droughts, storms, floods, insects, and crop diseases can threaten farmers in all areas of the world. Some communities may also face political unrest, war, and poverty. How do these factors affect where Canadians settled in the past? In the present?

Urban Settlements

You probably live in an **urban settlement.** Eighty percent of Canadians now live in cities or towns. **Urbanization**, which is the growth of urban places, has been one of the most important changes in human geography patterns since about 1950. That year, only a little more than 25 % of the world's population was urban. By 2007, according to United Nations estimates, 50 % of the world's people lived in urban settlements.

All around the world, people are leaving rural areas and moving to urban centres in search of opportunities for a better life. Often, cities in developing nations fail to meet the hopes of these rural migrants. Rapid urban growth can also cause other types of problems in developed nations. Housing shortages, high-cost housing, and the "tent cities" of the homeless—those who live without water services or electricity—are also found in countries such as Canada.

WORDS MATTER

urban settlement a community where 1000 or more people live close together

urbanization the increase of urban areas, usually the spread of cities and large communities into rural areas

During **READING**

Checkpoint
Remember to add this information to your fishbone organzier.

WEB LINK •·············
For more information about city populations around the world, visit our Web site.

In some cities in developing nations, housing shortages are severe and conditions are very crowded. Most rural migrants cannot afford to pay for water or electricity. Unemployment rates are usually high, leaving many residents in poverty. If you were the mayor of this city, what could you do to improve the lives of these people?

Housing shortages can also affect Canadian cities. In the case of Fort McMurray, Alberta, an employment boom led to so many new arrivals that there was a shortage of housing. Hundreds of workers scrambled to find homes. Many ended up living in trailers.

WORDS MATTER

developed nation a country where there is a higher level of income, industrialization, and modernization

suburban settlement newer communities found at the edges of established cities

Suburban Settlements

Does your family have more than one car? Two-vehicle households are common in the suburbs of North America. The growth of suburbs has been a population trend in **developed nations** since about 1950. Widespread car use is both a cause and a result of urban growth and **suburban settlements**—residential areas on the outskirts of urban areas. Suburbs have grown because the car makes travel easier and more convenient. However, families often rely on their vehicles to travel to work, stores, and other activities. Increased use of cars adds to air pollution, as well as decreasing the exercise a person might get from walking or cycling to their destinations. Suburban growth can also gradually connect separate cities together.

The Greater Ottawa Area

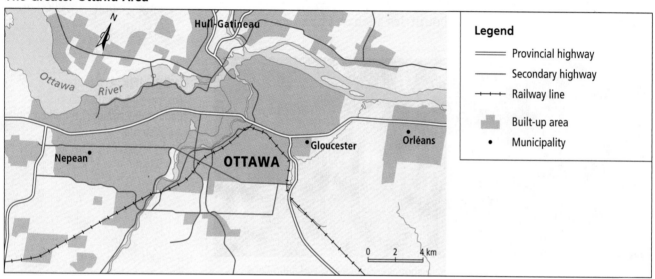

Legend

═══ Provincial highway

─── Secondary highway

┼┼┼ Railway line

▮ Built-up area

• Municipality

Which areas on the map have suburban settlement? How do you know?

WORLD RECORDS

Megalopolis, U.S.A.

Imagine an urban area with over 50 million people in it! The world's first mega-city stretches along the American east coast from Boston, Massachusetts, south to Washington, D.C. The heart of this megalopolis is New York City. Can you guess why geographers call it "Bosnywash?"

THINKING It Over

1. Use the text and table of contents to make a web that identifies examples of patterns in human geography. How does the web help you better understand the topic? *it helped me to get an idea of what is going to com*

2. a) Why are cities in the developed nations growing so fast? *the economy grew because*
   b) Why have suburbs grown so rapidly in the developed world? *there is more population*
   c) How has suburban settlement helped to create "Bosnywash?" *the people from the city moved* *more populatio*

3. Make a chart organizer to summarize the following information from the photos in this section: a) a description of the photo, b) challenges faced by the community shown.

Where Communities Locate

Would you like to visit Walt Disney World in Florida? Better still, how would you like to live there year-round? Imagine life in Celebration, a unique community planned and built by the Disney Corporation. This Orlando suburb is located near the gates of Walt Disney World, and is designed to create the neighbourly feeling of a small town. Many people who have enjoyed the theme park want to move to Celebration. To them, it is the perfect community, with an ideal **site** and **situation**.

What makes the location of Celebration, Florida, so popular? How might locations in Canada compare?

During READING

Checkpoint
You may want to reserve a section of your notebook for geography terms. It will be your own personal glossary. Try defining the terms in your own words.

What Is Situation?

In geography, situation describes the regional surroundings of a community. Favourable situation factors help explain why a community is growing and prospering. This "big picture" of location includes landforms, waterways, labour force, and highways. Communities in the same region often share the same situation factors. For example, Celebration is one of many Florida communities that enjoy a warm and sunny winter climate.

Physical Situation Factors	Human Situation Factors
• landforms	• population
• climate	• labour force
• waterways	• transportation
• natural resources	• market

Checkpoint
Find the main ideas and
supporting details in this
section. Add them to your
fishbone organizer.

What Is Site?

Every community has a site, or the exact spot where it is located. The
site has certain characteristics that attracted people to build there in
the first place, such as reasonably flat land for homes and a fresh
water supply. Aboriginal communities were often near water (lakes,
rivers, and seacoasts). In addition, there are four kinds of sites which
have favoured the growth of communities. As you read, discuss some
possible drawbacks that each site may have.

Harbour Site	Natural Resource Site
Many cities in the world have developed around natural harbours. Deep, ice-free harbours shelter boats from storms, and provide space to build docks and warehouses. Think of San Francisco, California, and Halifax, Nova Scotia.	Communities develop where natural resources are either gathered or processed, such as near mines or waterfalls. Minerals might be processed on site. Think of gold mining communities such as Kalgoorlie, Australia, and Dawson City, Yukon Territory.
Strategic Site	**Meeting Point Site**
During times of strife, people build defences and settlements at strategic sites. These places provide protection as well as control over territory. These locations are often sites where elevated land overlooks an important route. Think of Edinburgh, Scotland, and Québec City, Québec, both of which grew around a citadel placed on a hill.	Settlements develop at transportation junctions. In the past, crossroads were a favoured location to build rural schools, places of worship, and community halls. Basic commercial services soon followed. Meeting point sites could also occur along waterways. This is the case for London, England, and Thunder Bay, Ontario.

Site Factors
• natural harbour
• meeting point of transportation routes
• access to a resource
• elevated land
• flat land for building
• fresh water supply

Hamilton emerged as Canada's major steelmaking centre more than a century ago.
Using the list as a guide, what site factors can you identify in this photo? What are the
potential challenges of this location?

Map Skills and Location

An atlas includes many **thematic maps** covering different regions and themes. These include landforms, waterways, population, transportation, and other aspects of situation. Before you use an atlas to determine the situation of a place, let's review map-reading skills.

Symbols and Legends

Geographers can read maps by interpreting meaning from symbols, colours, and designs. They use map legends to identify the meaning of three types of symbols—area, line, and point.

Area Symbols	Line Symbols	Point Symbols
Colours used for larger areas such as natural features, lakes, parks, and cities	May connect places (roads, railroads, rivers) or divide them (boundaries)	Small designs used for towns, lighthouses, and other human activities

Direction and Distance

To use a map, you must understand where places are in relation to one another, and how far apart they are. The direction from one community to another is determined using compass direction. One way to describe the **relative location** of a place is to describe its direction and distance from some other place. For example, Hamilton is located southwest of Toronto, 69 kilometres by road. The **compass rose** represents the major directions pointed out by a magnetic compass. The top centre of most maps is located at north (unless it is marked differently).

A compass rose. Since Hamilton is located southwest of Toronto, what direction would you travel to go from Hamilton to Toronto?

Look for the map **scale** if you want to measure distance on a map. There are three types of scale:

- statement scale: 1 cm = 1 km means that every centimetre on the map represents one kilometre on the earth's surface

- ratio scale: 1:100 000 means that each unit on the map (for example, one centimetre) represents 100 000 of the same unit on the earth's surface (that is, 100 000 centimetres or one kilometre)

- line scale: a ruler can be placed along this type of scale to measure map distance. Look at the diagram for an example.

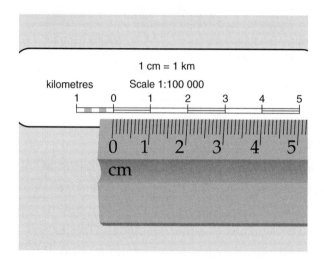

Absolute Location

The **absolute location** of a place can be found using two different systems. The easiest one is the **alphanumeric grid**, which uses lettered squares along one edge and numbered squares along the other. Another location method is **latitude and longitude**. With this system, you use the lines to find location, not the squares, as with the alphanumeric grid. This method is ideal in determining site.

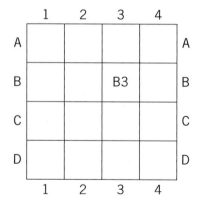

Place	Page	Grid Location	Latitude	Longitude
Rio de Janeiro, Brazil	123	E4	22° 50' S	43° 17' W
Lunenburg, Canada	72	C2	43° 23' N	64° 19' W

Pearson School Atlas, 2003

Hamilton: Situation Factors

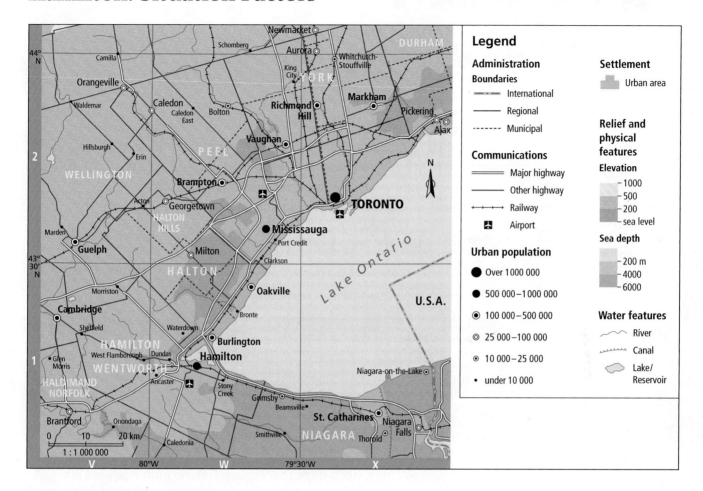

THINKING It Over

1. Identify the absolute location of Hamilton using the alphanumeric grid and approximate latitude/longitude.

2. Use compass directions to describe Hamilton's location in relation to a) Toronto, b) Niagara Falls, c) Guelph.

3. Use the map scale to measure the distance from the Hamilton airport to the centre of each of the three cities in question 2.

4. Use the map to record information about Hamilton's situation in southern Ontario:
   - Physical factors: landforms, waterways, climate, natural resources
   - Human factors: transportation, electrical energy, labour force, customers for products

GEO SKILL

Using a Topgraphic Map to Analyze Site

You used a regional map on page G 13 to interpret Hamilton's situation factors. It has a ratio scale of 1:1 000 000, a view from above that you might see from a high-altitude jet. The map on the next page is 1:250 000 in scale. This view is much closer to the earth, like the view from a helicopter. This is a **topographic map**, ideal for analyzing a city site.

WORDS MATTER

topographic map a very detailed map showing physical and human features through the use of contour lines and other symbols

Step 1 Identify Physical Symbols and Patterns

Physical features are shown in the colours most common in nature: brown, green, black, and blue.

Area colours	Line symbols	Point symbols
body of water	— elevation contour	∴ sand
forest	~ stream	

Look closely at the map on the next page. What do the tightly bunched brown contour lines forming a pattern around Hamilton Harbour indicate? The main part of the city is located below these cliffs, which are part of the Niagara Escarpment, a steep ridge that crosses Ontario from Niagara Falls to Manitoulin Island.

Step 2 Identify Human Symbols and Patterns

Pink, red, and black are the colours commonly used for human features on topographic maps.

Area colours	Line symbols	Point symbols
built-up area	⊨403⊨ divided highway	⊙ Com 333 communiation tower
	___ secondary highway or major street	⊙42 chimney

Examine the map. How have major transportation routes been affected by the Niagara Escarpment in the Hamilton area?

Analyze the Site

Use the map symbols to identify physical and human features.
What makes this an ideal city site? What are the possible limitations?
Explain.

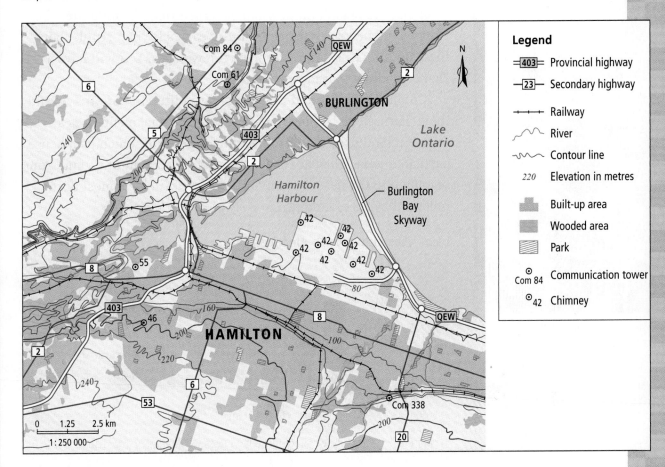

APPLY It

1. Use the physical symbols to list and briefly explain site factors for Hamilton. 📕

2. Use the human symbols in the same way. 📕

3. Find the location of the photograph from page G 10 on this map. How can you tell? Why are the steel mills located here? 📕

4. Make a simple sketch map of the Hamilton area. On it, draw and label the city site factors you identified in the preceding questions. 📕

Patterns Inside Communities

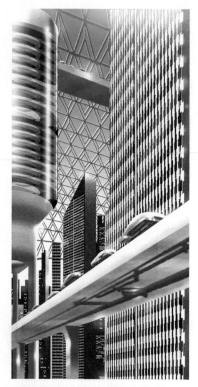

What factors might affect city planning in the future?

WORDS MATTER

land use the purpose for which people use a particular area

During **READING**

Checkpoint

Refer back to the wish list you created at the beginning of this chapter. Do you have new information that might change your list?

Imagine that you could design the perfect community. How would it be different from the place where you live now? What sorts of attractions and services would be available? How would people get from place to place, and how much "green space" would there be? How would people in the community earn a living? Think about these questions as you read the next few pages. You will have a chance to draw that ideal community.

Communities around the world have different patterns within them. Farm fields, homes, a park, or commercial businesses are all different land uses. **Land use** is the purpose for which people use a particular area. The patterns differ within a community, and from one town to the next. But any urban place will have most of the following types of land uses.

Land Uses in the North American City

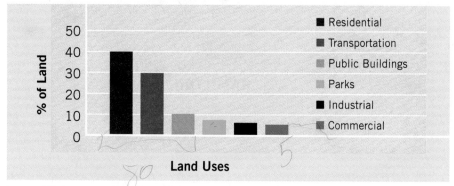

In your ideal community, which of these land uses would take up more space? Which would use less space?

Simplified Land Use Pattern

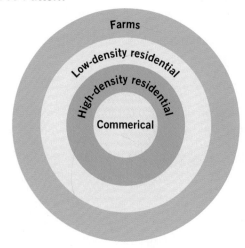

Where do you think industries would most often be located in this diagram? Where would you put parks and open space?

Check Your Neighbourhood

Look close to home to learn about land use patterns. In a rural area, there may be agricultural land all around you. In an older urban centre, streets may be laid out in a grid pattern of straight lines, with stores and services at major intersections and along **traffic arteries**. Schools and places of worship are likely in these locations too. There may not be much parkland or open space, unless the older neighbourhood is near a river valley or a shoreline. Older urban areas usually grew without much planning.

Land use patterns are different if your home is in a newer suburban area. Residences there are often located on quiet crescents and courts to reduce local traffic, while the whole area is designed around schools and parkland. Curving streets that lead into the neighbourhood connect it with local shopping centres and other services. The land use patterns here didn't just happen—they were planned before anything was built. Community planning in Canada has only happened in the last sixty years.

In Canada, land use is controlled. **Urban planners** prepare a land use map showing uses for different areas. When the land use map is approved by the local government it becomes law, called the Official Plan. Only land uses which conform to the Offical Plan are permitted in each part of the community.

Urban planners also plan for people's needs. Wheelchair users, for example, need ramps and wider sidewalks to make public spaces accessible.

WEB LINK • • • • • • • • • • • • • • • •
Discover the community patterns of Toronto using an interactive map. Visit our Web site.

Land Use Patterns

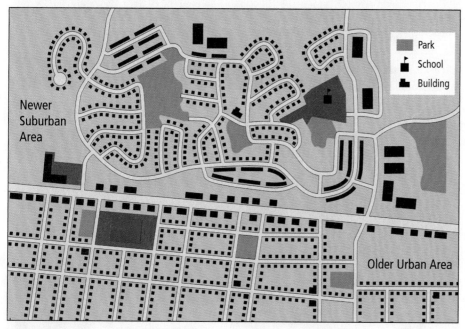

Park
School
Building

Newer Suburban Area

Older Urban Area

How do land use and street patterns differ in the older and newer parts of a community?

Community Land Uses

Residential

Communities often include different types of residential land use. They can range from detached houses on big estate lots to linked homes or high-rise apartments. Apartment buildings are often located along major streets with good access to stores and public transportation. What types of residential land use are found near your home?

Transportation

Streets, highways, and parking lots cover nearly one-third of the space in a typical North American city. People and products continually flow along transportation systems. Highways, railways, and water routes carry raw materials and finished products between manufacturers and customers. What are the main transportation routes near your home?

Institutional

There are many different types of public buildings in a community including schools, hospitals, religious centres, libraries, public arenas, and government offices. Often, the largest institutions are located in or near the downtown area. Many public buildings, such as schools and places of worship, are scattered throughout the community, to better serve the public. Which institutional land uses are located near your home?

Parks and Open Space

Residential land uses are often close to parks and open space. Urban planners also use parkland to screen residential areas from the noise of traffic or industry. Parkland along trails and streams may divide one urban neighbourhood from another. How far is your home from open space?

Industrial

Industrial land uses bring business into the community and create jobs. They often cover large areas of land close to important transportation routes. Older industries may be located near the centre of the community, along waterways or railroads. New clusters of manufacturing and warehousing businesses, called industrial parks, are usually built along major highways on the outer edge of town. Where are the industrial areas in your community?

Commercial

Most places have a central business district located in the middle of the community. Some communities have thriving downtown areas, while others are dying out because of competition from shopping malls and "big box" stores in the suburbs. Like industrial parks, these commercial areas use up large amounts of land. How far do you live from the nearest large shopping centre?

Planning "Greener" Communities

How can communities become more **sustainable**? "Greener" places in which to live can use clean alternative energy sources and extensive public transportation systems. They could have more efficient garbage disposal and recycling, and feature natural areas. Should care for the environment be part of community planning? How might a small community deal with environmental concerns *and* new economic opportunities?

Make a "greener communities" web chart. Share knowledge or do research to add details or examples for each topic.

WEB LINK • • • • • • • • • • • • • • • • • • •

For more information on sustainable cities, visit our Web site.

WORDS MATTER

sustainable the use of resources at a rate which meets the needs of the present generation but also ensures plenty for future generations

Communities Change

The photos on the previous pages show some important changes taking place within communities. Green space is now used to separate land uses such as industry and homes. More industries locate on the urban edge than in the city centre, and many downtown businesses struggle to survive against suburban mall competition.

Changes also take place in rural communities due to the growth of "cottage country" or economic development. The diagram below shows factors that create change in communities. Are any of these factors changing land use in your community? Which types of change are shown in the news story below?

Types of Change

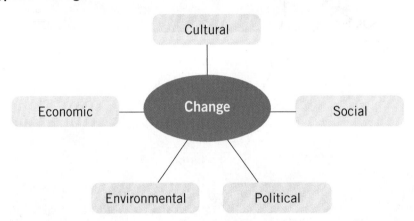

City's Downtown Population Surges

October 26, 2007
John Spears *Toronto Star*

The explosion of high-rise condominiums in Toronto's downtown isn't an illusion. The population of the downtown core has grown by 65 percent in the past 30 years, and nearly 10 percent in the past five.

That makes downtown Toronto one of the fastest-growing communities in Greater Toronto, says a new report by the city's planning staff.

And the newer residents are wealthier, better educated, and less likely to have children than their downtown neighbours.

"Downtown may be the fastest-growing area of the city, but it's not sucking the life out of other neighbourhoods," said Barbara Leonhardt, director of policy and research in the planning department. "We're seeing growth in other areas as well—all the areas where we want to see it happen: the North York centre, the Scarborough centre, the Etobicoke centre and along the avenues."

A photo of Rio de Janeiro, Brazil, appeared at the beginning of this chapter. Like some cities in developing countries, its land use patterns are quite different from those of Canadian cities. Large urban places in Latin America, Asia, and Africa have experienced tremendous migration from rural areas. Migrant newcomers are not always supported, and the cities can be encircled by large slums where there is high unemployment and few basic services. By contrast, the outlying suburbs in North American cities are usually well-planned neighbourhoods with services such as garbage collection, sewers, water, and electricity. Most people commute to work.

Latin America has some of the largest cities in the world. There is great contrast between the wealth in the city centre and the poverty in the outer edges. Most of the commercial activity and employment in Mexico City, São Paulo, Buenos Aires, and Rio de Janeiro is found downtown. Many tall office buildings and luxury apartments are also downtown, surrounded by high-quality housing. Between these homes and the outer slums is a middle zone, where people who came to the city years before are gradually improving their homes.

Five Biggest Cities, 2005 (Population in millions)	
1. Tokyo, Japan	35.2
2. Mexico City, Mexico	19.4
3. New York, USA	18.7
4. São Paulo, Brazil	18.3
5. Mumbai, India	18.2
– Buenos Aires, Argentina	12.6
– Rio de Janeiro, Brazil	11.5

THINKING It Over

1. Describe your neighbourhood street and land use patterns. Are they rural, urban, or suburban? Explain. 🔵 🔵

2. How do cultural, environmental, and political changes affect your community, or another location in this section? Do more research if necessary. 🔵

3. Use a chart organizer to compare city land use patterns in Canada and Latin America as follows: a) the city centre, b) the outer edges, c) the zone in between. 🔵 🔵

4. Draw a map or a diagram to show your ideal community or neighbourhood. Include at least four different land uses, as shown in the photos on pages G 18 and G 19. 🔵 🔵

PUTTING IT ALL TOGETHER

You have seen that many community patterns are different around the world. Rural, urban, and suburban places each have their own characteristics and problems in both developed and developing countries. You learned that all communities form at a location that offers certain advantages of site and situation. You also saw that inside each community there are different land use patterns that make each place unique. These patterns continually change for a variety of reasons. Finally, you learned that land use patterns in developing countries can be different from those in developed countries such as Canada. This information helped you in your study of the unit's Big Idea: **How do patterns in human geography affect people around the world?**

After READING

Use the Main Ideas to Summarize the Text

When you summarize a text, you should show the important ideas and information. In this chapter, you studied the differences between communities. Now summarize the information in the chapter by using your fishbone organizer. How do the main ideas relate to the concept that "communities are different?" What details support the main ideas? Create your summary by writing a short paragraph in your own words. All of the main ideas on the fishbone should be included in the summary.

THINKING It Through

1. Describe Québec City's location on the map of eastern Canada on the opposite page. Where is it situated in relation to waterways and human transportation? Is Québec City well situated for trade and shipping? Why or why not? Explain. **k m a**

2. Examine the close-up map of Québec City. Use map evidence to prove that the city developed as a) a harbour site, b) a meeting point site, and c) a strategic site. **k m a**

3. a) Imagine that a magnetic compass sits in the centre of the close-up map. Use the eight directions of the compass and the term "middle" to describe locations for these land uses in Québec City: i) parks and open space, ii) industrial, and iii) central business district. Explain your reasons by using map evidence. **k m a**

   b) Name three different examples of institutional land uses you can read from the map of Québec City. **k m a**

Québec City: Situation Factors

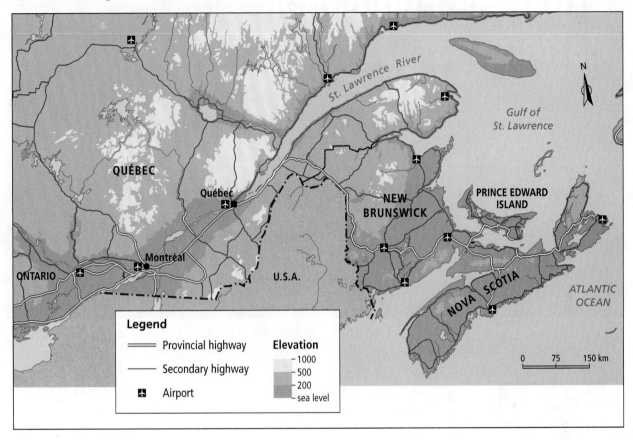

St. Lawrence River

Gulf of St. Lawrence

QUÉBEC

Québec

NEW BRUNSWICK

PRINCE EDWARD ISLAND

Montréal

ONTARIO

U.S.A.

NOVA SCOTIA

ATLANTIC OCEAN

N

Legend
- ═══ Provincial highway
- ─── Secondary highway
- ✈ Airport

Elevation
- 1000
- 500
- 200
- sea level

0   75   150 km

Québec City: Site Factors

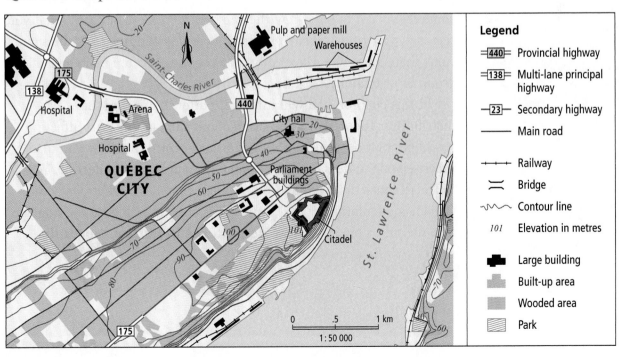

Saint-Charles River

Pulp and paper mill

Warehouses

175

138

Hospital

Arena

440

City hall

20

30

Hospital

QUÉBEC CITY

Parliament buildings

40

50

60

100

101

Citadel

70

90

80

St. Lawrence River

60

70

N

175

0   .5   1 km

1 : 50 000

Legend
- ═440═ Provincial highway
- ═138═ Multi-lane principal highway
- ─23─ Secondary highway
- ─── Main road
- ╫╫╫ Railway
- ═ Bridge
- ∿∿∿ Contour line
- *101* Elevation in metres
- ◼ Large building
- Built-up area
- Wooded area
- Park

CHAPTER 2

Exploring Population Patterns

Thousands of people enjoy a sporting event in England

Before READING

Making Connections

Think about your neighbourhood. Where are most homes located? Why is this? Now, look at a population map of Canada. Using your knowledge of physical geography, predict why you think certain areas have larger communities.

People are complex social animals. They can live, work, and play in big crowds, but they need some privacy and quiet too. Are you a person who likes the excitement and commotion of busy places or big events, or would you rather take a quiet walk? Do you prefer living, working, and playing in large or small groups? There are some regions of the world with such great numbers of people that you regularly find yourself surrounded by crowds and noise. At the same time, there are regions so empty that you would often be in a small group or even alone.

In this chapter, you will interpret patterns of population distribution and density, and learn about the main factors affecting world population trends. A strategic card game will allow you to practise your understanding of population growth and decline. You will also construct a population pyramid to make predictions about Canada's population in the future. This chapter will give you insight into the unit's big idea: **How do patterns in human geography affect people around the world?**

Gardens can offer space for quiet reflection.

Questions to Consider as You Read this Chapter

- What do linear, scattered, and clustered settlement patterns tell about population and land use?

- What factors can I use to compare places with high and low population densities?

- What are the main factors affecting population distribution?

- How can I predict job skills that will be needed as Canada's population grows?

- How can I construct population pyramids to predict population trends?

Thinking About Literacy

Reading Graphs

At the end of this chapter you will be asked to create a population pyramid. A population pyramid is a type of graph that shows information about age groups of people in a country. As you go through this chapter, you will see different types of graphs used to study and present geographical information. You can read more about graphs in the Skills Tool Kit, page S 16.

While you read: Add to the following chart for each graph you find in this chapter.

Page #	Graph/Type	Notes

Population Distribution and Density

Rate your views on each population issue below using a scale from 1 to 5, as shown in the margin. Record your answers by letter and number in your notebook. Afterward, compare your views with others.

1 Agree strongly
2 Agree somewhat
3 Unsure or no opinion
4 Disagree somewhat
5 Disagree strongly

a) A small community is the ideal place to live.

b) The population of our community is too large.

c) A country with a large population is more important in the world.

d) At 33 million, Canada already has enough people.

e) The earth has the resources to support a larger population.

f) At 6.6 billion, our world is dangerously overpopulated.

Canada had 1/200th of the world population in 2007.

There are no right or wrong answers to these questions. For example, the earth does have abundant natural resources, but there are two basic problems—many people badly misuse these resources, and each person in a developed country like Canada uses a much greater share than someone in a developing country such as Nigeria. You will learn more about this imbalance in Chapter 3.

WEB LINK •••••••••••••••••••••
To study maps of Canada's population, visit our Web site.

Type of Place	Typical Population	Examples	Population (2006)
hamlet	Fewer than 200	Scandia, AB Ballymote, ON	137 100
village	200–1000	Saint-Célestin, QC Burk's Falls, ON	762 893
town	1000–10 000	Lillooet, BC Smooth Rock Falls, ON	2324 1473
small city	10 000–50 000	Moose Jaw, SK Kenora, ON	32 132 15 177
city	50 000–100 000	Red Deer, AB Sault Ste. Marie, ON	82 772 74 948
metropolitan area	More than 100 000	Halifax, NS Ottawa, ON	372 858 812 129

Which type of community do you live in? How might this have affected your answers to the questionnaire at the top of the page?

Population Distribution

Rural, urban, and suburban communities would look different if you saw them on a **dot distribution map**. This type of map uses dots to show the spread of population. Each dot represents a certain number of people. For example, in the maps on these pages, one dot represents 200 people. Larger populations mean a greater concentration of dots. The arrangement of dots may form a pattern following a natural or human feature, such as a shoreline or a highway. Geographers use dot distribution maps to identify three **population distribution** patterns: scattered, clustered, and linear.

Scattered Population

Picture this TV commercial. A man struggles through Canada's treeless northern tundra. He finally reaches an isolated store, only to find that his favourite soft drink is not sold there. Disappointed, he begins to search for another place that sells his brand.

He will not find another store soon, because people are far apart in the North. **Scattered population** occurs where resources are limited and can support only small numbers of people. Australia's interior is mostly dry desert, where people may work on isolated ranches or in mining towns. The settlement pattern of northern Canada is similar, but for different reasons. Cold conditions and rocky terrain have resulted in a scattered pattern of settlement, based on hunting, mining, and support services. Aboriginal populations in the past also followed this population pattern.

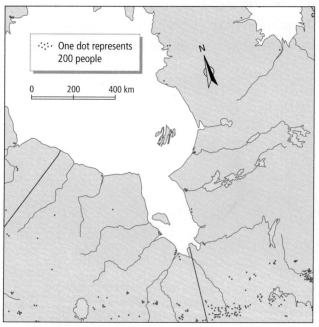

Scattered Population
Use a map of Canada to find the area shown here. Then, suggest two reasons why this region has a scattered population.

WORDS MATTER

dot distribution map a map that uses dots to show population

population distribution the pattern of where people live

scattered population a population distribution in which there are few people in a large area. Vast areas with scattered resources can produce a scattered population pattern.

During READING

Checkpoint
Imagining a picture in your mind is called visualization. Good readers visualize whenever they read.

Our Environment

Fragile Environments
Regions with widely scattered populations often have fragile environments easily affected by human activity. Permanently frozen ground called permafrost underlies large areas of northern Canada. Global climate change is melting the upper layers of the permafrost zone, causing buildings and roads to sink and collapse.

Use information on climate change in Canada to make a flow chart showing the effects of climate change on the arctic environment.

Clustered Population

WORDS MATTER

clustered population a population distribution in which many people live in a small area of closely spaced houses or communities

census metropolitan area an urban area with a population of at least 100 000

Clustered Population

Clustered population patterns form when many people settle together in a relatively small area. This may happen where there is a favourable climate, rich natural resources, and major transportation routes. These situation advantages draw people and industry. There are 27 **census metropolitan areas** in Canada, from Victoria, British Columbia, to St. John's, Newfoundland and Labrador. Metropolitan Toronto is the largest, with 5 406 300 people (2006).

During **READING**

Checkpoint

Connect the word **linear** to your math vocabulary: linear means *line*.

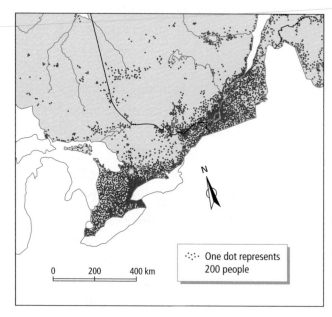

0   200   400 km

⁘ One dot represents 200 people

Clustered Population
Use a map of Canada to find the area shown here. Suggest two reasons why this region has a clustered population.

WORDS MATTER

linear population a population distribution which is arranged in a narrow line, perhaps along a road, river, or valley

Linear Population

A **linear population** pattern occurs where natural and human-made routes cause settlement to be arranged in a line. Rivers such as the St. Lawrence in Canada and the Nile in Egypt have communities along their banks. These settlements probably developed when the

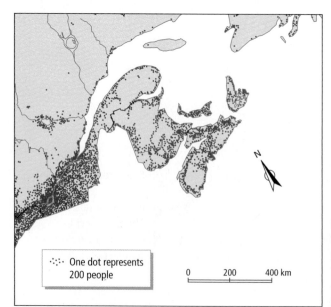

⁘ One dot represents 200 people

0   200   400 km

Linear Population
Use a map of Canada to find the area shown here. Then, suggest two reasons why this region has a linear population.

rivers were the main transportation routes. When railways were built across the Canadian West, stations were built at intervals along the lines. Communities developed at most of these places because the trains stopped there for passengers and grain shipments.

World Population Densities

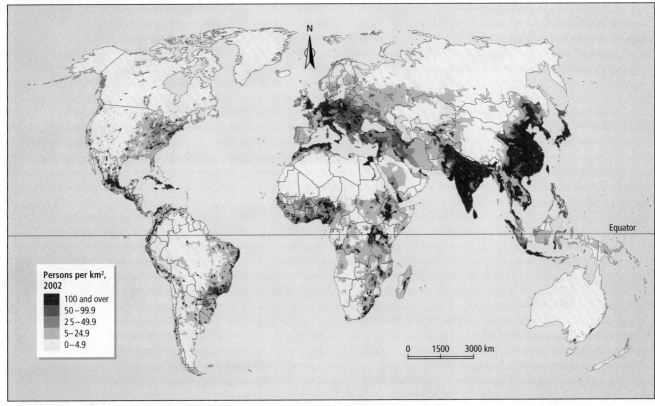

How does Canada's population distribution and density compare to other areas of the world? What factors can help explain this?

Population Density

Population density is a measure of how many people occupy an area of land. Your classroom has an area of about 100 m². When just one person is in the classroom, the population density of the room is 1 person per 100 m². This is the same as 10 000 people per km².

Bangladesh, in Asia, has about 1100 people per km², one of the highest densities in the world. Each person in Bangladesh has less space than one small school—just 9 classrooms. The small Asian territory of Macau has an amazing density of 16 205 people per km². Each person there has only as much space as about half of your classroom.

In contrast, Canada's population density is only about 3 people per km², one of the world's lowest. That is like having one person wandering through 3000 empty classrooms!

Formula for Population Density

$$\frac{\text{Population}}{\text{Area in km}^2} = \frac{\text{people}}{\text{per km}^2}$$

WORDS MATTER

population density number of people occupying a certain area, calculated using the formula above

**High Density: India
(Above 150 people per km²)**

Area: 3 287 263 km²

Population: 1 134 403 000

Density: 345 people per km²

Urban centres in India are densely populated. Millions have left rural areas and added to the soaring populations of cities such as Mumbai, Kolkata, or Delhi. High population density means that many farms are too small to allow rural families to achieve a decent standard of living.

**Moderate Density: Egypt
(Between 50 to 150 people per km²)**

Area: 1 000 250 km²

Population: 72 850 000

Density: 73 people per km²

Deserts cover large areas of Egypt, so the population is not evenly distributed. Instead, it is concentrated in the valley and the delta of the Nile River. The community shown here, Port Ghalib, is on the Red Sea. The cities of Cairo and Alexandria are very densely populated compared to isolated desert communities.

**Low Density: Australia
(Below 50 people per km²)**

Area: 7 682 300 km²

Population: 20 310 000

Density: 2.6 people per km²

Vast areas of Australia's interior desert are completely uninhabited or support only tiny populations. Most of the north is tropical rain forest where few people live. Australians largely occupy only the eastern edge and the southeastern and southwestern corners of the continent. Five cities alone hold half of Australia's total population.

How Is Population Density Used?

The profiles of Egypt and Australia have shown you how uneven population density can be. Even relatively empty Australia is crowded along the beautiful beaches of its famous "Gold Coast." Dividing a country's population by its area gives a very general picture. However, density is useful when comparing countries to one another. Population densities of regions and cities help governments plan hospitals and other services where they are needed most.

Macau: The Highest Population Density

Area: 28.2 km^2

Population: 456 989

Density: 16 205 people per km^2

Macau is located on the coast of China. It is almost entirely urban; most food, water and energy must be imported. Tourism and manufacturing pay for these necessities. However, Macau is changing as it works to reclaim land from the sea.

Country	Area (km^2)	Population (2005)	Population Density
Afghanistan	652 225	25 067 000	38.4 low
Albania	28 748	3 154 000	109.7 mo
Algeria	2 381 741	32 854 000	13.7 low
Angola	1 246 700	16 095 000	12.9 low
Argentina	2 766 889	38 747 000	14.0 low
Australia	7 682 300	20 310 000	2.6 low
Austria	83 855	8 292 000	98.8 mo
Azerbaijan	86 600	8 352 000	96. mo.
Bahamas	13 939	323 000	23.17 low
Bahrain	691	725 000	

$$\frac{\text{population}}{\text{area in km}^2} = \text{people per km}^2$$

1049.2 high.

THINKING It Over

1. Use a provincial road map to locate examples and record the population of a hamlet, village, town, small city, city, and metropolitan area. Who might need to know this information? Explain.

2. Which type of settlement pattern does the region around your community have: scattered, linear or clustered? Using a map, suggest three reasons why this type of pattern is found in your area. Find a region in another country that has a similar pattern. Why are the patterns similar?

3. Construct a chart organizer for India, Egypt, Australia, and Macau. Include facts about population, distribution, and density. Use this information to assess and justify which location you would prefer to live in.

4. Calculate the population densities from the table above, and classify them as high, moderate, or low. Locate and label these places and the others from this section on a world map. Use three different colours to represent low, moderate, and high population density.

What Factors Affect Population?

You have seen that patterns of population distribution and density differ from place to place. In this section, you will explore five factors that combine to explain why some regions have more people than others.

During READING

Checkpoint
Look back at the predictions you made in the Before Reading exercise on page G 24. Assess your ideas as you go through this section.

Population Factors

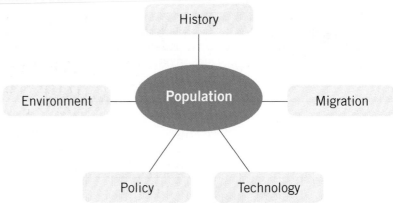

Most Favourable Environments
• fertile agricultural land
• abundant natural resources
• water: coastlines and rivers
• city sites: meeting points, natural harbours

Least Favourable Environments
• mountains and infertile soils
• scarce natural resources
• extreme climate conditions: desert, polar
• isolated locations: continental interior

Environment and History

The environment may shape human choices, but it does not rule them. People are inventive and can use technology to overcome obstacles. For example, air conditioning has supported a population explosion in hot and humid Florida. Technology such as sleds and weapons also allowed the Inuit to populate the North. There are certain locations that are more attractive to people because they offer features such as a mild climate, fertile soil, fresh water, and natural transportation routes. That is where people are found in greatest numbers.

Historically, populations first expanded where agricultural civilizations prospered. Ancient empires in the Middle East, India, and China were established on fertile soils that could produce food. Great cities grew there at a time when many other regions still relied on hunting and gathering. In 680 BCE, China already had about 12 million people, a number which has multiplied more than 100 times since then. In fact, China and India have populations of over a billion; together the two countries have more than one-third of the world's population. How do you think these large populations affect the agriculture industry of the world today?

Migration

Throughout history, people have moved in search of a better life. Much of Canada's early European population chose to come here from France and Britain.

Immigration is the act of coming into a new country as a permanent resident. **Emigration** means leaving a home country to take up permanent residence elsewhere. An emigrant could be a Canadian actor moving to the United States in search of a big break. It could be someone coming to Canada for a few years, then returning to his or her homeland. **Net migration** measures the real effect of migration on population. A positive net migration means that more people moved into the country than the number who left in the same year. Comparisons between countries use a calculation called "net migration per 1000 population." This makes it easy to compare countries with high and low population density. Below is an example using data from 2005. How might migration have an effect on the populations already present in the destination country?

WORDS MATTER

immigration the arrival of people into an area or country to live

emigration the departure of people from an area or country to live elsewhere

net migration the effect of migration on the population of a region or country

Immigration
– Emigration

Net Migration

Country	Immigration	Emigration	Net Migration	Net Migration Per 1000 Population
Australia (population 20 310 000)	131 593	67 853	63 740	3.91

Technology and Policy

Technology can affect population by allowing people to make environments more livable. For example, irrigation systems in the California desert allow dry but fertile soil to produce crops. Technologies also influence human life and death, directly affecting population.

WEB LINK •••••••••••••••••••••
Check a map of world migration on our Web site.

Natural Increase

The **birth rate** is the number of babies born each year for every 1000 people, while the **death rate** measures deaths per 1000 people. These rates can change due to catastrophes such as flood or war, but technology also has a great effect. Modern medicine, hospitals, and the reduction of disease have helped newborns survive and the elderly live longer. **Natural increase** uses birth rate and death rate to measure a country's actual growth.

WORDS MATTER

birth rate the number of births per 1000 people per year

death rate the number of deaths per 1000 people per year

natural increase the birth rate minus the death rate

China, Natural Increase, 1950–2005

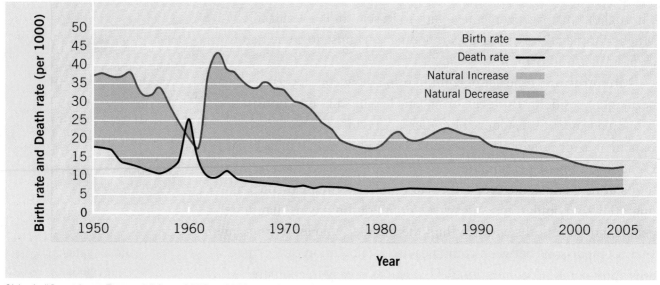

China's "Great Leap Forward," from 1958 to 1960, emphasized heavy industry at the expense of agriculture. How do you think this government policy affected population patterns?

Birth rate
− Death rate
―――――――――
Natural increase

Natural increase
+ Net migration
―――――――――
Population change

Government policies can also affect population, as in the case of China's "Great Leap Forward." China also created the One Child Policy. This policy was introduced in 1979 to limit the pressure of population increases on society. The policy continues today; couples are permitted only one child. Having a second child will result in heavy fines. China's rate of natural increase has dropped, but the One Child Policy has also had negative effects, including child abandonment. What could be the long-term effects of this policy—both positive and negative?

THINKING It Over

1. Calculate the overall population change in 2005 for these countries.

Country	Birth Rate per 1000	Death Rate per 1000	Net Migration per 1000
Canada	10.8	7.7	5.9
Mexico	21.0	4.7	−4.6
Mali	49.6	16.5	−6.3
Russia	9.8	14.5	1.0

2. Use a world map or an atlas to identify environmental characteristics of regions with high and low population density (as shown on the map on page G 29 of this chapter). Organize your findings in chart form using "High Density Regions" and "Low Density Regions" as headings.

China's One Child Policy has helped reduce the problems created by overpopulation, including strains on the health care system and on the environment. An earlier campaign used by the Chinese government during the 1970s encouraged couples to wait to have children, and to have more time between them. Together, these policies have succeeded in preventing China's population from reaching a staggering two billion. However, the One Child Policy does raise important questions about personal freedoms. State-run orphanages care for many thousands of abandoned children, the great majority of them girls. While thousands are adopted by Chinese or international families each year, many more grow up in the institutions.

In January of 2002, Mike and Sherri Boyd travelled to China to adopt a 10-month-old baby girl.

Sherri: We first met Jade in the restaurant at the hotel in Changsha, the capital city of Hunan Province. Other international families were staying there too. When the babies and their nannies arrived, the room was full of happy families meeting their daughters for the first time.

Mike: We were told that Jade had been abandoned at a street market and found when she was one day old. She was taken to the police station, and then to an orphanage. An adoption agency in Canada organized everything. A social worker did a home study and interview to see if we would be suitable.

The information went to China and we waited for 13 months until we heard that we could adopt.

Sherri: We know that Jade was cared for while she was in China. Her birth family must wonder how she is and what became of her. We love her so much and wish we could share with them what she is doing every day.

Jade and her family today

THINKING It Over

1. Write down four questions you would like to ask if you could meet the Boyds. Direct some questions to Jade. ⓣ

2. Write a paragraph weighing the pros and cons of China's One Child Policy. Discuss your conclusions about it in a small group. ⓒ

3. What effects could the policy have on rural communities in China? On city communities? ⓚ ⓣ

Day 1   **Day 14**

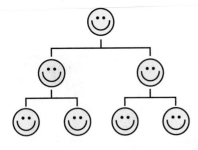

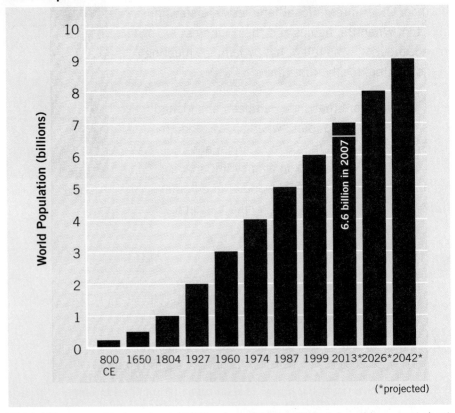

One day, thirteen-year-old Kwame offered to help more around the house. He asked for just a penny per day, to be doubled each day that he did a good job. His family laughed at Kwame's idea, but after two weeks they didn't find it so funny anymore. By then, he was asking for more than $80 per day for his chores!

Population can multiply in the same way. For example, a large family can develop if a couple has two children and those children each have two children. By the time they reach their sixties, the couple will have two children and four grandchildren—six descendants. Of course, this describes only the birth rate. In reality, the death rate puts a natural check on population growth. In this section, you will see that world population has increased dramatically in the past two centuries. While natural increase rates are low today in developed countries, they remain much higher in most of the developing countries.

In 2007, the population of the world reached 6.6 billion people. Only two centuries ago, the world population was a mere one billion! Look at the graph below. Compare the milestone years for each billion to get a sense of how fast global population has multiplied.

During READING

Checkpoint
Remember to add to your organizer while reading this graph.

World Population

World Population (billions)

| 10 |
| 9 |
| 8 |
| 7 |
| 6 |
| 5 |
| 4 |
| 3 |
| 2 |
| 1 |
| 0 |

6.6 billion in 2007

800 CE 1650 1804 1927 1960 1974 1987 1999 2013* 2026* 2042*

(*projected)

Which billion was added most quickly? How long did it take? What does this suggest about the growth rate since then?

The Population Boom

What happened to cause world population to grow so fast? To understand this, you must consider the **technological revolutions** that improved life and lowered death rates.

Three Revolutions

A revolution is a period of rapid change. Some are sudden political movements, while others are far-reaching technological changes. The revolutions in the chart below have caused great changes in world population. All three resulted in a sharp decline in death rates in Europe, where the revolutions first took place. From the early 1700s on, people began to migrate by the millions, especially to North and South America and Australia. Since 1850, the birth rate gradually fell in most countries as the **infant mortality rate** dropped due to advances in medicine. People could choose to have fewer children, as it was more likely that the children they did have would live to adulthood.

WORDS MATTER

technological revolution sweeping changes brought about by new technology

infant mortality rate the rate of death for infants less than one year old

WEB LINK ••••••••••••••••••••
Study world population information on our Web site.

Time Period	Revolution	Description
1650–1800	Agricultural	Changes in animal breeding, crop rotation, and the use of simple farm machinery to increase food production
1750–1900	Industrial	Inventions such as steam-powered machinery used to produce large quantities of factory-made goods
1850–2000	Scientific (modern)	Scientific advances in chemistry, medicine and medical practices, public health knowledge, and food

In the Developing Countries

After the Second World War, the benefits of the revolutions spread. The United Nations, governments in developed countries, and the Red Cross began a movement to fight disease and lower the infant mortality rate. Death rates in the developing countries fell very quickly between 1950 and 1980, while birth rates remained high. On the graph you can see that birth rates fell too, but not until about 20 years later. Eventually people realized that families were becoming larger because of the sharp decrease in infant mortality. Meanwhile, some countries had already doubled their populations.

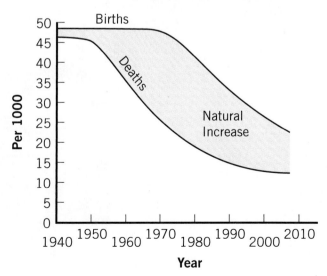

Typical Population Growth in Developing Countries since 1950

When did the death rate in developing countries begin to fall? Why?

Effects of the Population Boom

Changes in world population can have both global and local effects. How do you think the changes illustrated here might affect you and your future? What job skills might be in demand in Canada in the future because of changes in population?

People born during the 1945–1964 "baby boom" are the largest age group in most developed countries. As they grew up, their purchases of music, clothing, cars, and homes helped drive economic growth. As they grow older, they introduce greater numbers into the health care system. How can health care systems respond to such growth?

The population boom affects natural areas such as rain forests, which are home to two-thirds of the planet's animal and plant species. Many rain forest plants are being studied as the source of new medicines. However, about half the area of these forests has been cleared since 1950. The Brazilian government encourages settlement of the Amazon rain forest. How can the rain forests be saved if populations continue to grow?

The population boom has put great pressure on food supply, especially in drier environments such as northern and southern Africa. Here, the ability of the land to feed the people (called carrying capacity) has been exceeded. War, natural disaster, climate change—any threat to food production—can soon cause famine and death. How should the world respond to such crises?

Predicting Population Change

The map below shows different rates of change in world population by continent. The small graph indicates an overall trend—a projected decrease in the *rate* of world population growth. The rate rose in the early 1960s due to a drop in the death rate. But since then, population birth rates have also dropped. Why do you think experts expect this trend to continue?

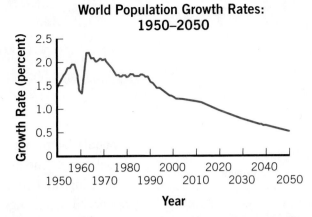

World Population Growth Rates: 1950–2050

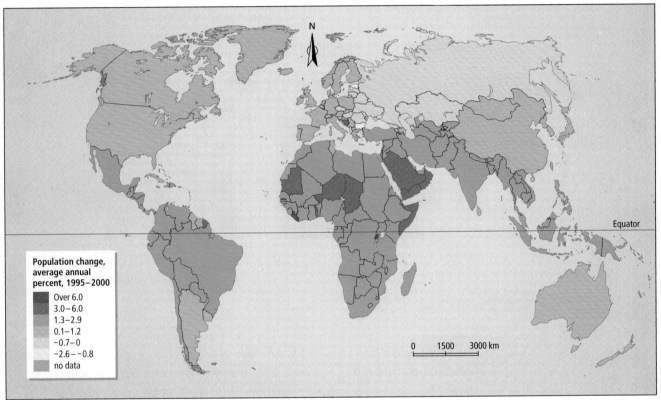

Population change, average annual percent, 1995–2000

- Over 6.0
- 3.0–6.0
- 1.3–2.9
- 0.1–1.2
- −0.7–0
- −2.6–−0.8
- no data

Where are populations still growing rapidly? Where are they actually declining?

THINKING It Over

1. **a)** Use the bar graph of world population growth on page G 36 to calculate how many years it took for each doubling of world population. Start with .25 billion and continue to 6 billion.

   b) Briefly explain how the three revolutions—agricultural, industrial, and scientific (modern)—caused this accelerated growth rate.

2. What is your opinion about each of the questions asked for the three photos on page G 38? Compare views with a partner.

3. Use the world map of population change above to record observations by continent. How can you explain the patterns you see?

4. Go back to the questionnaire on page G 26 and review your answers. Have you changed any of your opinions? What have you learned to improve your understanding of the topic?

GEO SKILL

Drawing and Interpreting Population Pyramids

A **population pyramid** is a graph that provides a snapshot of a country's population at one point in time. It can be used to find patterns by comparing two countries or two time periods. Most importantly, it can predict future changes in a society—something very useful as you consider your own career possibilities.

During **READING**

Checkpoint

Use your organizer to make sure your graph has all of the right information.

Canada Population Pyramid, 1991

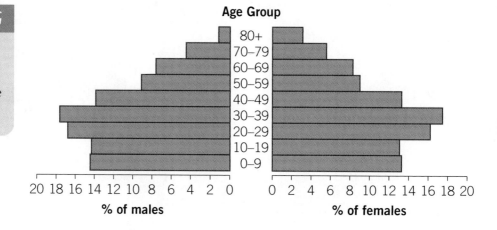

Step 1   Set Up the Graph Page

A population pyramid is two horizontal bar graphs in one. The vertical scale shows the age groups in the population. Here you will be using ten-year groups: ages 0 to 9, 10 to 19, 20 to 29, and so on. The scale along the bottom shows the percentage of the population in each age group. The left side of the graph shows males and the right side females. The percentages increase in each direction from the centre point.

Step 2   Plot the Right Side of the Graph

You will find it easier to put the female data on the graph first, because you normally make a graph by working to the right of the vertical scale. After plotting points for each age group, use a ruler to make straight bars.

Step 3 Plot the Left Side of the Graph

Next, plot the points for each of the male age groups. Remember that these percentages increase as you move to the left of the vertical scale. Use a ruler to draw the bars.

Step 4 Finish the Graph

Label the graph, using the 1991 example as a model. It is always important to include the year of the population data.

Canada: Population, 2006

Percentage of Males	Age Group	Percentage of Females
11.5	0–9	10.8
13.5	10–19	12.6
13.6	20–29	13.0
14.4	30–39	13.8
16.8	40–49	16.3
13.6	50–59	13.6
8.4	60–69	8.8
5.3	70–79	6.4
2.6	80+	4.9

APPLY It

1. Follow the steps to draw and label a population pyramid for Canada in 2006. Use the 1991 example as a guide. *m*

2. Compare the two graphs. What difference do you notice between Canada's population above and below the age of 40 in 1991 and in 2006? *m*

3. Use the two graphs to decide how Canada's population pyramid might look in ten years (2016). How might this affect the plans of someone your age to be a) a kindergarten teacher? b) a doctor? c) a business person? Explain. *m* *t*

4. Make a list of four questions you could ask to investigate why Canada's population characteristics changed between 1991 and 2006. *t*

5. Do some research into career areas that are expanding as Canadian baby boomers age. Choose one that interests you and find out about its educational requirements. *t*

The game winner combines the factors of birth, death, immigration, and emigration to create the largest total population increase for the country.

What You Will Need

A shuffled deck of 52 cards plus two Jokers

Spades	Hearts	Clubs	Diamonds
♠	♥	♣	♦
Death rate per 1000	Birth rate per 1000	Emigration rate per 1000	Immigration rate per 1000

Card Values

- All cards numbered 2 through 10 have their marked value.

- The face cards (Jack, Queen, King) are worth 11 points. Aces and Jokers have no value but do affect the game.

- An Ace allows the player to take any card from the person to the right, exchanging it for any card they hold.

- When a player draws a Joker, the round is finished and points are tallied.

How to Play

A. Play with 2, 3, or 4 people. First, remove Aces and Jokers from the deck before dealing out any cards.

B. Deal each person 6 cards. Players organize their cards into four groups by suit and put them face up. To the left, position the Hearts (births) above the Spades (deaths). On the right, position the Diamonds (immigration) above the Clubs (emigration).

C. Mix the Aces and Jokers back into the deck, shuffle and turn upside down.

D. Start with the oldest player and go clockwise. Each player discards one card and draws another from the top of the deck. Aim to maximize population score by discarding high black cards (death rate, emigration) in hopes of drawing high red ones (birth rate, immigration). If an Ace is drawn, discard it after exchanging cards.

E. When a Joker is drawn, the round ends. Players can then calculate their population scores. Start by adding together the values of any Hearts, Spades, Diamonds, and Clubs held. If no card of a particular suit is held, that sum is equal to zero.

Natural Increase = the sum of the Hearts minus the sum of the Spades.
Net Migration = the sum of the Diamonds minus the sum of the Clubs.

F. Record the population points on the score sheet. Calculate population change by adding the Natural Increase and Net Migration scores. Play another round. Continue for either three rounds or a time limit set by the teacher.

Sample Score Sheet

Round 1	Jillian M.
Natural increase (Hearts – Spades)	+ 12
Net migration (Diamonds – Clubs)	– 7
Population Change for the round	+ 5 per 1000 (i.e., .5%)

THINKING It Over

1. What strategies helped you to improve your score in the game?

2. Explain how this game could be played for the winner to have the greatest population *decrease*.

PUTTING IT ALL TOGETHER

This chapter has explored population patterns and trends around the world. You learned the difference between population distribution and density by using maps of Canada and the world. You saw how population around the world is affected by environment, history, migration, technology, and policy. Then, you used statistics, graphs, and a map to examine global patterns of population growth. You have also had the opportunity to examine how trends in population growth might affect you. Above all, you have gained a better understanding of the unit question, **How do patterns in human geography affect people around the world?**

After READING

Analyze Graphs to Synthesize Information

Using your organizer, review and analyze the graphs in this chapter. Which country has the most geographical challenges for human survival? How do you know? What could the Canadian government, your community, and/or your family do to help?

Country A	Information (2004)	Country B
21 040 km²	Area	41 532 km²
6 948 073	Population	16 407 491
26.1	Birth rate per 1000	11.1
5.6	Death rate per 1000	8.7
67.5	Infant mortality per 1000	5.1
−3.5	Net migration	2.8

THINKING It Through

1. Using the chart above, calculate the following for each country: a) population density, b) natural increase rate, and c) overall population change. **k a**

2. Decide which one is a developed country and which one is a developing country. Explain your choices. **t**

3. Use the information provided to explain whether or not there would be a pressing need for a) more schools, or b) more hospitals, in each country. **k a**

4. Write a paragraph describing the effects of two population issues each country might soon face. **k c a**

CHAPTER 3

Comparing Development Patterns

The Kariba Hydroelectric Dam, Zimbabwe

Making Connections

When you read a photograph in geography, ask yourself questions. For example, what does the photo show about the land areas (physical features)? Are there people in the photo? What are they doing, and why? Using the photographs on these pages, discuss these questions with a partner.

What are your first reactions to these two photos? Are you impressed by a gigantic engineering project that can create so much electricity and deliver fresh water to dry farmland? Do you laugh at the thought of a playground toy being used to pump clean water from a well? Both approaches are used today to improve people's lives. In fact, there are places where a human-powered pump is the best way to pump water. The choice depends on the level of economic and social development found in the area, as well as the demands of the environment.

In this chapter you will compare global development patterns. You will construct a scatter graph and explore whether or not developed countries, such as Canada, are doing enough to aid developing nations. Chapter 3 will complete your investigation of the unit Big Idea, **How do patterns in human geography affect people around the world?**

This PlayPump in South Africa uses the energy of children's play to pump clean water from deep in the earth.

Questions to Consider as You Read this Chapter

- In what ways do people seek to improve the quality of their lives?

- How do countries compare when I evaluate factors that affect quality of life?

- How do countries compare on the Human Development Index?

- What criteria can be used to assess the aid given to developing nations?

- How do I construct and interpret a scatter graph?

Thinking About Literacy

Predict and Infer

In this chapter, you will use your prediction and inference skills to preview the main ideas and make connections. Skim the chapter to preview headings, highlighted words, photographs, diagrams, and maps. Use a chart like this one to list your observations. List any connections you think there may be between the main ideas. Then use the preview and your prior knowledge to predict what you think the chapter will be about.

Main heading	What I see	Connections	What I think
What Affects Quality of Life?			

What Affects Quality of Life?

What do people need in order to live a decent life—one with some quality? These headlines suggest some key ideas: safety from danger, an environment with clean air and water, food, and education. What other things do people need for a life with quality?

Food Bank Running Low

Environment Tops Worry List

Literacy Test Scores Up at Local Schools

Daily Life Dangerous in Baghdad

CANADIAN WOMEN LIVE TO 83

During READING

Checkpoint
Scanning is reading up and down and zig zag, without reading every word. Scan this page and note headings and features in your preview.

WEB LINK ••••••••••••••••••••
Learn more about John Peters Humphrey on our Web site.

The Universal Declaration of Human Rights

You might be surprised to learn that a Canadian played a very important part in identifying what people really need (and have a right to). The United Nations (UN) was founded in 1945. The following year, Canadian lawyer John Peters Humphrey formed its Human Rights Division. He worked with a small group of people who drew up a list of basic human rights. The stamp on this page shows Humphrey in his role as Human Rights Division director, penning final changes to the list. The United Nations adopted his final version of the Universal Declaration of Human Rights in 1948.

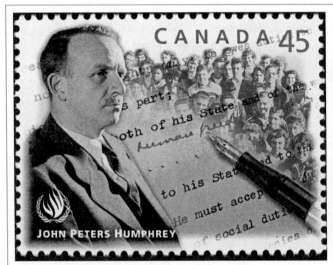

Why do you think Canada issued this stamp depicting John Peters Humphrey?

The United Nations flag, on which olive branches symbolizing peace surround the world's continents

Selections from the Universal Declaration of Human Rights

Article 1: All human beings are born free and equal in dignity and rights. They are endowed with reason and conscience and should act towards one another in a spirit of brotherhood.

Article 2: Everyone is entitled to all the rights and freedoms set forth in this Declaration, without distinction of any kind, such as race, colour, sex, language, religion, political or other opinion, national or social origin, property, birth or other status.

Article 25: Everyone has the right to a standard of living adequate for the health and well-being of himself and of his family, including food, clothing, housing and medical care and necessary social services.

Article 26: Everyone has the right to education. Education shall be free, at least in the elementary and fundamental stages. Elementary education shall be compulsory.

WEB LINK •••••••••••••••••••••
Read the full text of the Universal Declaration of Human Rights on our Web site.

The Three "L"s

When the UN Declaration speaks of health, well-being, and education, it is highlighting the importance of the Three "L"s: life expectancy, living standard, and literacy. Each one is a measure of quality of life. **Life expectancy** shows how long a person can expect to live. Long life indicates a society with a strong health care system. **Living standard** estimates the average purchasing power a person has, based on where they live. Of course, there are actually great differences in personal wealth within most countries. The **literacy rate** is a measure of basic education, expressed as a percentage of people who can read and write. Use the photographs on the next page to learn more about these quality of life ideas.

WORDS MATTER

life expectancy the average number of years a person is expected to live

living standard the amount of goods and services people can purchase

literacy rate the percentage of people with the ability to read and write

Life Expectancy

Country	Average Life Expectancy (years)	Country	Average Life Expectancy (years)
Canada	80	Costa Rica	77
United States	78	Panama	75
Mexico	75	Cuba	77
Guatemala	69	Haiti	57
Belize	68	Dominican Republic	73
El Salvador	71	Jamaica	73
Honduras	69	Bahamas	65

Given what you know right now, how can you explain the differences in life expectancies between Canada and Haiti?

Life Expectancy

Life expectancy is extended by access to safe water and food supplies. Improved medical technology and hospital care affect the most fragile members of society—infants and seniors. In the developed nations, infant mortality rates are very low, while at the same time life expectancy has reached an average of 75 years or more. What obstacles might limit these improvements in some developing countries?

Living Standard

The homes people live in are often a good reflection of living standards in a society. Houses in good repair with effective plumbing and sanitation systems indicate that people have incomes high enough to maintain their dwellings and help pay for public services. In Chapter 1, you learned that as urban migrants in developing countries found jobs, they upgraded their homes. Why do people often want a better home?

During **READING**

Checkpoint
Remember that photographs can be part of your chapter preview.

Literacy

Children need a basic education to at least learn how to read and write. These skills will give them an alternative to working in traditional rural livelihoods, such as farming and fishing. With some education, young people in developing countries can access better-paid employment in transportation, tourism, and other service jobs. What level of education do students in developed countries, like Canada, need for a good career?

Basic Freedoms

Quality of life means more than just health, wealth, and education. Do you watch or read the world news? Many people around the world do not have the basic freedoms which you enjoy in Canada. There are cases in which human rights are being violated. News of warfare, terrorist bombings, and military governments are a reminder that there can be differences between the quality of life you experience in Canada and the dangers faced by people in other parts of the world.

Selections from the Universal Declaration of Human Rights

Article 18: Everyone has the right to freedom of thought, conscience and religion....

Article 19: Everyone has the right to freedom of opinion and expression....

Article 20: Everyone has the right to freedom of peaceful assembly and association....

Article 21: Everyone has the right to take part in the government of his country, directly or through freely chosen representatives....

THINKING It Over

1. Construct a declining-order bar graph to compare life expectancies, using data from the chart on page G 47. Use three colours to show countries from North America, Central America, and the Caribbean. Provide an explanation for any pattern you see.

2. With a partner, record and discuss answers to the questions with the photos on page G 48.

3. Using current events, complete a discussion sheet to record Canadian and world situations in which specific Universal Declaration of Human Rights articles

   a) are very much in evidence.

   b) seem largely to be ignored.

   Do you think the UN Declaration is being followed in the world today? Explain your views.

Our Environment

Quality of Life

Protecting the earth and its resources is vital to quality of life. Without clean air, fresh water, and fertile soil you could not live on the planet. Quality of life also comes from green open spaces that offer the chance for physical and mental rest. Almost one-eighth of Canada has been set aside as nature reserves, parkland, and wilderness areas.

Does your region have enough parkland and open space? Write a concise letter to the editor supporting your viewpoint.

Canoeists in Algonquin Park

GEO SKILL

Draw and Interpret a Scatter Graph

WORDS MATTER

correlation the connection, or relationship, between two things. Finding a correlation can help geographers study cause and effect.

scatter graph a graph that shows the relationship between two related sets of data

Geographers find patterns to help make sense of a complex world. One way to do this is to compare two related things to find the **correlation** between them. A **scatter graph** can be used to find these correlations. Here you will learn to use scatter graphs to study the relationship between quality of life and population.

Step 1 Pick Two Related Topics

It is important to choose two sets of numbers that might be related, with one as cause and the other as effect. Here you will compare birth rate and average income levels. What do you expect to find when you compare the two?

Step 2 Set Up the Graph Scales

Look at the numbers you will be graphing when you set your graph scales. The chart on the next page shows that the highest birth rate is 36 (Guatemala), and the highest income level is $34 142 ($US). On the side of the graph, make a birth rate scale from 0 to 40. Along the bottom, make an income scale from $0 to $40 000.

Step 3 Plot the Number Sets

Each dot on the graph will represent one country. First find the numbers for the country on each scale, then place a dot where these two numbers intersect on the graph. Use the graph below as a guide.

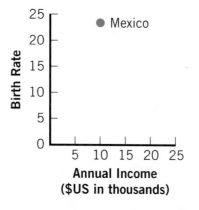

In this example, Mexico has 22 births per year per 1000 people, measured up the vertical axis. The average annual income in Mexico is $9023, measured along the horizontal axis. The dot for Mexico is plotted where the two values intersect on the graph.

Step 4 Fit a Straight Line to the Points

Move a ruler over the graphed points until you find the line of "best fit." That will be where a straight line can be drawn through the points to get as many as possible close to the line.

Step 5 Describe Your Findings

There can be three possible results:

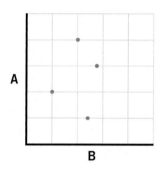

No relationship

There is no correlation between A and B because a "best fit" line cannot be drawn.

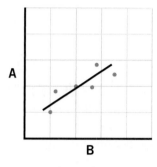

Direct relationship

There is a direct correlation because as A increases so does B.

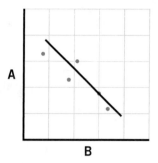

Inverse relationship

There is an inverse correlation because as B increases, A decreases.

Country	Birth Rate (per 1000)	Purchasing Power per Person ($US)	
Canada	11	27 840	✓
U.S.A.	14	34 142	✓
Mexico	22	9 023	✓
Guatemala	36	3 821	✓
Belize	31	5 606	✓
El Salvador	25	4 497	✓
Honduras	32	2 453	✓
Nicaragua	27	2 366	✓
Costa Rica	20	8 650	✓
Panama	21	6 000	✓
Trinidad and Tobago	15	8 964	✓
Haiti	34	1 467	✓
Dominican Republic	24	6 033	✓
Jamaica	18	3 639	✓
Bahamas	19	17 012	

APPLY It

1. Use the chart above to construct a scatter graph comparing birth rate and average income levels for countries in North America, Central America, and the Caribbean. 🔟

2. Describe the correlation that you see between the two sets of numbers. Which one is cause and which is effect? Suggest reasons to explain this connection. 🔟

HDI: The Bottom 8, 2006	Countries
170	Ethiopia
171	Chad
172	Central African Republic
173	Guinea-Bissau
174	Burkina Faso
175	Mali
176	Sierra Leone
177	Niger

UN report on best places to live in the world

10 November 2006

This week, the United Nations once again named Norway as the best place to live, a title it has enjoyed since 2001. Norway is able to provide its 4.5 million citizens with high-quality and low-cost education, health care, and social services, thanks to substantial income from oil exports.

Next in the list, placing second through eighth, are Iceland, Australia, Ireland, Sweden, Canada, Japan, and the United States.

Annually since 1990, the UN Development Report Office has compared the 177 countries for which statistics are available. Data used to create the rankings relate to the ability of people to reach their full potential—to be healthy and live long lives, to be able to read and write, to have access to resources like clean water, and to be able to participate freely in the decisions of their community. In those countries near the bottom of the ranking list, these basic needs often go unmet.

During **READING**

Checkpoint

As you scan this section, take note of how the author has organized the information.

WORDS MATTER

Human Development Index a comparison of countries that measures health, education, and wealth of each nation's citizens; life expectancy, literacy, and standard of living are measured

You may be wondering why Canada didn't rank first. After all, we led the United Nations' annual ratings for five consecutive years before Norway took the lead. However, Canada is in the top 3%, next to some very strong competition. That's a lot like making it to the finals for the Stanley Cup or the World Series. Now take a look at the chart in the margin showing the bottom eight countries on the HDI list. What do these countries have in common? How are they different from the top ranking countries listed above? Think of this in terms of geographical and environmental factors such as location, natural resources, industry, and climate.

Keep these factors in mind as you learn more about the UN **Human Development Index** in the following pages. Patterns of life expectancy, literacy, and living standard will be compared on a series of world maps, ending with one showing the Human Development Index. Keep an eye on Canada's place in these different measures.

Global Life Expectancy

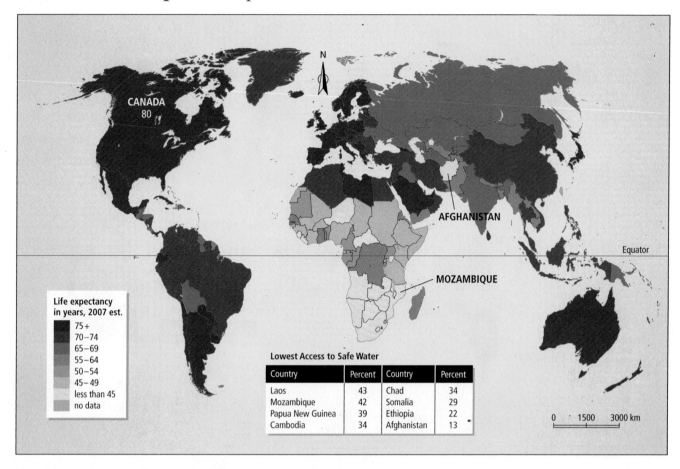

Life expectancy in years, 2007 est.
- 75+
- 70–74
- 65–69
- 55–64
- 50–54
- 45–49
- less than 45
- no data

CANADA 80

AFGHANISTAN

MOZAMBIQUE

Equator

N

0   1500   3000 km

Lowest Access to Safe Water

Country	Percent	Country	Percent
Laos	43	Chad	34
Mozambique	42	Somalia	29
Papua New Guinea	39	Ethiopia	22
Cambodia	34	Afghanistan	13

What supports a long, healthy life? Genetics and healthy choices are not the only things that affect life expectancy. In a country such as Canada, a wealth of natural resources and an advanced economy mean that most people have access to clean water and food. If someone gets sick or injured, they have access to health care. The system is not always perfect, but on average, Canadians live long lives.

However, in many countries of the world, average life expectancy is low. Life can be short in nations torn apart by years of war and political turmoil—countries such as Afghanistan or Mozambique. Many countries face problems that contribute to lower life expectancy. The lack of clean drinking water or famines caused by drought can result in **malnutrition** and disease. Severe shortages of hospitals, medicine, and doctors reduce the odds of recovery for someone who is ill or injured. Parts of Africa face another huge threat to life expectancy—the **AIDS epidemic**. AIDS has caused the deaths of large numbers of adults in many African countries and has lowered life expectancy to 40 or less.

WORDS MATTER

malnutrition an often fatal condition caused by an inadequate diet

AIDS epidemic the occurence of AIDS and HIV. In parts of Africa, more than 20 million people live with HIV, the virus that causes AIDS. AIDS has also been called a pandemic, meaning that it affects populations worldwide.

Global Literacy

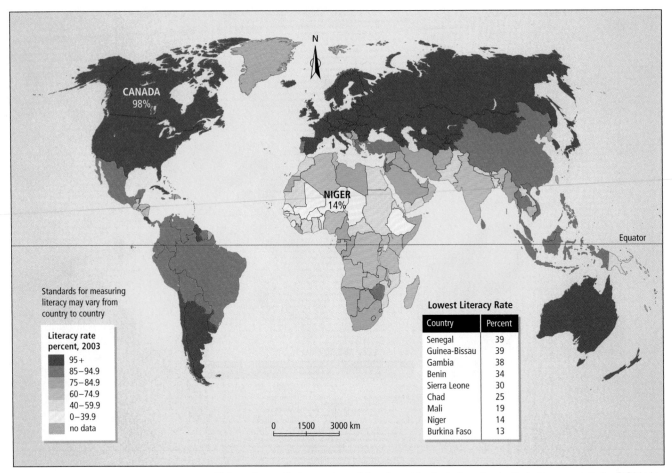

Standards for measuring literacy may vary from country to country

Literacy rate percent, 2003
- 95+
- 85–94.9
- 75–84.9
- 60–74.9
- 40–59.9
- 0–39.9
- no data

CANADA 98%

NIGER 14%

Equator

0   1500   3000 km

Lowest Literacy Rate

Country	Percent
Senegal	39
Guinea-Bissau	39
Gambia	38
Benin	34
Sierra Leone	30
Chad	25
Mali	19
Niger	14
Burkina Faso	13

Did you know that some countries do not include females in their literacy statistics? Girls in those countries often receive little or no education.

Literacy is a good measure of access to education. While the UN Declaration states that everyone has the right to at least elementary schooling, the map above shows that this is not happening in many parts of the world. In Niger, for example, fewer than one person in six has basic literacy skills.

Nations with low literacy levels often lack many basic requirements for schools. Shortages of money, building materials, school supplies, and trained teachers are immediate problems. As well, there may be a lack of roads, power, and other services to support a school. In many developing countries, rural families need their children at home to help with crops, animal care, and household tasks. In these societies, anything more than basic schooling is a luxury that many cannot afford. This can limit opportunities for people, generation after generation. Think about your school experience up until now. How does a country such as Canada support education and literacy?

Global Living Standards

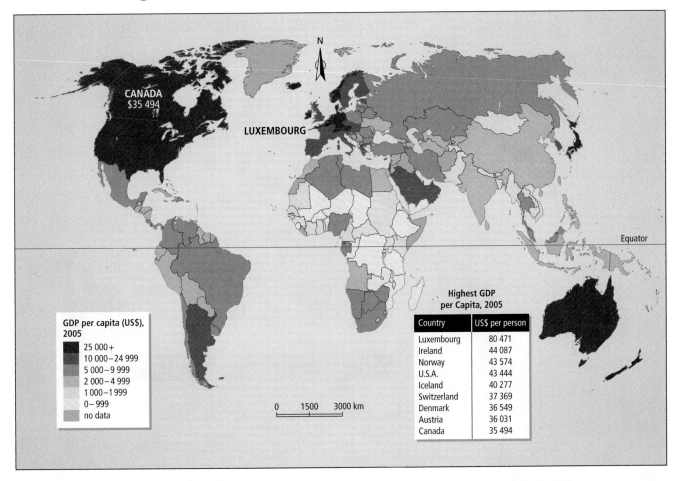

GDP per capita (US$), 2005

■	25 000+
■	10 000–24 999
■	5 000–9 999
■	2 000–4 999
■	1 000–1 999
■	0–999
■	no data

Highest GDP per Capita, 2005

Country	US$ per person
Luxembourg	80 471
Ireland	44 087
Norway	43 574
U.S.A.	43 444
Iceland	40 277
Switzerland	37 369
Denmark	36 549
Austria	36 031
Canada	35 494

Gross domestic product (GDP) and **gross national product (GNP)** are two similar ways to describe the value of all goods and services produced by the people of a country in one year. They are used to measure the size of a country's economy, and can indicate the living standards of the country. GDP and GNP can also be calculated per person, or "per capita." In 2005, Canada's **GDP per capita** was $35 494 ($US), ninth in the world. But don't ask for your share to spend. GDP per capita refers only to the production of goods and services, not the actual amount you can spend on things. It is a national average, including everyone from millionaires to Grade 8 students.

How does GDP per capita show living standard? Improvement in a country's economic performance can mean better public services, a cleaner environment, and better protection for workers. However, this is not always completely true. What might happen if economic wealth was not distributed evenly among all citizens?

Compare this map to the literacy and life expectancy maps you just used. You will see that all three of these global patterns share many similarities.

WORDS MATTER

gross domestic product (GDP) the value of all goods and services produced in a country in one year

gross national product (GNP) the value of goods and services produced by a country in one year, including those produced outside the country

GDP per capita gross domestic product per person

Human Development Index

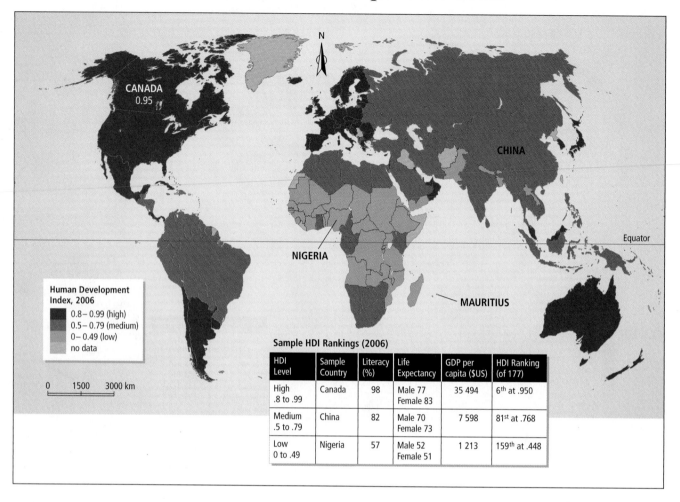

Human Development Index, 2006

■	0.8 – 0.99 (high)
■	0.5 – 0.79 (medium)
■	0 – 0.49 (low)
■	no data

0   1500   3000 km

Sample HDI Rankings (2006)

HDI Level	Sample Country	Literacy (%)	Life Expectancy	GDP per capita ($US)	HDI Ranking (of 177)
High .8 to .99	Canada	98	Male 77 Female 83	35 494	6th at .950
Medium .5 to .79	China	82	Male 70 Female 73	7 598	81st at .768
Low 0 to .49	Nigeria	57	Male 52 Female 51	1 213	159th at .448

The UN Human Development Index brings all the measures of education, health, and wealth together into one big picture. It is a bit like the scoring system used in Olympic competition, with a 1.0 (similar to the Olympic 10) seen as perfection on each measure. The different scores for each country are added together and averaged as one final number. For example, in 2006, Canada scored .950. The map above groups countries into three categories based on their scores— High, Medium and Low. It can be a way to identify the world's "haves," "have somes," and "have nots."

What might an HDI score mean to a country? If you were leading a country's government, what would you do if your nation were awarded a very high or a very low HDI score? How might that score affect your popularity and power among the people?

The maps on pages G 53–G 56 may have indicated that most of Africa is in difficulty, but the small island nation of Mauritius shows that a country can make dramatic improvement. It is one of only two African countries with a Human Development rating in the High category. (The other is Seychelles, another small nation made up of tiny islands.)

Since the early 1500s, Mauritius has been inhabited and ruled by the Portuguese, the French, and the English. Until 1968, Mauritius was a British colony with a high birth rate but a low standard of living. Sugar exports, an industry that began in the early 1700s, still created most of the island's income. That changed after Mauritius became an independent country with a stable democratic government.

The government of Mauritius has taken advantage of its unique location to make big changes in quality of life. This includes moving from a reliance on sugar exports to a more **diversified economy**. Improved roads, an international airport, and a seaport all attract foreign investment. Beautiful beaches, coral reefs, and a tropical climate make it a tourist destination. Mauritius's economic and political stability also make it an ideal headquarters for companies operating in Africa and India. As a result, the country has one of Africa's highest per capita incomes.

Area	2 040 km²
Population	1 245 000
Density	610 per km²
Life expectancy	Males: 68, Females: 76
Literacy	84%
GDP per capita	12 800 ($US)
HDI rating	63rd of 177: .800

Port Louis, the capital city of Mauritius

THINKING It Over

1. Use the Life Expectancy map on page G 53 to compare Africa to the rest of the world. List five reasons that can explain this pattern. **k π**

2. Compare the maps of Literacy and Living Standard. What patterns do you observe? What explanations can you give? **k π**

3. What is the Human Development Index? Use the map to rank the continents in declining HDI order. (Record Europe and Asia separately.) **k π**

4. Could Mauritius' formula for success be applied in other developing countries? Compare ideas with a partner. **t c**

WORDS MATTER

diversified economy an economy that is based on more than one resource

Imagine that you could do something to improve the quality of life in some part of the world. What important changes would you make? How would you get your message out to others? In 2005, top music performers donated their talents for *Live 8* rock concerts in the leading developed countries, including Canada. They wanted to raise awareness of world poverty and urge developed countries to contribute more to solutions. At the end of this chapter, you'll be identifying problems in one region of the world and making your own plan to improve conditions there.

In the summer of 2007, *Live Earth* concerts drew attention to global climate change. They were televised from every continent, including Antarctica. Do you think that celebrities should use their popularity to speak out on issues like climate change and poverty? How can it help?

Types of Aid

Foreign aid describes the flow of assistance between governments. Money, loans, trained people, supplies, and equipment can move from one nation to another. The following questions will review what you need to know to plan a development project.

What Is Bilateral Aid?

"Bi" means two. **Bilateral aid** connects two countries together: a donor and a recipient. Countries may have bilateral aid ties with strategic military allies or with former colonies. At other times, aid may be a response to a crisis. Canada's official foreign aid is handled by CIDA, the Canadian International Development Agency. In 2004, CIDA coordinated the Canadian effort to help countries affected by the tsunami in South Asia.

What Is Multilateral Aid?

"Multi" means many. **Multilateral aid** comes from more than one country. The best-known multilateral aid organization is the United Nations. Contributing countries work together to support thousands of development projects around the world. Organizations such as the World Health Organization (WHO), the Food and Agriculture Organization (FAO), and other agencies are employed to bring humanitarian aid where it is needed.

What Is Tied Aid?

Tied aid comes with conditions that tie the receiving country to the donor. It is like a gift card which must be spent at one store, whether you want to shop there or not. Tied aid requires the receiving country to buy supplies and equipment from the donor country. For example, money needed to help fight AIDS in Africa may only be given if that money is used to buy the necessary drugs from the donor country.

What Is an NGO?

Non-governmental organizations are aid agencies which are not part of any government. You may be familiar with some NGOs, such as the International Red Cross and Oxfam. Others carry out small-scale projects. For example, Sarnia's Rayjon Share Care supports rural schools in Haiti in order to help improve literacy.

What Is the World Bank?

The **World Bank** is a multilateral organization that supports international development. Governments and banks invest large amounts of money in the International Monetary Fund (IMF). The World Bank then lends this money to countries for specific projects. Between July 2006 and June 2007, the World Bank distributed 24.7 billion dollars ($US).

WORDSMATTER

tied aid economic aid that has conditions on where and how it must be used

NGO (Non-Governmental Organization) an aid agency that is independent of any government

World Bank an international banking organization with a mandate to reduce world poverty

WEB LINK •••••••••••••••••••
Look at an interactive world map showing World Bank data on different countries on our Web site.

Heroes and Villains | *The World Bank*

The World Bank is a large source of foreign aid loans. Officials say they are successfully fighting poverty, while critics claim the bank is actually causing it. For example, farm poverty is widespread in developing countries, but between 2001 and 2005, only one-tenth of World Bank funds went to rural development projects. Critics point out that loans for large-scale projects, such as dams, pipelines, and airports are favoured instead. Loan conditions are strict. Sometimes countries must cut social services (e.g., schools and hospitals) in order to continue making payments. For these reasons, protestors gather whenever the World Bank meets with global leaders. Research current events concerning the World Bank. Do you think the actions of the World Bank reflect its purpose, or not? Explain.

Checkpoint
Using the information you have already gathered, record how this section might connect to those you have previously scanned.

WEB LINK •••••••••••••••••
Read stories about the use of appropriate technology on our Web site.

WORDS MATTER

appropriate technology
technology that is suited to the environmental, cultural, or economic situation it is intended for

Technology and Development

Some of the criticism of the World Bank is one-sided. It overlooks how large-scale projects could support long-term economic growth. For example, if a country has petroleum deposits, construction of a pipeline would allow it to export oil. This might improve living standards, but there is no guarantee. The African nation of Nigeria exports oil but remains near the bottom of the UN Human Development Index. Airport construction is another type of World Bank project that critics dislike. However, an important part of economic growth for Mauritius was the construction of an international airport. This opened the island to commercial tourism, increased trade, and raised the GDP per capita.

Appropriate Technology

Does large-scale technology always benefit everyone? Think about the photos at the beginning of the chapter. Big projects such as hydroelectric dams cost a lot of money, and sometimes the benefits do not filter down to people in rural areas. An approach to development called **appropriate technology** has become increasingly popular. The PlayPump is an example of this type of technology, which focuses on the real needs and skills of people. It is called "appropriate" because the technologies use locally available materials or power sources. Appropriate technology does not require large investment, high-tech equipment, or fossil fuels. It aims to improve people's ability to feed, clothe, and shelter their families.

Solar Power
In isolated rural areas, many people must use kerosene, candles, or batteries for light. Low-cost solar equipment is now becoming more available. Tibet is known as "The Roof of the World," and can have more than 3000 hours of sunlight each year. There, solar power is used to run lights and stoves. What are the benefits of solar power?

Cycle Trailers

Small cycle trailers made in local village workshops can carry up to 200 kg. The trailer shown here is being used to carry a passenger and produce in Cambodia. Farmers also use bicycles to transport produce to market. Cycle trailers also carry water, firewood, or even a mobile library! How is this an example of appropriate technology?

Biogas Cooking

Odourless and smoke-free, biogas is made from decomposing crop or livestock waste. This biogas "plant" in India serves an entire village. Also in India, Dr. Anand Karve has invented a much smaller plant which can be used by individual households. In just hours, biogas plants can turn food and animal waste into clean-burning gas. Why might this be better than a wood- or oil-burning stove?

Appropriate technology can make people's lives better. All the examples shown here have the added advantage of being "green"— they are based on renewable energy sources.

WORDS MATTER

biogas fuel produced from organic matter

THINKING It Over

1. Describe and explain examples of the following types of development projects:

   a) bilateral tied aid, b) multilateral aid from an NGO, c) locally-made appropriate technology

2. What is the difference between large-scale aid projects and appropriate technology? Work with a partner, and use the photos at the beginning of the chapter and in this section to create a chart showing the advantages and shortcomings of each type of development.

3. How might you convince the World Bank to direct more of its loans to appropriate technology solutions?

Are Canadians Helping Enough?

Yes

In 2006, the Canadian government spent more than $3 billion on foreign aid. That amounts to about $100 for every Canadian. This is proportionally much higher than developed nations like the U.S. and Japan. As well, individual Canadians and NGOs respond very generously to international relief efforts, such as the Asian tsunami disaster in late 2004.

No

The United Nations recommends that developed countries give 0.7% of their Gross Domestic Product (GDP) to foreign aid. That amounts to 7 cents on every $10. Canada pledged to meet this goal, but currently gives just 0.3% of the GDP. Most European countries exceed Canada's rate, and five of them met the United Nations standard in 2006.

Make Poverty History is one of many Canadian NGOs that want to end poverty worldwide. Their goals include increasing Canada's foreign aid to 0.7% and canceling the huge debts owed by developing nations. The organization urges people to support fair trade by purchasing **fair trade** products, such as coffee, clothing, and craft goods. What is happening in your community to fight poverty?

WEB LINK •
Learn more about fair trade on our Web site.

WORDS MATTER

fair trade trade that gives fair prices to small, independent producers of a wide variety of goods

What Do YOU Think?

What is your view? Hold a class debate to discuss the following. *t c*

- Canada must increase its foreign aid level to 0.7% of its national income.

- Both large and small retailers in Canada should support fair trade.

For help with debates, check page S 11.

PUTTING IT ALL TOGETHER

This chapter completes your exploration of the key question for Unit 1, **How do patterns in human geography affect people around the world?** Here, you have seen the tremendous global differences found in education, health, wealth, and human development. You began by identifying human needs for a life of quality and read the United Nations Universal Declaration of Human Rights. Unfortunately, the human right to a decent life with basic freedoms is absent in many parts of the world. You learned that different forms of development assistance are available. But the question remains whether or not the developed countries are doing enough to assist countries in Africa, south Asia, and South America.

After READING

Revise Your Predictions

Now that you have read and worked through the chapter, go back to your original predictions. With a partner, share your predictions chart. Note similarities and differences. Then, revise your chart to bring in any new ideas or information you now have since you read the chapter. How accurate were your predictions?

THINKING It Through

Pick one of these regions from the quality of life map series used in this chapter (pages G 53–G 56):

- Central America (south of the U.S. and north of South America)

- Africa (south of the Sahara Desert and north of the equator)

- Southeast Asia (south of China and east of India)

- East Africa (along the coast, by the Indian Ocean)

1. Use the maps to prepare a half-page summary identifying how serious the development problems faced by your region are. *m a*

2. Prepare a detailed list of three key things which would improve the quality of life in your chosen region. Some research will be necessary to focus on specific information. Refer to page S 6 in the Skills Tool Kit to review researching a topic. *k t*

3. Write a one-page development plan explaining steps you would take to meet each of the three needs you identified in question 2. Include Canada's role in contributing to your project. *c a*

4. Make a map of your region, naming the countries that your plan covers. *m*

Back to the Big Idea

How do patterns in human geography affect people around the world?

Throughout this unit, you have:

• looked at the main factors that influence population distribution and land use

• examined patterns of community, population, and economic development around the world

• compared Canada's patterns in human geography with other places

• identified and assessed ways to aid developing nations

Use a graphic organizer to answer the key question, **How do patterns in human geography affect people around the world?** Consider: population, settlement, land use, and economic development.

"Somewhere": Percentage of Population, 2000		
Age Group in Years	Percentage of all Males	Percentage of all Females
0–9	13.0	12.8
10–19	13.6	12.4
20–29	14.3	13.1
30–39	14.9	14.3
40–49	14.5	14.1
50–59	11.9	11.4
60–69	8.8	9.4
70–79	6.6	8.7
80+	2.4	5.0

"Elsewhere": Percentage of Population, 2000		
Age Group in Years	Percentage of all Males	Percentage of all Females
0–9	22.9	22.7
10–19	27.0	27.3
20–29	17.5	17.9
30–39	12.1	12.7
40–49	9.1	9.1
50–59	5.9	5.3
60–69	3.3	3.1
70–79	1.6	1.4
80+	0.5	0.4

The populations of two different types of countries. Which one is the developing nation? How can you tell?

Show That You Know

Use your knowledge of population pyramids to construct, interpret, and compare two different countries. Use the information to make predictions about each country's future needs.

Step 1 Construct population pyramids ✈

Work with a partner to draw and label pyramids of the population data shown on the facing page.

Tip: Use the same scales for the pyramids so they can be compared more easily.

Step 2 Compare the two countries ✈

Use the following chart to compare the total percentage of the population of each country found in three different age groups.

Age Groups	"Somewhere"	"Elsewhere"
Children and Youth (age 0–19)		
Working Adults (age 20–59)		
Seniors (age 60 and older)		

Step 3 Classify the pyramids

Work with your partner to identify which type of population change is shown in each case. Identify the developed and the developing countries.

Tip: Review the textbook section about population pyramids on pages G 40 and G 41 before you make your final decisions.

Step 4 Make predictions

Imagine that you are a government official in one of the countries. Your partner holds the same position for the other one. Use the pyramids and chart organizer to predict what your country's needs will be ten years from the date of the population data for each of the following:

- Education for young people (age 10–19)
- Infant care for young mothers (age 20–29)
- Home construction for growing families (age 20–39)
- Medical care for seniors (age 60 and older)

Tip: Make predictions by determining the present age of the population group. For example, the future young mother group is currently age 10–19 on each pyramid.

Step 5 Write a short report

Write a page or two to state your predictions for your country, and explain your reasons. Identify what you think should be done to prepare the country for each of these four changes in the population.

Tip: Create an introduction and a conclusion to frame your report.

World Economic Systems

> How do economic systems influence industries across Canada and the world?

This family uses horses to herd cattle at their ranch near Longview, Alberta. How would these ranchers decide how many cattle to raise? What factors can affect the price consumers pay for beef at the grocery store?

What types of work can you do at home or in your community? Which jobs do you prefer? Why?

What's the Big Idea?

In Unit 1, you explored patterns of settlement, land use, and the living conditions of communities and countries around the world. Each of these societies has a type of economic system that produces, uses, and distributes goods and services. These systems vary depending on many factors, including resources, industries, traditions, government policies, and trade relationships.

How are you a part of the Canadian economic system? Perhaps you provide a service when you help out at home or volunteer in the community. Or you may get paid working for a neighbour or a family business. All of these activities reflect part of the Canadian economy. How would this be different if you lived in a society in another part of the world?

Key Terms

economy, entrepreneurial, traditional economy, command economy, market economy, mixed economy, supply and demand, production, goods and services, consumer, market, distribution, imports, exports, land, capital, primary industry, secondary industry, tertiary industry

What You Will Learn in this Unit

- What are the characteristics of different types of industry and business?

- How could I decide on the best location for a successful new industry or business?

- How do factors such as access to resources and markets influence economies?

- How do different societies produce and distribute goods and services?

- How does Canada's economic system work?

- How can I use thematic maps to show economic patterns?

- How could a new business affect the economy of my local region?

CHAPTER 4

Different World Economies

The financial heart of Canada is located in Toronto, where most of the major banks have their head offices.

Before READING

Rapid Writing

Think about types of businesses that you think would work in the region you live in. Then brainstorm and write as much as you can on this question:

What type of business would you start, and why?

WORDS MATTER

economy the system of production, consumption, and trade of goods and services

economic system the production, distribution, and consumption of goods and services in a particular society

production the creation of products and services for consumption

distribution the marketing, transporting, merchandising, and selling of any item

Have you ever seen the glow of Toronto's downtown at night? The shimmering chrome, bronze, and black towers of Canada's biggest banks are very striking. Every day, decisions and transactions are made in these buildings that affect the **economy** and the lives of most Canadians. Money constantly moves between banks, industries, and people.

Throughout the world, you will find different **economic systems**. Many people live outside the world of banks, investment, and paycheques. Their everyday decisions are often shaped by various factors, such as traditions, barter, or government control of **production** and **distribution**. Comparing these different types of economies will help you answer the key question for Unit 2: **How do economic systems influence industries across Canada and the world?**

A traditional rural economy in a developing country.

Questions to Consider as You Read this Chapter

- What are the basic questions all economic systems must answer?

- How would I plan a business of my own based on these questions?

- What are the different types of economic resources, and how do they influence the success of a region?

- What are the characteristics of market, traditional, and command economies?

- How can I use a thematic map to draw conclusions about labour?

Thinking About Literacy

Organize Ideas with a Concept Map

Creating and using a concept map while you read is a good way to find and remember important information. Use a concept map to summarize the main ideas of this chapter. The example below shows how your concept map might start. Fill in the blanks as you read. Add more circles or other shapes when you need to.

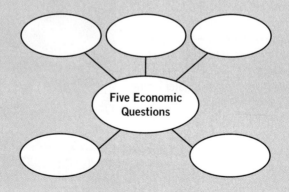

Operating Your Own Business

What activities do you enjoy? What skills do you have? Your answers to these questions could launch you into a business of your own. You may enjoy writing or drawing, which could lead you to a career in freelance writing or illustrating. Do you like fashion and shopping? You might own a retail business, such as a trendy clothing store. If you enjoy music, you could become an **entrepreneur** like Michele Stokley, a concert organizer whom you'll meet in this section.

The Five Economic Questions

Some businesses produce **goods** (cars or beauty products) while others provide **services** (car repairs or hairstyling). There are five basic economic questions that every business person needs to consider.

1. Who Produces Goods and Services?

Artists, farmers, dentists, and electricians all provide different types of goods or services. The quality of these products and services reflects the abilities of the individuals who produce them. Even people born with a talent must get an education to better prepare them for the work they'll do. What sort of business might you like to operate? What interests and talents could you bring to this business?

2. What Goods and Services Are Produced?

Geography often determines which goods can be provided and what services are needed. Florida farmers produce oranges and grapefruit because winter temperatures there are warm enough to protect the fruit from freezing. Companies along the Ottawa River offer whitewater rafting because of the long stretches of rapids. What sorts of goods and/or services would your dream business provide? How might they be affected by geography?

3. How Are Goods and Services Produced?

Most automobiles are mass-produced using the **assembly-line technique** pioneered by Henry Ford. This cuts production costs. Vehicles like Ferraris are hand-built using small-scale **production team methods**. Production costs are much higher, but so is the quality of the finished cars. Of course, the selling price of a Ferrari is much higher too. Would you sell mass-produced or hand-made products? Or would you provide services such as car repairs? Explain.

4. For Whom Are Goods and Services Produced?

Businesses must carefully study the wants and needs of potential customers before they make new products or offer services. Dog walkers, for example, might customize their services according to the needs of the pets and the desires of the pet owners. They might offer related services such as grooming. What are the characteristics (e.g., age, gender, income) and preferences of your potential customers?

5. How Are Goods and Services Distributed?

Large companies such as Canadian Tire and Tim Hortons use truck fleets to carry products to their stores and outlets. The brightly-painted trailers act as rolling advertisements. Canadian Tire moves products to its stores across Canada from a distribution centre in Brampton, Ontario. Tim Hortons trucks carry products from distribution centres in Ontario, Alberta, Nova Scotia, and British Columbia. How would you advertise and distribute products or services in your own business?

economic resources factors (land, labour, capital, and entrepreneurship) needed for the economic success of a region

land natural resources which are the raw materials of industry and business

Four Economic Resources

The answers to the five economic questions are keys to the success of a business. They are also important to the countries or regions in which these activities are carried out. Within each country or region, there are also four **economic resources** that are vital to its economic system.

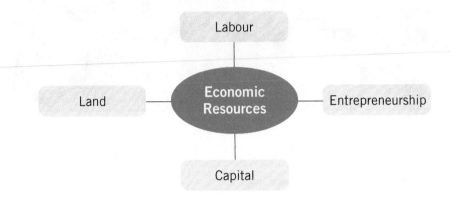

During **READING**

Checkpoint

Create a concept map with "The Four Economic Resources" in the centre. Add details as you read about each resource.

WEB LINK
Check facts and statistics on Canada's land resources. Visit our Web site.

Land Resources

In economic terms, the word **land** means more than property. It means the resources of the earth—the raw materials of industry and business. Natural resources include soils, water, forests, animals, minerals, and energy sources. Some places, such as Canada, have an abundance of different resources. Other regions must rely upon a more limited "land" factor. While some places, such as the Netherlands, may overcome obstacles such as a lack of arable land, other places may struggle. Nepal, in South Asia, is dominated by a mountain range—the Himalayas. Average incomes and living standards there are low.

Labour Resources

People are very important in the production of goods and services when their skills are combined with other economic resources. For example, India has iron ore and coal, the key land resources needed for steel production. Alone, this is not enough. Skilled labour to manage and operate steel mills is also necessary. Today, there are more than one billion people in India, and the country has a good system of education to train industrial managers. India has become one of Asia's major steel producers, and has also developed industries that produce trucks, bicycles, and other items made of steel.

The Ekati diamond mine, Northwest Territories. Canada produces more than $1 billion worth of diamonds each year, about 8 percent of the world's supply.

Capital Resources

In economics, the word "**capital**" means investment money *and* all that it can buy. Therefore, capital includes not only money, but also such **capital goods** as transportation equipment. In Canada, capital resources come from both private and public investment. When starting up a business, you can invest your own money or offer investors a share of the company. Some capital goods are already in place, such as transportation and communication systems. These are investments made in the local economy by the government, as was the case for India's steel mills.

Industrial construction can cost many millions, sometimes requiring **foreign investment**. However, profits earned by outside investors often go back to their home countries, instead of being reinvested into the local economy. This can be a problem for developing countries, who may find that their resources and labour are being used to profit companies from other countries.

Identify examples of capital goods in this steel mill photo.

Entrepreneurship

An entrepreneur is like a captain who must unify a sports team in order to win. If **entrepreneurial** abilities are weak, the business will fail. The entrepreneur recognizes a business opportunity and is able to combine land, labour, and capital to make a profit. If this person (or group) can create a successful business, the whole region can benefit. However, if they misuse the environment, pay poor wages, or run short of capital, the entire area may suffer. Entrepreneurship is found in Canada and nations with a similar economic system. In other countries, the government or a national or international corporation may make the business decisions.

WEB LINK ••••••••••••••••••••
Read stories about Canadian entrepreneurs. Visit our Web site.

Michele Stokley is an entrepreneur. For the past ten years, she and her husband have organized Bayfest, a four-day outdoor rock concert in Sarnia, Ontario. Every July, acts such as Aerosmith, Blink182, and Toby Keith perform. In 2007, attendance rose to 77 000.

Q: What got you into the concert business?

A: My father owned a company that promoted and marketed events. I thought it was the most exciting job in the world. My husband and I started the Sarnia Bayfest after someone suggested that we have an event in the park beside our restaurant. Now, it gets bigger every year.

Q: How do you decide which acts to include?

A: Bayfest fans range from 8 years old to 80. We decide our line-up based on requests and performer availability. There's always a balance of rock and some country. Nickelback and the Tragically Hip have been here twice due to popular request.

Q: What's involved in pulling it all together?

A: It's a year-round job. As it gets closer, we're working 18 hours a day. There are 30 people at the office and another 50 setting up. This year we had a $300 000 stage, four stories high. We hire more than 250 people for security, concessions, and clean-up.

Q: What is it like dealing with the performers?

A: Special trailers are brought in for the acts and all of the people travelling with them. Caterers are hired to prepare special food requests, some of them unusual.

Q: How does Bayfest affect the community?

A: The festival fills up every hotel room in the area, and brings tremendous restaurant and shopping business. The local tourist bureau estimates that Bayfest adds at least $10 million to the area economy during the four days. And I promise that next year's event will be even bigger and better than the last one.

Nickelback performed at Bayfest in 2007. How might local businesses prepare for such a large, four-day event in their community?

THINKING It Over

1. Add the bold-faced words covered in this section to a personal dictionary. Write your own definitions. Include a sentence using the term to help you remember it. **k**

2. Develop ideas about operating your own business by answering the caption questions found with the five photos on pages G 70–G 71. Design your own business plan. **k t**

3. Prepare a brief oral presentation to convince others to invest in your business idea. Include your responses to the five economic questions, use of resources, and how the business will benefit the local area. Try adding a chart or illustrations. **c a**

The Market Economy

How do economies differ? What you have learned so far in this chapter is based on the type of economic system found in Canada. However, there are other ways to answer the five economic questions. The diagram below uses the story of a person with a cow in different economic systems found around the world.

During **READING**

Checkpoint
Create a concept map answering the five economic questions for the market economy.

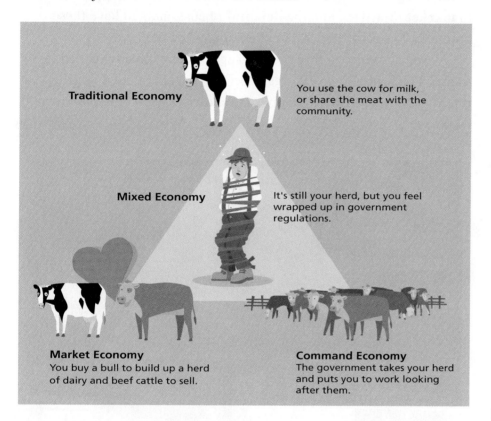

Traditional Economy — You use the cow for milk, or share the meat with the community.

Mixed Economy — It's still your herd, but you feel wrapped up in government regulations.

Market Economy — You buy a bull to build up a herd of dairy and beef cattle to sell.

Command Economy — The government takes your herd and puts you to work looking after them.

Now look at the **market economy**. What do you think about the statements below? Use the chart in the margin to rate your views on a scale from 1 to 5. Do the survey privately. Afterward, you can compare your opinions with others and keep your survey results to use later.

WORDS MATTER

market economy a system in which businesses and consumers decide what they will produce or purchase

1. Canada is a land of opportunity where almost anyone can be successful.

2. Wealth is a good measure of a person's achievement.

3. Government rules make it hard for businesses to grow.

4. People should be paid for work done in the family (e.g. housekeeping).

5. Our community needs more jobs if it is to grow and prosper.

Survey Opinion Scale
1 Agree totally
2 Agree somewhat
3 Not sure/no opinion
4 Disagree somewhat
5 Disagree totally

Our Environment

Reusable Shopping Bags

Since the 1970s, most store
purchases in North America
have been packed in plastic
bags made from non-
renewable material. Recently,
many retailers have
introduced reusable bags.
Environmentally conscious
shoppers can buy them for
just 99 cents. Reusable bags
prevent more plastic from
going into landfills. What are
other ways people can reduce
waste?

How can environmentally
friendly products affect
businesses? How can they
affect consumers?

Driven by Profit

In a market economy, answers to the economic questions will be
influenced by profit. People will make and distribute products or
services that can be sold at a price greater than the production costs.
When you shop, you are participating in the market economy—you
decide whether or not the product or service is worth the asking
price. This is an economic system that dates back to the earliest days
of the village marketplace. Prices were decided by the **supply** brought
to **market** by sellers, and the **demand** of customers to have these
products. The same two forces affect prices today.

Are all activities within the market economy directly related to
profit? Think of non-profit organizations that act in the public
interest. They still employ people, purchase services, or support small
businesses.

Considering the concept of supply and demand, suggest why front row seats at a
game or performance cost more. Would you pay extra to see an event up close?
Why or why not?

In 1776, Scottish professor Adam Smith was the first to describe
the market economy in his book, *The Wealth of Nations*. Smith was a
witness to the Industrial Revolution in Great Britain. He saw worth
in a market system where producers and consumers both tried to get
the best price for goods and services. Smith wrote that all people
should be free to pursue this self-interest, as long as their actions did
not harm others.

At that time, the British government had many laws controlling trade with its colonies. Smith thought that a country would be more successful if government did not interfere with business. Decisions about goods and services in a market economy should only be made by those directly involved in business and industry—people seeking to make a profit.

Market Economy Problems

Market economies expanded rapidly in the 19th century as the Industrial Revolution spread. The aggressive actions of powerful entrepreneurs led social critics to call them "robber barons." These businesspeople owned and operated factories, railway lines, and power plants. Their investments created immense fortunes, and the entrepreneurs and their families lived in luxury. Meanwhile, most working people laboured long hours for very little pay. Since then, labour unions and other organizations have sought better pay and working conditions for all workers.

Market economies also go through cycles of decline, called an **economic depression**. During the Great Depression of the 1930s, factories were forced to close, workers were laid off, and ten years of widespread poverty set in. Between 1929 and 1939, the market economies of the world were unable to correct themselves. In many countries, governments stepped in to help their economies by investing in work projects and supporting some businesses. Many governments continue to play an active role in business and industry today.

What do you think motivated Adam Smith to write *The Wealth of Nations*?

Profit or Environment?

Choosing between protecting the environment and allowing the growth of business can be very difficult. Communities want jobs and growth, but damage to the environment can have long-term effects on everyone. Responsible companies seek to limit their impact on the environment. For example, they may replant trees or reduce waste by recycling. However, many companies find these practices too expensive, and choose cheaper options. This is a continuing problem in market economies.

Canadian financier Sir Henry Pellatt built Casa Loma, a 98-room mansion overlooking the city of Toronto. Why were wealthy entrepreneurs called "robber barons?"

How Free Should the Market Economy Be?

The United States is a good example of a market system, with millions of consumers and companies active in the economy. Americans spend and make trillions of dollars every year. However, the government plays an important role in its economy. For example, the government provides important services, such as national defence, assistance programs, and the construction of highways.

During the Great Depression, when thousands of people were out of work, U.S. president Franklin D. Roosevelt's government borrowed heavily to fund massive work projects. These projects included the building of many of the international bridges connecting the U.S. and Canada. Today, thousands of federal and state government agencies regulate most aspects of American business and industry. The U.S. Department of Commerce is the largest.

There is strong debate about the role of government in the free market in the United States. Which one of these opposing points of view do you find more acceptable?

A. The government is needed in business. Laws have two purposes. One is to protect us from people who may cheat customers or clients, or sell dangerous products. The other is to provide a good business environment for the companies that give us necessary products and services.

B. The government limits business. Sometimes it actually creates more problems, and makes business too hard for small entrepreneurs. We need less control—maybe even no government interference at all—in order for business to flourish. This would be a truly free market economy.

The Canadian government also sponsored work projects during the Great Depression. This photo shows construction of the Big Bend Highway in British Columbia.

What Do YOU Think?

1. Discuss the two points of view found at the left. Which one do you favour? Why? *t c*

2. What was the importance of each of the following to the market economy? *k*
   a) Adam Smith, b) the "robber barons," c) Franklin D. Roosevelt

3. Go back to the survey on page G 75. Have any of your opinions changed? Have any of them become stronger? If so, explain what changed your mind. *t*

Sometimes people work for free. For example, you may help your friends, do small favours for neighbours and relatives, or help at home without expecting payment in return. Unpaid work also happens in a market economy, even when most goods and services are offered at a price. In the **traditional economy**, most production is for shared use by a group or family. Profit is not the goal of production and little, if any, money changes hands. Cultural and religious values often shape economic decisions in this system.

Hunting and Gathering

A traditional economy is one which answers the five economic questions by relying on the familiar customs of the past. It still exists in some cultural and religious groups, although it is disappearing in many areas. In the past, the Aboriginal peoples of Canada organized hunting, fishing, and farming to provide for the whole group. At places like Alberta's Head-Smashed-In Buffalo Jump, the community cooperated to guide a herd of buffalo toward a cliff. The buffalo were stampeded over the edge, and the kill was shared. Today, this kind of sharing is becoming lost. Simon Akpaliapik, an Inuit Elder in Nunavut, speaks of the change which he has seen in his own lifetime:

In a camp many years ago we were all related and we all worked together. We shared everything. Now, in the communities, that cooperation is gone. In some places hunters are selling their meat, even to relatives.

MATTER

traditional economy an economic system in which decisions are based on customs, beliefs, or religion, within a strong social community

During **READING**

Checkpoint
Create a concept map answering the five economic questions for the traditional economy.

Traditional economies rely on group production and the sharing of goods, such as in this buffalo jump. How do the five economic questions apply to the buffalo jump?

Subsistence Agriculture

The traditional economy still exists within countries where subsistence farming is practised. **Subsistence farmers** work full time to produce their own food. Often the family works for its own survival, rather than cooperating with the community. If there is a surplus above the needs of the family or group, the extra produce or livestock is traded or sold.

Subsistence farmers may own a small plot of land where they raise a mixture of crops and livestock. Families work together. Children look after animals and gather firewood, while adolescents and adults do the heavier farm work. Elderly adults often care for the children, and give valued advice on issues affecting the family, farm, and community.

Sample Countries	GDP per Capita ($US)	Agriculture (% employed)	Manufacturing (% employed)	Services (% employed)
Ethiopia	1044	88	2	10
Rwanda	1406	92	3	5
Tanzania	801	84	4	12
India	3737	67	13	20
Cambodia	3170	75	5	20
Laos	1575	78	6	16
Canada	**35 494**	**4**	**20**	**76**

Countries with subsistence agriculture often have very little manufacturing and few available services. Compare the first six countries with Canada. What factors might explain the difference?

During READING

Make Connections

What are your basic needs? What could you do without? What would life be like if you could only have nothing except your basic needs?

Subsistence farming takes place in developing countries where commercial farms and large plantations often make use of the best lands to grow export crops. Nomadic herders and shifting cultivators move through **marginal lands** to produce their food. These areas are too rugged, dry, or isolated for successful commercial farming. However, subsistence farming can produce enough for their families and their community. Subsistence agriculture is often carried out on tiny fields like those shown on the cover of this book.

At one time, most countries had traditional economies. Today, no government bases its economic decisions on tradition. Most nations have been influenced by the worldwide movement of people, products, and information, and operate either market or command economic systems. However, traditional economies are still found within developing nations, among people who rely on hunting and gathering or subsistence agriculture for their survival. It is not only the geography of an area or available resources that affect their economic decisions—cultural values and religious tradition are also major factors.

What types of tools or technology might be used in subsistence farming? Explain.

Economic Questions   **Economic Systems**

Economic Questions	Market Economy	Traditional Economy
1. Who produces goods and services?	Entrepreneurs, professionals, and employees	Members of the family or the cultural group
2. What goods and services are produced?	Goods and services that can be sold to create a profit	The materials needed to provide food, clothing, and shelter
3. How are goods and services produced?	Modern technology and methods are used to cut production costs and improve quality	Traditional technology and methods passed down from generation to generation
4. For whom are goods and services produced?	For paying consumers	For members of the family or community
5. How are goods and services distributed?	Advertising attracts customers to retail outlets and the Internet	Either by sharing necessities or by bartering (trading) surplus goods with others

During **READING**

Checkpoint
Check your understanding of the connections between the five economic questions and the market and traditional economies. Compare your concept maps with the table on this page.

WEB LINK •••••••••••••••
Read about a subsistence farmer in Zambia. Visit our Web site.

THINKING It Over

1. Think about paid and unpaid work in Canada. Work with a partner to create questions for a simple survey to find out what work is done by family members for free and what is done to earn income. What do your survey results tell you about work?

2. Discuss how people in a traditional economy might deal with these issues: a) whether or not to try new agricultural methods being introduced in a nearby area, b) how to survive a devastating natural disaster which has ruined the season's crops, c) how to settle conflicts between farmers or hunters claiming the same lands, d) whether or not to migrate to the nearest city in hopes of a better life.

3. Use the information in this section as a starting point for a drawing or collage about food production in the traditional economies of Africa or Asia.

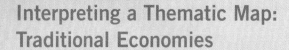

Interpreting a Thematic Map: Traditional Economies

Many people in traditional economies support themselves and their families directly from farming, forestry, and fishing. In this Geo Skill, you will learn to connect map, graph, and numerical information to draw conclusions about traditional economies.

Step 1 · Review the Map Colours

This map uses two shades of colour. You will notice that the darker shaded countries have small circle graphs showing employment structure.

Step 2 · Interpret the Circle Graphs

The legend indicates that circle graphs show the proportion of agricultural, industrial, and service employment in the sample countries. Focus on the proportion of people working in agriculture (which on this map includes fishing and forestry).

Step 3 · Look for Map–Graph Patterns

Some countries on the map have high agricultural employment. Describe their map locations in relation to latitude and the continents. Are high proportions of farm labour found at certain latitudes or in certain continents or regions of the earth?

Step 4 · Look for Map–Number Table Patterns

There is a direct connection between labour and living standards. Compare the agricultural countries on the map to the Gross Domestic Product per Capita chart. What pattern can you see?

Step 5 · Test Your Observations

Check your findings by looking at the map, graph, and number table in a different way. Describe the locations of countries with very high employment in service industries. These jobs range from entertainers to surgeons. Compare the GDP per capita of these countries to those with a high proportion of agricultural employment.

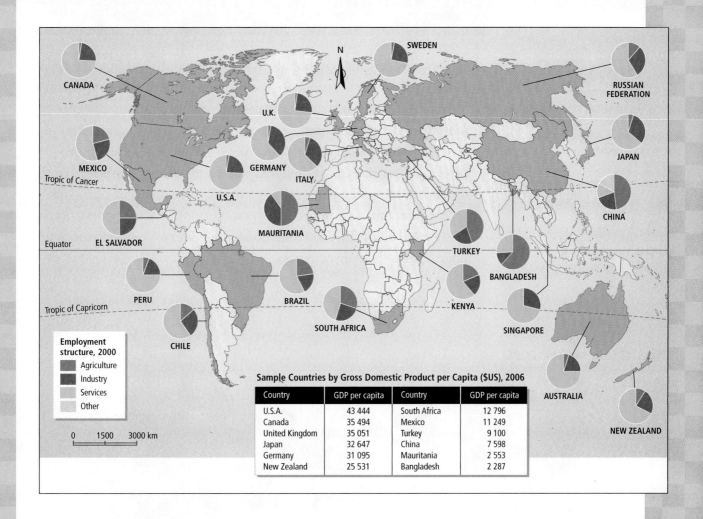

Employment structure, 2000
- Agriculture
- Industry
- Services
- Other

0   1500   3000 km

Sample Countries by Gross Domestic Product per Capita ($US), 2006

Country	GDP per capita	Country	GDP per capita
U.S.A.	43 444	South Africa	12 796
Canada	35 494	Mexico	11 249
United Kingdom	35 051	Turkey	9 100
Japan	32 647	China	7 598
Germany	31 095	Mauritania	2 553
New Zealand	25 531	Bangladesh	2 287

APPLY It

1. Where are the countries with the highest proportion of agricultural labour located? Note a) latitudes, and b) continent or regions. Why might this occur?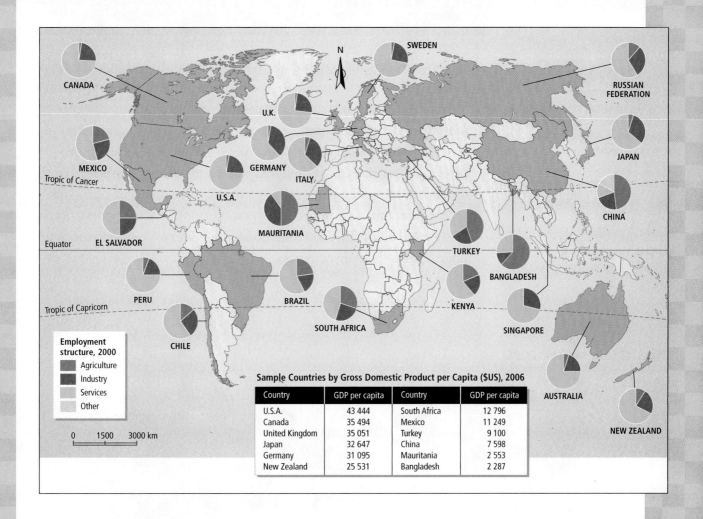

2. Compare the countries with the highest percentage of the labour force in agriculture with the GDP per capita of those countries. Is there a relationship between these numbers? Explain possible reasons for this pattern.

3. Predict what might happen to income levels in these countries if they shifted to more service employment. What obstacles stand in the way of this change?

During **READING**

Checkpoint
Create a concept map
answering the five economic
questions for the command
economy.

Economic decisions are not always made by individuals, companies, families, or cultural groups. In a **command economy**, production and distribution are directed by one person or a small group of people who form the government. Suppose you are part of a group making T-shirts for a special event. If one person takes over the whole project, it becomes a command system. That person makes all of the decisions, while the rest of the group follows orders. In countries with command economies, one person or political party dictates the answers to all of the economic questions. Everyone else's role is to obey or face the consequences.

Types of Government, 2006

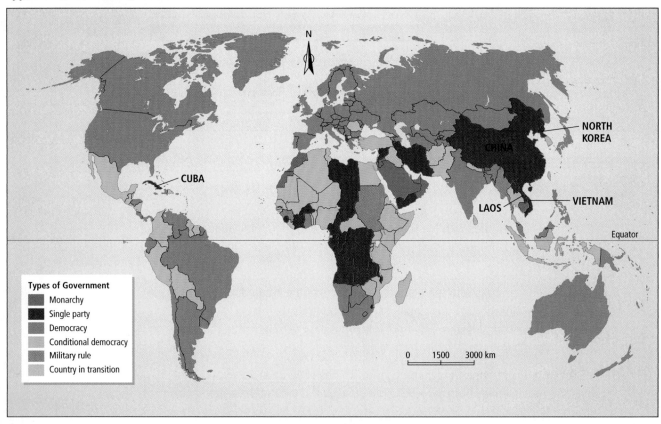

Command economies are usually found in countries without freely elected governments.
These countries are governed by a monarchy, a single political party, or by military rule.
Where are these governments found?

Military Spending

Some command economies are also military dictatorships or nations at war. The government of a **military dictatorship** is controlled by the armed forces. A military leader makes decisions about production and distribution of goods and services. There are several countries in Africa and Asia with this type of government today.

In many of these dictatorships people live in poverty, with little chance for an education or access to health care. Many countries that spend heavily on their military often do not leave much for social services. There are some exceptions. The following table includes some countries with high military spending and also a high standard of living. Also, note that Israel, Canada, India, and the United States are **democracies** and do not have command economies.

WORDS MATTER

military dictatorship a form of government in which the military holds political power

democracy a form of government in which elected people fill government offices

Military and Educational Spending

African Countries	Military Spending (% of GDP)	Education Spending (% of GDP)	Middle Eastern and Asian Countries	Military Spending (% of GDP)	Education Spending (% of GDP)
Angola	21.2	3.0	Israel	8.0	8.0
Brunei	7.6	4.0	Kuwait	8.2	6.0
Burundi	5.4	4.0	Oman	9.7	4.0
Eritrea	22.9	5.0	Yemen	5.2	7.0
Ethiopia	9.4	4.0	China	4.3	2.8
			India	2.5	4.4
U.S.A.	4.1	4.7	**Canada**	1.2	6.0

What pattern do you notice about the spending priorities of these governments compared to Canada? Why would governments make such decisions?

In some regions, years of conflict are matched by high levels of military spending.

How did Canada's government answer the economic questions during World War II (1939–1945)?

WORDS MATTER

communism a system that supports common ownership of the means of production

Canada at War

During the First and Second World Wars, Canada's economy was temporarily controlled by the government under the War Measures Act. Canada and other nations involved in the war switched to an economy centred on the production of weapons and military equipment. Factories that normally made cars, farm machinery, and home appliances made military necessities instead. To do so, governments abroad and in Canada switched from a market to a command economy during the war years. What does this imply about the Canadian government's priorities during the wars?

Communist Economies

About 160 years ago, German philosopher Karl Marx introduced a new type of economic system. It promised: "From each according to his ability; to each according to his need." Marx was the founder of **communism**, an economic and political system in which people would work together to produce goods and share them fairly. Communist political revolutions took place in Russia in 1917 and in China in 1949. Later, Marx's economic system spread to several nations in Asia, Africa, and the island of Cuba. Today, communist governments are still found in five countries: China, Cuba, Laos, North Korea, and Vietnam. (See the map on page G 84.)

Heroes and Villains | *Karl Marx*

Karl Marx aimed for a cooperative economic system created by political revolution. He predicted that eventually, "the state would wither away," leaving the people with freedom. In practice, however, communism has always brought a command economy. Strong dictators and Communist Party officials have made all the economic decisions. Tanks and missiles have been more important than decent housing and consumer goods. In recent decades, Russia has rejected communism and adopted the market economy, while communist China has relaxed government control of production and distribution. Was Karl Marx wrong, or have communist leaders misused his ideas?

Cuba: A Communist Command Economy

More than 11 million people live on the island of Cuba. Until 1957, American companies invested heavily in Cuban sugar, tobacco, and fruit plantations. However, they took the profits home. Most Cubans were very poor, with little access to education or medical care. In 1958–59, Fidel Castro's communist forces overthrew the Cuban government and seized American-owned businesses and property on the island. To this day, the U.S. forbids its citizens from visiting Cuba, and will not allow American companies to trade or invest there.

International tourism, especially from Canada and Europe, has become a very important source of income for Cuba's economy.

In Cuba, the government decides what to produce and how to distribute goods and services. Individuals lack many freedoms and choices. The economy struggles, partly because the island nation must do without American trade and investment. Cubans live with only the basic necessities, and deal with shortages of consumer products. However, the government provides free education, daycare, and health care for all Cubans. Today, more than 95 % of Cubans can read and write, and many are engineers or skilled technicians.

THINKING It Over

1. Use the world map on page G 84 to identify the following.

   a) The continents in which most command economies are located

   b) The type of command economy found in most of those countries.

2. Why are American citizens and companies not allowed to have contact with Cuba? How has this affected Cuba's economy? Why do Canadians often visit Cuba?

3. Work with a partner to construct a chart showing how a command economy might answer each of the five economic questions.

PUTTING IT ALL TOGETHER

This chapter has taken you on a tour of the world of economic systems. You used the five economic questions of production and distribution to consider a business that you could operate some day. You met an entrepreneur who combines economic resources to offer entertainment. You also compared decisions about production made in market, traditional, and command economic systems. Above all, you looked into the unit's key question: **How do economic systems influence industries across Canada and the world?**

After READING

Visualize Ideas with a Concept Map

Choose one of your concept maps. Find pictures online or in magazines and newspapers to create a visual concept map. Replace the outer circles with the pictures, and use your notes to write a caption for each picture.

THINKING It Through

1. Describe the pattern of the map on page G 89:
   a) In which regions do women generally make up more than 40% of the labour force? **m**
   b) In which regions do women generally make up less than 30% of the labour force? **m**
   c) Identify a region of the world with traditional economies. Use information from the chapter to explain your choice. **k m**

2. Which of these factors would help explain the world pattern of women's paid employment, and which would not? Explain why or why not. a) literacy, b) landforms, c) social customs, d) living standards, e) child care **t**

3. What are the differences and similarities between the two photos on the next page? Classify each of the photos as representing either a market or traditional economic system. Use information from the photo and the chapter to explain each choice. **t k**

4. Write a half-page summary about working women in different regions of the world. Refer directly to the economic question, "Who produces goods and services?" and to the economic resources of labour and entrepreneurship. **k c**

World: Women in the Labour Force

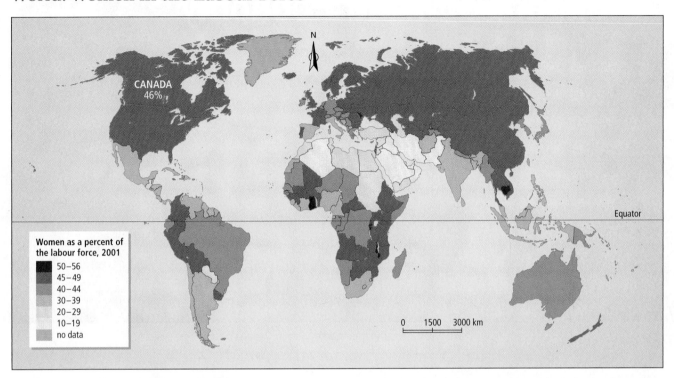

CANADA
46%

Equator

Women as a percent of
the labour force, 2001
- 50–56
- 45–49
- 40–44
- 30–39
- 20–29
- 10–19
- no data

0   1500   3000 km

CHAPTER 5

Canada's Mixed Economy

What role does the free market play in Canada's economic system?

Making Connections

Look at the products you bring to school (clothes, notebooks, pens, pencils, or calculators). With a partner, discuss where the products are made. What materials are they made of? Where do those materials come from?

WORDS MATTER

mixed economy an economy that combines different economic systems, such as the market and command systems

A re you an avid shopper, or do you just buy something when you need it? Do you pay full price for what you need, or do you look for bargains? No matter what your shopping habits, you are a consumer—a driving force behind Canada's economy. The market brings together sellers and buyers to decide prices based on supply and demand. Sometimes the supply is greater than the demand for a product, and it will likely go on sale. Other times the demand is greater than the supply. In this case, the price of the product may rise.

Governments enter the economy by promoting growth and setting the minimum wage. They also pass laws to regulate commerce and protect consumers. Governments collect taxes and spend heavily. They even own and operate huge companies, such as VIA Rail and Hydro One. Like many countries, Canada combines the market and command systems in a **mixed economy**. In this chapter you will be investigating the mixed economy as part of the unit's Big Idea: **How do economic systems influence industries across Canada and the world?**

Why is government such an important part of Canada's economic system?

Questions to Consider as You Read this Chapter

- How does the mixed economy work in Canada?

- What are the three different types of industry?

- How has technology changed industry in the past century?

- How do I research and communicate information about an industry?

- How do I interpret a map of industrial location factors?

Thinking About Literacy

Comparing Information and Finding Ideas

Create charts to compare economies and industries as you read this chapter. Use headings and subheadings to choose topics for your chart, like the example below. As you read the chapter, include your ideas on the importance and meaning of the topics.

Mixed Economy

Traditional and Market	Traditional and Command	Market and Command	Importance/ Meaning
Traditional crafts sold to tourists			People in this country have learned to earn money from their traditional ways

You just picked out a snack at the variety store. At the cash register, your 99¢ item suddenly jumped to $1.12 with the addition of two government sales taxes. Welcome to Canada's mixed economy! Canada is not the only country with a mixed system. In fact, most nations today have some combination of the basic types: traditional, market, and command. Mixed economies are everywhere.

Traditional and Market: Around the world, you will find traditional economies that also have marketplaces in which goods are offered by vendors. Services such as local taxis or repair work are also available to those who can afford them. Also, traditional craftspeople make many different handicrafts to sell directly to tourists or for export. Fair trade goods are increasingly popular with Canadian consumers.

Traditional and Command: Among the five communist governments that remain today are four Asian nations: China, North Korea, Vietnam, and Laos. Many people in these countries rely on subsistence agriculture. It would be very difficult for these governments to successfully change traditional farming methods adapted to the land.

Market and Command: There are no longer any "true" market economies in the world. Even the best examples of the free market—the United States, Taiwan, and Singapore—have some degree of government regulation of business. At the other end of the scale, some European countries like Sweden and Norway have market economies with a great deal of government planning and taxation.

During **READING**

Checkpoint
Check pages S 12–S 13 to review analyzing photos. What do you see in these pictures? What clues can you use to answer the question in the caption?

How can you tell which type of mixed economy is best represented in each of these photos?

Canada's Mixed Economy

Business, government, and consumers all play a part in Canada's economy. Every day, news headlines show the important role each group takes in our mixed system. All three have the power to influence the production and consumption of goods and services.

Ontario Government to Close Coal-Fired Plants

Telus Corporation Eyes Bell Canada for Merger

Imperial Oil Bids on Arctic Natural Gas

Police Probe Store Open on Holiday

Consumer Group Claims Gasoline Overpriced

Which of these news headlines show the actions of a) business, b) government, and c) consumers?

Governments Tax and Spend

All levels of government in Canada affect the economy because they tax and spend. You may not pay income taxes yet, but you contribute to government **revenue** every time you pay the GST (Goods and Services Tax) and the PST (Provincial Sales Tax) on purchases. The federal government in Ottawa collected more than $220 billion in 2006 from all sources. Ottawa then chooses how to spend this money for the benefit of Canadians and the world.

Revenue Collected by Canadian Federal Government (2006)

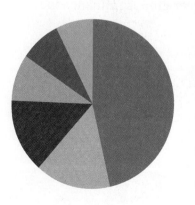

- Personal Income Tax
  $103.7 billion
- GST (Goods and Services Tax)
  $33.0 billion
- Corporate Income Tax
  $32.0 billion
- Other revenues and earnings (e.g., VIA Rail)
  $19.6 billion
- Taxes on imports, energy, tobacco, alcohol
  $17.7 billion
- Contribution to Employment Insurance plan
  $16.5 billion

How does government revenue collection affect you?

Spending by Canadian Federal Government (2006)

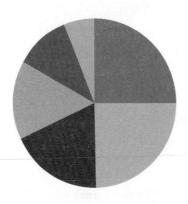

- ● Program expenses (e.g., defence, public safety) $56.9 billion
- ● Transfers to persons (e.g., old age security) $55.6 billion
- ● Transfers to provinces (e.g., health care) $41.0 billion
- ● Interest payments on the national debt $33.8 billion
- ● Other transfers (e.g., foreign aid) $24.9 billion
- ● Paying down the national debt $13.2 billion

How does government spending affect you?

WEB LINK •························
Learn about consumer rights in Canada. Visit our Web site.

Consumer and Producer Groups

Did you ever buy something that didn't work? Was there anything you could do about it? **Consumer** groups in Canada represent the interests of consumers, which includes protecting them from inferior products. At the same time, there are producer groups that look after the interests of sellers. Both meet with governments to influence regulations affecting the economy.

Consumer Groups

Buyers take a direct interest in the quality, safety, and value of products and services as **consumer advocates**. Organized groups, like the Consumers' Association of Canada (CAC) and the Canadian Toy Testing Council, are more than 50 years old. The CAC tackles food and health issues, as well as product standards and prices. For example, they monitor gas prices, and call for government investigation if prices are too high. The Toy Testing Council tests toys every year and rates them in an annual *Toy Report*. Consumer groups have also pushed CD and video companies to post Parental Advisories on their music and game products. Consumer groups influence the marketplace in Canada's mixed economy.

Producer Groups

Farmers and other producers have organized **marketing boards** to improve product quality while ensuring the income of their members. Suppose farmers brought huge quantities of eggs or milk to market at the same time. They would receive very low prices because of the oversupply of their product. To help prevent this problem, marketing boards organize farmers to regulate the production of their goods. This creates a fairly even supply, which helps stabilize prices. They also use advertising to inform consumers about farm products and to protect the interests of Canadian farmers.

WORDS MATTER

marketing board an organization created by producers to promote their product and to maintain fair prices by controlling supply

WEB LINK ••••••••••••••••••••••
For links to producer groups visit our Web site.

MILK PRODUCTS — AN ESSENTIAL PART OF HEALTHY LIVING

Every year, the Dairy Farmers of Canada publish the Milk Calendar, which is distributed free in print and online. Recipes inside the calendar are centred on milk products and are based on Canada's Food Guide. How is this effective advertising?

THINKING It Over

1. What is a mixed economy? Answer the caption question found with the photos of mixed economy combinations on page G 92.

2. Examine the two loonies showing Ottawa's revenue and spending on pages G 93 and G 94.

   a) Identify one fact from each diagram that you found most surprising. Explain why.

   b) Use examples from your community to explain why government taxing and spending are so important in Canada's economic system.

3. Based on the two loonies, construct circle graphs of your weekly or monthly revenue and spending. How might this graph be useful to you?

Three Types of Industry

Everyday life can be very different in various parts of the world. While you are in school, or perhaps spending part of your day helping out in the family business, other young people are working many hours a day. Girls your age are knotting handwoven carpets. Young boys must sometimes work in dangerous conditions in factories. In Canada, most people work in service occupations—for example, electricians, ski instructors, and fashion designers. Education and training are very important in service-based economies.

Most people think of industry and manufacturing as two words for the same thing. To geographers, **industry** is any type of work people do to make money. Carpetmaking and metalworking are industries—they manufacture products. Teaching and designing are also industries—they provide services. If a ski instructor is giving a lesson, that's industry. When she skis on her day off, her skiing is leisure, not work. There are three types of industry:

- **Primary industry** is work based on harvesting natural resources, such as animals, crops, trees, or minerals.

- **Secondary industry** makes commercial products from these resources, through manufacturing or construction.

- **Tertiary industry** provides personal, social, and commercial services, as well as transportation and public utilities.

With a compound bar graph, the bar segments are stacked one on top of the other for a particular year. It is a useful way to see overall changes in detailed information.

Canada: Employment by Industry, 1941–2006

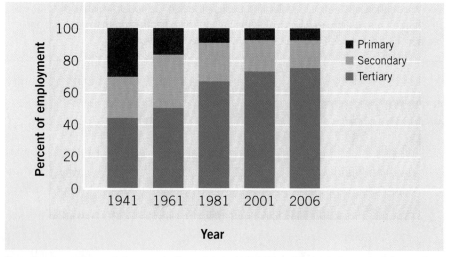

Describe the pattern of changes in Canada's industrial employment shown in this graph.

Primary Industry

In Grade 7 Geography you learned about Canada's natural resources and the industries that process them. You might think that these industries make up a large part of the Canadian economy. However, you might be surprised to know that farm, fish, forest, and mineral production accounts for less than 6% of the total value of Canadian goods and services. Only about 1 Canadian employee in 25 works in these activities. Farming, fishing, forestry, and mining are called **primary industries** because each one gathers natural resources, the first stage of industrial production. Use this chart to learn the main characteristics of the four primary industries.

Farms	Forests
• cultivating, planting, and harvesting crops, raising livestock and farming specialized products such as honey or nursery plants • cleaning and packaging fruit and vegetables and other products	• harvesting trees for manufacturing or retail sale, as well as planting seedlings • includes sawmills, which make building materials (cut lumber and plywood) for construction
Fish	**Minerals and Fossil Fuels**
• catching, cleaning, and packaging fish and all varieties of shell fish, such as lobsters or clams, from the wild or from aquaculture • processing may be done on "factory ships"	• extracting any type of mineral from the earth, from diamonds to gravel, along with petroleum and natural gas • includes any refining which purifies minerals before use in manufacturing

Industry Combinations

Sometimes primary industry may combine with another type of economic activity. Clovermead Apiaries, near Aylmer, Ontario, has been owned and operated by the Hiemstra family since 1975. Besides producing honey, they have also created a small pioneer village on their farm that attracts school groups and tourists. Special festivals related to honey production and a country store round out the Clovermead operation. Tourism, education, and retail sales are all services, and examples of tertiary industry. The Hiemstra family business is a combination of industry types.

Our Environment

Environment and Industry

All primary industry takes natural resources directly from the earth. Producers must harvest a **sustainable yield**, leaving plenty for future use. They must also prevent damage to the environment through pollution or waste. Poor farm practices, over-fishing, clear-cut logging, and poisonous mine wastes are all environmental threats.

Create a poster to increase awareness of environmental threats in one primary industry.

WORDS MATTER

sustainable yield the amount that can be taken from a natural resource (e.g., cod stocks) without reducing the resource's ability to maintain itself

primary industry the collecting of raw materials for use in industry

The annual "bee-beard" competition at Clovermead Apiaries attracts many visitors. Don't try this at home!

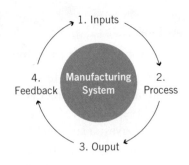

1. Inputs
Manufacturing System
2. Process
3. Ouput
4. Feedback

Secondary Industry

If you play or watch sports, you know that a good team uses winning strategies. Before games, players practise strategies. Afterward, the coach reviews what worked and what didn't. Manufacturing follows a similar system. **Input** and **process** steps are like the game plan, while **output** and **feedback** stages are like the game results. Use the information about the clothing industry on this page, and the *Zoom In* feature about the automobile industry on pages G 104–G 105 to understand more about **secondary industry**.

Fashion: Input and Process

The manufacturing game plan calls for a new line of clothing. First, several important imputs are required. Company designers study the latest fashion trends before creating their own designs. Suitable fabrics, leather, buttons, and thread are purchased from suppliers. Pattern templates for the cutters to use are prepared in every clothing size. The process of actually making the clothing differs from company to company. Some use mass production methods in order to sell inexpensive garments, while others focus on quality, perhaps having one skilled sewing machine operator produce an entire outfit. Some produce the goods locally, while others use **offshore companies**, such as garment manufacturers in Mauritius or China. The choice to use off-shore companies is usually made because of lower labour costs.

Fashion: Output and Feedback

Clothing manufacturers employ sellers who arrange contracts with stores. If the store buyers like the new products, they place big orders. As a result, manufacturing output is large, and extra labour is hired to increase production. On the other hand, the designers may have misjudged consumer tastes. Fewer sales contracts result in lower manufacturing output for the season. The volume of sales provides company management with important feedback. After discussions with the store buyers, managers may reward successful fashion designers, and let others go. This feedback will help the company have a better game plan for next season. Manufacturers are like coaches—they don't like to lose.

WEB LINK • • • • • • • • • • • • • • • • • •
Explore an interesting Web site about jeans—history, production, and ads. Visit our Web site.

Industrial Factors in the Fashion Industry

Montréal and Toronto are Canada's most important fashion design and manufacturing centres. Industrial factors such as raw materials, labour force, and markets explain why the clothing industry is located in these places.

During **READING**

Checkpoint
Create a chart to organize your notes on the fashion industry. Add your ideas on how input, process, output, and feedback relate to the primary, secondary, and tertiary aspects surrounding the fashion industry.

WEB LINK •••••••••••••••••••
Learn about Toronto's fashion industry at our Web site.

Inputs: Raw Material
Montréal and Toronto are well situated to receive shipments of fabric, leather, and other materials. Highways speed the movement of container freight shipments from around the world. Care must be taken so that the materials do not become damp or musty in transit or storage. Why are quality materials so important in the garment industry?

Process: Labour Force
Canada's two largest cities are leading garment centres based on a large, skilled workforce. Many fabric cutters and sewing machine operators have been immigrant women. Colleges in both cities train designers. What skills would a successful fashion designer require?

Output and Feedback: Market
The large populations of Montréal, Vancouver, and Toronto make them the consumer base of Canada's garment market. Fashion shows are used to present the new lines to store buyers, and their response shapes the production volume for the season. Why do international designs usually get their first Canadian showings in Montréal and Toronto?

Tertiary Industry

Making a guitar: secondary industry. Selling a guitar: tertiary industry. Teaching guitar players: tertiary industry.

WORDS MATTER

tertiary industry the providing of services, such as customer support, distribution, or retailing

outsourcing sending work to an outside provider, usually to cut costs

The store buyers and models at a fashion show are not producing anything; instead, they are buying and selling the finished products. People behind the scenes are providing services too—truck drivers, stage technicians, advertisers, and caterers. This is different from the designers and machine operators who actually turned the cloth into clothing. In Canada, there are about four service workers for every manufacturing job. All developed countries have economies heavily based on **tertiary industries**.

Now look at tertiary industry in daily life. Do you ride a bus to school? If so, that is tertiary industry: transportation. After school, you might have a guitar lesson, or buy milk, or mail a letter. All personal and commercial services are tertiary industries, as are communications activities like the mail system. It is not hard to understand why about three-quarters of all Canadian employees work in tertiary industries.

A recent trend in tertiary industries is **outsourcing**. Companies that offer services such as accounting or computer support are hired by companies in other countries. Often it is cheaper for companies to outsource these tasks, rather than have their own employees deal with them. How can this affect Canada's tertiary industry? Why is outsourcing often a concern for Canadian employees?

Tertiary Industry in Canada, 2006

Category	Value (% of GDP)
Finance, insurance, real estate	19.2%
Education, health, social services, government	15.5%
Retail and wholesale trade	12.8%
Professional, scientific, and technical services	4.5%
Information and cultural services	4.1%

Value in Canada's Economy, 2006

Industry Category	Value (% of GDP)
Primary Industry	5.8%
Seconday Industry	22.0%
Tertiary Industry	72.2%

The Multiplier Effect

Some communities in Canada have economies based almost entirely on tertiary industry. These are tourist centres such as Niagara Falls, Whistler, and Peggy's Cove. They have a high proportion of businesses offering tours and activities, food and lodging, shopping, and souvenirs. Tourists bring money, and the tourism businesses circulate the money through the local economy. Business owners and their employees then use their profits or wages to pay for food, clothing, and shelter. Geographers call this the **multiplier effect**. It occurs in every type of community. Many communities seek manufacturing opportunities because this also results in a high multiplier effect—it promotes other manufacturing and more services. Local economies also prosper when resource industries sell their grain, fish, wood, or minerals.

Outsiders buy local resources, products, or services

(e.g. stores, offices)

(e.g. farming, tourism)

Local resources, products, and services

Local employers and workers

Local businesses and services

$ spending

How is the multiplier effect like throwing a stone into a pool of water?

THINKING It Over

1. Classify each of these activities as primary, secondary, tertiary, or non-economic. Explain your choices. a) delivering newspapers, b) making steel rods for the construction industry, c) working on a ranch, d) fishing with friends, e) making woven carpets, f) babysitting for neighbours.

2. Fashion moves across Canada from Toronto and Montréal. List examples of goods and services that flow into these two cities from each region of Canada (e.g., oil from Alberta).

3. Apply the terms input, process, output, and feedback to an industry such as building construction in an isolated First Nations community.

4. a) Explain the multiplier effect in your own words.

   b) How can the multiplier effect change a region? Discuss how discoveries of precious minerals, such as diamonds, affect Canada's North.

GEO SKILL

Interpreting Industrial Location from Maps

Area Symbols	
	urban area
	wooded area

Line Symbols	
~180~	elevation contour
/\/\	stream
+++	railway track
—•—	power line
=407=	divided highway
——	major street

Point Symbols	
	large buildings

The Chrysler Corporation operates a huge auto assembly plant in Brampton, in the Greater Toronto Area (GTA). Here you will learn to interpret the location factors for this industry from topographic and road maps.

Step 1 Review the Meaning of the Map Symbols

You will need to know how to interpret area, line, and point symbols, particularly those used on a topographic map. Use Chapter 1 to review topographic map reading skills.

Step 2 Locate the Industry on the Maps

You can spot the assembly plant on the topographic map as a large three-part building near the northeast edge of the Brampton urban area. Find this place on the road map.

Step 3 Find Industrial Location Information on the Maps

- Flat land: a large area with few contour lines (for buildings and completed cars)
- Raw materials: expressways to bring auto parts to the plant in transport trucks
- Labour supply: a large population of workers in the surrounding region
- Market: a large population of customers in the surrounding GTA region, and railway tracks to transport cars to more distant customers

Step 4 Make a Sketch Map

A sketch map is a simple hand-drawn map that shows only certain details related to a topic. Use the topographic map to make a sketch map which shows only the industrial location factors for the industry. Start with a blank page and follow the steps found in "Using and Making Maps" on pages S 14–S 15 of the Skills Tool Kit.

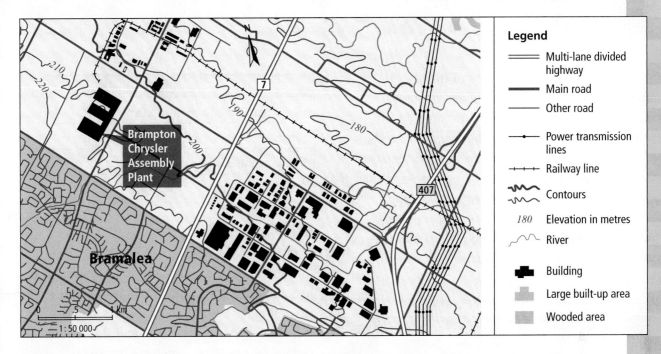

Legend

- ═══ Multi-lane divided highway
- ━━━ Main road
- ─── Other road
- •─•─• Power transmission lines
- ┼┼┼┼ Railway line
- ∿∿∿ Contours
- *180* Elevation in metres
- ∿∿ River
- ■ Building
- ▨ Large built-up area
- ▨ Wooded area

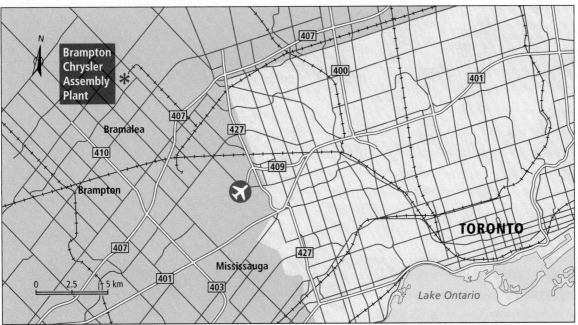

APPLY It

1. Use the maps to record the industrial location information listed in Step Three for the Brampton assembly plant. 🔵

2. Make a simple labelled sketch map to show this location information. 🔵

3. Vehicles are carried from Ontario across Canada by truck or rail. Give examples of raw materials that reach Ontario from specific provinces by a) ship, b) rail, c) transport truck, and d) pipeline. 🔵

The automobile industry is one of the leading manufacturing activities in Canada. Motor vehicles and parts are Canada's leading export products, greater in value than wheat, lumber, or minerals. The industry is concentrated in southern Ontario, where it has a tremendous effect on the economy of the region. More than a quarter of Ontario's manufacturing employees work in some phase of the auto industry, either producing auto parts or assembling the actual vehicles.

Brampton Assembly Plant: Facts and Figures (2006)
Floor area: 278 711 m^2 (the size of 40 football fields!)
Production: 968 vehicles per day (two shifts)
Employment: 3 500 people
Robotics: 507 robots

Economic Resources

Chrysler Canada was formed in 1925. Today, Chrysler Canada operates two major assembly plants in southern Ontario, one in Windsor, and the other in Brampton. The Brampton plant was built in 1986. It produces the Chrysler 300 and Dodge Magnum sedans for the North American market.

The Brampton assembly plant is huge—more than half a kilometre wide! However, this factory does not make any parts. Instead, car parts manufactured in communities all across southern Ontario (and some in the United States), are assembled into completed cars. Brampton is an excellent site for an assembly plant for several reasons. A large supply of trained labour is available in the Greater Toronto Area, as well as land and capital resources. And as you have seen, the plant is well located in relation to transportation routes. (See page G 103.)

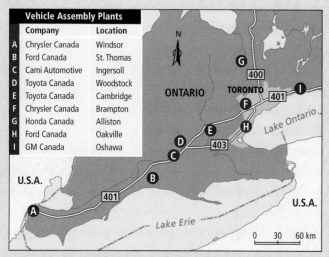

Vehicle Assembly Plants

	Company	Location
A	Chrysler Canada	Windsor
B	Ford Canada	St. Thomas
C	Cami Automotive	Ingersoll
D	Toyota Canada	Woodstock
E	Toyota Canada	Cambridge
F	Chrysler Canada	Brampton
G	Honda Canada	Alliston
H	Ford Canada	Oakville
I	GM Canada	Oshawa

Where are automobile assembly plants located? Why?

The Brampton Chrysler assembly plant

Input and Process

Chrysler has a reputation for progressive designs from their high-tech Design Institute in Detroit, Michigan. Like the fashion industry, new ideas are featured at international auto shows to test public reaction—the input stage of manufacturing. The process stage uses the assembly line. Three separate lines begin moving in different areas of the plant: the engine, chassis (or frame), and body lines. When both the engine and chassis are complete, powerful **robotic** arms fit the engine into the chassis. Later, other robots lower the completed body onto the chassis. Painting, upholstery, glass, tires, and trim are all added along the continuously moving final assembly line.

Output and Feedback

A new vehicle rolls off final assembly every few minutes. This output is distributed to Chrysler dealers in two ways. Delivery within a few hundred kilometres is completed using trucks with open trailers that can each carry ten cars. They are a common sight along Highways 407 and 401. More distant delivery uses covered triple-stack railway units, specially designed for the purpose. Consumer feedback is all-important. The popularity of the retro-styled Dodge Charger led Chrysler to develop a similar concept car, the Dodge Challenger. It drew rave reviews and is scheduled for production at the Brampton plant in 2008.

In what other ways might technology affect industry in the future?

WORDS MATTER

robotics mechanical arms which can repeat simple operations over and over with precision.

THINKING It Over

1. Suggest why robotics are used to a) combine the three assembly lines, b) paint car bodies, c) install windshields. **t**

2. With a partner, make a chart to compare the manufacturing systems for clothing and cars. Consider both similarities and differences. **k t**

3. All of Canada's major vehicle assembly plants are in Ontario. Explain why. Then, look at atlas maps to identify why certain resources or goods are produced in a) British Columbia, b) the Prairies, c) the North, and d) the Atlantic region. **k m**

WORDS MATTER

technology the application of mechanical arts and sciences to producing goods and services

microchip a tiny integrated circuit on which computer technology relies

high technology equipment and methods based upon computers, robotics, and space research

During **READING**

Checkpoint

Create a new chart for this section. Use the three economic eras for your column headings.

Would you rather have a cellphone or a land line? An iPod or a portable radio? A laptop or a desktop PC? If you picked the cellphone, iPod, and laptop, it's probably because they are smaller and more portable than the other choices. They also use more advanced **technology**. Twenty-five years ago, people would have been happy with the choices you rejected, because the cellphone, iPod, and laptop were not yet available to consumers. The electronic systems that operate them had just entered the marketplace in the Commodore 64 computer. The age of cheap **microchip** circuits was only beginning in the early 1980s.

Economist Nuala Beck identifies three stages in Canada's economic and industrial development, each with its own technology. The Commodity Economy lasted until 1918, and relied on coal for energy and steel production. Next was the Mass-Manufacturing Economy, with wide-scale secondary industry based on cheap supplies of petroleum. Beck believes Canada entered its third economic stage in 1981, what she calls the Technology Economy. It continues today, driven by inexpensive microchips, computers, and the telecommunications industry. You live in an era with technology that was not available when your parents and grandparents were young.

New technology changes the equipment and methods that society uses to gather and process natural resources. In the past hundred years, Canada and the other developed countries have moved quickly from steam engines to computers. New machines and methods have made it possible to produce more goods using fewer people. **High technology** is being applied to most types of industry. For example, computer-aided design (CAD) and robotic assembly have become vital parts of the automobile industry. Even the vehicles themselves are controlled by internal computer systems.

Canada's Economic Eras

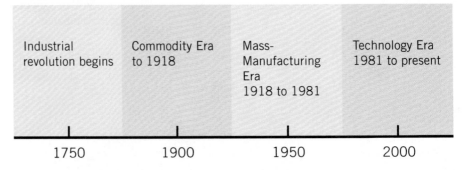

Industrial revolution begins	Commodity Era to 1918	Mass-Manufacturing Era 1918 to 1981	Technology Era 1981 to present
1750	1900	1950	2000

New Technologies Change Primary Industry

Computerized Mining

Mining takes place throughout Canada, but three-quarters of Canada's metallic mineral production happens in Ontario, British Columbia, Saskatchewan, and Québec. In some Canadian mines, underground equipment is controlled by operators on the surface. Watching television monitors, they control mining equipment using joysticks. Inside the mine, an operator watches over two or three machines in one area. Mining companies also use "virtual reality" simulators to train workers.

Precision Farming

The majority of Canada's grain farming happens in the three prairie provinces. On these large farms, precision farming combines satellite technology and computers. A yield monitor and a global positioning unit are attached to a combine. This equipment records how much grain is harvested from each part of the field. Computer software then makes a yield map, showing which areas were most productive. This allows the farmer to improve the soil with lime or fertilizer only where needed.

High-Tech Forestry

Cut-to-Length (CTL) logging systems are used to cut more than 30% of the world's wood. This technology is also used in Canada's foresty industries, in such provinces as New Brunswick and British Columbia. The harvester machine grabs a tree and cuts it at ground level. Then a sharp collar strips off the branches before the machine slices it to length. Then a forwarder machine picks up and piles the logs for removal.

Technology and Tertiary Industry

Technology has increased production while reducing the need for workers. This sounds like a recipe for unemployment, but that hasn't happened, because technology creates new jobs too. Skilled technicians are needed to install and repair new high-tech equipment. Increased production has also brought wealth to developed nations, and living standards have risen a great deal. This has led to the rapid growth of tertiary industry, as people use a wider range of services. Internet use is a good measure of the level of technology available in a society. The map below shows that developed nations dominate the Internet.

World Internet Use

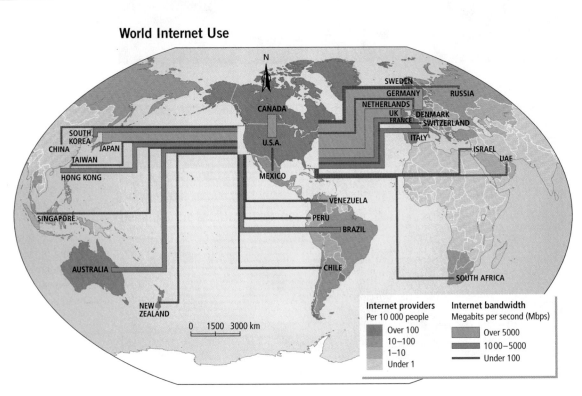

With which countries does North America have the most Internet traffic? What does this suggest about technology and living standards?

THINKING It Over

1. Work with a partner to make a chart comparing the benefits and problems of each of the three new technologies in the photos on page G 107.

2. How might technology change the economy of Canada in the future? Consider a) production, b) jobs, c) living standard.

3. In a small group, discuss the extent to which rapid technological change has been a good thing or a bad thing for the Canadian economy. Rate your personal overall opinion on a scale from 1 (very good) to 5 (very bad).

PUTTING IT ALL TOGETHER

Canada has a mixed economy that combines market and command characteristics. You examined the importance of government, business, and consumers in this system. You also learned how three types of industry—primary, secondary, and tertiary—operate in this business environment. Finally, you saw how much technology has changed Canadian industry. These ideas were all part of the unit question, **How do economic systems influence industries across Canada and the world?**

After **READING**

Synthesize Information from the Chart

Consider the unit question. Using the information from your charts (especially in the importance/meaning column), write down what you know about the factors that affect industries. Continue adding to these notes as you read the last chapter of this unit.

THINKING It Through

1. Choose one of the industries listed here as a research topic. Carefully record four good primary and secondary sources of information about your topic. Use charts to support and organize your research. **t**

2. Prepare a map to show the location of the industry in relation to raw materials, labour, and markets. **m**

3. Prepare an organized report describing the characteristics of the industry. Answer the question: Why has this industry been successful? Use chapter vocabulary, and apply the concepts of input, process, output, and feedback where you can. **k c a**

- wheat farming in the Prairies
- nickel mining in the North
- salmon fishing in British Columbia
- newsprint manufacturing in New Brunswick or Northern Ontario
- steel manufacturing in Ontario
- aerospace manufacturing in Québec
- a major homebuilder in your local region
- a major bank in your local region
- a major retailer in your local region

CHAPTER 6

Canada's World Trade

The Port of Vancouver container terminal. How would having container ports in Vancouver, Montréal, and Halifax affect trade between Canada and other countries?

Before READING

Making Connections

Think about the products that you use at home or at school. Where were these items made? Did any come from other countries? How would these items have made their way to you? Discuss with a partner.

You might be surprised to know that Canada is locked in a continual struggle with other global powers. It isn't a military battle—it is more like a constant strategic game. Like most countries, Canada's businesses and government compete to win export sales contracts. Industries continually aim to improve their efficiency and their products. Government officials (e.g., from Canada's Department of External Affairs) work hard to arrange trade agreements with other nations. Some countries win and some countries lose in these economic battles.

In this chapter, you will evaluate Canada's world trade connections. You will find out how well our country has been faring in the intense competition for export sales. You will also play a board game based on world trade groups. This chapter will complete your exploration of this unit's question: **How do economic systems influence industries across Canada and the world?**

Should consumers buy Canadian products or imported goods? Why?

Questions to Consider as You Read this Chapter

- What economic systems are best suited for successful world trade?

- How can I explain which factors benefit the top trading nations?

- How can I use primary and secondary information sources to describe trade?

- What are the pros and cons of Canada's major trade agreements?

- How can I use a map to draw conclusions about trade between countries?

What Is Balance of Trade?

First, a few personal questions: Can you keep track of your spending? Do you always seem to owe money to friends or family? Do you have money in the bank earning interest? The governments of countries have to ask themselves similar questions. Like people, some countries have growing debts because they spend more than they earn. Their **balance of trade** is negative because they sell (**export**) fewer goods than they buy (**import**). This is called a **trade deficit**, and it must be made up with cash payments or loans. Meanwhile, other countries are in better shape with respect to trade. They have a **trade surplus** by exporting more than they import. These countries are profiting from international trade. In this section, you will compare six major trading countries. Here is a sneak preview of two of them:

Trade Item	Canada, 2006 ($US)	U.S.A., 2006 ($US)
Value of Exports (sales)	405.0 billion	1024 billion
Value of Imports (purchases)	353.2 billion	1869 billion
Trade Balance	51.8 billion	845 billion
Trade Surplus or Deficit	**Surplus** +$51.8 billion	**Deficit** –$845 billion

WORDS MATTER

balance of trade the relationship between the value of a country's exports and imports; also called trade balance

exports goods or services that are sold to another country

imports goods or services that are brought into the country

trade deficit a negative trade balance (more imports than exports)

trade surplus a positive trade balance (more exports than imports)

International Carriers

Many different products move between countries. The method of transportation chosen depends upon the locations of the trade partners and the type of material moved. Countries located next to one another or on the same continent can use trucks and trains to move bulky freight. Energy supplies can be carried through pipelines and electric power wires. Trade across the oceans is a different matter. Supertankers, cargo vessels, and container ships transport different types of cargo. Planes also carry a very limited amount of lightweight, high-value goods such as diamonds.

Supertankers

Supertankers are the largest ships ever built. They are sometimes longer than four football fields from end to end! Pipelines may carry oil across continents, but supertankers are used to transport oil across oceans. Their huge capacity makes shipping fairly inexpensive. However, terrible environmental damage occurs when oil carriers run aground. In 1989, the *Exxon Valdez* spilled more than 40 million litres of oil on the Alaskan coast, causing great loss of fish and wildlife. Why is this issue important?

Container Freight

Canada has major container ports on both the Pacific and Atlantic coasts. Standard-sized metal containers are widely used for international cargo because they are secure and flexible. They are easily transferred from ships onto flatbed trucks or rail cars. Loss is minimized because containers can be tracked by using the Global Positioning System (GPS). However, since they are stacked high on the decks of ships, containers occasionally break loose during severe storms. Do you think container ships are a good way to transport goods? Why or why not?

Electric Power Lines

Energy is an important part of international trade. Oil and natural gas flow through pipelines, but electricity can also cross borders. Power plants in Ontario and Québec sell surplus energy to nearby American states. Their systems are connected as a single power grid. In August of 2003, a power failure in Ohio caused a massive blackout across northeastern North America. It continued for several days. Do you predict there will be other cases of power failures in the future, or not? Explain.

United States (2006)	
Population	301.1 million
GDP per capita (2005)	43 444 $US
Human Dev. Index	.948 (8th)
Economic System	Market
Value of Exports	$1024.0 billion
Value of Imports	$1869.0 billion
Trade Balance	–$845.0 billion **deficit**

Germany (2006)	
Population	82.4 million
GDP per capita (2005)	31 095 $US
Human Dev. Index	.932 (21st)
Economic System	Mixed
Value of Exports	$1133.0 billion
Value of Imports	$916.4 billion
Trade Balance	+$216.6 billion **surplus**

Which type of economic system do you think has been most successful in world trade? Which countries do you think have the best trade balances? After you've guessed, check your answers by skimming over the top five countries profiled in this section. Canada has been included too, but currently ranks ninth in world trade. Not in the top five, but not bad for a country with only a small fraction of the world's population!

The United States

The United States is a large country with many natural resources and huge agricultural production. Its wheat exports are the largest in the world. American industry produces a great variety of products, including technology, automobiles, chemicals, and electronics. However, many U.S. manufacturers cannot compete with less expensive foreign imports. American labour costs are much higher. To counter this, many businesses rely on off-shore companies to produce the goods and services they sell. As well, the U.S. uses more energy than it produces, and must import fuel and electricity at great cost. Huge imports make the U.S. trade deficit a serious problem.

Germany

The value of German exports is the highest in the world. Although the nation has a limited range of natural resources, it has earned a global reputation for high-quality manufactured products, such as automobiles, machinery, and consumer goods. Its $216 billion trade surplus proves that the demand for German products is strong. The country must import some raw materials for its steel industry, along with oil and natural gas. The former communist country of East Germany and market-based West Germany united in 1990. Since then, there has been heavy investment to improve outdated factories in the former East Germany.

China

China is almost as large in area as Canada, and has a wide range of natural resources. The government of this command economy has relaxed its tight control since about 1990, with resulting increases in manufacturing output. However, there are still serious human rights violations against people who oppose the communist government's policies. China is different from the other top trading countries in this section. It is a rapidly developing country, with a huge, low-cost labour supply that produces many inexpensive items for export. As a result, China has a large and growing trade surplus. How might this rapid development affect China's trade in the future?

Japan

Japan and Germany are global economic giants, yet both are smaller in size than most Canadian provinces. Japan has to import almost all of its mineral and energy resources, but has developed into an industrial and technological leader. The country's real strength is people—entrepreneurs and workers known for their technical skills, motivation, and teamwork. Manufactured products make up 97% of Japan's exports, particularly high-quality machinery, automobiles, and electronics. Japan is very crowded, but the rate of population increase is low. As a result, Japan has an aging workforce. This has become a growing problem as companies struggle to hire from a shrinking workforce.

China (2006)	
Population	1 321.8 million
GDP per capita (2005)	7 598 $US
Human Dev. Index	.768 (81st)
Economic System	Command
Value of Exports	$974.0 billion
Value of Imports	$777.9 billion
Trade Balance	+$196.1 billion **surplus**

Japan (2006)	
Population	127.4 million
GDP per capita (2005)	32 647 $US
Human Dev. Index	.949 (7th)
Economic System	Mixed
Value of Exports	$590.3 billion
Value of Imports	$524.1 billion
Trade Balance	+$66.2 billion **surplus**

As Japan's labour force ages, it might not be able to export as many goods to Canada. What market opportunities might this create for Canadian producers?

United Kingdom

United Kingdom (2006)	
Population	60.8 million
GDP per capita (2005)	35 051 $US
Human Dev. Index	.940 (18th)
Economic System	Mixed
Value of Exports	$468.8 billion
Value of Imports	$603.0 billion
Trade Balance	−$134.2 billion **deficit**

The United Kingdom has a limited range of natural resources. However, the country has large supplies of energy—oil and natural gas from the nearby North Sea. Its agriculture is very efficient and produces about 60 % of the nation's food needs. Many of the United Kingdom's factories are outdated, and this part of the economy is in decline. As a result, the nation buys more automobiles, machinery, and other products from neighbouring European countries than it sells to them. This has caused a large and growing trade deficit.

Traditional products, like these fabrics, are still made in the U.K. Why can Britain no longer rely on such export products in today's world economy?

Canada

Canada (2006)	
Population	32.8 million
GDP per capita (2005)	35 494 $US
Human Dev. Index	.950 (6th)
Economic System	Mixed
Value of Exports	$405.0 billion
Value of Imports	$353.2 billion
Trade Balance	+$51.8 billion **surplus**

Canada ranks behind France, Italy, and the Netherlands in world trade. Like many large countries, its natural resources are plentiful. Canada's top exports include lumber, aluminum, natural gas, petroleum products, and hydroelectricity. Canada is also a leading exporter of grain. Its labour force has a greater percentage of college- and university-educated young adults than any other nation. Motor vehicles and parts are Canada's largest single export, most of them sold to the United States. In fact, more than 80 % of Canada's exports go to the United States. However, Canadian producers have been hurt by some U.S. policies aimed at blocking competing lumber and farm imports.

Trade and Industry

Now compare the top trading countries. The U.S., China, and Canada are large and have abundant natural resources. Germany and Japan produce high-quality products, while China is a developing country that specializes in low-cost goods. On the map below, all the top traders except China are called "Industrialized high income economies." The large group of countries with "Agricultural low income economies" plays a very minor part in international trade.

During **READING**

Checkpoint
Add information from this page to your Venn diagram comparing two top traders. Remember to include information from the map.

World Industrialization, 2000

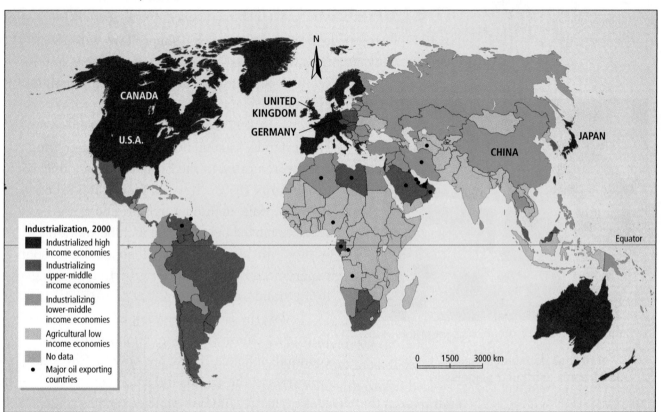

Industrialization, 2000
- Industrialized high income economies
- Industrializing upper-middle income economies
- Industrializing lower-middle income economies
- Agricultural low income economies
- No data
- • Major oil exporting countries

0   1500   3000 km

THINKING It Over

1. Use a chart to compare the advantages and disadvantages of the international carrier methods described on page G 112. Add your own information for airplanes or pipelines.

2. Use the map to identify the continental locations of a) major international traders, b) minor international traders. What primary and secondary resources could you use to check your answers?

3. Make a bar graph comparing the trade balances of the six countries in this section. Place deficit bars below the base line.

4. In a small group, prepare final report cards for the six countries described on pages G 114–G 116. Choose three criteria to compare. Include grades, comments, and recommendations.

During **READING**

Checkpoint
Create a new Venn diagram to compare the EU and OPEC. Add how these alliances affect trade around the world.

There is security in numbers. You may prefer to be with your friends or family when you are in new surroundings. That way, you don't feel alone or vulnerable. In Canada, trade alliances were formed between Aboriginal groups, and later between the First Nations and European traders. Today, alliances are very important in the global trade wars. They also have important effects on the Canadian economy.

The European Union

In 1945, Europe's economy was in terrible shape. Two world wars had left many countries with damaged factories, huge debts, and a reduced population. Politicians urged longtime enemies to cooperate for the benefit of their citizens. By 1957, France, Belgium, the Netherlands, Luxembourg, West Germany, and Italy were united in the European Economic Community (EEC). It was a **free trade** union—raw materials, manufactured products, and services moved between the member nations without **duties** or **tariffs**. All six countries soon experienced rapid economic growth and rising living standards.

Why would the new European Union be a significant issue to these European students in 1957?

Today, the EEC has developed into the European Union (EU)—much more than an economic alliance. There are now 27 European countries in the group, and a democratic parliament that decides on many common policies such as trade, development, and security. A common currency—the euro—makes it easier to conduct trade.

The European Union is an example of a **trade bloc**, a large area operating under a free trade agreement. You already learned that Germany, Britain, France, Italy, and the Netherlands are five of the world's top eight international traders. They help make the European Union the world's largest trading power. By uniting economically, the European Union has become a huge trade competitor for Canada. For example, Canadian manufacturers often bid against major European firms for international sales contracts. How is Canada at a disadvantage if the sales contract is for a member of the European Union?

WORDS MATTER

free trade trade without duties or tariffs

duties/tariffs taxes on imported goods

trade bloc a large free-trade area made up of two or more countries

OPEC: Controlling an Energy Resource

Suppose you and a friend were the only ones to bring snacks to a party. You control the snack supply, so you can decide how to distribute it. Countries that produce oil have this kind of power in the world export market. The Organization of Petroleum Exporting Countries (OPEC) is an alliance of twelve nations with economies that rely heavily on crude oil exports. Put together, these countries control more than 70% of the world's petroleum reserves. This is a vital energy resource that every country needs, and OPEC controls much of the supply. This very powerful group of suppliers is called a trade **cartel**.

Before OPEC was formed in 1960, the price of petroleum averaged only about $2.50 per barrel. In 2007, the price reached more than $90 US a barrel. These twelve oil producers have unified their oil policies to ensure "a steady income to producers and a fair return." OPEC controls both the price and the supply of oil. This trade strategy has resulted in an economic boom for OPEC's major producers, found in the Middle East and Venezuela.

Canada has the world's second-largest oil reserves. Our economy has benefitted directly from the world price of oil. Although consumers see high gas prices, there are economic benefits for some provinces. How might the environment benefit from higher consumer prices for fossil fuels?

OPEC Members (2007)	
Africa	Libya, Algeria, Nigeria, Angola
Asia	Indonesia
Middle East	Qatar, Iran, Saudi Arabia, United Arab Emirates, Iraq, Kuwait
South America	Venezuela

Our Environment

Fossil Fuel Energy

Our society is addicted to fossil fuel energy, especially oil. Canadians use more than one million barrels of oil per day by using gas and products made from oil, such as plastics. Pollution and global warming make our oil addiction a serious environmental concern.

Record five ways you and your family could conserve fossil fuel energy. What could be the environmental impact if everyone made these changes?

What are the advantages, for producer groups like OPEC, of supplying their products slowly? Would other groups, such as fruit producers, be so successful? Why or why not?

Interpreting a Proportional Flow Map

A **proportional flow map** is a special type of thematic map, useful for showing the movement of people, products, or information. The flow arrows on the map are most important. Not only do these arrows show the direction of movement, but also, their widths indicate the volume of flow along the transportation routes. Follow these steps to interpret a proportional flow map of world petroleum.

Step 1 Read the Map Legend

You will see that line and point symbols are used on the map:

- line: fine black lines show national boundaries; brown arrows represent trade in oil

- point: small purple spots show the location and size of oil fields

Step 2 Look Closely at the Flow Arrows

The flow arrows show both the directions of oil export movement and their approximate volume. First of all, the arrowheads point at the countries to which oil is sold. Secondly, the width of each arrow is proportional to the volume of oil transported.

Step 3 Identify the Map Patterns

Use the direction and width of the flow arrows to identify map patterns. These questions will help you to focus on the flow patterns:

- Which countries or regions are major oil exporters? (Hint: They sell, and are the starting point of many wide arrows.)

- Which countries or regions are major oil importers? (Hint: They buy, so the widest arrows end there.)

- What do the arrows indicate about the market for Canadian oil? (Hint: Look for arrows flowing in or out of Canada.)

Step 4 Interpret the Graph and Number Table

Use the information surrounding the map to discuss the present and future place of OPEC members and Canada in world petroleum trade.

World Oil Trade Flow

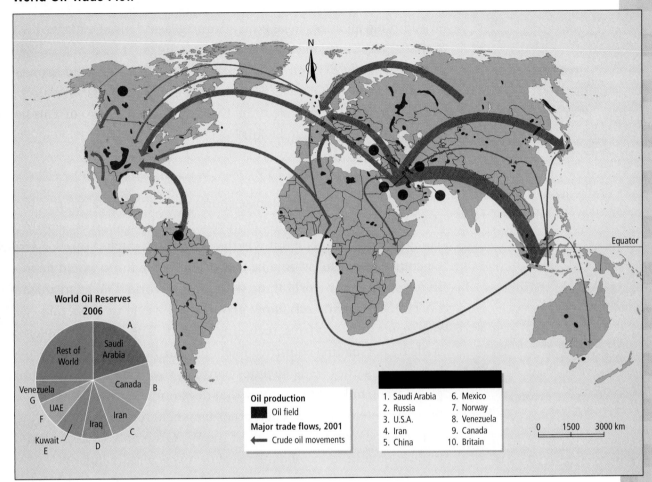

World Oil Reserves 2006
- Rest of World
- Saudi Arabia — A
- Canada — B
- Iran — C
- Iraq — D
- Kuwait — E
- UAE — F
- Venezuela — G

Oil production
■ Oil field
Major trade flows, 2001
◄— Crude oil movements

1. Saudi Arabia	6. Mexico
2. Russia	7. Norway
3. U.S.A.	8. Venezuela
4. Iran	9. Canada
5. China	10. Britain

0   1500   3000 km

Equator

APPLY It

1. Answer the three questions in Step 3 on page G 120 to identify petroleum export patterns on the map. Discuss the regional effects on Canada. *m*

2. With the map, identify two examples each for petroleum exports which may use a) oil supertankers, and b) oil pipelines. *k m*

3. Use the map and other information provided here to comment on the importance of OPEC in a) the present pattern of oil flows, and b) the future pattern of oil flows. *t m*

Canada's Trade Links

WTO
- Promote free trade
- Settle trade disputes
- Organize trade talks

World trade alliances have both advantages and disadvantages for Canada. First the good news: Canada has huge oil reserves and will benefit from OPEC's oil trade policies. The bad news: the European Union is a large and powerful free trade group that sets very high standards. Can Canada meet the EU's challenge? Above all, can fierce global trade competition be fair?

What Is the WTO?

Imagine playing a really intense sports game without a referee. Would the home team decide whether or not a penalty should be called? Should the fans scream out whether or not the pitcher threw a strike? Of course, the result would be chaos. The same thing would happen in the struggle for world trade without the World Trade Organization (WTO). This **trade advisory group** was formed in 1995, and represents 151 countries, including Canada. The WTO promotes free trade by persuading countries to abolish tariffs and other trade barriers. It settles trade disputes between governments and organizes global trade talks. Any country that does not obey WTO rulings faces **trade sanctions**, when other members refuse that country's imports or exports. As a result of the WTO's involvement, world trade competition may be intense, but it is generally fair.

What Is NAFTA?

Canada's answer to the European Union has been to join in a trade alliance with the United States and Mexico. In the past, Canadian industries were protected from American companies by import tariffs. Any manufactured goods crossing the border from the U.S. into Canada were taxed. This would raise the cost of U.S. products and hopefully encourage people to buy Canadian products instead. This policy of protecting Canadian industry from cheaper imports is called **protectionism**. While it promoted Canadian industry, protectionism made goods expensive for consumers at the same time.

WORDS MATTER

trade advisory group an organization that supervises trade

trade sanctions trade penalties imposed on one country by another

protectionism the policy of adding taxes to imported goods to protect a country's home industries

WEB LINK •••••••••••••••••••
Learn about Canada's relationship with the WTO and NAFTA. Visit our Web site.

In 1994, the North American Free Trade Agreement (NAFTA) was signed between Canada, the United States, and Mexico. It created a trade bloc to rival the European Union—although the NAFTA countries do not share a common currency or a common political system. Debate about NAFTA was very heated in Canada, because of fears that industries would be lost and the U.S. would dominate trade. Some Canadian manufacturing plants have closed, especially traditional firms making furniture, clothing, and footwear. Other companies in transportation, communication, and high-tech industries have successfully competed against imported goods and have even expanded their exports into the huge U.S. market. The flow of goods between Canada and Mexico is small but increasing.

During **READING**

Checkpoint
Reread the text on Canada's trade links. Create a Venn diagram to compare the WTO and NAFTA. Compare the purposes of these organizations. How do they affect Canada's world trade?

Tariffs

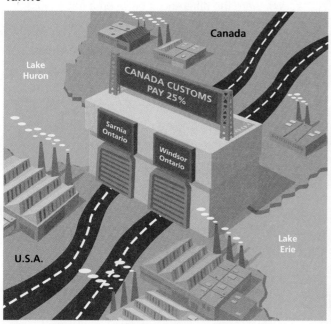

Free trade

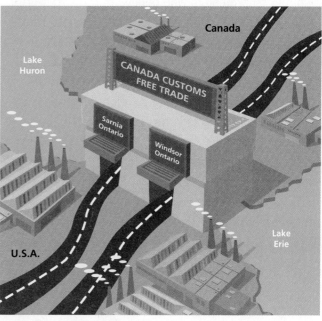

Tariffs vs. free trade. How would free trade affect the production of goods in Canada?

NAFTA: Divided Opinions

The outflow of business has been phenomenal... We need to abdicate [end] the agreement. Otherwise we will ...become a nation of warehouses [and no factories]. –Maude Barlow, Chairperson, Council of Canadians	*Dow Chemical expects to benefit in the long run from a larger free-trade zone. Protectionism [tariffs on imports] creates small, inefficient plants that fail when restrictions are removed.* –Bob Child, Vice President, Dow Chemical of Canada	**Public support for NAFTA:** Canada: 70% Mexico: 64% U.S.A.: 47% **Who benefits most from NAFTA?** Canadians: U.S.A. benefits Mexicans: U.S.A. benefits Americans: Mexico benefits

Canada is a member of the world's most prestigious economic club: the G8. The name stands for "the Group of Eight," the most powerful industrialized democracies in the world. The organization was formed in 1975, and Canada joined a year later. G8 members take turns hosting annual meetings at which foreign policy and economic issues are discussed.

Remember the criticisms of the World Bank you read about in Chapter 3? Meetings of the G8 are also met by protestors who believe that this powerful group wants to dominate world trade policies. The G8 certainly does look after its own interests, but it also deals with global issues like international terrorism and crime. Some critics believe that the G8 should be doing more for developing nations. For example, during the June 2007 meetings in Germany, Irish musician and political activist, Bono, accused Canadian prime minister Stephen Harper of blocking efforts to increase aid to Africa. The prime minister denied the charge, saying that Canada was on target to meet all of its African aid commitments.

G8 Members	
United Kingdom	Italy
Canada	Japan
France	Russia
Germany	U.S.A.

THINKING It Over

1. What are the differences between a trade bloc, a cartel, and a trade advisory group? **k**

2. Make a chart to compare the European Union, OPEC, and NAFTA. Use these four guiding questions: a) Why was the group formed? b) How extensive is the organization? c) Which nations are the leading members? d) How effective is the organization? **k c**

3. What is your opinion of NAFTA? Write a paragraph in which you state your opinion and reasons for it. Or, you can express your views by drawing a political cartoon or writing a letter to the editor. **c**

4. Create four questions that could be used to investigate whether or not belonging to the G8 benefits Canada. **t**

WEB LINK ••••••••••••••••••••••••••••••••••
Read summaries of G8 meetings from Canada's point of view. Visit our Web site.

A group photo of the G8 leaders in Germany, 2007. Given the information provided, what questions would you like to ask Prime Minister Stephen Harper and political activist Bono to better understand their points of view?

What You Will Need

- Game board and one die
- Three small coloured moving pieces per player

How to Play

1. Four players each start from a different corner of the board. Aim to move one of your trade items to each corner, with an exact roll to land. Deliver all three pieces first to win, then play again.

2. Take turns rolling one die and moving one playing piece in any direction away from your corner. You cannot move pieces back toward your corner. All three pieces can be in play. Each roll counts for only one piece.

3. The trade routes are filled with hazards and rewards on the specially marked spaces. Read the board symbols to lose a turn, gain a turn, or return the piece home.

4. There are fewer hazards through the centre, but if you take that route you must visit the World Trade Organization with an exact roll. Remain there having your trade dispute heard until you roll 1 to exit.

What Do YOU Think?

1. What have you learned in this chapter that connects to the game?

2. How was the game like the real world? How was it different?

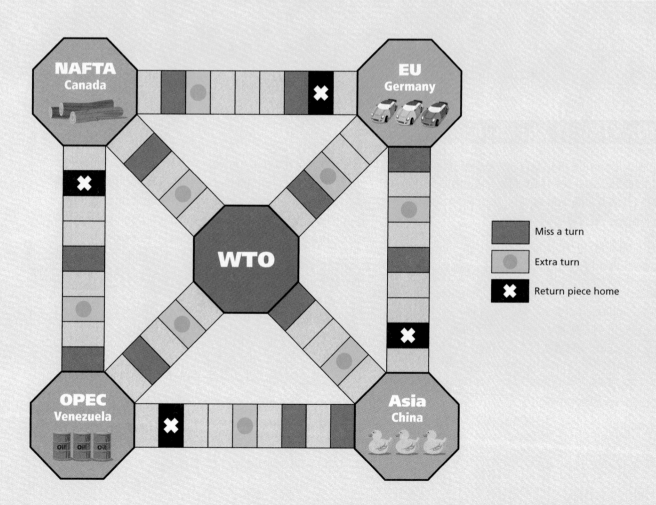

Miss a turn

Extra turn

Return piece home

PUTTING IT ALL TOGETHER

Canada ranks ninth in world trade even though it ranks only 36th in population. Our country has been successful in global trade competition because of abundant natural resources and a highly educated labour force. The majority of Canada's international trade is with the United States, one of our partners in the North American Free Trade Agreement. Canada is also a member of the G8 and the World Trade Organization, groups that advise and direct member countries. Canada will continue to face powerful economic rivals, including the European Union, and the Organization of Petroleum Exporting Countries. You've learned information that will help answer the unit question: **How do economic systems influence industries across Canada and the world?**

After READING

Analyze Differences and Similarities

Analyze each of the Venn diagrams you made for this chapter. What can you infer from these comparisons? Record your ideas by writing a short paragraph below each diagram.

THINKING It Through

1. How is the world map on page G 127 different from others you have seen? Explain why this type of map was chosen after you have answered the other questions. **k m**

2. Use the map to record four important conclusions about Canada's export trade. **m**

3. Based on the information on the map, explain how important each of these groups is to Canada's export trade: a) NAFTA, b) the European Union, and c) OPEC. **k t m**

4. Work on a map provided by your teacher. Use the information in the Top Ten Export Partners chart to draw proportional flow arrows from Canada to each country. Base the width of your flow arrows on the map scale—the more trade, the wider the arrow. Complete your map with a legend and an appropriate title. **m c a**

Canadian Export Partners, 2006

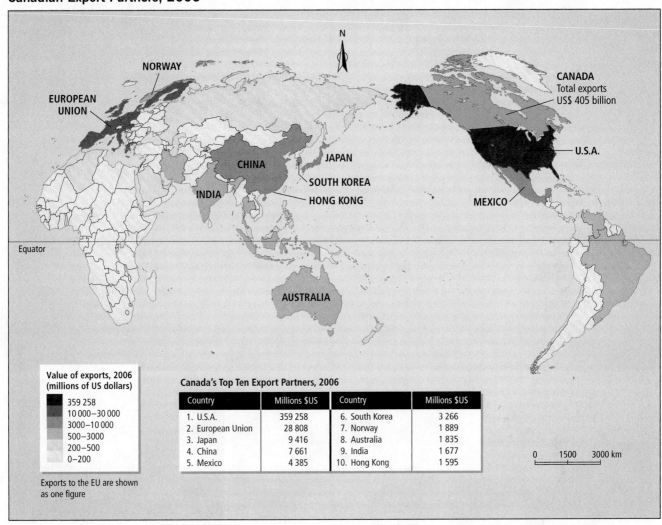

Value of exports, 2006 (millions of US dollars)

- 359 258
- 10 000–30 000
- 3000–10 000
- 500–3000
- 200–500
- 0–200

Exports to the EU are shown as one figure

CANADA Total exports US$ 405 billion

0   1500   3000 km

Canada's Top Ten Export Partners, 2006

Country	Millions $US	Country	Millions $US
1. U.S.A.	359 258	6. South Korea	3 266
2. European Union	28 808	7. Norway	1 889
3. Japan	9 416	8. Australia	1 835
4. China	7 661	9. India	1 677
5. Mexico	4 385	10. Hong Kong	1 595

Back to the Big Idea

In Unit 2 you learned that societies make different decisions about making and distributing products and services. Canada has a mixed economy, combining characteristics of the market and command systems. You saw that economic activities in our country are both "free" and "regulated" at the same time. Look back over your notes to review your findings about the Big Idea: **How do economic systems influence industries across Canada and the world?**

- Complete a graphic organizer to compare four different economic systems: traditional, market, command, and mixed.

- Examine your predictions (from page G 67) about the comparisons between Canada's mixed economy and systems in other countries. Were the differences you expected present? What other comparisons did you discover?

How is the price of beef decided in a market economy? How is this decision made in a command economy?

How are economic decisions made in a command economy? What priorities are often apparent in this system?

Which type of economic system is shown here? How are economic decisions made in this system?

Show That You Know

In this unit you learned that industry and businesses are found at locations that meet important requirements. Now, you will work as part of a team to decide whether your local region is suited to a particular type of economic development. You will also assess how the arrival of this business might affect your local community.

Step 1 Choose an economic activity

Work in a small group to consider the four choices given on this page. Choose a topic, either one per person or one per group.

Step 2 Generate ideas

Use a chart organizer like this one to focus on each type of activity.

General Requirements	Best Local Location	Effects on the Community
•	•	•
•	•	•

Step 3 Become an "expert"

Have each member of the group use different types of geographic sources to investigate the topic more closely, using the chart above.

Step 4 Report your findings

- Create a point-form summary of the general requirements for each type of economic activity (or for the one which your group focused on).
- Produce a map to show the best location for this particular business activity.
- Write a page which reviews the possible effects of this type of business on the local community.

Step 5 Compare the possibilities

As a group, decide which of the four activities would be best for the community. You may want to use a comparison organizer to work out this decision.

Activity Choices

- a recreation centre (e.g., swimming, boating, camping, fishing, skiing, theme park, or museum)
- a computer-based business (e.g., video arcade, retail store, Internet provider, or Web page design)
- a manufacturing plant serving the automotive industry (e.g., engine parts, electronics, upholstery, or aftermarket parts)
- an activity suited to the region and decided by the group (e.g., a horse farm, "big box" store, mine, or a fish-based or forest-based industry)

Tip: Use maps of the local area and other information to choose suitable locations for the business.

Tip: Review the skill "Making a Map" on page S 14.

Tip: Consider these effects:
- number of jobs
- number of tourist visitors (if any)
- impact on local merchants
- impact on local schools and other services
- impact on competitors (if any)
- impact on the environment

UNIT 3

Mobility, Migration, and Culture

> How do migration patterns affect people and communities in Canada and the world?

In 2007, *MoneySense* magazine chose Ottawa as the best Canadian place to call home. What do you think makes a community a good place to live in?

Halifax ranked second in the survey. What questions would you ask to identify the best place to live in Canada?

Québec City came third. The top three Canadian communities are all capital cities. How would you explain the attraction of a capital city as a place to live?

What's the Big Idea?

For more than a century, about 20% of Canada's population has been made up of people born in other countries. Think about the original reasons your family, or someone else you know, came to Canada. Within the country, the Canadian population is very mobile—people often move to new locations. What effects would moving to a new home, community, province, or territory have on you? In this unit, you will learn about the challenges and opportunities migration presents for people around the world, and the effect it has on Canada's identity.

Key Terms

accessible, barrier, migration, mobility, immigration, emigration, refugees, modes of transportation, push factors, pull factors

What You Will Learn in this Unit

- Where would I most like to live in Canada?
- What are the main factors that affect the movement of people? How do these factors affect individuals and communities?
- How has technology increased human mobility?
- How does human migration affect Canada's geography and culture?
- How can I make and use thematic maps to show migration patterns?
- How could I promote Canada as a destination for immigrants?

CHAPTER 7

Canadians on the Move

Crowded highways are a common sight in Canada's big cities.

Making Connections

How many times have you moved? Have you travelled to other communities, provinces, or countries? How are they the same or different than where you live now? Take a class survey. How many people in your class are from another country, have parents from another country, or grandparents from another country?

Canadians live in a mobile society. We could be shoulder-to-shoulder in the bus or subway, or driving down a quiet country road. We travel a great deal, and many of us move frequently too. On average, Canadians move to another home about every dozen years. Sometimes it is a move across town. Sometimes it is a complete change of scene to a different city or another province.

In this chapter, you will interpret data and construct maps and graphs using Canada's most recent census. You will learn that different factors play a role in people's decision to move. You will also find out about Canadians' favourite residential locations. In the process, you will explore many aspects of the unit Big Idea, **How do migration patterns affect people and communities in Canada and the world?**

What are the advantages and disadvantages of moving to a new place?

Questions to Consider as You Read this Chapter

- How would I go about choosing an ideal place to live in Canada?

- How has the movement of people within Canada affected development?

- How can I explain the impact technology and mobility have on migration?

- How would I construct and use a map to show the flow of migrants between regions?

How Do People Decide Where to Live?

Where-to-Live Factors
- jobs
- weather
- housing prices
- cost of living
- safety
- health care

During **READING**

Checkpoint

Consider these factors when you rank each detail in your chart, and when you complete the ranking ladder at the end of the chapter. What do you consider most important on this list? Discuss with a classmate. Did you pick the same one?

WEB LINK ·············
Learn more about weather conditions in different regions of Canada. Visit our Web site.

Do you consider your community a good place to live? Does it attract new families to move there, or is it a place people are leaving? What makes one place more desirable than another? There are many factors to weigh, but let's start with just six. Later, you will use these six factors to rate Canadian communities, including your own.

Employment

Why do many people rate job prospects as the top factor in choosing a new community? Large urban centres attract people because they offer a variety of jobs and opportunities. Communities outside of densely populated areas are generally shrinking in size. Many are based on natural resources, and offer only a small percentage of the jobs in Canada. One major exception is Fort McMurray, a booming small city near the Alberta oil sands.

Nice Weather, Eh?

Canada is a cold country in winter—one of the reasons that 90 % of the population lives within 160 km of the country's southern border. Many people think that if a community has a mild winter, it's a better place to live in. What can you infer from the map below about Canada's winter temperatures? How does temperature affect where most people live in Canada?

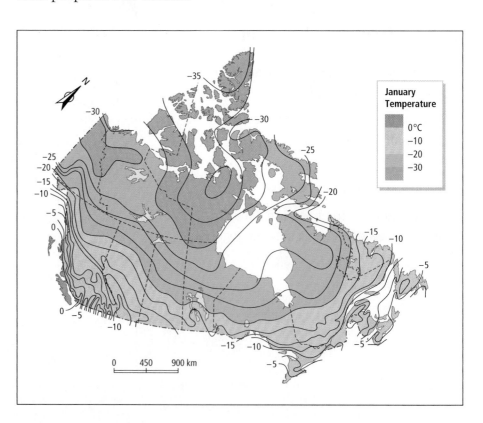

Which temperature zone would you prefer to live in? Why? How does the map help you rank places to live in Canada?

Affordable Homes

For most Canadian families, **shelter cost** takes over one-quarter of the monthly budget, sometimes more. Home prices and rents are very high in cities like Toronto and Vancouver. Home prices in British Columbia are especially high. Prices are also high in "boom" communities where there is a great demand for the little housing available.

Cost of Living

A budget has two parts: income and expenses. Money left over after necessary expenses such as taxes, shelter, food, and transportation is called **discretionary income**. This income is usually spent on non-essential things like movies and vacations. Some places are more expensive than others in terms of necessary expenses. How might this affect the discretionary income of people who live there?

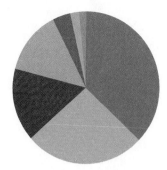

- Food and Shelter
- Taxes, Insurance
- Discretionary Income
- Transportation
- Clothing
- Education
- Health Care

This graph shows typical divisions in a family budget. What is the largest single item in your own personal budget?

Safe Neighbourhoods

Why would some people consider safety—a low crime rate, or a high police presence for example—the most important factor on the list?

Health Services

Access to health care professionals is important to everyone, but especially to young families and seniors. Specialized services may be less available in areas with low populations. Urban places have hospitals, research laboratories, and teaching centres. While communities compete to attract doctors and nurses, most of these professionals are drawn to large cities.

WORDS MATTER

shelter cost the cost of owning or renting a home

discretionary income part of the family budget that can be used on savings or non-essentials such as entertainment or vacations

Canada's Top Ten

In 2007, *MoneySense* magazine ranked 123 Canadian communities with populations over 10 000. The places were ranked against one another, from best to worst, 1 to 123. A score of 1 was always the best situation: for example, safety and a low crime rate. The magazine also counted factors such as population growth rate and attractions such as sports teams and theatres. The results below show the score of the top ten cities in the six factors we have examined. Remember, a lower score is better. Are all these cities good choices for everyone? Why or why not?

MoneySense Magazine Ranks the Top Ten Canadian Cities

Top Ten Cities	Jobs	Weather	Housing Prices	Discretionary Income	Safety	Medical Services
1. Ottawa, ON	33	33	73	9	43	22
2. Halifax, NS	24	79	55	26	77	4
3. Québec City, QC	56	27	29	73	12 (tie)	15
4. Guelph, ON	30	49	77	17	12 (tie)	16
5. Fredericton, NB	37	77	24	7	44 (tie)	34
6. Kingston, ON	73	10	58	32	51	1
7. Moncton, NB	33	106	25	10	44 (tie)	41
8. London, ON	67	40	49	36	8	5
9. Victoria, BC	7	4	122	102	75	10
10. Gander, NL	44	118	7	51	1	3

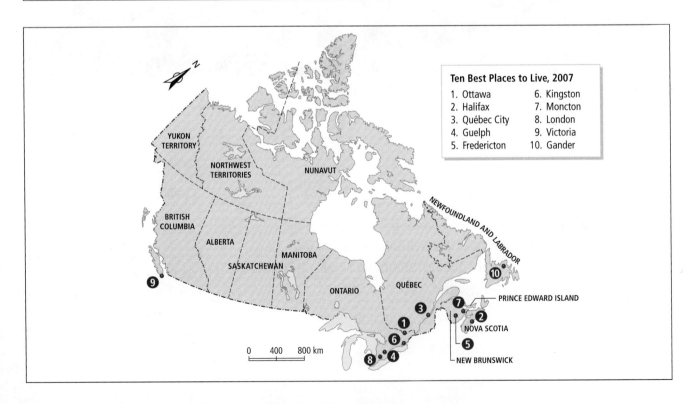

Ten Best Places to Live, 2007

1. Ottawa   6. Kingston
2. Halifax   7. Moncton
3. Québec City   8. London
4. Guelph   9. Victoria
5. Fredericton   10. Gander

While Ottawa's winters can be very cold and snowy compared to those in some other Canadian cities, it is considered a wonderful place to live. The city did not score at the top of any single measure, but it did rank in the top third in almost all categories.

More than a million people live in the National Capital Region, which includes Gatineau, located across the river in Québec. As Canada's fourth-largest metropolitan area, Ottawa-Gatineau offers many attractions. A professional hockey team, museums and art galleries, and fine restaurants and shopping give it a "big-city" flavour.

Urban planners work to include parks, walking paths, and transportation links. The National Capital Commission (NCC) was set up in 1959 to build the region into a source of pride and unity for Canadians. It preserves green space within the city. For example, the historic Rideau Canal curves through Ottawa, offering pleasant walks and summer canoeing. When it freezes over in the winter, people can even skate to work on it!

How would access to recreation, restaurants, and public spaces influence your decision about where to live?

THINKING It Over

1. Which of the six factors discussed in this section do you consider most important in choosing a place to live? Why? 🜛 🜚

2. The Top Ten would be different if only the six factors we examined had been used. Use the chart on page G 136 to add together the results. How do the cities rank now? How did Ontario communities rank? 🜚

3. Rate your own community as a place to live. Use a scale from 1 (Excellent) to 5 (Poor) to rate each of the six factors discussed in this section. Are there other ranking factors you can suggest that would apply to where you live? 🜚 🜛

4. Where would you like to go for a one-day trip? First, make a list of four local possibilities. Then, decide on three criteria for judging each possibility (e.g., cost). Last, use a chart to rank each option. Which choice received the best score? 🜚 🜛

Rate Your Community
1. Excellent
2. Very good
3. OK or not sure
4. Not very good
5. Poor

During **READING**

Vocabulary Review

Remember that *urban* means city and *rural* means countryside or small town. Do you live in a rural or urban area? Has your area changed from rural to urban in the last five years?

Have you and your family moved in the past five years? Or have you lived in the same home for most of your life? About nine million Canadians moved to another home between 2001 and 2006. Most of those moves took place within the local community. Many others were to another location in the same province. However, over 300 000 Canadians moved to another province in 2006.

Migration is the movement from one place to live in another. Some migration is permanent, and some is temporary. For example, immigrants may come to Canada with no intention of returning to their home country. Meanwhile, some retired Canadians migrate to Florida or Arizona each winter, returning in April. This is called **seasonal migration**, and these people are nicknamed "snowbirds."

Another example of temporary migration relates to seasonal workers, many of whom come to Canada from the Caribbean region and Mexico to help harvest fruit and vegetable crops in the summer. In this chapter, you will be examining migration within Canada.

The Rural-Urban Shift

A great deal of movement from the countryside to towns and cities has occurred during Canada's history. Because of this **rural-urban shift**, Canadian society is now overwhelmingly urban.

Canada: Rural and Urban Population, 1871–2006

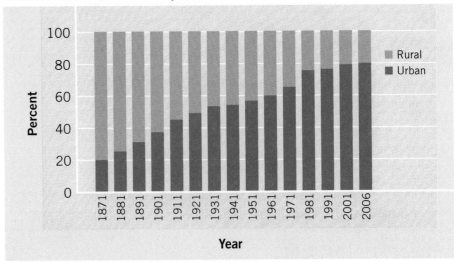

How has the rate of change been different in the last five years? What does this indicate?

In Chapter 1, you learned that an urban place is a cluster of at least 1000 people. Generally, this includes towns, cities, and metropolitan areas. Rural areas include farms as well as small settlement clusters like hamlets and villages. Rural areas are usually based on the primary industries: agriculture, fishing, mining, or forestry. A century ago, most people classed as rural were farming families, but today, only a tiny percentage of Canadians live on farms. Despite this great population shift, Canada's farmers are able to produce more food than ever. Let's look at these changes more closely.

Why People Left the Land

In the past, rural families were usually large, because children could help out with the labour required in farming or fishing. As technology advanced, new inventions reduced the need for much of this tough work. By the early 1900s, for example, huge steam-driven threshing machines were doing the work of ten people at harvest time. During the 1900s, many rural families have sold their farms to more prosperous farmers or developers and moved into nearby towns and cities. In doing so, they gained better access to services such as schools and hospitals. Look at the following survey of Saskatchewan farmers. What effects do you think this rural-to-urban shift had on local communities?

Why have so many farm families left the land? Look at this image. Where do you think the people who farmed here live now?

Why Did Farmers Leave the Land? Saskatchewan Survey, 1953

Reasons for Moving to Town	Response (%)
Access to eduction: e.g., school too far away, closed	30
Roads: e.g., blocked in winter, poor roads	16
Health: e.g., must be near medical care	14
No conveniences: e.g., no power or water	12
Farm housing: e.g., poor repair, overcrowded	9
Isolation: e.g., neighbours gone	5
Employment: e.g., have business in town and a farm	5
Forced off farm: e.g., rental expired, went broke	3
Other reasons: e.g., son taking over farm	6

During **READING**

Checkpoint
Add the factors on internal migration to your chart as you read this section.

The Shift Continues

WEB LINK • · · · · · · · · · · · · · · · · ·
Find a description of the Canadian population in 2006 on our Web site.

Canada's population is still growing in the 21st century, but not outside of the major cities. Most resource-based communities which rely on primary industries are either just holding on or slowly dying. Their mines, mills, and processing plants may be as busy as ever, but technology has replaced human labour with more efficient machines. (See Chapter 5, page G 107, for examples of technology in primary industry.) As a result, there are fewer and fewer jobs available. Often, only the most experienced workers have any measure of job security at all.

Across Canada, hamlets, villages, and small towns are shrinking as young people leave and do not come back. The only exceptions are rural communities close to cities. They have become what geographers call **dormitory towns**. Some use the term "bedroom community." People live in these places but commute to jobs, shopping, and services in the nearby large urban centres.

WORDS MATTER

dormitory town a community that is mostly residential, from which people commute to jobs or shopping in another community

How are people affected when local businesses close?

Make Pictou County Livable, Says Expert

Jennifer Vardy, *The Evening News,* New Glasgow, Nova Scotia

In the past 20 years, about seven percent of Pictou County's population has left the area.

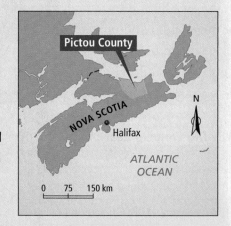

"It's part of the writing on the wall—there's a definite trend of out-migration of youth from rural areas and into urban areas," said David Bruce, the director of rural and small town programs at Mount Allison University. "There are so few people left behind when half or two-thirds of a graduating class leaves for Halifax or other urban cities."

That creates a challenge to rural municipalities to create a situation where they can attract youth to return and have families. "People choose to live where it's livable," Bruce said. "The challenge, I think, is not how to get more people here, but instead looking at what it takes to make Pictou County livable."

For some, he said, economic opportunities will convince them to return, while others want services and a good quality of life.

Metropolitan Areas: Population Magnets

In the newspaper story, David Bruce mentions that half or two-thirds of the local graduating class was leaving for Halifax and other cities. Halifax is the largest city in the Atlantic region, fast approaching 400 000 in population. It is a metropolitan area, one of today's population magnets.

The six biggest metropolitan areas in Canada have nearly 45 % of Canada's total population. Together, they accounted for almost all of Canada's population growth between 2001 and 2006. If the next three largest (Québec City, Winnipeg, and Hamilton) are added, more than half the people of Canada are clustered in just nine big urban centres!

Would you rather live in a small community or in a large metropolitan centre? Many young people are attracted to cities by opportunities for college and university educations and good jobs. Cities have entertainment attractions and shopping malls. They are lively, multicultural places that are interesting to visit and to live in. No wonder large urban areas are growing quickly.

WEB LINK • · · · · · · · · · · · · · · · · · ·
Read about why young adults choose to move to urban centres. Visit our Web site.

Growth of Canada's Largest Cities, 1951–2006

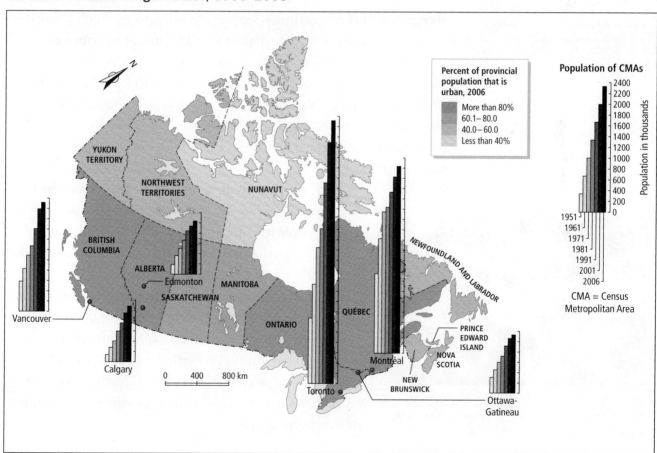

Rank the top three cities from largest to smallest. Why are they growing so quickly?

Interprovincial Migration

Try this: without talking to anyone else, decide whether or not you think each of the provinces listed below would be a good place to live. Give each province a number from 1 to 5, according to the ratings scale given in the margin. Record at least one reason for each response. Then, discuss your views with others and explain reasons for your opinions. How do your ideas compare? What was the basis of your opinions? How might such opinions affect migration between provinces?

Rate the Provinces

1 An excellent place to live
2 A good place to live
3 It might be OK/I'm not sure
4 Not a good place to live
5 I would never live there!

Newfoundland and Labrador
Nova Scotia
Québec
Ontario
Alberta
British Columbia

WORDS MATTER

interprovincial migration moving from one province to another

At the beginning of this chapter, you read that getting a job is an important reason why people move to a new community. **Interprovincial migration** is very much affected by employment prospects. About 1% of Canadians move to another province every year, and this percentage doubles among people between the ages of 20 and 29. Young people are often more willing to leave family and friends to get a good job. Some of them may only move temporarily. They may intend to return home after they have gained work experience or finished school, but some will decide to stay in their adopted province.

Interprovincial migration is directly shaped by the economy. The Atlantic Provinces have been steadily losing people to Ontario and western Canada for the past fifty years. Atlantic industries, such as fishing, do not offer enough jobs. Ontario either gains or loses interprovincial migrants depending on the state of its manufacturing. British Columbia's net migration also varies with the state of the economy. Only Alberta has experienced continual growth, because of the oil industry. In this chapter's Geo Skill feature, you will construct a map to show which provinces have gained or lost population.

The 1992 closure of the cod fishery in Newfoundland and Labrador left thousands of people without work. Many stayed, finding work through government programs or catching other types of fish. However, many young people left the province.

Alberta Bound

How did you rate Alberta as a place to live? It certainly is a good place to get a job, as the provincial economy is driven by the demand for oil. In 2007, world oil prices rose to almost $100 a barrel, pushing the Alberta oil sands to maximum production. Edmonton is the oil capital of Canada. Calgary is the headquarters for Canada's natural gas industry—another fossil fuel found in Alberta. The multiplier effect is evident here: every job in Alberta's booming energy industry creates other jobs in retail, social services, and communications. No wonder so many Canadians have moved to Alberta! Alberta's population increased by more than 10% between 2001 and 2006. This was the fastest growth of any province in Canada.

WEB LINK •·····················
For more information about the Alberta economy, visit our Web site.

Alberta, Interprovincial Migration, 2001–2006

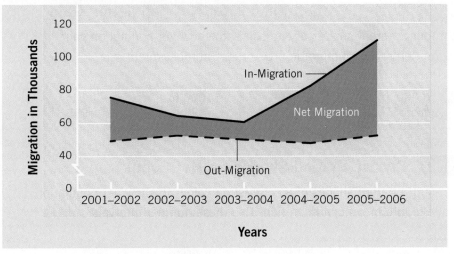

THINKING It Over

1. Analyze the newspaper story about rural Nova Scotia on page G 140. What is the main point that the expert makes? How does he suggest achieving this? What is your view of his advice?

2. Identify three important patterns on the urbanization map, page G 141. What do you notice about the population growth rates of the largest cities? Why is this happening?

3. Research the six provinces listed on page G 142. Then rate them again. Explain your "best province to live in" choice to a group of classmates.

4. Imagine that you are one of the people in Saskatchewan who left their farm. Write a one-page diary entry to express how you feel about leaving, and what you expect from the future.

GEO SKILL

Making a Thematic Map of Migration

A thematic map highlights one particular topic. Here you will use a political outline map of Canada's provinces and territories to show population changes caused by interprovincial migration.

Net Migration, 2006	
Alberta	+ 57 105
British Columbia	+ 3 779
Nunavut	+ 104
Ontario	– 21 391
Saskatchewan	– 9 073
Manitoba	– 8 635
Québec	– 8 155
Newfoundland and Labrador	– 4 368
Nova Scotia	– 3 930
New Brunswick	– 3 788
Northwest Territories	– 1 327
Yukon Territory	– 194
Prince Edward Island	– 127

Step 1 Review the Graded Shading Map Technique

On page G 141, four shades of green are used in the map to show provincial urbanization. The darker the colour shade, the more urban the province.

Step 2 Choose Graded Shades for Net Population Gain

Select four different shades of one colour to show net population gain through interprovincial migration. Use these number intervals:

+10 000 or more	+5000 to +9999	+1000 to +4999	+1 to +999

Step 3 Choose Graded Shades for Net Population Loss

Select four different shades of a contrasting colour to show net population loss due to interprovincial migration. Use these number intervals:

–10 000 or more	–5000 to –9999	–1000 to –4999	–1 to –999

Step 4 Construct and Complete the Map

Use the number table as a guide to apply your colours to the map. Then, complete it with a legend, title, and other map requirements.

APPLY It

1. Use the steps to colour and label a map of Canadian interprovincial migration. *m*

2. Describe the pattern of your completed map. Suggest possible reasons for this pattern. *k m*

3. Use the patterns to predict how you think population will change due to interprovincial migration over the next 10 years. *t a*

How Do Mobility and Technology Impact Migration?

While migration means moving to live in a new place, **mobility** refers to the ease of travelling from one place to another. How do you travel to school? Walking, cycling, skateboarding, busing, and driving are all different **modes of transportation**. Each method has its own pros and cons, and new technology is always changing that balance. Improved running shoe designs can make the walk easier, while hybrid vehicles make the drive to school better for the environment.

Canada is huge, but during the past two centuries transportation developments have improved mobility. Today it is possible for people, products, and information to move around faster and more easily than in the past. Technological improvements enabled the growth of Canada's railways, highways, and air routes. Nineteenth century inventions such as steam engines made railways the best way to transport people across the country. The 20th century brought automobiles and the construction of paved highways. Today, cars and airplanes have largely replaced trains as primary passenger carriers.

WORDS MATTER

mobility travelling from one place to another

modes of transportation different ways to transport people or goods

During **READING**

Checkpoint
Add factors from this section to your chart.

Canada, Mobility Timeline

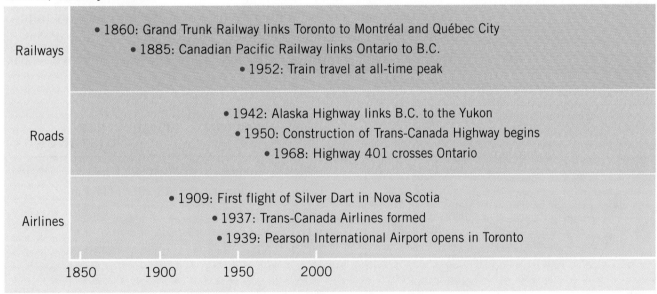

Railways	• 1860: Grand Trunk Railway links Toronto to Montréal and Québec City
	• 1885: Canadian Pacific Railway links Ontario to B.C.
	• 1952: Train travel at all-time peak
Roads	• 1942: Alaska Highway links B.C. to the Yukon
	• 1950: Construction of Trans-Canada Highway begins
	• 1968: Highway 401 crosses Ontario
Airlines	• 1909: First flight of Silver Dart in Nova Scotia
	• 1937: Trans-Canada Airlines formed
	• 1939: Pearson International Airport opens in Toronto

1850   1900   1950   2000

Why do you think railway passenger travel has dropped since 1952?

Examine the case studies of journeys in Canada on the next two pages. How has technology improved our mobility in the past 200 years?

How Far Could Canadians Travel in One Day?

Across the Prairies by Canoe, 1810

Fur traders of the North West Company left Fort William (today Thunder Bay, Ontario) in spring to travel to Fort Chipewyan, in what is now northern Alberta. On Lake Superior, the Métis traders kept a paddling rate of 45 strokes per minute, up to 18 hours a day. On one section of the Winnipeg River, each canoe and its heavy cargo had to be carried over 10 portages in a single day. In Fort Chipewyan, they rested for a few days and completed their business. They then began the return journey to Fort William, laden with furs.

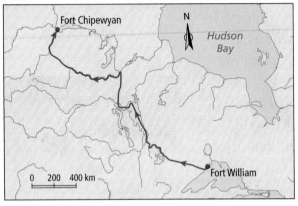

Journey: Fort William to Fort Chipewyan and return, 1810

Total Journey Time: 75 days one way
Average Daily Travel: 35 km
Average Hourly Travel: 2.2 km
Distance: 2600 km

Across Southern Ontario by Train, 1876

Passengers travelled by steam-powered Great Western Railway train from Windsor to Buffalo, New York. There, they could catch a New York Central passenger train headed east to Rochester. The whole trip took one day.

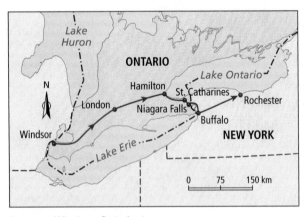

Journey: Windsor, Ontario, to Rochester, New York, 1876

	STATION	TIME	TRIP DISTANCE
Depart	Windsor	05:00	
Arrive	London	08:20	117 km
Arrive	Hamilton	11:20	298 km
Arrive	St. Catharines	12:27	350 km
Arrive	Niagara Falls	12:55	368 km
Arrive	Buffalo, New York	13:45	403 km
Depart	Buffalo	15:00	403 km
Arrive	Rochester	16:15	505 km

Total Journey Time: 11 hours, 15 minutes one way
Average Daily Travel: 505 km
Average Hourly Travel: 45 km
Distance: 505 km

Across British Columbia by Airplane, 1943

By the early 1940s, airplanes were becoming an accepted method of travel in Canada. Although too expensive for the average person to consider, air travel was relatively safe and reliable in small twin-engine passenger planes. Regularly scheduled flights were offered by many airline companies, including Canadian Pacific Airlines.

	AIRPORT	TIME	TRIP DISTANCE
Depart	Vancouver	09:00	
Arrive	Prince George	11:30	540 km
Arrive	Fort St. John	13:00	830 km
Arrive	Fort Nelson	14:40	1140 km
Arrive	Whitehorse	18:00	1880 km

Total Journey Time: 9 hours one way
Average Daily Travel: 1880 km
Average Hourly Travel: 209 km
Distance: 1880 km

Journey: Vancouver, B.C., to
Whitehorse, Yukon, 1943

Across Four Provinces by Car, 1959

By the late 1950s, most of the Trans-Canada Highway system had been built. Very little of it was a four-lane divided highway, but there were plenty of gas stations, restaurants, campgrounds, and small motels or tourist cabins along the way. By driving thirteen hours per day, a vacationing family could reach Ottawa from Edmonton after four long days of driving.

Total Journey Time: Four days one way
Average Daily Travel: 895 km
Average Hourly Travel: 70 km
Distance: 3580 km

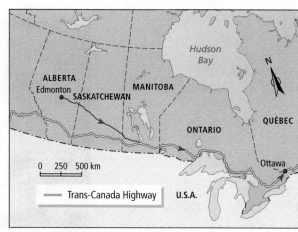

Journey: Edmonton, Alberta, to
Ottawa, Ontario, 1959

The Past Half-Century

The first satellite launched into space was Russia's Sputnik, in 1957. Today, there are hundreds of satellites orbiting the earth, monitoring the weather and transmitting television, radio, and other communications signals. Mobility has been improved a great deal by satellites used for Global Positioning Systems (GPS). When a satellite picks up signals from a GPS unit, it can pinpoint the exact position of the unit. This can help a driver decide on the best route to a destination. It also allows trucking companies to keep track of vehicles. Hand-held GPS units can be essential devices for people finding their way in the wilderness.

Design technology has made great improvements in both the machines and the networks that help our mobility. The use of lightweight, space-age materials has increased the strength of airplanes. Larger and faster planes that can carry more passengers have helped to make airline flights cheaper than ever. New automobiles make use of complex computer systems and lightweight parts to improve safety, performance, and fuel efficiency. Highway design has made it easier and quicker to get from one city to the next. Multi-lane divided highways with core lanes and exit ramps link nearly every community in Ontario with 50 000 or more people.

New Airplane Technology: The Boeing 787 Dreamliner
Seating: 290 passengers
Speed: 1000 km/hr
Range: 15 000 km
Fuel Use: 20% more efficient than current airplanes of this type
Production: late 2008

During **READING**

Topic Sentences
The topic sentence is often the first or second sentence in a paragraph. Can you find and note the technological improvements these paragraphs will be discussing?

A view of the interchange between Highways 407 and 427 in Ontario. What impact do additional highways have on people? The environment?

New Technology on the Move: Hybrid Vehicles

The word "hybrid" means that something has features from two different origins. Hybrid vehicles combine fossil fuel (gasoline) and electric energy to achieve the lowest levels of fuel consumption on the road. The first hybrid vehicles were introduced to commercial markets in the late 1990s. Today, the most popular model is still the original one—the Toyota Prius. These energy-efficient vehicles sell as fast as manufacturers can produce them.

Toyota's concept vehicle, the Hyrbid X, was introduced in 2007. What could the hybrid vehicle mean to car manufacturers in the future?

Hybrid Vehicle Timeline

1997	The first commercial gasoline-electric hybrid, the Toyota Prius, is introduced to the Japanese market.
1999	Honda releases the lightweight two-door Insight coupe, the first hybrid car to hit the mass market in North America.
2000	Toyota releases the Prius in North America, a small four-door family sedan.
2002	Honda introduces the Honda Civic Hybrid, its second commercially available hybrid car.
2004	The Toyota Prius II wins Car of the Year awards from *Motor Trend* magazine and the North American Auto Show. Ford releases the Escape Hybrid, the first built in the U.S.
2008	Hybrids are available from other manufacturers, including Lexus, Nissan, Mazda, and Saturn.

THINKING It Over

1. Make a master chart to compare the four journeys described in this section. Put the four methods of travel across the top, and down the left side enter a) date, b) daily travel, and c) average speed. When your chart is finished, work with a partner to add sections d) advantages, and e) disadvantages, for each travel method.

2. Has improved technology made our lives easier or more complicated? Present your views either as a statement or as an editorial cartoon.

3. Use the web link to learn more about hybrid vehicles. If you were buying one, which would you choose? Why?

WEB LINK •••••••••••••••••••••
Learn more about hybrid vehicles and alternative fuels. Visit our Web site.

PUTTING IT ALL TOGETHER

Canada is a nation on the move. You learned that people often choose new communities by the quality of life they offer. Canadians move within their community, province, territory, or across the country to find better jobs, better health care, or better opportunities. Canada's rural-to-urban shift has been happening for more than a century. Small rural communities struggle to survive as their young people leave. Interprovincial migration has a general westward direction as people from the Atlantic region head for Ontario, while Ontarians move to Alberta. Technology continues to improve our mobility. Automobiles and airplanes have become our favourite means of travel. This chapter has introduced you to some important aspects of the unit question, **How do migration patterns affect people and communities in Canada and the world?**

After READING

Create Your Ranking Ladders

Use the information in your chart to create several ranking ladders. Write the least important factor/idea/effect on the bottom rung, and the most important on the top rung. Decide the order of the middle ideas.

You will want one ladder for each of the following topics:

• Where to live factors

• Migration: best cities or provinces to live in

• Internal migration

• Effects of technology

Your teacher may ask you to complete this in groups of 2–4. Then, discuss the charts with a partner in your class. How are your charts similar and/or differerent?

THINKING It Through

1. Using the chart on the next page for data, draw and label a multiple line graph of Ontario's interprovincial migration. You can use the graph showing Alberta's Interprovincial Migration (page G 143) as a guide. **a**

2. Compare your completed graph to that of Alberta. Identify two important differences between the graphs. Use information from this chapter to explain the differences. **k t**

3. Look at the map and city graphs of Ontario on the next page. Divide the communities into a) those that grew fastest between 1991 and 2006, and b) those that grew more slowly. What pattern do you notice when you compare the size and location of the two groups? Suggest two reasons for your observations. **m t**

4. Write an organized paragraph about the effects of migration on Ontario. Consider both interprovincial migration and the rural-urban shift. Refer to the maps and graphs on the next page, and other information from this chapter. **k c m**

Interprovincial Migration, Ontario, 2001–2006

Year	In-Migration	Out-Migration
2005–2006	64 000	86 000
2004–2005	59 000	71 000
2003–2004	57 000	64 000
2002–2003	64 000	64 000
2001–2002	70 000	65 000

Metropolitan Growth in Ontario, 1991–2006

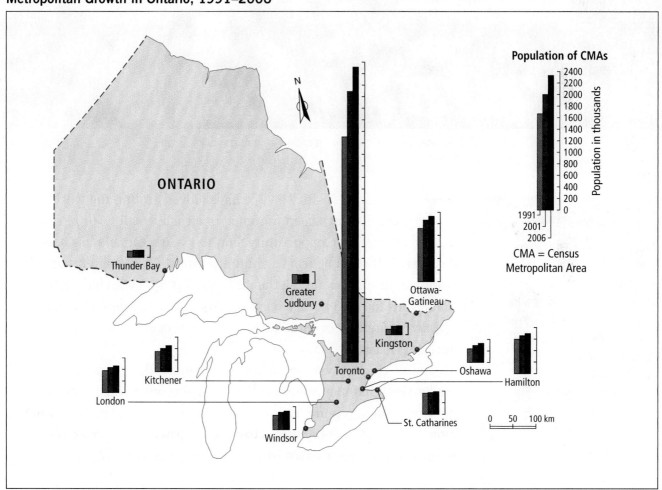

CHAPTER 8

The Decision to Migrate

Asia has become the leading source of immigrants to Canada.

Making Connections

Look in the index of this book for *push* and *pull* in the History section (or skim Chapter 8 in History). Review push and pull factors that influenced people's decisions when moving to a new location. Write the information in the organizer provided in this chapter's Thinking About Literacy.

Throughout history people have moved around the world. Families have been uprooted in a rush to safety, or in search of economic opportunity. For 400 years, Canada has been a destination for people from around the world. You, a parent, or a grandparent may be among the millions of people who have left their homelands to come here. Except for Aboriginal peoples, Canadians all have immigrant origins. The main difference is how long ago our ancestors arrived.

In this chapter, you will learn why people want to move despite the barriers that may stand in their way. You will compare past and present Canadian immigration patterns. And you will come to know more about the unit Big Idea, **How do migration patterns affect people and communities in Canada and the world?**

In 2004, a tsunami devastated part of Sri Lanka, leaving over a million people without homes.

Questions to Consider as You Read this Chapter

- How do push and pull factors influence people to move?

- What effects do different types of barriers have on the decision to migrate?

- What are the opportunities and challenges faced by past and present immigrants?

- How can I construct and use a proportional flow map of immigration to Canada?

Thinking About Literacy

Make Connections Between Geography and History

Show how geography played a role in the history of Canada. As you read, note factors that affected immigration in the past and today. Note the impact each factor has had on Canada. You may want to refer to Chapter 7 in this Geography section, or to Chapter 8 in the History section.

Today	Past	Impact (including policies, past and present)

Why Do People Migrate?

During *READING*

Making Inferences
This paragraph and the photos below introduce the factors of push, pull, and policy. Based on what you know now, how do you think these factors affect migration?

People leave their homelands in search of better conditions. They want to improve their quality of life. However, people cannot simply pack up their belongings and move. Immigrants can act legally to move to a different place only if the government welcomes them. The photographs below shows the Three "P"s—push, policy, and pull—that affect migration. Read more about push and pull factors in the next few pages. Policy factors are found in "Barriers to Migration," on pages G 161 to G 162.

PUSH	**POLICY**	**PULL**
(Homelands)	(Government)	(New Opportunities)

Look closely at the the photographs and the headings. What can you infer about the relationship between the Three "P"s?

Push Factors

Did you ever feel unsafe because of some very real danger? Have you ever felt threatened by someone bigger than you, or by a menacing group of people? You probably made the wise choice to get away immediately, if that was possible. Each of these situations is an example of a **push factor**. Think of more examples from your life at home or in school. In migration terms, a push factor is a negative situation that drives people from their homeland:

- a natural disaster that claims lives and destroys communities

- political violence and war that threatens safety and disrupts the economy

- poor living conditions such as poverty, which people can no longer tolerate

WORDS MATTER

push factor the social, political, economic, and environmental forces that drive people away from where they live

Natural Disasters

Nature can unleash tremendous energy. It can provide the force to move people from their homes. Volcanoes, earthquakes, and tsunamis create instant widespread destruction. In December 2004, an earthquake in Southeast Asia caused massive tsunami waves. These waves took 230 000 lives and left millions homeless. Many people who worked near the sea chose to move farther inland, where they felt safe. However, they have now lost their livelihoods. Extreme events such as tsunamis, hurricanes, or floods can create this kind of mass migration as survivors struggle to regain their lives.

Political Violence

It is hard to follow world news without seeing images of war or terrorism. It is even harder for farmers, store owners, and other business people to maintain their livelihoods in war-torn lands. Political upheaval can ruin businesses and disrupt lives. It can lead to discrimination and loss of freedom, which are also push factors for many people. Many current examples are found in South Asia, Africa, and the Middle East. Command economic systems have also been the cause of mass migrations. For example, more than 6.5 million people fled Vietnam in the late 1970s when the country fell to communism.

Poverty

Poverty can be made worse by natural disasters and political violence. In Chapter 3, you learned that poverty in developing countries can be the result of too many mouths to feed from too little land. Debt from loans to pay for seed, animals, and basic necessities often takes away any surplus a farmer produces. To find work, many **guest workers** from North Africa and the Middle East arrange temporary permits to take jobs in Europe. Canada also employs seasonal farm labourers from Mexico, Central America, and the Caribbean.

About 18 000 guest or migrant workers come to Canada to work in fields, orchards, and greenhouses every year. This man lives and works for six months in Ontario, sending money home to his family.

WEB LINK •••••••••••••••••••••••
Learn more about Vietnamese refugees in the 1970s. Visit our Web site.

WORDS MATTER
guest worker a person who works temporarily in a foreign country

Natural Disaster: Escaping Katrina
Hurricane Katrina flooded New Orleans, Louisiana, in August of 2005. The Superdome football stadium became a refuge for downtown residents who could not leave the city before the storm hit. This photo shows people leaving the Superdome after the storm. Hundreds of buses were sent to evacuate thousands of people. Most people were taken to communities in Texas and Oklahoma. Many have not returned to New Orleans. Why do you think that is the case?

Political Violence: Fleeing Iraq
Since the 1990s, about 2 million of Iraq's residents have fled the country due to violence and war. Most have escaped to neighbouring countries, such as Jordan, Lebanon, and Syria. Many people continue to sell their possessions and journey through the desert to United Nations refugee camps. More than a million people have also fled to safer communities within Iraq. Why is this issue significant to Canadians?

Poverty: Leaving Mexico
The U.S.–Mexico border is almost 3200 km long, crossing mountains and deserts. It is marked by walls and fences. Living standards are very different on either side of the border. Most of the 11 million illegal immigrants in the U.S. come from Mexico. Every day hundreds more make their desperate bid for the "American dream" by crossing the border any way they can. What might Mexian immigrants—both legal and illegal—believe they will achieve in the United States?

Pull Factors

In Chapter 7, you learned that certain Canadian cities scored better than others on job prospects, safety, and discretionary income. These are examples of **pull factors**—the characteristics of a place that attract migrants. Pull factors offer some solutions to the problems shown in the previous pages.

Safety

Natural disasters and human conflict are life-threatening situations. People may need to be evacuated to places where they can find shelter, food, medicine, and water. Armed violence sends families into hiding or across borders to safer areas. People who move because of a need for protection from danger or persecution are called **refugees**. People arriving in Canada claiming refugee status are allowed to stay here until their case can be judged.

Economic Opportunity

People constantly strive to improve their living conditions. In History class, you may have learned that Canada attracted immigrants by offering free land to settlers in Ontario and the West. Many who came were British, European, and American farmers, eager for land. There were also those who received land but were not experienced farmers. They were full of hope for a new life, but some of them failed. Many of today's immigrants are drawn by opportunities for jobs, or the chance to start a successful business in Canada.

Reuniting Family

As people immigrate, something called **chain migration** often happens:

- young adults, usually males, will emigrate to find work in a new country. They will then

- send money home to help support direct family members left behind, and also

- save money to help pay for the eventual immigration of additional family members.

Canada supports **family reunification** through family class immigration. Currently, about one-quarter of immigrants who enter Canada are sponsored by relatives who agree to support them for three to ten years, depending on the newcomer's age.

During **READING**

Summarize
Create a paragraph summary. First, find the topic sentence. Find two or three details that support the topic sentence. Conclude with a point stating the impact of this information. Write your notes into a short statement, creating your summary.

WEB LINK •••••••••••••••••••••••
For more information about Canada's refugee policies, visit our Web site.

WORDS MATTER

pull factor the social, economic, and environmental attractions that draw people to move to a particular place

refugees people who flee to a foreign country for safety from political upheaval or war

chain migration when people immigrate to a new country after relatives have already established citizenship there

family reunification an immigration policy that acknowledges the right of a family to be together

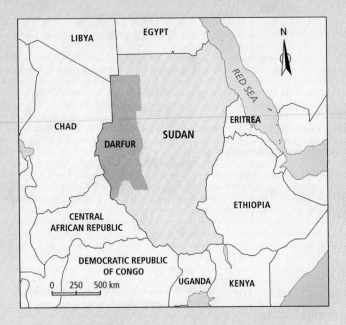

Darfur is an isolated region in North Africa, and the scene of a devastating humanitarian crisis. At least 400 000 people died between 2003 and 2007, and another 2 million to 2.5 million have been forced to migrate. They have fled their homes into safer territory. Most have moved to refugee camps in Chad.

The Darfur crisis is complicated, with racial, environmental, and political roots. Both Arab and non-Arab peoples live in Sudan, and there is a long history of conflict between the groups. Darfur, an arid territory on the western edge of Sudan, has suffered from decades of drought and famine. This created conflict over the remaining water sources. The recent crisis between Darfur's farmers and nomadic Arab herders began over land and water rights.

In 2003, rebel groups in Darfur declared independence from Sudan, stating that the government was oppressing non-Arab peoples. The government replied with army and air force attacks on rebel villages. The government has also been accused of supplying weapons to the mostly Arab Janjaweed fighters, who attack non-Arab villages and refugee camps. The United States government has called their actions **genocide.** International aid workers have been killed, and food and medical supplies stolen. However, the United Nations has been slow to take action because the Sudanese government denies any connection with the Janjaweed. A small African peacekeeping mission was attempted with little success. When full UN involvement was announced in June, 2007, many felt that it came much too late.

What point is the cartoonist making about the United Nations? Use information about the Darfur situation and images in the cartoon to explain your answer.

WEB LINK •
For more information on the crisis in the Sudan, visit our Web site.

WORDS MATTER

genocide the deliberate and systematic extermination of a national, racial, political, or cultural group

The environment of the Darfur region has been greatly affected by climate change. Drought has been identified as one of the root causes of the conflict. Ban Ki Moon, appointed Secretary General of the United Nations in 2007, has discussed how the problem of global climate change has affected Darfur.

As the drought continues, experts fear that continued conflict and the refugee camps may do even more harm to the environment. Millions of refugees use up scarce water supplies and cut down trees for firewood. How could this affect the future of the region?

A Climate Culprit in Darfur

By Ban Ki Moon
Saturday, June 16, 2007
Washington Post

...Amid the diverse social and political causes, the Darfur conflict began as an ecological crisis, arising at least in part from climate change.

Two decades ago, the rains in southern Sudan began to fail. According to UN statistics, average precipitation has declined 40 percent since the early 1980s. Scientists at first considered this to be an unfortunate quirk of nature. But subsequent investigation found that it coincided with a rise in temperatures of the Indian Ocean....from man-made global warming.

It is no accident that the violence in Darfur erupted during the drought. Until then, farmers would welcome herders as they crisscrossed the land, grazing their camels and sharing wells. But once the rains stopped, farmers fenced their land. For the first time in memory, there was no longer enough food and water for all. Fighting broke out. By 2003, it evolved into the full-fledged tragedy we witness today....

THINKING It Over

1. Work with a partner to apply the Three "P"s to an example of natural disaster, political violence, or poverty found in the media today.

2. a) Explain the factors pushing people from the Darfur region. Discuss the environmental cause in detail.

   b) Make a poster or write a letter to draw attention to the situation in Darfur.

3. Work with a small group of students to make a dramatic presentation based on one of the migration situations described in this section.

What Are Barriers to Migration?

Personal Barriers
- emotional
- financial

You may want to go to a sports event or a shopping centre, but cannot get a ride. This is a barrier in the way of your plans. You must overcome this obstacle, or give up your outing. The same is true with moving from one country to another. Personal, national, and legal migration **barriers** often stand in the way of people's plans.

Personal Barriers

Immigration is a huge risk. No one knows what life will be like in another country. The thought of leaving friends and relatives behind is a real emotional barrier. When families move to another continent, they may never see their loved ones again. Immigration is very expensive too, and many people cannot afford the cost of applications, **entry visas**, and airplane tickets. Immigrants often need a sponsor in the new country to provide good advice and financial support until they find work. Above all, people find it very difficult to start life over again at the bottom of the economic ladder. Barriers to migration can discourage or prevent a person from moving to another country. Government immigration and refugee policies can act as major barriers. This is why "Policy" is one part of the Three "P"s model you examined on page G 154.

A family carries their possessions as they cross the Khyber Pass from Afghanistan into Pakistan in 2001.

A Dangerous Journey: Refugees Flee Afghanistan

The country of Afghanistan is currently one of the top sources of refugees coming to Canada (the others in the top five are Sudan, Iran, Colombia, and Congo). The refugees from Afghanistan who are fleeing the oppressive rule of the Taliban also seek refuge from political upheaval and civil war.

Most Afghan refugees undertake a dangerous journey to find freedom and peace. With no visas or passports, they have to enter another country illegally. Those going into Pakistan face long climbs on foot through mountain passes. Some families have to hide from the Taliban in mountain caves for days or even weeks.

Once in Pakistan, the most dangerous part of their journey is over. Now, they can think about where to go next. Some will stay in Pakistan, and some hope that one day they will be able to return to Afghanistan. Others have a different dream—a home in Canada, where they can work, go to school, and raise their children without fear.

National Barriers

Physical and political factors present major obstacles to migration. Two countries may be located very far apart, or they may be separated by mountains or deserts. Physical separation makes it more difficult, dangerous, or costly to migrate. You just read that many Afghan refugees had to make their way across a mountain range to reach the border of Pakistan.

The greatest national barrier to overcome is political **policy**. For example, a command society may not let people leave the country. This was the situation in Russia and communist-controlled Eastern Europe between 1945 and 1989, although it is quite different now. In the same way, opportunites in a new country can only be a dream when that country's entry doors are closed.

Before 1967, Canada accepted very few immigrants from regions other than Europe and the United States. That year a **points system** was introduced to assess potential immigrants, almost like a report card. This "test" was based on language skills in English or French, education and useful work experience, age, and sponsorship by residents. The graphs below show how this policy change opened immigration doors that were closed before 1967.

National Barriers
• physical
• political

WORDS MATTER

policy government laws and regulations that may create a barrier to immigration

points system an assessment system used to evaluate potential immigrants

Immigrants to Canada, 1960 and 1980

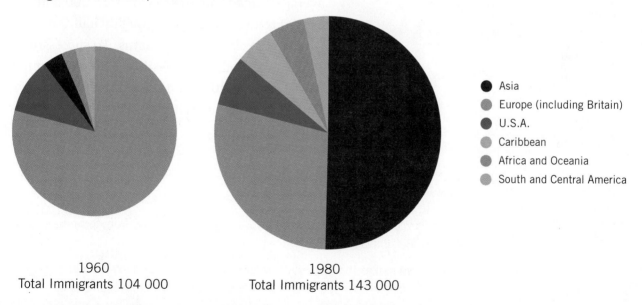

1960
Total Immigrants 104 000

1980
Total Immigrants 143 000

Asia
Europe (including Britain)
U.S.A.
Caribbean
Africa and Oceania
South and Central America

Why is one circle larger than the other? What do the other major differences between the graphs tell you?

Legal Barriers

Migration within and between countries is regulated by international law. The United Nations Universal Declaration of Human Rights includes freedom of movement. However, these statements have not always been practised by individual countries.

> Article 13: 1) Everyone has the right to freedom of movement and residence within the borders of each state. 2) Everyone has the right to leave any country, including his own...

> Article 14: 1) Everyone has the right to seek and to enjoy in other countries asylum [protection] from persecution....

Canada: Top Sources of Refugee Claimants, 2006

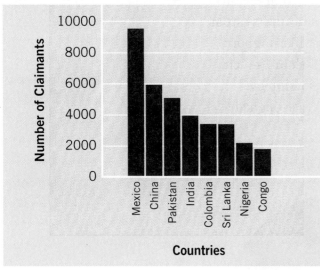

In 1951, the UN expanded these statements in the Convention Relating to the Status of Refugees. When refugees come to Canada, they declare refugee status under this Convention. They are allowed to stay in Canada until their case is presented at a legal hearing. If immigration officials decide that a person or a family can safely return to their country of origin, they are sent back, or deported. On average, Canada accepts between 15 000 and 50 000 refugees each year, roughly half the people who claim refugee status. To successful refugees, Canada is **accessible**. The others must leave Canada, although they are free to re-apply under the same or another immigration category.

WORDS MATTER

accessible in terms of migration, when a person is able to gain entry to their desired destination

THINKING It Over

1. How did Canadian immigration patterns differ in 1960 from those in 1980? Explain why.

2. What makes the news story and photo on page G 160 interesting? Do you or other students in the class have family immigration stories? Write out either your story or an interview with a classmate in about 150 words.

3. Make a world map showing the top countries of origin of people who claim refugee status in Canada. Discuss the reasons you think the refugees came to Canada. If you are unsure, what resources might you use to find out more?

PLAY — **Immigration Barriers**

Overcome immigration barriers to reach Canada first.

What You Will Need:

• One die, game board, small marker for each player

How to Play:

A. Roll one die and move a marker along the direct route to Canada. If you land on a coloured Detour Space, you must visit that Barrier Zone on your next turn. However, if you roll a 1 on your next turn, continue to Canada. You need an exact roll to land on Canada.

B. An exact roll is not required to enter a Barrier Zone. However, each zone tells you the number that must be rolled to leave. If you land on a Detour Space on the way out of a Barrier Zone, you must turn around and go back on the next turn (unless you roll a 1).

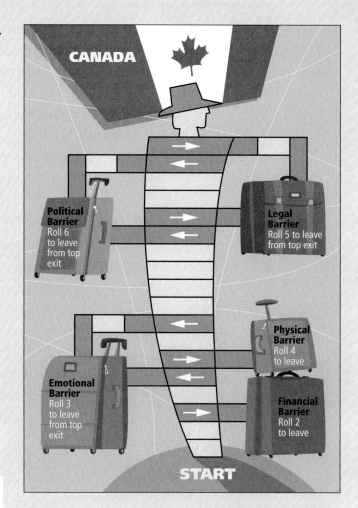

What Do YOU Think?

1. Describe your experiences in this game. Did you find it frustrating at times? Explain.

2. How might your experiences in this game compare to the real world? Identify some similarities and differences.

3. Ask three questions to create discussion about the main barriers to Canadian immigration today.

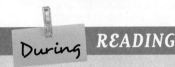
Checkpoint

Include this information in your organizer. What barriers existed in the past, and what impact did they have on Canadian policy?

In the early 21st century, Canada's population has grown faster than all the leading developed countries. Much of this growth came from net migration, with about 250 000 new immigrants arriving each year (and relatively few people leaving). During this time, the Canadian economy grew steadily and the government's policy was to welcome qualified newcomers. If a quarter-million more people each year seems like a lot to you, remember that Canada is the world's second-largest country by area. Canada still has plenty of room and many opportunities for people to start a new life.

Past Immigrants

In the 50 years following Canada's Confederation, there was a major effort to populate the vast prairie region with settlers. Immigration agents went to Europe and the United States to lure settlers to the "Last Best West." Advertising posters used this phrase because by 1890 there was no more land available in the American plains. Immigrants could get 65 hectares (160 acres) of prairie land by paying a small registration fee and farming for three years. It was a powerful pull factor. The policy doors were open—to those who came from approved areas, such as Central and Eastern Europe. The Minister of the Interior, Clifford Sifton, wanted farmers. He especially wanted those from Ukraine, Romania, Hungary, and Poland, where agricultural and climatic conditions were similar to those in western Canada.

The population graph on the next page shows the success of Canada's campaign to attract immigrants. More than 8 million people came during the first century after Confederation, with the greatest number of them arriving between 1900 and 1930. After 1930, there were serious problems that slowed immigration to a trickle. The Great Depression brought the Canadian and world economy to a standstill. The Second World War almost halted international movement completely.

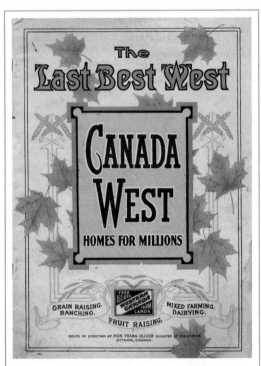

Which potential immigrants would be drawn by this advertisement? Why? What impact do you think this policy of increasing immigration to Canada would have on people already living here, such as Aboriginal peoples?

WEB LINK •

Look at a multimedia presentation about immigration to Canada. Visit our Web site.

Immigrant Arrivals in Canada, 1860–1959

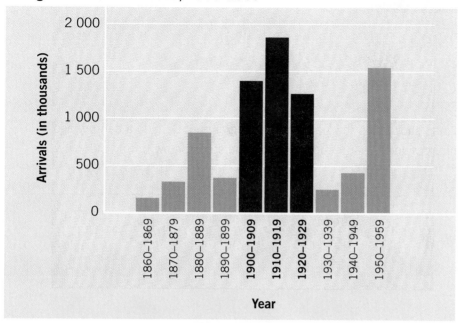

A century ago, almost all of Canada's immigration came from the U.S., Britain, and Europe. Canadian policy at that time blocked most immigration from Asia, Africa, and South and Central America. Open hostility toward Chinese, Japanese, and Sikh migrants led to entry restrictions, such as the "head tax" Chinese immigrants were required to pay from 1885 to 1923. People with disabilities were not welcome either. Even immigrants from Central and Eastern Europe could never be sure how they would be treated by their neighbours.

The Irish Migration

Irish farmers relied on potatoes, both to take to market and for their families. From 1845 to 1847, the Irish potato crop completely failed, and 750 000 people starved. Huge numbers of survivors filled any ship bound for North America in one of the biggest mass migrations ever. Irish immigrants swelled the populations of Boston, New York, Montréal, and Toronto. Today, their descendants form large populations in the United States and Canada.

Olga Seibot Remembers

My parents knew war was coming. I was 13 when they sold everything and went by ship to Halifax. In 1937, we bought a farm near Alvinston, Ontario, where there were other Slovaks. We helped each other, but we were so isolated. Canada was cold and snowy, and we had to live on white beans and milk at first.

There were seven in our family and we all joined in the farm work. Friends from our country shared machines at harvest time and helped us to fix broken equipment. We went to the same church, and that brought us together too.

I didn't know English, so I was put into Grade 1. I felt so awkward. We couldn't speak Slovak in public because people thought we were Nazi spies. Some boys even shot pellet guns at us.

Life was hard for everyone. There's a saying: "If the countries were connected by a bridge, people would have walked back."

Olga Seibot came to Canada in 1937. Later she married a Canadian war veteran, raised a family, and worked as a nurse's aid. She still participates in local Slovak activites. Why is community so important to most Canadian immigrants?

Making a Proportional Flow Map of Immigration

This map shows the flow pattern of immigrants to Canada a century ago. Is immigration the same today? Follow the steps below to find out.

Immigration to Canada: 1901–1911

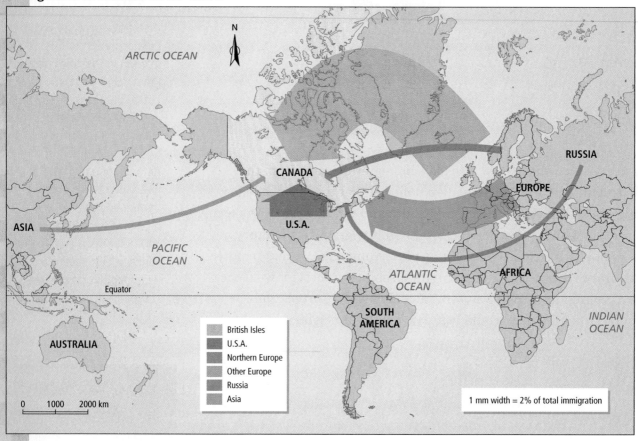

Legend:
- British Isles
- U.S.A.
- Northern Europe
- Other Europe
- Russia
- Asia

0   1000   2000 km

1 mm width = 2% of total immigration

Tip:

- For a review of proportional flow maps, go to the Geo Skill in Chapter 6, pages G 120–G 121.

Step 1 Label the Source Countries

To show worldwide immigration to Canada, choose a map that places North America and South America in the middle. Label Canada and the source countries on the map.

Step 2 Draw Flow Lines to Canada

Flow lines look best as smooth, curving lines ending at Canada's western, southern, or eastern borders, depending on the location of the source country. Do not space the flow lines too close to one another, because you will be widening them in Step 4.

Step 3 Create a Flow Scale

The flow lines will be widened to represent the number of immigrants from each country. In this map, every millimetre of width represents 2000 people. Since China was the source of about 33 000 people in 2006, the flow line will be 16.5 mm wide (33 000 ÷ 2000 = 16.5). These widths have been calculated for you in the immigration chart below.

Step 4 Apply the Flow Scale to the Lines

Use a ruler to measure the width of each flow line. Then, carefully draw them onto the map. Finish them with colour, with an arrowhead at the Canadian end.

Tip:
- Remember to finish your map with a title, a legend, and a scale.
- Use the example flow map as a guide.

Canada: Top Ten Sources of Immigration, 2006

Source countries	People	Flow line width
China	33 080	16.5 mm
India	30 753	15.4 mm
Philippines	17 717	8.9 mm
Pakistan	12 332	6.2 mm
United States	10 943	5.5 mm
Iran	7073	3.5 mm
United Kingdom	6542	3.3 mm
Korea, Republic of	6178	3.1 mm
Colombia	5813	2.9 mm
France	4915	2.5 mm
Top 10 countries	135 346	—
Other countries	116 303	—
Total	251 649	—

APPLY It

1. Follow the steps to make a flow map of immigration to Canada. Use the chart above to construct your arrows. 🄜

2. Describe the pattern of your completed 2006 immigration map. Which continent is Canada's major source of immigrants? 🄜

3. Compare this pattern to the map on the previous page, showing Canadian immigration a century ago. Suggest reasons for the differences between the patterns. 🄚 🄐

Immigration Today

Do you have family or friends overseas? Would you like them to think about moving to Canada? Here is some good advice that you can give them. They need to apply at a Canadian visa office outside of Canada before coming here (unless they qualify as refugee claimants, or are caregivers to people already in Canada). Tell them that Canada accepts immigrants who qualify under these criteria:

WEB LINK •·····················
Learn more about the experiences of new immigrants in Canada on our Web site.

- Skilled workers and professionals with education and experience

- Investors or entrepreneurs who can start a business in Canada

- Family members sponsored by permanent residents of Canada

Canada's *Immigration and Refugee Protection Act* has three main aims: protecting refugees, contributing to the economy, and reuniting families.

Patterns Since 1980

What conclusions can you make by examining the graph below? Economic immigrants are those accepted because of their skills, education, investments, or entrepreneurship. This class of immigrant has grown significantly since the mid-1980s. However, the numbers vary a great deal from year to year. This is because fewer economic immigrants are accepted when Canadian unemployment rates are high. This explains the small number in this class entering Canada between 1982 and 1986.

To find the number of immigrants of each type, look at the width of the band in one year. For example, in 1980, the economic immigrants zone starts at 50 000 and ends at 100 000. There were 50 000 in this class that year. How many economic immigrants were there in 2006?

Canada: Immigrants by Category, 1980–2006

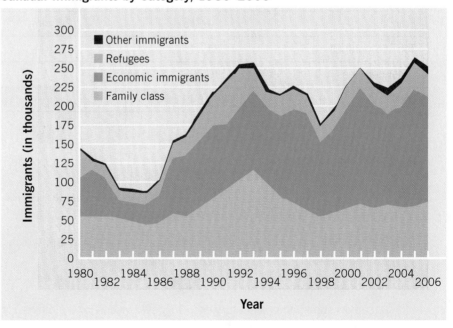

Big City Bound

Between 2001 and 2006, about 1.2 million people immigrated to Canada. The graph below shows that half of them came to Ontario in 2006, mostly in the region around the west end of Lake Ontario, from Oshawa to Niagara Falls. The Greater Toronto Area (GTA)—in the centre of this Golden Horseshoe region—has Canada's greatest concentration of new immigrants. Altogether, about 85% of newcomers chose just three provinces—Ontario, Québec, and British Columbia. It is no coincidence that Canada's three biggest cities— Toronto, Montréal, and Vancouver—are located there. Immigrants go to these places for jobs and to join family and friends already in Canada. Here, they can live and work within a cultural community with familiar language and customs.

WEB LINK •·····················•
Read about services and information offered to immigrants arriving in Vancouver, Montréal, and Toronto. Visit our Web site.

Immigrant Destination by Province or Territory, 2006

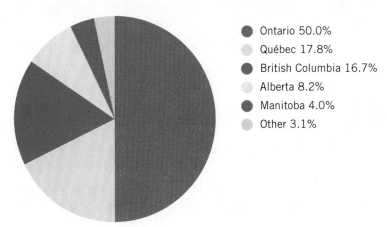

- Ontario 50.0%
- Québec 17.8%
- British Columbia 16.7%
- Alberta 8.2%
- Manitoba 4.0%
- Other 3.1%

Which four provinces are the main immigrant destinations? Why are these provinces so popular with newcomers?

THINKING It Over

1. **a)** Compare the origins of immigrants to Canada in the past and today. How do policy changes explain the difference?

   b) Compare the destinations within Canada of immigrants a century ago and today. How can you explain the difference?

2. Make a Venn diagram to show either, a) similarities and differences between the experiences of Afghan refugees and Olga Seibot, or b) comparisons between your family's immigration experiences and an Afghan refugee's or Olga's.

Is Canada Failing Its Immigrants?

Immigration can be a difficult experience. Read the following information to help you decide whether or not Canada is failing its immigrants.

Immigration Targets Go Beyond Numbers

Editorial, *Toronto Star*
March 18, 2007

Canada has done a remarkable job of attracting new immigrants from around the world to offset the brewing demographic storm sparked by an aging population and a declining birth rate.

Despite our growing need for immigrants, though, Canada does not always offer a warm welcome to these newcomers. Many white-collar professionals wait for years to have their credentials recognized. Their talents go unused because too many of Ontario's 34 regulated professions throw huge barriers in the way of qualified foreign-trained applicants, denying them the chance to practise their skills in fields which the province desperately needs.

In the meantime, they must struggle to hold two or three part-time jobs in order to pay the rent and feed their families.

At the same time, they face language barriers, racial discrimination and an insistence on "Canadian experience." Given the increasing importance of immigration to the country's future, Canada must do more to welcome these needed immigrants or risk losing them to other countries. As University of Toronto demographics expert David Foot put it: "Just bringing in immigrants and dropping them down in Canada is not sufficient."

Immigrant Welcome Centres

In June 2007, a new immigrant Welcome Centre opened in suburban Toronto. It is the first of five Ontario centres planned by the provincial and federal governments. An extra $920 million will be spent over five years to help newcomers find homes and jobs and improve their language skills. The Vaughan location expects to help about 3500 new immigrants in its first year alone.

What Do YOU Think?

1. What is the main idea of the news editorial? List three examples of evidence used to support this idea. **k**

2. To what extent do you agree with the editorial—completely, partly, a little, or not at all? Write down two reasons for your views. **t**

3. Is Canada failing its immigrants? Discuss your opinion and reasons with others in a small group. How is Canada aiming to improve the situation? What barriers remain? **t c**

PUTTING IT ALL TOGETHER

In this chapter you have investigated this unit's Big Idea: **How do migration patterns affect people and communities in Canada and the world?** You have read information in this chapter to help you find your answer to this question. You have learned that people have come to Canada because of various push, pull, and policy factors. Immigrants have had to overcome personal, national, and legal barriers to complete the journey.

In the past, Canadian policy favoured British, American, and European applicants. Today's immigrants come from around the world, particularly from Asia. More than 80% of immigrants settle in big cities in Ontario, Québec, and British Columbia.

After READING

Summarize Your Connections

Use the information in your chart to summarize this chapter and show the connections between history and geography. Information from the impact column can be used to write the conclusion to your summary. Remember that a summary should be fairly short and in your own words. Use only a few quotations from the chapter.

You may want to organize your summary this way:

- Topic sentence (topic plus opinion)
- Three to five details that support the topic sentence
- Conclusion, based on the impact column, stating what important changes were made to Canadian polices around immigration

THINKING It Through

In which period would it be more difficult for people to migrate to Canada—now, or a century ago? Consider the barriers faced by immigrants as you follow the steps below to answer this question.

1. Write down some good questions to help you form an opinion. For example, you could ask "When was the journey to Canada more difficult?" *t*

2. Write a three-paragraph report to answer the question. Clearly state your viewpoint in the opening sentence of the first paragraph, then use factual information to support it. Restate your view in the last sentence of the third paragraph. *k c t a*

3. Create a graph, map, or graphic organizer to illustrate your report and support your view. *m a*

4. Provide a detailed bibliography of three sources of information you used to answer the question. At least one must be a primary source. *c t*

CHAPTER 9

Canada's Cultural Imprints

Toronto's annual Caribana Parade and festival

Before READING

Making Connections

Canada is often called a mosaic, while the United States is often called a melting pot. What do each of these terms suggest to you?

In 1995, U.S. President Bill Clinton said, "Canada has stood for all of us as a model of how people of different cultures can live and work together in peace, prosperity and understanding." At the time, he was talking about how Canada's English and French populations work together in one country. He could also have been talking about Canada's current policies, which encourage cultural understanding.

At one time, Aboriginal peoples and immigrants were expected to blend in with the majority groups—the English and French. Most cultural practices were discouraged or banned. Today, both the federal and provincial governments support a wide range of cultural events, such as Caribana. As you explore these changes, you will continue to investigate the unit's Big Idea: **How do migration patterns affect people and communities in Canada and the world?**

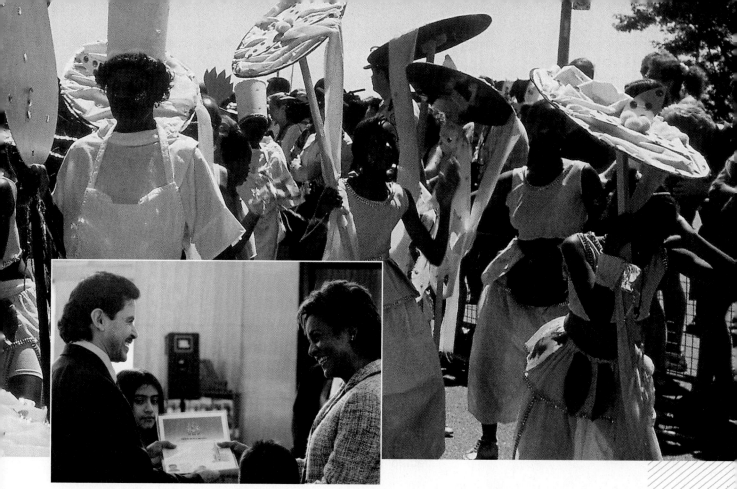

Canada's Governor General Michaëlle Jean congratulates new Canadian citizens in 2007.

Questions to Consider as You Read this Chapter

- How does migration affect Canada's culture?

- What comparisons can be made between the experiences of minority groups in Canada, past and present?

- How can I become more aware of the cultural origins of people in my community?

- How can I interpret a map of population distribution and cultural origins?

Thinking About Literacy

Inferences: Making Meaning Through Context Clues

Create a personal dictionary. You will use the words and phrases in your dictionary at the end of this chapter. Write any bold or italicized words in the first column (and any other words you are not sure of) then write the definition. In the third column, explain how you actually see this in Canada.

Word/Phrase	Definition	How do I see this in Canada?
culture		
core values		

Culture has different meanings to different people. To some it means art or music, while others think of it as food or clothing. Others connect culture with language and beliefs. In fact, culture is all of these things and more. A **culture** is the collected values, customs, beliefs, artifacts, and arts of a group of people. In this section, you will examine culture and consider how it has shaped Canada.

WORDS MATTER

culture learned behaviour of people, which includes their belief systems, social relationships, organizations, and material goods (e.g., food, clothing, buildings)

core values the central beliefs that influence how a group thinks and acts

secular values ideas that are based on an individual's morals, reason, and experience, instead of religion

A Model of Culture

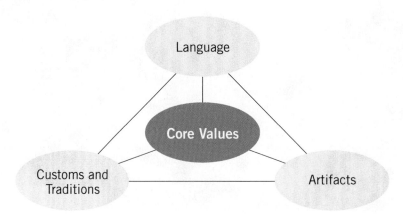

During **READING**

Making Connections
Brainstorm public celebrations or festivals that take place where you live.

Core Values

Core values are the basic ideas that explain how a group thinks and acts. Does a culture value success above happiness? Does it strive for conquest or peace? Religious beliefs remain very important in shaping core values. Major world religions include Hinduism, Islam, Buddhism, Judaism, and Christianity. There are also people with **secular values**, which are not based on religious beliefs (although their values may not always be different). Secular values can include the belief that religion and politics should be separate.

Customs and Traditions

Cultural customs and traditions come directly from core values. In December, you may participate in Hanukkah, Kwanzaa, or Christmas, depending on your cultural roots. Cultural celebrations would be incomplete without traditional foods, such as those eaten at the Passover seder or Christmas dinner. In Canada today, it is common for cultural groups to invite the whole community to share in some of their customs.

Artifacts

You may think that artifacts are old objects, such as arrowheads or Roman coins. In fact, an **artifact** is any object produced within a cultural group. This includes buildings, clothing, and tools. Artifacts often provide clues about the core values of the culture which produced them. In some cultures, women wear specific clothing that covers their hair or face. These artifacts reflect core religious values. The same is true for head coverings worn by men.

Language

Language is extremely important to culture. It is one of the ways in which values and customs are passed between generations. Young people learn their culture through language. Their parents, relatives, and Elders are their first teachers, long before they go to school. When children do not learn the important stories, lessons, and songs of their culture, they cannot pass them on to their own children later. The culture may begin to die.

These students in Iqaluit can learn using their first language, Inuktitut. Along with English and French, Inuktitut is recognized as an official language in Nunavut.

English and French are the two official languages of Canada. Many families find it hard to preserve other languages after a few generations in this country. Typically, grandparents speak the **heritage language** best. Sometimes children have little interest in learning the language because they do not need it at school or with their friends. That's why some groups have organized heritage language classes. By teaching the language, they hope to keep the culture alive.

During **READING**

Connecting Text to Self
Elders can include family or community members. In Aboriginal communities, Elders are those who pass on their wisdom and experience to others. Who would that include for you?

WEB LINK •
For information about many different cultural groups in Canada, visit our Web site.

WORDS MATTER

artifact an item that reflects the culture of a group, either modern or historical

heritage language a language that originates in another country, and which is learned and used at home; it may not be the dominant language of the community in which the speakers live

WEB LINK •••••••••••••••••
Learn more about Aboriginal cultures in Canada by taking a virtual tour on Canada's Aboriginal Portal Web site. Visit our Web site.

WORDS MATTER

reserves land that is set aside for the exclusive use of First Nations people

residential schools schools where First Nations children were expected to give up their language, spirituality, and culture

Canada's Aboriginal Cultures

The Aboriginal peoples of Canada include the First Nations, the Inuit, and the Métis peoples. In the 2006 Canadian census, these three groups numbered more than one million—about 3% of Canada's population.

The Inuit

The Inuit live in northern Canada—Nunavut, the Northwest Territories, the Yukon, and northern Québec and Labrador. The Inuit first encountered European explorers and traders about 400 years ago. In recent years, the Inuit have successfully negotiated shared control of Nunavut and a large area of northern Labrador. A national organization called Inuit Tapiriit Kanatami (ITK) works to preserve Inuit language and culture. This is difficult because the Inuit way of life has changed a great deal.

The First Nations

The First Nations are found throughout Canada. They have negotiated land treaties for traditional territories with Canadian government officials. More than half of the First Nations live on **reserves** as part of those land agreements. Further treaty discussions and land claims disputes have yet to be settled. Only about 19% of First Nations people can still speak the language of their ancestors. This is largely a result of the **residential schools** system, which began as early as 1874 in Canada, and lasted until the 1990s. First Nations children were taken from their families to be educated in English or French. They were forbidden to speak their first language.

The Métis

The Métis are people of mixed First Nations and European ancestry. Their culture draws on their diverse origins, including Scottish, French, Ojibwe, and Cree. The Métis have no treaty agreements with the government of Canada. You may have learned in Grade 7 that the Métis culture was closely tied to the fur trade, especially in the West, where many Métis people worked as traders or transporters. In the past, the Métis struggled for their land rights, and were often cheated out of lands to which they were entitled. Today, many live in urban communities where their cultural traditions may be lost.

The summer solstice—the longest day for the Northern Hemisphere—usually falls on June 21. Some Aboriginal groups in Canada have always celebrated the **solstice**. The idea of a nationally recognized day for Aboriginal peoples in Canada was first proposed in 1982 by the National Indian Brotherhood (now the Assembly of First Nations). A Royal Commission on Aboriginal Peoples also recommended a National First Peoples Day. In 1996, then-Governor General Romeo LeBlanc made it official.

> WHEREAS the Aboriginal peoples of Canada have made and continue to make valuable contributions to Canadian society and it is considered appropriate that there be, in each year, a day to mark and celebrate these contributions and to recognize the different cultures of the Aboriginal peoples of Canada....
> THEREFORE, His Excellency the Governor General in Council... hereby directs that a proclamation do issue declaring June 21 of each year as "National Aboriginal Day."

> "Everything that is going on today is in recognition of the contributions made by Aboriginal people. It's a day to come together and celebrate. A day to educate non-Aboriginal people about the different cultures and diversity."
>
> **Lisa Nidosky, Métis, Regina**

National Aboriginal Day is an invitation for all Canadians to learn about Aboriginal heritage by attending their celebrations. The day reflects Canada's commitment to **multiculturalism**—recognizing the value of all cultures.

Boys drum during National Aboriginal Day at Curve Lake First Nation near Peterborough, in 2006.

THINKING It Over

1. Apply the four parts of culture to your own background or to secular society in Canada. **k a**

2. Work with a small group to apply the model of culture on page G 174 to the Inuit, the Métis, and the First Nations. Use the Web Link (page G 176) to find out more information to share with your group. **t c**

3. What effect does learning about other cultures have on you? Do you now see great differences, or appreciate the other culture more? Explain. **t**

WORDS MATTER

solstice the name given to the longest day (summer solstice) and the shortest day (winter solstice) of the year

multiculturalism the preservation of culturally distinct groups within a society

Culture and the Environment

Ecological Footprints

An ecological footprint measures the imprint which people have on the environment. Aboriginal hunters and fishers had very limited effects on the earth. However, modern peoples can leave a much deeper ecological footprint. Some people view the earth as an endless storehouse of natural resources. This attitude contributes to today's environmental problems.

Work with a partner to make a Venn diagram comparing resource use in past and present societies.

Every culture is affected by its surroundings—the land and the climate. People make tools, gather food, and build homes according to their needs and their level of technology. When European explorers first encountered Canada's Aboriginal peoples, they found cultures well-adapted to an environment that was sometimes harsh.

Many of the ways the Inuit, First Nations, and Métis adapted to the environment have become part of Canadian society today. Originally, all of the items below were drawn from the natural resources available to Aboriginal peoples. Today, some are produced using newly developed materials, such as Kevlar or titanium. Many are still made using traditional materials and methods.

- **Transportation:** canoes, snowshoes, and kayaks
- **Clothing:** moccasins, boots, parkas, and beaded clothing
- **Foods:** pumpkins, squash, corn, and beans
- **Tools and equipment:** paddles, bows and arrows, lacrosse sticks, and woven baskets
- **Remedies:** herbal medicines to cure many common illnesses, aches, and pains

European and Aboriginal cultures were both changed by their contact with one another. The First Nations and Inuit hunters received useful manufactured products, such as pots and cloth. In return, they traded furs, which were sent to Europe. The First Nations became working partners in the fur trade for the next several hundred years. They also passed along important cultural knowledge about the environment to Europeans. For example, during the winter of 1535–1536, members of Jacques Cartier's settlement at Stadacona (Québec) had scurvy, an illness caused by a lack of vitamin C. Ten men had already died. The Mohawk First Nations saved the rest by showing them how to make a tea from white cedar bark, a traditional remedy.

Lacrosse, a game invented by First Nations peoples in North America, is now played all over the world. This photo shows a Canada vs. Finland game at the Lacrosse World Championships, held in Ontario in 2006.

What Is a Cultural Imprint?

Cultures also have an impact on the environment. The way that culture affects the earth's surface is called **cultural imprint**. This imprint can last for a long time. Today, the imprints of many cultures can be seen on the land, giving a distinctive character to Canada's different regions.

The Canadian environment presented Aboriginal peoples, explorers, and immigrant settlers with many obstacles. Canada's climate can be extreme, with hot summers and frigid winters. The maritime coastal climates can be very wet, while the interior may be very dry. Add extreme weather such as blizzards, hailstorms, and the occasional Atlantic hurricane into the mix. Landforms also presented challenges. Many pioneer farmers spent years trying to farm the Canadian Shield. Nature is still reclaiming all of their abandoned cabins and stony fields. Soon their cultural imprint will be gone forever.

Canada's environment also provided opportunities for Aboriginal peoples and newcomers to feed, clothe, and shelter themselves. Different cultures found ways to make a living by farming, fishing, forestry, and trading. They created **cultural landscapes**—areas of the land changed by human activity. Their homes, communities, and ways of life have all contributed to the unique regional character of Canada. On the next two pages, you will see photos that show how different cultures, past and present, have left their imprint on six regions of Canada.

The Welland Canal, built to allow large ships to bypass the Niagara Escarpment, is an example of a cultural landscape.

THINKING It Over

1. How can the environment be an obstacle to culture? How can it be an opportunity?

2. Use examples to explain the terms *ecological footprint* and *cultural imprint.*

3. How did the arrival of Europeans affect Aboriginal societies? Create a chart using the same headings as the list on the previous page to show the trade of cultural knowledge, materials, and tools between European and Aboriginal peoples.

Cultural Imprints from Coast to Coast

The cultural makeup of each region of Canada is different. This reflects Aboriginal settlement and the waves of immigrants that have entered the country in the past 500 years. These pictures highlight cultural differences which give each region its own unique character.

The Atlantic Provinces

Newfoundland attracted seasonal European fishers five centuries ago. Just as the First Nations had, the European fishers settled along the rocky coast. Most communities are Irish, English, or French in origin. With the collapse of the cod fishery in 1992, these places fell on hard times. Some now use their unique cultural imprint to attract tourists. This photo shows the Battery, a neighbourhood of the city of St. John's.

Québec

Québec was settled by France four centuries ago. Montréal and Québec City have often been described as a bit of Europe in North America. The combination of cafés, historic buildings, and the French language and culture can make visitors feel that they are overseas. This photo was taken in downtown Montréal.

Ontario

The Toronto area was home to the Huron and the Iroquois before the arrival of European settlers. It has become the favourite destination of immigrants to Canada since the mid-1900s. Today, 49% of the city's population was born in another country. International events send many Toronto neighborhoods into wild celebration, such as in this Greek neighbourhood after the EuroCup in soccer.

The Prairie Provinces

There are more than one million Canadians of Ukrainian origin, with the greatest numbers found in the Prairie Provinces. They were among the groups that Clifford Sifton favoured for western settlement. Ukrainian settlers built homes of sod to live in during their first years on the land. Soon, they were building traditional churches across the Prairies. This church is in Insinger, Saskatchewan.

British Columbia

British Columbia has a large Chinese population, much of it in Vancouver. The first wave of Chinese immigrants came as railway workers in the late 1800s. In the early 1900s, the Canadian government discouraged Chinese immigration with the "head tax"—a fee imposed only on Chinese immigrants. Most of Canada's Chinese immigrants have come in the past twenty-five years. Vancouver has the largest Chinatown district in Canada.

The North

Communities in the North are often based on traditional camping or meeting places where the Inuit people would hunt and fish. The town of Inuvik, in the Northwest Territories, was first built in the 1950s. The most well-known building in Inuvik is the church, built in the shape of an igloo. Now more than 40 years old, the building reflects the tradtional heritage of the Inuit population, as well as the ingenuity and creativity of the community.

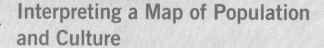
Interpreting a Map of Population and Culture

The map and circle graphs on the next page will help connect what you have learned about Canada's population patterns (in Chapter 2) and cultural origins. Use this information to see why each of the photos on the previous pages was chosen to represent a particular cultural imprint.

Step 1 Become Familiar with the Map

Identify the meanings of the symbols and colours used on the map. Note that the map has divided Canada into six large regions, divided by heavier boundary lines than the provincial or territorial boundaries.

Step 2 Identify Population Patterns by Region

Review the small maps on pages G 27 to G 28, where you learned to identify scattered, clustered, and linear population patterns. These terms can be used to describe the most common population pattern(s) in each of Canada's six regions.

Step 3 Compare Cultural Origins by Region

Look at the circle graphs positioned close to each region. They do not show the number of people in each region, just their cultural origins. Note how the cultural origins follow the same order in each circle. This makes it easier to compare the six different regions.

APPLY It

1. Review the terms *clustered*, *scattered*, and *linear* population in Chapter 2. Then describe the main population pattern(s) of each region using these terms. Suggest reasons for these regional population patterns based on your knowledge of Canada's land and people. **k m**

2. Use the circle graphs to record one unique cultural characteristic of each region. **k**

3. Use either the map or the circle graph to explain why each photo on pages G 180 and G 181 was chosen to represent the culture of the region. **t m**

4. Which of these six regions do you find most interesting? Is it the physical landscape or the cultural imprint that affects you? **t**

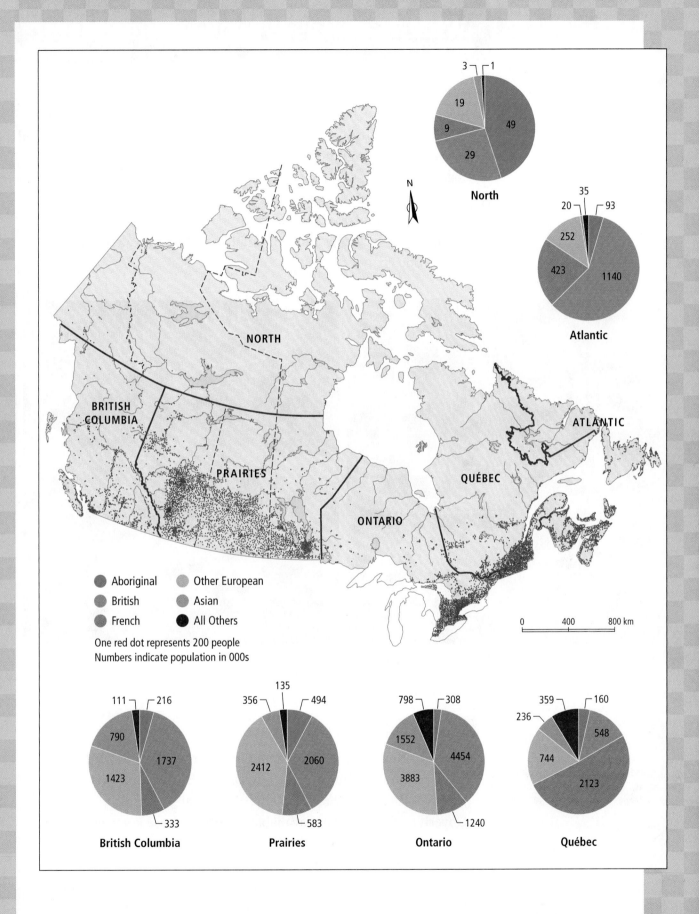

North

3 1
19
9
49
29

Atlantic

35
20 93
252
423
1140

N

Aboriginal
British
French
Other European
Asian
All Others

One red dot represents 200 people
Numbers indicate population in 000s

NORTH

BRITISH
COLUMBIA

PRAIRIES

ONTARIO

QUÉBEC

ATLANTIC

0   400   800 km

British Columbia

111 216
790
1423
1737
333

Prairies

135
356 494
2412
2060
583

Ontario

798 308
1552
3883
4454
1240

Québec

359 160
236
548
744
2123

What Happens When Cultures Meet?

When cultures meet, various things can happen. Some cultures, such as the Amish and the Hutterites, want to keep their core values and beliefs unchanged by secular values. They do so through **cultural isolation**—for example, by speaking mainly German or living together in close-knit communities. Contact with other cultures is kept to a minimum by more conservative groups. At the opposite extreme is **globalization**, a world trend that is changing cultures. International trade has spread products, values, music, and language worldwide.

Why have familiar restaurants and cafés expanded globally? When and where have you experienced eating international foods in Canada?

Cultural Assimilation

When cultures meet, one is sometimes overcome by the other. This is called cultural **assimilation**. For example, English and French are the two official languages of Canada's federal government. Government services are available in both of those languages, but not in every language spoken in the country. Although people are not expected to give up their heritage language, it is easier to get by if they learn English or French. People also join Canadian society when they become citizens. While Canada does not expect immigrants to completely assimilate, it was not always this way.

In 1867, 80% of Canada's population was either British or French in origin. For the next century, all other cultures were expected to adopt British language and customs, except in Québec, where French language and traditions dominated. There was little interest in learning about other cultures, and only limited tolerance for public displays of other traditions. Schools taught children "Canadian" ways. It was common for immigrant teenagers to learn basic English by attending classes with much younger children. English as a Second Language (ESL) classes were a thing of the future.

Aboriginal children were often separated from their families and cultural surroundings by being placed in residential schools, which operated until the 1990s in Canada. Abuse was a serious problem in the schools. Children were taken far from home and could not wear traditional clothing, speak their own language, or practise their spiritual traditions without being punished. They were expected to earn their keep through physical labour. Hunger, illness, and overwork were common. Total assimilation was the real aim of these institutions.

WORDS MATTER

enemy alien a person who is a citizen of a country that is at war with the country in which they currently live. In the case of the Japanese Canadians in World War II, this was not completely true, as the majority were Canadian citizens.

WEB LINK •••••••••••••••••••••
Read more about residential schools, and watch videos about this issue. Visit our Web site.

Heroes and Villains | Mackenzie King and His Ministers

William Lyon Mackenzie King served 22 years as prime minister of Canada between 1921 and 1948. King and his ministers led Canada through part of the Depression and all of the Second World War. His government introduced unemployment insurance and the family allowance. However, many of his government's policies were prejudiced, even racist. Unfortunately, their views reflected the views of many, but not all, Canadians at the time.

Prime Minister King: During the Second World War, Japan was an enemy of Canada. King ordered all people of Japanese ancestry be moved from the west coast into isolated camps. Although most were Canadian-born citizens, they were called **enemy aliens**. Their possessions were confiscated and never returned.

Frederick Charles Blair, Director of Immigration: During the Second World War, Jewish refugees escaping Nazi Germany asked to be admitted into Canada. Blair refused them.

Duncan Campbell Scott: Deputy Superintendent of Indian Affairs: In a speech supporting the assimilation of Aboriginal peoples, Scott declared that "Our objective is to continue until there is not a single Indian in Canada that has not been absorbed into the body politic...."

What were the consequences of these leaders' beliefs and actions? How would you respond to their ideas about other races and cultures?

Checkpoint

Remember the last section that talked about assimilation. Why would the government now have to vote on multiculturalism?

Multiculturalism

By the time the last residential schools closed, a lot of damage had been done to individuals and to the cultures of Aboriginal peoples. Since then, the outlook favouring assimilation has been mostly replaced. Instead, the government, and most Canadians, have become committed to multiculturalism. This new perspective on culture and citizenship has become an important characteristic of Canada today. When Prime Minister Pierre Trudeau brought a new policy of multiculturalism to a vote in 1971, everyone in Parliament supported it! Here is what the prime minister said:

> *It is the view of the Royal Commission, shared by the government...[that] there is no official culture, nor does any ethnic group take precedence over any other. No citizen or group of citizens is other than Canadian, and all should be treated fairly....A policy of multiculturalism...[is] the most suitable means of assuring the cultural freedom of Canadians.*

Just what did the prime minister mean? And where did he get his ideas? During the 1960s, there were many social changes occurring in Canada. Canada was busy revising its immigration policy to a points system that would open the country to migrants from all continents. Canada was also trying to cope with a more independent attitude from Québec. In 1963, Canada set up a Royal Commission on Bilingualism and Biculturalism (i.e., two languages and two cultures) to develop new government policies. The Commission travelled across

WEB LINK •

What is the Canadian government doing to support multiculturalism? Visit our Web site.

This monument in downtown Toronto was donated to the city by the Italian Canadian community as a tribute to multiculturalism. It was unveiled on Canada Day in 1984. How is multiculturalism recognized and celebrated in your community?

Canada, listening to people's views. They heard from many immigrant groups who argued that Canada was not bicultural, but *multi*cultural. They knew that their ancestors had also contributed to the building of the nation.

What Is Multiculturalism Policy?

There are many multicultural countries around the world. For example, Brazil has a very wide mix of peoples and cultures. Britain, France, and Australia are all becoming more multicultural. The United States has an even greater cultural mix than Canada, including many people of African and Latin American heritage. These are all multicultural countries, but Canada is the only one with an official policy of **multiculturalism**. Look at the diagram below to compare the policies of Canada and the United States.

Campaigns against racism are an important part of Canada's multiculturalism policy.

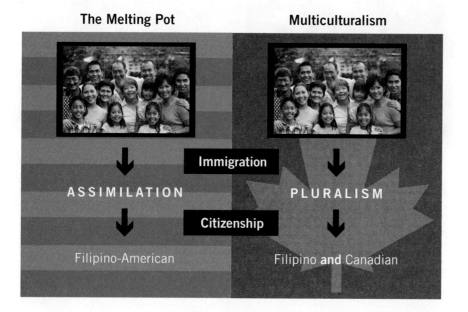

Having a multiculturalism policy means that Canada officially recognizes and supports all cultures living in Canada. The government gives financial support for parades, festivals, and other events. The government also supports cultural exchanges between different groups, and actively fights racism.

In Canada, immigrants become citizens without having to leave their own culture behind. In other words, a person can be Polish or Arab *and* Canadian. This is different from the **melting pot** of the United States, where newcomers are assimilated. In the U.S., there is no federal multicultural policy to support cultures. Instead, it is seen as a personal matter. People can call themselves Polish-American or Arab-American if they feel it is important. In fact, many do.

WORDS MATTER

multiculturalism policy
government policy which supports the preservation of distinct cultural groups

melting pot a system which supports the blending together of many cultures

During READING

Checkpoint
Return to what you said about the melting pot in the Before Reading section of this chapter. Were you right?

What Do You Think?

You live in a multicultural society. What do you think about Canada's multiculturalism policy? How important is your own cultural background to you? Compare your thoughts with those of your classmates.

I've been to other parts of the world, and none of them have nearly the level of diversity we have. But some people don't believe we have any problems. Like they've been blinded by the accolades [praise] we've received from the world.

Robert Haggon, Toronto high school student, 2001

The future is bright for Canada. In fifty years, because of our multicultural mix, we will all be called Canadians. This will be our unique Canadian experiment for the future, a far cry from the past.

Fred Concisom, a retired teacher who immigrated from Malaysia in 1970

What it is to be a Canadian, I think, ultimately becomes what it is to be a citizen of this earth. And how we do as a country is going to be judged globally.

Baltej Dhillon, a Sikh who immigrated to Canada in 1983. When he joined the RCMP, he won the right to wear his turban on the job.

THINKING It Over

1. How did Canada's multiculturalism policy come about? What does the government do to support it? What do you do?

2. What are the cultural imprints in your community? Choose a community in another region that is about the same size as yours. Do some research to find out how the cultural imprints of each community compare.

3. With a small group, discuss the quotations about Canada today on this page, along with the quotation from Bill Clinton on page G 172. What does each one mean? Which one do you agree with most? Write your own group statement about multiculturalism.

PUTTING IT ALL TOGETHER

This chapter completes your investigation of the unit key question: **How do migration patterns affect people and communities in Canada and the world?** In this chapter, you examined culture closely, using a model to show how values, customs, artifacts, and language are connected. You applied these ideas to Canada's Aboriginal peoples, then used maps, graphs, and photos to compare cultural imprints in different regions of Canada. The chapter ended with a comparison of assimilation and multiculturalism in Canada.

After READING

Show Meaning Using Words and Visuals

Draw a picture or create a collage of Canadian identity. Use your own photos or those from magazines to create your collage. Then write a poem using at least 10 words from your personal dictionary that explains what your work says about Canadian identity.

THINKING It Through

Work with a partner for this assignment, ideally someone with a different cultural background from your own. Each person will have the opportunity to ask questions and exchange information.

1. Use different print and electronic sources to gather information about the cultural heritage of your partner. Use the model on page G 174 as a guide. Draw a model of the culture to show your information. Carefully record your sources. **k c a**

2. Interview your partner to find out how their culture may have been changed by experiences in Canada. What parts of their culture remain unchanged in Canada? How long have they, their family, or their ancestors been living in Canada? **k c**

3. Prepare an organized report based on your findings from this interview. **k c**

Back to the Big Idea

Throughout this unit, you have:

• Examined the forces that affect migration, both within Canada and around the world

• Identified the Three "P"s (push, pull, and policy)

• Looked at how technology affects migration and mobility

• Compared and studied multiple cultures in Canada

Look back over the unit to assess what you have learned. Use a graphic organizer to answer the question: **How do migration patterns affect people and communities in Canada and the world?** Consider mobility, migration, and immigration.

Show That You Know

Canada is a very promising destination for people wanting to start a new life. Imagine that you have been hired to produce promotional material to attract immigrants to Canada. You can work alone on a limited assignment or as part of a team on a big production. Your work will be judged on both your research and your creativity.

Step 1 Choose your medium

The choices for the assignment include a large poster, a folding brochure, a computer slide show, a video, or a dramatic presentation. Choose the medium with which you are most comfortable.

Tip:
- See pages S 4–S 5 of the Skills Tool Kit to review primary and secondary information sources

Step 2 Research the topic

Use a variety of sources to research the pull factors and immigration regulations involved in drawing immigrants to Canada.

Tip: Review map skills using the Skills Tool Kit, pages S 14–S 15.

Step 3 Construct a map

Make a map of either Canada or Ontario to include in your promotional materials. Include the following information:

- population distribution
- major urban centres
- 2007 best places to live

Tip:
- Poster: Use bold images and a simple message, both of which can be seen clearly from a distance.
- Brochure: Plan a different topic or theme for each panel, using bold titles and clear visuals.
- Computer presentation: Use projection software and test the computer equipment before your presentation.
- Video: Edit your material so that the best information is shown in just 5 to 10 minutes.
- Dramatic presentation: Keep your scene(s) simple and be sure that everyone speaks clearly, projecting their voices toward the audience.

Step 4 Use unit vocabulary

Terms about migration and mobility from Unit 3 will improve the quality of your promotional materials and your score on the activity.

Step 5 Appeal to your audience

Communication skills are very important in this assignment. Plan your presentation to appeal to your classroom audience, and practise it ahead of time.

GLOSSARY

Words that appear in blue are your unit key terms.

absolute location the position of a place that can be expressed by a grid reference

accessible in terms of migration, when a person is able to gain entry to a desired destination

AIDS epidemic the occurrence of AIDS and HIV. In parts of Africa, more than 20 million people live with HIV, the virus that causes AIDS. AIDS has also been called a pandemic, because it affects populations worldwide.

alphanumeric grid an interlocking system of letters and numbers used to determine location

appropriate technology technology that is suited to the environmental, cultural, or economic situation it is intended for

artifact an item that reflects the culture of a group, either modern or historical

assembly-line technique a construction method in which the item is moved along a production line to stations where workers add one part or a group of parts

assimilation when one culture is absorbed by another

balance of trade the relationship between the value of a country's exports and imports; also called trade balance

barrier something that may discourage or prevent a person from migrating

bilateral aid given by the government of one country directly to another

biogas fuel produced from organic matter

birth rate the number of births per 1000 people per year

capital money available to be invested to increase production or wealth

capital goods goods such as factories or transportation systems, that are used in the production of other goods

cartel a group of suppliers who agree with each other to maintain high prices and control production

census metropolitan area an urban area with a population of at least 100 000

chain migration when people immigrate to a new country after relatives have already established citizenship there

clustered population a population distribution in which many people live in a small area of closely spaced houses or communities

command economy an economic system in which the government controls all production and distribution of goods and services

communism a system that supports common ownership of the means of production

compass rose a figure showing the major directions pointed out by a magnetic compass

consumer a person or organization that purchases and uses products or services

consumer advocate a group or person who protects consumers from fraud, inferior products, false advertising, etc.

core values the central beliefs that influence how a group thinks and acts

correlation the connection, or relationship, between two things. Finding this correlation can help geographers study cause and effect.

cultural imprint ways in which culture has shaped the land

cultural isolation the preservation of a distinct culture by avoiding contact with other cultures

cultural landscape landscapes which have been changed by human societies

culture learned behaviour of people, which includes their belief systems, social relationships, organizations, and material goods (e.g., food, clothing, buildings)

death rate the number of deaths per 1000 people per year

democracy a form of government in which elected people fill government offices

developed nation a country where there is a higher level of income, industrialization, and modernization

developing nation a country where most people have a lower standard of living and less access to goods and services than people in developed nations

discretionary income part of the family budget that can be used on savings or non-essentials such as entertainment or vacations

diversified economy an economy that is based on more than one resource

distribution the marketing, transporting, merchandising, and selling of any item

dormitory town a community that is mostly residential, from which people commute to jobs or shopping in another community

dot distribution map a map that uses dots to show population

duties/tariffs taxes on imported goods

economic depression a time of unemployment, low prices, low profits, and loss of business

economic resources factors (land, labour, capital, and entrepreneurship) needed for the economic success of a region

economy the system of production, consumption, and trade of goods and services

emigration the departure of people from an area or country to live elsewhere

enemy alien a person who is a citizen of a country that is at war with the country in which they currently live. In the case of the Japanese Canadians in World War II, this was not completely true, as the majority were Canadian citizens.

entrepreneur a person who starts or organizes a business

entrepreneurial having the ability to recognize business opportunities, take on the risk of starting a new business, and combine the factors necessary to make the business successful

entry visa a document that grants a person the legal right to immigrate to a country

exports goods or services that are sold to another country

fair trade trade that gives fair prices to small, independent producers of a wide variety of goods

family reunification an immigration policy that acknowledges the right of a family to be together

feedback the last stage of manufacturing, in which the product and process are judged

foreign aid economic help provided to countries as a response to disaster or to achieve a larger goal

foreign investment money invested by people or organizations in a country other than their own

free trade trade without duties or tariffs

GDP per capita gross domestic product per person

genocide the deliberate and systematic extermination of a national, racial, political, or cultural group

geography the study of the earth and people's relationship to it

globalization the idea that the entire world is becoming one community with interconnected needs and services

goods physical objects or merchandise

gross domestic product (GDP) the value of all goods and services produced in a country in one year

gross national product (GNP) the value of goods and services produced by a country in one year, including those produced outside the country

guest worker a person who works temporarily in a foreign country

heritage language a language that originates in another country, and which is learned and used at home; it may not be the dominant language of the community in which the speakers live

high technology equipment and methods based upon computers, robotics, and space research

Human Development Index a comparison of countries that measures health, education, and wealth of each nation's citizens; life expectancy, literacy, and standard of living are measured

immigration the arrival of people into an area or country to live

industry work that provides income for people

imports goods or services that are brought into the country

infant mortality rate the rate of death for infants less than one year old

input the first stage of the manufacturing system, in which decisions are made

interprovincial migration moving from one province to another

land natural resources which are the raw materials of industry and business

land use the purpose for which people use a particular area

landmark a prominent object or landform, such as a hill or building, that identifies a place

latitude and longitude locations measured in degrees north and south from the equator (latitude) and east and west of the prime meridian (longitude)

life expectancy the average number of years a person is expected to live

linear population a population distribution which is arranged in a narrow line, perhaps along a road, river, or valley

literacy rate the percentage of people with the ability to read and write

living standard the amount of goods and services people can purchase

malnutrition an often fatal condition caused by an inadequate diet

marginal lands areas too hilly, rocky, or dry for large-scale commercial use

market the area of trade or business

market economy a system in which businesses and consumers decide what they will produce or purchase

marketing board an organization created by producers to promote their product and to maintain fair prices by controlling supply

melting pot a system which supports the blending together of many cultures

microchip a tiny integrated circuit on which computer technology relies

migration the movement of people from one place to another, for the purpose of settlement

military dictatorship a form of government in which the military holds political power

mixed economy an economy that combines different economic systems, such as the market and command systems

mobility travelling from one place to another

modes of transportation different ways to transport people or goods

multiculturalism the preservation of culturally distinct groups within a society

multiculturalism policy government policy which supports the preservation of distinct cultural groups

multilateral aid given by the government of a country to an international organization, such as the World Bank

multiplier effect the effects of spending in a local economy

natural increase the birth rate minus the death rate

net migration the effect of migration on the population of a region or country

NGO (Non-Governmental Organization) an aid agency that is independent of any government

offshore companies foreign firms that supply goods and services for export to companies in other countries, such as Canada

output the third stage of manufacturing, in which products are distributed to customers

outsourcing sending work to an outside provider, usually to cut costs

points system an assessment system used to evaluate potential immigrants

policy government laws and regulations that may create a barrier to immigration

population density number of people occupying a certain area, calculated using the following formula: Population / Area in km^2 = People per km^2

population distribution the pattern of where people live

population pyramid a graph showing the distribution of population by age and gender

primary industry the collecting of raw materials for use in industry

process the second stage of manufacturing, in which the product is made

production the creation of products and services for consumption

production team method an assembly technique in which the item remains in one place for a small team of highly skilled workers to add parts

proportional flow map a type of thematic map which shows the movement of goods, people, or information

protectionism the policy of adding taxes to imported goods to protect a country's home industries

pull factor a social, economic, or environmental attraction that draws people to move to a particular place

push factor a social, political, economic, or environmental force that drives people away from where they live

refugees people who flee to a foreign country for safety from political upheaval or war

relative location the position of a place described in relation to another place

reserves land set aside for the exclusive use of First Nations people

residential schools schools where First Nations children were expected to give up their language, spirituality, and culture

revenue the amount of money a company or government receives as income

robotics mechanical arms which can repeat simple operations over and over with precision

rural areas sparsely settled areas

rural-urban shift the pattern of movement of people from rural areas to urban areas

scale on maps, the measurement that represents an actual distance on the earth's surface

scatter graph a graph that shows the relationship between two related sets of data

scattered population a population distribution in which there are few people in a large area. Vast areas with scattered resources can produce a scattered population pattern.

seasonal migration moving from one place to another according to the seasons; e.g., temporarily moving south to enjoy warmer weather in the winter

secondary industry manufacturing and construction activities

secular values ideas that are based on an individual's morals, reason, and experience, instead of religion

services the performance of any duties or work for another person; a helpful or professional activity

shelter cost the cost of owning or renting a home

site the specific physical features defining the location of a place

situation the location of a place in relation to other places or larger features

solstice the name given to the longest day (summer solstice) and the shortest day (winter solstice) of the year

subsistence farmers people who work their own small farms to feed their families

suburban settlement newer communities found at the edges of established cities

supply and demand the relationship between the production and consumption of goods and services

sustainable the use of resources at a rate which meets the needs of the present generation but also ensures plenty for future generations

sustainable yield the amount that can be taken from a natural resource (e.g. cod stocks) without reducing the resource's ability to maintain itself

technological revolution sweeping changes brought about by new technology

technology the application of mechanical arts and sciences to producing goods and services

tertiary industry the providing of services, such as customer support, distribution, or retailing

thematic map a map which shows one subject or theme, such as population or climate

tied aid economic aid that has conditions on where and how it must be used

topographic map a very detailed map showing physical and human features through the use of contour lines and other symbols

trade advisory group an organization that supervises trade

trade bloc a large free trade area made up of two or more countries

trade deficit a negative trade balance (more imports than exports)

trade sanctions trade penalties imposed on one country by another

trade surplus a positive trade balance (more exports than imports)

traditional economy an economic system in which decisions are based on customs, beliefs, or religion, within a strong social community

traffic artery a major street along which there is a large volume of traffic

urban planners people who are trained to design communities and public spaces

urban settlement a community where 1000 or more people live close together

urbanization the increase of urban areas, usually the spread of cities and large communities into rural areas

World Bank an international banking organization with a mandate to reduce world poverty

INDEX

Credits

The publisher would like to thank the following people and institutions for permission to use their © materials. Every reasonable effort has been made to find copyright holders of the material in this text. The publisher would be pleased to know of any errors or omissions.

Photo Credits

bg/i: background/inset
t/c/b/l/r: top/centre/bottom/left/right

Front Cover: Jeff Spielman/Iconica/Getty; **G2 t** 22DigiTal/Alamy; **b** Giles Robberts/Alamy; **G3 l** Freeman Patterson/Masterfile; **r** Anders Ryman/CORBIS; **G4 G5 bg** Blaine Harrington III/Alamy; **G5 i** David Norton Photography/Alamy; **G6 l** imagebroker/Alamy; **r** First Light/Getty Images; **G7 t** Images of Africa Photobank/Alamy; **b** AFP/Getty Images; **G9** AA World Travel Library/Alamy; **G10** Simon Wilson/ Klixpix/First Light; **G17** David Young-Wolff/Photo Edit; **G18 t** Zoran Milich/Masterfile; **c** Michael Klinec/Alamy; **b** Arco Images/Alamy; **G19 t** Megapress/Alamy; **c** Paul A. Souders/Corbis; **b** Bill Brooks/Alamy; **G24 G25 bg** Christian Liewig/TempSport/Corbis; **G30 t** Thierry Prat/Sygma/Corbis; **c** Reinhard Dirscherl/Alamy; **b** blickwinkel/Irlmeier/Alamy; **G35** Courtesy of Mike and Sherri Boyd; **G38 tl** Masterfile Royalty-Free; **tr** Donald Nausbaum/Getty Images; **b** Per-Anders Pettersson/Getty Images; **G44 G45 bg** Michael Nicholson/Corbis; **G45 i** Courtesy of playpumps.org; **G46 l** Canada Post Corporation, November 22, 2007. Reproduced with Permission; **r** tompiodesign.com/Alamy; **G48 tl** Corbis Royalty-Free; **tr** Alan Marsh/First Light; **b** Mark Downey/Lucid Images/Corbis; **G49** JUPITER-IMAGES/Comstock Images/Alamy; **G57** John Hay/Lonely Planet Images; **G58** Tim Larsen/AP/CP PHOTO; **G59** Reuters/CORBIS; **G60** Liu Quanlong/Xinhua Press/Corbis; **G61 r** R. Ian Lloyd/Masterfile; **b** Peter Arnold Photography; **G62** Courtesy of Make Poverty History; **G66** Dave G. Houser/Corbis; **G67** Eric Aldwinkle/Rare Books and Special Collections, McGill University; **G68 G69 bg** Rudy Sulgan/Corbis; **G69 i** Roman Soumar/Corbis; **G70 t** B&C Alexander/First Light; **b** Robert Llewellyn/Corbis;

G71 t Vittoriano Rastelli/Corbis; **c** JUPITERIMAGES/ Thinkstock/Alamy; **b** Photo courtesy of Tim Hortons; **G72** Courtesy of BHP Billiton Limited; **G73** Hans Blohm/Masterfile; **G74** CP PHOTO/*Sarnia Observer*, Glenn Ogilvie; **G76 l** Courtesy of Shirley DesRivieres; **r** Dave Sandford/Getty Images Sport; **G77 t** Bettmann/Corbis; **b** CP PHOTO/Boris Spremo; **G78** Glenbow Archives NA-4868-180; **G79** Courtesy of Canadian Heritage Gallery #10045; **G81** Dennis Cox/Alamy; **G85** Pavel Wolberg/epa/ Corbis; **G86** Bettmann/Corbis; **G87** Jose Fuste Raga/Corbis; **G89 l** Keith Dannemiller/Corbis; **r** Lindsay Hebberd/CORBIS; **G90 G91 bg** John Hasyn/First Light; **G91 i** CP PHOTO/Sean Vokey; **G92 l** Atlantide S.N.C./MaXx Images; **r** Miles Ertman/Masterfile; **G95** 2007 DAIRY FARMERS OF CANADA, Design by Allard Johnson Communications Inc., Photography by Philip Rostron, Instil Productions; **G97** Clovermead Bees & Honey, Aylmer, ON, Canada www.clovermead.com; **G99 t** Photo By F. Sierakowski/Rex Features Rolls of cloth HABERDASHERY MATERIAL; **bl** Jose Luis Pelaez, Inc./CORBIS; **br** CP PHOTO/Aaron Harris; **G100** Elvele Images/Alamy; **G104** Courtesy of DaimlerChrysler Canada Inc.; **G105** George Haling/Stone/Getty Images; **G107 t** Courtesy of Fifth Dimension Technologies; **c** Brian Sytnyk/ Masterfile; **b** Peter Essick/Aurora/Getty Images; **G110 G111 bg** Bayne Stanley/First Light; **G111 i** Bill Aron/Photo Edit; **G113 t** JUPITERIMAGES/Workbook/First Light; **c** Andrew McKim/Masterfile; **b** Radius Images/Alamy; **G115** CP PHOTO/AP Photo/Brian Kersey; **G116** Sandro Vannini/CORBIS; **G118** INTERFOTO Pressebildagentur/Alamy; **G119** Kevin Phillips/ Digital Vision/Getty Images; **G124** CP PHOTO/ Action Press; **G128 l** Dave G. Houser/Corbis; **c** Pavel Wolberg/epa/Corbis; **b** Roman Soumar/

Corbis; **G130 t** John Sylvester/Alamy; **it** Ralph Biggör/Shutterstock; **b** Bill Brooks/Alamy; **ib** Ralph Biggör/Shutterstock; **G131** John Arnold Images/ Alamy; **i** Ralph Biggör/Shutterstock; **G132 bg** Alan Marsh/First Light; **i** Carlos Davila/Alamy; **G135 l** Kleinhenz/Alamy; **r** Michael Matthews/Alamy; **G137** CP PHOTO/Jonathan Hayward; **G139** Gemstone Images/Getty Images; **G140** Richard Hamilton Smith/Corbis; **G142** CP PHOTO/Jonathan Hayward; **G148 t** CP PHOTO/Ted S. Warren/AP; **b** Peter Christopher/Masterfile; **G149** CP PHOTO/ AP/Nicholas Ratzenboeck; **G152 G153 bg** Jeff Greenberg/Alamy; **153 i** Mark Pearson/Alamy; **G154 l** liquidlibrary Images/Jupiter Unlimited Images; **c** Stockdisc Classic/Alamy; **r** Jim West/ Alamy; **G155** CP PHOTO/Jason Kryk; **G156 t** Smiley N. Pool/*Dallas Morning News*/Corbis; **c** Peter Turnley/Corbis; **b** Karen Kasmauski/Corbis; **G158** Courtesy of Greg Perry and the Sarnia *Observer*; **G159** CP PHOTO/AP/Alfred Montesquiou; **G160** CP PHOTO/AP Photo/Riaz Khan; **G164** Glenbow Archives NA-789-104(a); **G165** Courtesy of Olga Seibot; **G172 G173 bg** Peter Mintz/First Light; **G173 i** CP PHOTO/Fred Chartrand; **G175** Bryan & Cherry Alexander Photography/ Alamy; **G177** CP PHOTO/Clifford Skarstedt; **G178** CP PHOTO/Geoff Robins; **G179** Garry Black/ Masterfile; **G180 t** Hemis/Alamy; **c** Danita Delimont/ Alamy; **b** CP PHOTO/Aaron Harris; **G181 t** Terrance Klassen/Alamy; **c** Albert Normandin/Masterfile; **b** Robert Harding Picture Library Ltd./Alamy; **G184 l** Photo Japan/Alamy; **r** Black Star/Alamy; **G186** Rudy Sulgan/Corbis; **G187 l, c** Blend Images/Alamy; **r** Courtesy of Canadian Heritage; **G188** Roy Morsch/zefa/Corbis; **G190** M. Kathleen Kelly/Star Ledger/Corbis.

Literary Credits

t/c/b/l/r: top/centre/bottom/left/right

G20: Reprinted with permission—Torstar Syndication Services. From an article originally appearing in the *Toronto Star* October, 2007.

G47: From United Nations Universal Declaration of Human Rights. Adopted and proclaimed by General Assembly resolution 217 A (III) of 10 December 1948. Used with permission.

G49: From United Nations Universal Declaration of Human Rights. Adopted and proclaimed by General Assembly resolution 217 A (III) of 10 December 1948. Used with permission.

G79: From "Pond Inlet: An Inuit Community Caught Between Two Worlds," *Canadian Geographic*, Feb/March 1991, p. 51. Used with permission.

G136: Adapted from Phil Froats and Duncan Hood, "Canada's Best Places to Live," *MoneySense* (magazine),Volume 9, Number 2, May 2007, page 30. Used with permission.

G140: From "Make Pictou County Livable, says expert" Jennifer Vardy, *The Evening News* (New Glasgow, Nova Scotia). November 21, 2005. Used with permission.

G159: From "A Climate Culprit In Darfur", Ban Ki Moon, Saturday, June 16, 2007, *Washington Post*. Used with permission of the United Nations.

G162: From United Nations Universal Declaration of Human Rights. Adopted and proclaimed by General Assembly resolution 217 A (III) of 10 December 1948. Used with permission.

G170: From "Immigration Targets Go Beyond Numbers" Editorial, *Toronto Star*, March 18, 2007

G177: Governor General's Proclamation, Indian and Northern Affairs Canada, 1996.

G177: From "A Day to Remember the First People" by Mervin Brass, Sage Writer; *Saskatchewan Sage*, July 5, 1999. Used with permission.

G186: *Hansard*, October 8, 1971.

G188: (left) From "So where are you from?" David Trattles, *Canadian Geographic*, January/February 2001, Vol. 121, No. 1, page 37.

SKILLS TOOL KIT

CONTENTS

→ The Inquiry/Research Process

Start   Review what you already know

In Grade 7, you learned the six steps of the Inquiry/Research Process. Review these steps, listed below. In your own words, summarize the requirements of each step.

Step 1   Identify an issue

Narrow down one of the examples below to identify an issue.

A: History general subjects	B: Geography general subjects
Confederation	World population patterns
The Red River and Northwest Rebellions	Different types of industry
Canada's role in defending the British Empire	Cultural imprints in Canadian regions

Step 2   Ask questions

Select one of the examples from the chart above, and create six questions using the 5W + H model. Your questions will begin with each of the following words: who? what? when? where? why? how? These questions will guide your research on your subject.

Step 3   Gather information

You will look at a variety of materials to find the information you need to complete the Inquiry/Research Process. Possible sources include encyclopedias, atlases (maps, graphs, and statistics), books, journals and diaries, newspapers and magazines, Web sites, and personal interviews.

Continue with the subject you selected in Step 2. Visit a library, and do research on the internet. Find an example of four different types of information resources that would help you to solve the identified issues for your topic.

Step 4 Record information

Now, record information you have found about your topic. This will help you answer the six questions you posed in Step 2. Use a set of file cards, or create a computer file that contains the following items:

- the title of each source

- the library call number or the internet address of the Web site

- the date the source was published or the date that you located the Web site

- three pieces of key information from each source, together with their page numbers.

Step 5 Analyze information

Study the six questions you posed in Step 2, and the information you recorded in Step 4. How well have you answered your questions? If you have not found information to fully answer one or more questions,

- you can adjust one or more questions to get a better fit between the question(s) and the information, or

- you can do more research until you have information that will allow you to fully answer the question.

If you still have a mismatch, check with your teacher before proceeding.

Step 6 Communicate findings

There are many ways to communicate research findings. For this skill feature, create an organizer that allows you to communicate your findings about your topic.

APPLY It

Investigate the following topics.

History	Geography
General Subject: Canadian expansion and national confidence, 1867–1914	**General Subject:** Rural-to-urban migration in Canada
Identified Issue: Why did Canada expand and grow in national confidence between 1867 and 1914?	**Identified Issue:** What has been the effect of rural-to-urban migration in Canada since 1950?

Recognizing and Using Primary and Secondary Sources

Start **Review what you already know**

In Grade 7, you learned about the differences between primary and secondary sources. Review this information now. What are the key differences between primary and secondary sources?

Step 1 **Check the origin of your source**

- If it is a book, examine the front pages, which usually contain publication information. Who is (are) the author(s)? When was it published?

- If it is any other type of paper source (for example, a newspaper or magazine), find publication information about it.

- If it is an artifact, find who made it and when.

- If it is an electronic source (like a CD-ROM or a Web site), try to find who compiled the information and when. (Is it original material from another source, or was it specially created for the electronic source?)

Step 2 **Look for clues within the source**

- Secondary sources usually use quotation marks or special formatting when they borrow primary material from another source. (See pages H 11 or G 49 for examples in this book.)

- Secondary sources can include credit lines telling the reader where the primary information was taken from.

- Secondary sources are normally written in the third person and can use formal language.

- Primary sources often come from an earlier time. They may have an old "feel" to them, or use old-fashioned language or technical terms.

- Some primary sources, like letters or journals, have a personal feel to them, using words like "I" or "we."

Step 3 Examine primary sources for bias

All authors have their own bias about their subject. (What they choose to write about, or not write about, is just one example of bias.) For example, Sir John A. Macdonald made speeches about the benefits of Confederation to spread his views of the proposal. Similarly, critics of the World Bank have created Web sites and material to protest its policies. When using primary sources, ask yourself these questions:

- Who wrote or created this material?

- Why did the person write or create this material?

- How does this affect the importance of the material for me?

- What is the point of view of the person?

- What was the purpose of the material when it was created? How does that affect its meaning for me?

- What information can this material give me?

APPLY It

History

Choose one of the following topics:

- British North America in 1860
- the culture and lifestyle of the Métis
- women and the vote
- Henri Bourassa

Use the library and the Internet to find at least one primary source and one secondary source for your topic. Examine your primary source. Is it reliable or unreliable? Why?

Geography

Choose one of the following topics:

- different types of residential land use
- problems with the market economy
- China's current economic growth
- Canada's multiculturalism policy

Use the library and the Internet to find at least one primary source and one secondary source for your topic. Decide whether you consider your primary source reliable or unreliable, and explain why.

Researching a Topic

Start Review what you already know

Make sure you have completed the skill **Recognizing and Using Primary and Secondary Sources** (pages S 4–S 5). In your research, you should work with secondary sources before going to primary ones.

Step 1 Examine general secondary sources

Reference texts some-times have multimedia material with extra information.

It is best to start your research with general sources. They examine a broad range of topics, but in limited detail. They will give you an overview of your topic, without assuming that you know a lot about it. Some examples of general secondary sources are:

- encyclopedias and almanacs

- textbooks

- atlases

You can find these sources in the reference section of a library or on-line. Make notes on file cards or in a computer file as you proceed.

Step 2 Examine specific secondary sources

Once you have a general understanding of your topic, you need to explore it in greater detail. To accomplish this, you need to examine specific sources. These are sources that study a smaller topic in greater detail. Specific secondary sources examine:

- a small topic, or a small part of a larger topic

- a specific event

- an individual person or a small group of people (studies of individuals are called biographies)

Continue making research notes.

Examine primary sources

Once you understand the overview (Step 1) and the important facts (Step 2) of your topic, you can move on to primary sources. Sometimes, primary sources are difficult to understand because they often use old-fashioned or technical language. They also deal with a very small part of the topic. Complete your research notes at this stage.

There was one of two things I had a right to—liberty or death. If I could not have one, I would have the other for no man should take me alive.

An extract from a primary source

APPLY It

History

Imagine that you are researching the sinking of the *Titanic* in 1912.

a) Identify which of the following are general secondary sources, specific secondary sources, and primary resources.

b) Place them in the correct order of study, applying the principles outlined above.

- A history of marine disasters and shipwrecks with a chapter on the *Titanic*
- The official register containing the names of all the passengers who sailed on the *Titanic*'s fateful voyage
- A biography about the captain of the *Titanic*
- An encyclopedia of Canada with a short article about the Canadian passengers on the *Titanic*
- The official report of the commission investigating the *Titanic*'s sinking
- A history of Canada with a paragraph about the sinking of the *Titanic*

Geography

Imagine that you are researching the future of the world population.

a) Which type of resource is the graph below? How will it be useful to your research?

b) Examine Chapter 2 of the Geography textbook to identify two more examples of primary or secondary research sources on this topic.

c) Use the steps above to create a list of five research sources, including this graph and two others found in Chapter 2.

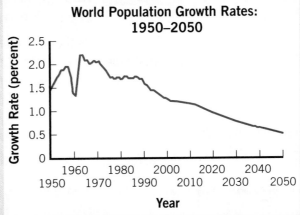

World Population Growth Rates: 1950–2050

Start Review what you already know

In Grade 7, you learned about the 5W + H model, and the difference between factual and opinion questions. Review these items now to make sure you fully understand them.

Step 1 Understand different types of research questions

You should use a variety of types of questions when you do research. You already know about factual and opinion questions, but there are other types of research questions to consider.

Question Type	History examples	Geography examples
Causal (look for causes of events)	What were the causes of the mass immigration of the 1900s?	Why is Alberta's population growing faster than that of other provinces?
Comparative (make comparisons)	How does Canada's world reputation today compare with its reputation in the 1890s?	What differences are there between Canada's immigration policy now and a century ago?
Speculative (infer the answer)	How might the development of the Prairies have been different if the CPR had not been built?	Which types of industry would be best suited to economic conditions in your local region?

Step 2 Recognize that key words and question types are different

The key words that begin research questions (5W + H) do not tell you what type of question it is. Refer back to the organizer above. Note how types of questions can start with different key words.

APPLY It

History/ Geography

1. Choose a general topic that you have recently studied in this book. Create two questions of each type shown in the organizer above.

2. Use your questions as a guide to do research about the person or topic.

3. Use a graphic organizer to show your questions and answers. Present your completed work to your classmates.

Recognizing Fact, Opinion, and Inference

Start **Identify different types of information**

As you study history and geography, you encounter many facts, opinions, and inferences.

Step 1 **Understand the meanings of the terms**

In order to understand what you hear and read, you need to be familiar with the meanings of *fact*, *opinion*, and *inference* in order to fully understand the information.

- **fact:** something that can be proven by hard evidence, and about which there is general agreement

- **opinion:** What someone thinks about a topic or question. The author might be trying to convince the reader to agree with a particular position.

- **inference:** a position that the reader comes to by making a deduction about the information—something that is not stated specifically

Step 2 **Recognize fact, opinion, and inference**

In the organizer below, identify fact, opinion, and inference.

History (See Zoom In: Henri Bourassa, page H 186)	Geography (See Exploring Points of View: Are Canadians Helping Enough?, page G 62)
Henri Bourassa was more of a fighting politician than Wilfrid Laurier.	Canada is falling short on its foreign aid commitments.
Bourassa was born in 1868.	Higher levels of foreign aid could improve the lives of people in developing nations.
Bourassa's firm position on conscription made it impossible for Laurier to find a compromise.	The United Nations recommended that developed nations contribute 0.7% of Gross Domestic Product to foreign aid.

APPLY It

History

Examine one of the following topics in this textbook. Identify one fact, one opinion, and one inference in the topic.

- Prince Edward Island's "absentee landlord" problem (Chapter 1)
- The North West Mounted Police (Chapter 6)
- The Reciprocity issue (Chapter 8)

Geography

Examine one of the following topics in this textbook. Identify one fact, one opinion, and one inference in the topic.

- Rural, urban, and suburban settlement (Chapter 1)
- Command economic systems (Chapter 4)
- Mobility and changing technology (Chapter 7)

SKILL

Detecting Bias in Sources

Start | **Judge Information**

Use this checklist to judge information that you see, hear, or read.

✓ Recognize fact versus opinion

Facts can be accepted as true. Opinions shape a set of facts to present a certain point of view. For example, it is a fact that there are about 6.6 billion people on earth. Some people believe that this is too many, and others don't. These are opinions.

✓ Watch for words that show bias

Bias means "a preference." These are preferences that can be unbalanced or unfair. Biased writing is also shown by what is *not* there— it may not give all the evidence or treat all sides with equal attention. Language that reflects a preference for certain races, cultures, genders, or some human groups over others is a type of bias called prejudice. Language that is very assertive or extreme can also show bias.

✓ Identify the author's purpose

Try to find out why the material was prepared. It may be intended to persuade others to agree with the author's opinion. Ask why the author might choose to ignore evidence or groups of people. Consider whether or not the author is a member of an interest group which holds a particular point of view about an issue.

APPLY It

Identify examples of fact and opinion in the following. How does the text show bias?

History

When European explorers discovered North America, they found a savage, empty wilderness. To bring the light of civilization to this world was a constant struggle. Imagine going from bustling cities and busy trade to empty forests and rocky coasts. However, there were riches—gold, furs, and timber. This was the great benefit of exploring the New World.

Geography

To the editor,

I am shocked and appalled to read stories about demands for reducing the populations of wild animals. The burden of the human population on the earth is the most pressing environmental problem we face today. No one would ever suggest that we get rid of people! Yet for some reason, some people think it is okay to do such a thing to animals.

SKILL

→ Debating an Issue

Start — Recognize the value of debate

History and Geography are filled with conflicting opinions. A debate is a good way to weigh different ideas, and help you make up your own mind.

Tip: There are features in this textbook which can give you good debate topics. They are **Exploring Points of View** and **Heroes and Villains**.

Step 1 — Identify an issue

An issue is a question about which there are different points of view. The issue should be presented so it can be answered by "Yes," "No," or "Unsure." For example:

- Why did it take so long for the RCMP to hire female officers?

- Was Karl Marx a hero or a villain?

Step 2 — Take a vote

Consider your first response to the debate question, then vote "Yes," "No," or "Unsure." After the vote is counted, sit in a horseshoe shape, seated according to how you voted.

Step 3 — Exchange points of view

Find out more about the debate topic, then take turns presenting the "Yes" and "No" points of view. If you are "Unsure," listen carefully and ask questions to help you make up your mind.

Step 4 — Take a final vote

After discussion, take another vote. You can still choose "Yes," "No," or "Unsure." The winning side is the one with the largest increase in votes. This measures how persuasive the presentations were.

APPLY It

Debate these issues using the steps above.

History

Was Maritime Union or Confederation with Canada the best solution to Nova Scotia's difficulties in the early 1860s? (Chapter 2)

Geography

Is the "One Child Policy" the best way for China to control its population growth? (Chapter 2)

Start Focus on images

This textbook is filled with many different types of visuals. They can give you as much information as the text that you read. Like reading material, visual images contain messages that reflect a point of view. They can also contain possible bias.

Step 1 Identify the image

There are many different types of images. Each has a different purpose.

• paintings, photographs, or posters are artistic expressions that contain a message or information	• drawings or diagrams are illustrations to simplify or explain a topic
• cartoon series or editorial cartoons give a message using humour	• maps, aerial photographs, or satellite images show patterns on the earth

When you see an image, read the title and caption that goes with it. See if you can find out when the image was created, and by whom.

Step 2 Read the image

A useful way to look at images is to identify what is in the foreground or the centre. This is probably the main subject, and the most important part. Next, examine the background or the edges of the image. This tells you the setting or context. Reading foreground and background will help you draw information from the image. Think as well about what may not be in the image. A photograph, for example, can be cropped to emphasize something within an image that was originally larger.

Step 3 Analyze the image

You have gathered information about the image and its content. Now you can ask yourself some important questions:

- What is the artist's **message**? How does he or she make this message clear?

- What is the artist's **point of view** about the topic? How can you tell? How is he or she trying to show a certain point of view?

- Why did the artist create this image? Why was it chosen for this publication?

Step 4 Evaluate the image

To evaluate something means to judge or assess it. Ask these questions to evaluate the image:

- Is the message easy to understand or difficult to identify?

- Is the artist's point of view current or out of date? Do you agree with it or not?

- Would another type of image have been as effective, or perhaps even better?

History

The Canadian Pacific Railway was the largest owner of land that could be sold to settlers. This poster was one way to promote immigration to Canada.

Geography

A Mexican couple looks at the border fence at the U.S.-Mexican border, near Tijuana, Mexico.

APPLY It

Answer these questions for each of the images above.

1. What type of image is shown? What is its purpose?

2. What information can be seen in the foreground and the background? What does this tell you about the subject? How does the caption help with understanding the image?

3. What is the artist's message? Identify the point of view.

4. How effectively is the message presented? Does it create an emotional response in the viewer? What other type of image could have been used instead? Why?

→ **Using and Making Maps**

Start **Know how to use maps**

People say that "a picture is worth a thousand words." This is especially true when you are examining or creating a map. A map is a specialized drawing which shows a simplified view of the earth (or part of it) from directly overhead. Maps use symbols, scale, direction, and location to convey their meaning.

Step 1 **Look at the legend**

Three major types of symbols unlock the stories told by maps. Use the map legend to find their meanings.

Area Symbols	Line Symbols	Point Symbols
Colours or patterns are used to indicate large parts of the map with common characteristics (e.g., oceans)	Lines of different colours and design divide places (e.g., boundaries) or join them (e.g., highways)	Small shapes and drawings identify specific places, such as cities, hospitals, and camp-grounds

Step 2 **Check the scale**

Three different types of scale can be used to show how much actual distance is shown on the map.

Statement Scale	Line Scale	Ratio Scale
The scale of the map is stated in a combination of words and numbers (e.g., 1 cm = 1 km)	A measured line is used, with map distance marked along the top and the actual distance along the bottom	Numbers show how much actual distance is represented (e.g., 1:100 000 means 1 cm = 1 km)

Step 3 **Identify direction and location**

Location on a map can be determined in two different ways. North direction is found at the top centre of a map (unless shown otherwise). Places can be located in relation to one another by combining distance and compass direction. For example, Ottawa is found about 350 km NE of Toronto. Some maps will also have a grid of lines, such as latitude and longitude, to give the location of places.

Step 4 | Make Your Own Map

- Decide what to show on your map. Is there particular information about a place that you wish to show?

- Start with a page of blank paper or a computer drawing program. Decide the best way to shape the map area.

- Frame the map area, leaving room for the map legend.

- Begin your map with the major outlines and line symbols. Then add point symbols. Fill in large areas of colour last.

- Complete your map with a title, a scale, a compass rose. Group symbols of the same type together in an organized legend.

Geography Example

History Example

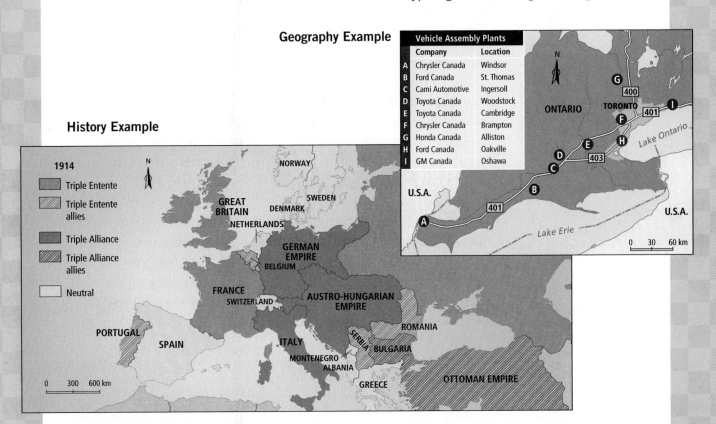

APPLY It

History

1. Why are Britain, France, and Russia all in the same colour?

2. How far is it from the most easterly point of Great Britain to the most westerly point in Russia?

3. How might this distance affect Britain's and Russia's abilities to act as effective military allies?

Geography

1. What do the blue circles represent? What other symbol do they coincide with? Suggest a reason for this pattern.

2. How far is it from B to I in a straight line? Explain why so many of these car plants are clustered near Toronto.

3. Use distance and direction to give these locations in relation to the centre of Toronto: a) GM Canada, b) Honda Canada

→ **Using Different Types of Graphs**

| Start | **Recognize that different graphs have different purposes**

In this textbook you will read and construct various types of graphs that show data. Graphs help you to identify patterns that would not otherwise be obvious. They are also effective ways to present your findings to an audience. There is a graph for every purpose.

| Bar Graph | **Bar Graph: Identifying different parts of a topic**

A **bar graph** is used to show data about a group of topics or places, usually at one point in time. This graph has two axes. The horizontal axis usually shows the different topics or places, while the vertical axis usually shows the units of measure. (Sometimes this will be reversed to create a horizontal bar graph.)

When you are reading a bar graph, check to see if the number scale starts at 0. Small differences between topics or places can be easier to read if the bars are arranged in declining order, from the largest to the smallest. The graph below has bars arranged by year, showing the pattern of immigration from year to year. You can use graph paper or computer software to create a bar graph.

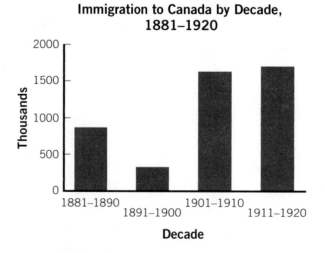

Immigration to Canada by Decade, 1881–1920

Pie Graph Comparing different parts to the whole

A **pie graph** is used to compare different proportions for one topic. In other words, a pie graph shows the size of individual slices in one pie. This type of graph is compact and easy to read, but the individual slices must add up to 100% to reflect the whole topic.

When reading a pie graph, find the largest slice first. Then look for the second-biggest one, and so on down to the smallest. The simplest way to create an accurate pie graph is to use a computer program.

Immigrant Destination by Province or Territory, 2006

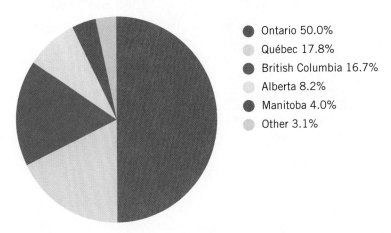

- Ontario 50.0%
- Québec 17.8%
- British Columbia 16.7%
- Alberta 8.2%
- Manitoba 4.0%
- Other 3.1%

Line Graph Identifying change over time

A **line graph** shows information about a topic for several different periods of time. The interval of time can be months, years, decades, or centuries. Every line graph has two axes. The horizontal axis marks off the time periods. The vertical axis shows the units of the topic being measured at different times.

When you read a line graph, identify the period of greatest change by finding the steepest slope of the line. Periods of little change are indicated by little or no slope of the line. When drawing a line graph, use either graph paper or a computer program.

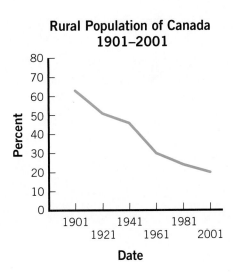

Rural Population of Canada 1901–2001

Comparing many times and topics

More complex information may require a multiple type of graph. A **multiple line graph** uses lines to show change in many topics during the same period of time. A **multiple bar graph** shows matching information at two or three different times. A **compound bar graph** (below) stacks different parts of a topic on top of each other. It is a useful way to compare parts of a topic at different times. The parts of the bars should be arranged in the same order for easier comparison. Use either graph paper or a computer program to create these graphs.

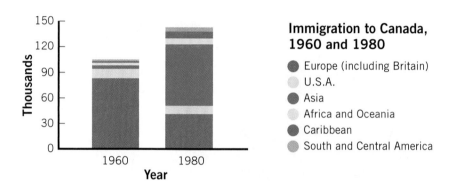

Immigration to Canada, 1960 and 1980

- Europe (including Britain)
- U.S.A.
- Asia
- Africa and Oceania
- Caribbean
- South and Central America

APPLY It

Which type of graph would be the best way to show the information below? Why?

History

Ontario Support for Political Parties, Election of 1911

Political Party	Percentage
Liberals	42.1%
Conservatives	56.2%
Others	0.7%

Geography

Alberta, Interprovincial Migration, 2001–2006

Year	In-Migration	Out-Migration
2005–2006	109 686	52 581
2004–2005	82 418	47 995
2003–2004	60 822	50 216
2002–2003	64 627	52 724
2001–2002	75 615	49 380

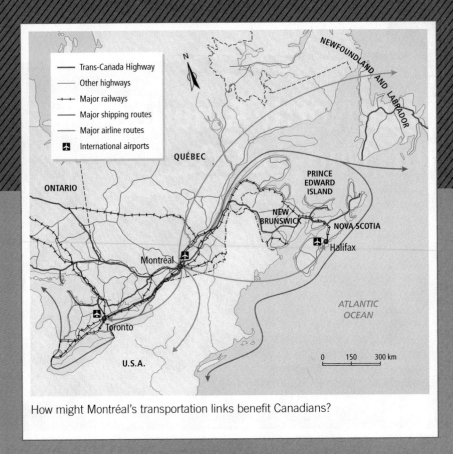

How might Montréal's transportation links benefit Canadians?

What's the Big Idea?

Canada is a land of many contrasts. The smallest province, Prince Edward Island, is 5684 km^2 in size. Québec, the largest province, occupies an area of 1 356 366 km^2.

There are more than 50 First Nations languages and more than 100 non-Aboriginal languages spoken in Canada, but only English and French are official federal government languages.

How do you think a country with so many differences came to be? Why are we not part of the United States? The answers to these questions lie in our history. In Unit 1, you will learn how the people of such a large area put aside their differences to create one country.

Key Terms
Confederation, conference, political deadlock, reciprocity, intercolonial trade, Corn Laws, Fenians, Manifest Destiny

What You Will Learn in this Unit

You will explore these aspects of the Unit 1 Big Idea:

- What political factors, people, events, and geographical realities led to the creation and growth of Canada?
- How was Canada in 1867 different from Canada today in terms of political, social, and other issues?
- How can I use the inquiry process to answer historical questions?

British North America in the Mid-1800s

Making Connections

- What provinces on the map do you recognize from today?
- How much time do you think it would take to travel across Canada in 1850? How long does it take to travel across the country today? Consider more than one travel method.
- Which provinces would you want to live in then and now? Why?

Add two questions of your own and discuss them with a partner. How did your partner's questions help you see more in the map?

Imagine you are planning a trip to Vancouver. Around 1850, the quickest way to travel from Halifax to Vancouver was to take a ship around the coast of South America, a journey that took months (see map on page H 15). Even going from Toronto, Ontario, to St. John's, Newfoundland, could take weeks.

The political map of North America was different than it is today. North of the United States, there were seven British colonies, one British government territory, and two large areas controlled by the Hudson's Bay Company. These areas had little to do with one another. There was little trade between them, and their populations were small. Why might such remote colonies consider forming a united country?

Historians study how things change over time. They not only describe the great events of history, but they also explore the background factors that led to these events. In this chapter, you will examine some of the similarities and differences between the colonies. You will learn why these colonies later formed the new country of Canada.

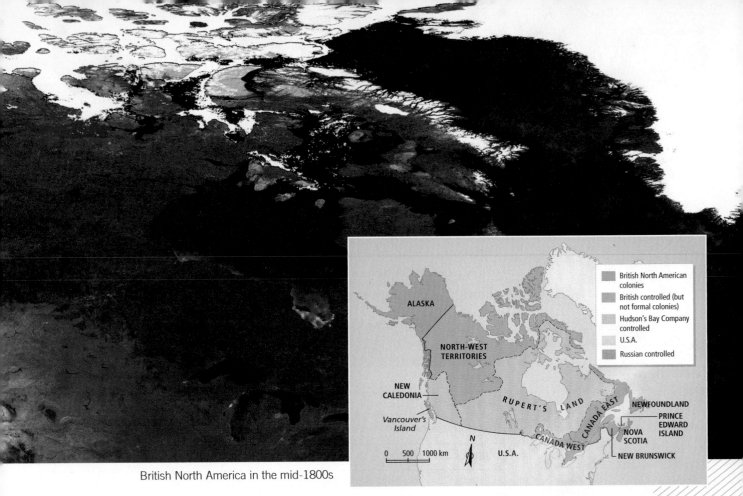

British North America in the mid-1800s

Questions to Consider as You Read this Chapter

You will explore these aspects of the Unit 1 Big Idea: **Why did some of the colonies put aside differences and create a new country—Canada?**

- What were the key social, physical, political, and economic characteristics of the British North American colonies between 1850 and 1860?

- What were the regional interests of each colony before the formation of Canada?

- Why is it important to use appropriate vocabulary when referring to historical events?

Thinking About Literacy

Taking Notes to Compare and Contrast

Use a chart like the one shown below to help you record facts about each of the colonies. Some boxes will have more than one point, and some will be left blank. Remember that a "feature" is a characteristic, or trait.

At the end of this chapter, you will be asked to put your notes into a Venn diagram to compare and contrast the differences and similarities between the British North American colonies.

Colony	Physical Features	Political Features	People	Economic Features	My Thoughts

Did you know that approximately 5 million people live in the Greater Toronto Area? That is about twice the number of people who lived in all of British North America in the 1850s. Then, people were spread out across the vast landscape. Historians have uncovered a lot of information about them.

The first survey of British North America's population was the **census** of 1851. After that, a population census was taken every 10 years until 1956, when it was changed to every five years. This table shows the distribution of people in 1851.

Colony (or Region)	Population	Percentage of BNA's Total Population
Newfoundland	101 600	4%
Nova Scotia	276 854	10.9%
New Brunswick	193 800	7.7%
Prince Edward Island	56 878	2.2%
Canada East (part of Québec today)	890 261	35.2%
Canada West (part of Ontario today)	952 004	37.6%
Rupert's Land and the Northwest Territories	5700	0.2%
New Caledonia	55 000	2.2%
Total	2 532 097	100%

The 1861 census showed that the population of British North America was 3 229 633. The population was overwhelmingly of British origin, as the following pie chart shows.

People of British North America

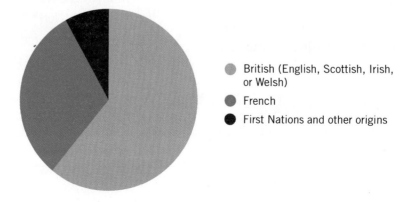

- British (English, Scottish, Irish, or Welsh)
- French
- First Nations and other origins

MATTER

census an official count of the population including information such as occupation, gender, age, religion, and ethnic origin

During **READING**

Checkpoint

Include the population numbers under the "People" column of the chart you began on page H 5. Under "My Thoughts," consider how census information might be useful for transportation, trade, and decision making in British North America.

Almost half of the people who live in Toronto today were born outside of Canada. Toronto is one of the most multicultural cities in the world. Why do you think this is?

This pattern varied from region to region. People of French origin were the majority in Canada East. In Canada West and the Maritimes, people of British origin were predominant. In the Prairies, First Nations people and the Métis were the largest groups. There were also some British and French fur traders living there. In British Columbia, the largest groups were people of British and American origin who had been attracted by a series of **gold rushes**.

Miners wait their turn to register their claims to gold-mining sites. Think of three questions you would like to ask the men in this photo.

The Great Migration

One factor that contributed to the population diversity was a mass migration of people from Europe in the 1830s and 1840s. Poverty and food shortages drove thousands of people to **emigrate**, many coming to what is now Canada. This increased the ethnic diversity of British North America. People from the Netherlands and Germany settled here. Others came here from Ireland because of the Great Irish Famine, when disease destroyed the country's main crop, potatoes. Many of the Irish who came were Roman Catholic and were hostile to Britain, but conditions in their homeland were so poor they needed to move in order to survive. You will read more about the Irish immigrants in Chapter 2.

Environmental Milestones

Diversifying Crops

In the early 1840s, potatoes were the staple food in Ireland. A strain of potato known as the "lumper" was the most popular because it gave a high yield. In 1845, a fungus infected the lumper potato. For three years in a row, the potato crop failed. In the resulting famine, thousands of Irish people starved. Others emigrated to North America. It was an environmental disaster that might have been avoided by growing a wider variety of crops.

The Underground Railroad

Another factor contributing to diversity was the Underground Railroad. Slavery had been illegal in British North America since 1833. About 30 000 American slaves escaped to Canada West and Nova Scotia. The secret network that helped runaway slaves was called the Underground Railroad.

Parade in Amherstburg, Ontario, marking the abolition of slavery in the British Empire

Mary Ann Shadd, a prominent member of the organization, was born as a free black woman (not a slave) in Delaware, a small state in eastern U.S.A. She later settled in Windsor, Canada West, where she wrote a pamphlet called *A Plea for Emigration*. She called on all free people to assist American slaves to settle in British North America. She wrote:

In Canada as in recently settled countries, there is much to do, and comparatively few for the work... If a coloured man understands his business, he receives the public patronage the same as a white man.

Harriet Tubman. How would you feel knowing that anyone could get a large reward for turning you in to the authorities?

Harriet Tubman was born as a slave in Maryland in the U.S. She escaped to Canada West where she became involved in the Underground Railroad, helping other slaves escape. Between 1850 and 1860, she made 19 secret trips to the American South. She risked her life helping approximately 70 people reach freedom in Canada West. Slave owners put a bounty of $40 000 (the equivalent of $750 000 today) on her head. Anyone capturing her could claim the bounty when they turned her over to the police. She wrote:

There was one of two things I had a right to—liberty or death. If I could not have one, I would have the other for no man should take me alive.

WEB LINK •••••••••••••••••••••
For more information on the Underground Railroad, visit our Web site.

Life in British North America was generally better for escaped slaves than the life they had come from; however, they were not always welcomed by white society. Many black people lived in separate communities rather than in established towns and villages.

The First Nations

Historians do not know exactly how many First Nations people were living in the colonies at this time. This is largely because First Nations people often lived on the fringes of settler society. They had once been valued allies of the British in the fight against the Americans and important suppliers of furs to the Hudson's Bay Company. However, there had been peace with the Americans for 50 years, and the significance of the fur trade was declining.

Blackfoot camp, 1880s. How might the First Nations have felt about the establishment of settlements?

The census of 1871 records 23 037 First Nations people in the population of Ontario, Québec, New Brunswick, and Nova Scotia. This figure probably underestimates the true figure because census officials did not consider it important to get an accurate count of all the First Nations people of the colonies. Why do you think the officials did not consider this important?

First Nations leaders realized they were no longer treated as friends and allies. Little Pine, chief of the Garden River Ojibwe near Sault Ste. Marie, wrote a letter to the governor of Canada in 1849:

> ...you have become a great people, whilst we have melted away like snow beneath an April sun; our strength is wasted, our countless warriors dead, our forests laid low, you have hounded us from every place as with a wand, you have swept away all our pleasant land, and like some giant foe you tell us "willing or unwilling, you must go from amid these rocks and wastes."

WEB LINK • • • • • • • • • • • • • • • • • • •
For more information on First Nations in the 1800s, visit our Web site.

THINKING It Over

1. Look at the 1851 population table on page H 6 and write down two general observations you can draw from it about where the people of British North America settled. Use your "My Thoughts" section to help you.

2. Summarize the cultural makeup of the colonies' population at the beginning of the 1860s.

3. How does learning about the population and people of British North America give you a better understanding of British North America compared to Canada today?

What Was Life Like in British North America?

During **READING**

Checkpoint

Add some of the information about the people of British North America to your chart. Under "My Thoughts," note how this information helps you know more about Canada. If you want, add a section to your chart for facts about people in all the colonies.

What are your responsibilities at home and at school? How do you think your life would be different if you lived in British North America?

Everyday Life

In the 1850s, roles were usually organized by gender. Women were responsible for most domestic chores, while men did most of the outside tasks. When it was necessary, however, everyone was expected to help with heavy agricultural jobs, such as clearing rocks to create farm fields.

Very young children did not normally have household roles, but by age five they were expected to take on simple tasks. Girls learned to spin, knit, sew, cook, work in the garden, milk the cows, and care for the younger children. Although every farm was unique, in general young boys helped with feeding livestock and gathering firewood. Older boys would clear fields, build fences, and harvest crops. From about 14 years of age, boys were expected to work a full day in the fields. Girls of that age were expected to be able to do any domestic job in the home. If you could choose, which work would you rather have done: a boy's or a girl's? Why?

Imagine yourself living the way people did in the mid-1800s. Their winter heat came from a wood stove, which meant cutting and hauling wood. Even in summer, the wood stove was used every day for heating water and cooking. People went to bed early because light came from candles and oil lamps. This light was too dim for much activity, and wax and oil were expensive. There was no indoor plumbing. People used basins to hold hand-pumped water. There were no flush toilets yet; they used outhouses or chamber pots.

A French-Canadian woman bakes bread in an outdoor oven in the late 1800s. Why might she have had an outdoor oven?

During the 1850s, many children were needed at home to work on farms or in workshops. In Canada West during the 1840s, Egerton Ryerson set up a system of free elementary schools, but many children attended school rarely or not at all. Some religious organizations provided education for children, but these often charged fees, which many families could not afford. It was not until the late 1800s that public schooling became available to everyone.

There was little entertainment. Newspapers were popular. People wrote long letters to each other describing their daily lives. Visiting friends and family was a favourite pastime. Going to religious services on Sunday was an event to be looked forward to; it was a relief from the hard work of everyday life and a time for socializing.

Frances Tweedie Milne and her husband farmed in Scarborough, now part of Toronto. What do you think her life was like? Base your answers on the following diary extracts.

May 24, 1869: William and I stuffed mattress. We sewed it all and did it very nicely. We both tied the twine. Didn't finish today.

August 2, 1869: Busy canning cherries, Jennie helping to stone them. Boiling 1/2 my vinegar.

November 11, 1869: Busy preparing for the [barn] raising tomorrow, beheaded two geese for it.

December 28, 1869: Killed seven hogs and got them salted before dark. Margaret and I got on very well alone and quite delighted that this job is over.

January to April, 1870: Busy at my rug and knitting sock in the evening... Finished rug... Started 2nd sock for Em... Cut my lilac print... Busy at my lilac print dress... Cut Wm.'s shirts.

August 21, 1872: Baby a week old today. It feels most fearfully lonesome and I can't get relief without a cry.

September 13, 1872: Am alone and baby cried some. I am feeling very sad sometimes.

WEB LINK •·················
For more information on life in the mid-1800s, visit our Web site.

Social Characteristics

British North American society was not the same everywhere. Canada East was mainly French-speaking and Roman Catholic. Canada West was mainly English-speaking and Protestant. There were communities of people of African descent, especially in Nova Scotia and in the south part of Canada West. First Nations people lived apart from European settlers.

Two things were common to all of the colonies. First, there were distinct class divisions. People spoke, dressed, and acted differently depending on which class of society they belonged to. Second, there was much movement of people into and out of settled areas. This was because people were constantly trying to improve their situation in life.

Compare the people in these two photographs. Focus your inquiry on their attire, surroundings, and what they are doing.

THINKING It Over

1. From what you have read, create a "day in the life of" timeline, outlining what your day might have been like in the 1850s.

2. Do research to compare the general conditions described in this section with the general conditions in Canada today. With a partner, compare them under the following headings: a) population, b) gender roles, and c) technological development. Discuss with your partner whether you think things are better or worse now than they were then, giving your reasons.

Understanding Continuity and Change

Why do we study history? Some might say we study history to see how things have changed. That is true; however, historians are also interested in studying continuity: how and why some things stay the same. For example, your textbook says that "in the 1850s, roles were usually organized by gender." Some of those gender roles have changed over time. Women today work outside the home much more than they did in 1850, and men do more work inside it. Some things have not changed, however. It is still true, for example, that women today still do more domestic work than men, and on average men get paid more than women for many kinds of work. Historians try to understand both how and why some things change while other things stay the same.

Let us look at an example from your everyday life. On a plain piece of paper, draw a map or floor plan of your school. Show as much detail as you can, and use a legend if it helps you show more.

Now take a look at the floor plan and short description of Melissa Johnson's school in Stanley, New Brunswick, around 1870.

> *As time was spent for the greater part at school I will try to tell you what the school house was like, and also tell you of the master, the only teacher I ever had. I will draw a map—a picture of the school house and a floor plan.*

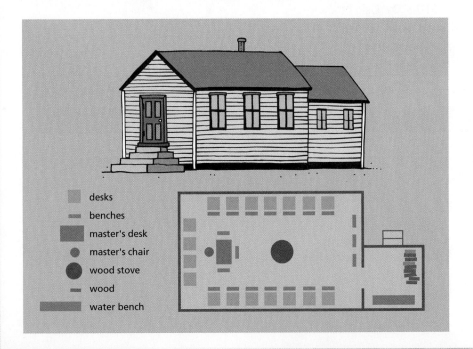

desks
benches
master's desk
master's chair
wood stove
wood
water bench

When we needed to write or cipher we turned in to the desk, and when just studying we turned out. The small children who were not yet using pencil or pen sat on the benches, where there were no desks.

Step 1 Find similarities and differences

Working in groups, fill out a chart like this one, showing differences and similarities between Melissa Johnson's school and yours.

Differences	Similarities
One room	Students used desks

Step 2 Analyze the similarities and differences

Write a paragraph describing how you think life would be different for students in this school than in yours, and another paragraph describing ways you think life would be the same.

APPLY It

Historians also study whether changes represent progress or decline. They ask the question, Have things gotten better or worse? Usually the answer is not simply either "better" or "worse," but a combination of both. Think about school and the lives of children since the mid-1800s. Using the section on Everyday Life from page H 10 of your textbook and the information you collected above, fill out a chart like this one.

Now use your chart to write a short essay answering the question, Is life better or worse for children in Canada today than it was in the mid-1800s? Remember, it is okay for your essay to say it is both better and worse.

Ways in which life is better for children today	Ways in which life was better for children in the mid-1800s

The settled areas in the colonies were separated by vast distances, bodies of water, and difficult terrain. Those who wished to unite the colonies would have to overcome obstacles imposed by the challenging landscape. William Lyon Mackenzie King, prime minister from 1921–1930 and 1935–1948, once remarked, "Canada has too much geography." What do you think he meant by this?

Vast Distances and Difficult Terrain

First Nations people moved and transported goods in all parts of Canada. They originally showed Europeans the routes from place to place, from one watershed to another, enabling Europeans to travel long distances before there were roads, railways, canals, and powerboats. If you drive from Halifax to Vancouver, your route covers 5876 km. Today, airplanes can connect these cities in a matter of hours. In the 1850s, it took months to make this journey. To make matters more difficult, some colonies were separated by geographical barriers, such as mountains and bodies of water. Developing a transportation system would be essential in order to create a united nation.

During READING

Checkpoint
Look up "challenging" in a dictionary. The word is not always used to describe land. Review physical maps of Canada. What makes the physical features of Canada's geography challenging? Add to the "My Thoughts" or "Physical Features" sections of your chart.

The voyage from Halifax to Vancouver in the 1850s involved travelling by horse, boat, and on foot. It would take even longer than going all the way around South America by ship.

What do you think the pros and cons would be if you had to travel on this ship?

Climate Extremes

Canadians sometimes call their country the "Great White North." This implies that Canada is frozen solid most of the year. In reality, the climate varies enormously from region to region. This table summarizes some of the differences.

Climate affects how societies develop. In areas where winters are milder, outdoor work is possible for a longer part of the year. The length of the seasons and the amount of precipitation influences the agriculture, and thus the economy, of a region.

Region	Airstreams	Summers	Winters
West Coast	Warm and moist	Warm and moist	Temperate and wet
Prairies	Cold winter/ hot summer	Hot and dry	Cold
Great Lakes– St. Lawrence	Cold winter/ hot summer	Hot and humid	Snowy and wind-chilled
Atlantic	Arctic and maritime	Warm and humid	Snowy and cold
North	Arctic	Cool and short	Long and cold

These images show contrasting climates in Ontario (left) and Iqaluit (right). In what ways does climate affect our lives?

THINKING It Over

1. Quote some figures and details about the physical features from this section to illustrate the great size and diverse geography of British North America.

2. In your own words, discuss with a partner why Mackenzie King might have said that Canada has "too much geography." Do you agree with him? Why or why not?

3. Assess what it would have been like to live in each region during the 1850s. Consider transportation, climate, and ways of life.

The British North American colonies had similar government structures. This may have made it easier for them to work together on matters of common interest.

The Government of the Canadas

In your previous studies, you examined the political structure of the Canadas. The diagram on this page may help remind you of what the government system there looked like. The **Crown** appointed the governor who, in turn, appointed the members of the legislative council and executive council. The executive council is the part of government that decides what bills will be introduced into the legislature. It is now called the cabinet. For a bill to become law, it had to be approved by the legislative assembly, the legislative council, and the governor.

The voters consisted of male property owners. They chose the members of the legislative assembly. Even though the legislative assembly was elected by the people, the Crown still held influence because it appointed the governor. The Crown generally chose a member of the British **nobility** to be governor. The governor tended to choose **conservative** people to be members of the legislative council. There was a mixture of influences in government: the Crown, the nobility, and men who owned property.

WORDS MATTER

Crown a symbolic term referring to the monarch of a country

nobility members of the highest class of society

conservative preferring what is safe and familiar rather than wanting change and risk

During **READING**

Checkpoint
In the "My Thoughts" section of your chart, note what allowing the Crown to choose members of the legislature tells us about Canada's society at the time.

The first legislature of Ontario, 1867. What groups of Canada's population are not represented here? Why do you think this is?

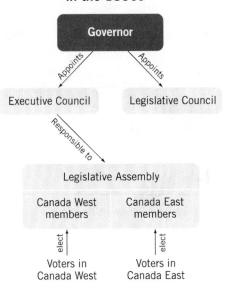

The Political System of the Canadas in the 1850s

Governor

Appoints → Appoints

Executive Council   Legislative Council

Responsible to

Legislative Assembly

Canada West members   Canada East members

elect   elect

Voters in Canada West   Voters in Canada East

Canada East and Canada West each had the same number of seats in the legislative assembly. This sometimes caused **political deadlock**, as the two sides fought with each other about the best way to solve the economic challenges of the colony.

Two issues tended to deadlock the legislative assembly: transportation and representation. Politicians from Canada West wanted to expand transportation facilities to increase trade and wealth; they were willing to spend government money to do so. Politicians from Canada East did not want to change their existing way of life; they felt that better links with Canada West would threaten their identity, and they resisted attempts to spend tax money on transportation improvements.

There was also deadlock over the representation issue. You may recall from Grade 7 that Canada West supported representation by population, while Canada East wanted to retain equal representation. Compromise seemed impossible.

This illustration shows a deadlock situation. How might you illustrate compromise?

Government in the Maritimes

Before 1784, there were only two colonies in the Maritime region—
Nova Scotia and Prince Edward Island. However, in that year, Nova
Scotia was divided in three, and the separate colonies of New
Brunswick and Cape Breton Island were created. Transportation was
slow and difficult. Today, Prince Edward Island, Nova Scotia, and
New Brunswick are Canada's smallest provinces.

By the late 1850s, many people in the region were talking about
joining New Brunswick and Nova Scotia into a single colony again.
Supporters of union said that a single government controlling this
larger population would have greater influence in North America.
The British government liked this idea because it would be less
expensive to have one colonial government rather than two. In fact, it
went a step further: Why not bring Prince Edward Island into the
united colony? the government asked. Now the population would be
more than 663 000, and two governments would be done away with,
saving even more money.

Why do you think it would have been relatively easy to create a
single colony in the Maritimes? All three of these colonies had the
same form of government. It was exactly the same form as in the
Canadas. By 1864, the Maritime colonies had scheduled a conference
in Charlottetown, P.E.I., to discuss Maritime union. You will return to
this story in Chapter 3.

The room where the Charlottetown Conference of 1864 took place

What Was Prince Edward Island's Absentee Landlord Problem?

In 1763, the British took over the French colonies in what later became Canada. At that time, they gave most of the land on Prince Edward Island to wealthy families who lived in Britain. Local farmers were mainly tenants. They rented the land from these absentee landowners, called landlords. In the other colonies, farm families could buy land relatively cheaply. In P.E.I., this was impossible. Island farmers formed a tenant union to push for change. They passed the following resolutions:

Resolved, That we the [tenant farmers will]... withhold... rent... to resist [being thrown off the land], seizure [arrest] and sale [of our property] to pay rent.

Resolved, That it is our duty to unite as tenants for mutual protection and sympathy in order to put an end to the leasehold system [having to rent land instead of being able to buy it].

Resolved, That every member provide himself with a bugle to summon the note alarm on the approaches of the rent-leeches [rent collectors].

What do you suppose the tenants would do when they heard a bugle warning that a rent collector was coming?

The absentee landlords issue was one of the reasons P.E.I. saw itself as different from the rest of British North America. In 1866, the *Charlottetown Examiner* wrote that P.E.I.'s legislature refused to join Confederation because of its "isolated, peculiar and exceptional position... as contrasted with the other British North American Provinces and Colonies."

THINKING It Over

1. Imagine you are a tenant farmer. Using information from the resolutions, explain in your own words what you want and what you are prepared to do to get it. **k c t**

2. With one or two partners, discuss why the farmers of P.E.I. would want to own their land, rather than rent it from absentee landlords. **c t**

The Distant Colonies

There were other colonies in British North America, but they were too far away to have close relations with the Canadas and the three Maritime colonies. In the East was Newfoundland. The sea crossing to Newfoundland across the Cabot Strait was dangerous and unpredictable. Newfoundland tended to go its own way, although it watched the Maritime union movement with interest.

In the West, there were two colonies: British Columbia (formerly New Caledonia before it became a colony in 1858) and Vancouver's Island (the original name of modern Vancouver Island). They were united into the single colony of British Columbia in 1866. All of these colonies had the traditional British government system. In B.C., there was strong American influence.

Many Americans came north into B.C. to join the gold rush movement of the 1850s. Some British Columbians felt that the rest of British North America was too distant. If the colony wanted to change its status, they argued, it should become part of the United States. Get rid of the Crown, these people said. They thought an American **republic** was better than a British monarchy.

Treacherous ocean waters made transportation from Newfoundland dangerous, increasing the sense of isolation from the other colonies.

What does the signpost in this political cartoon represent?

Sir James Douglas (1803–1877) was a senior official for the Hudson's Bay Company. He had a reputation for working hard and getting jobs done; however, he was also difficult to deal with.

In 1849, Douglas was appointed the Hudson's Bay Company agent on Vancouver's Island to supervise the fur trade. He had disputes with the governor, Richard Blanshard. In theory, Blanshard could overrule Douglas, but in practice Douglas had the real power. In less than a year, Blanshard resigned.

When the colony of British Columbia was created in 1858, Douglas became its first governor. He supervised the building of a 640-km road to the Cariboo region when gold was discovered there. In 1862, he got into trouble with Britain for taking out loans for the construction without permission.

His opponents began to complain that he was snobbish and a dictator. The British decided to end his governorship of the colony.

The story of Sir James Douglas brings up an important question: should people be judged by their achievements, or should their personalities be considered as well? Douglas achieved much professionally; however, his personality was grating. In what ways was Sir James Douglas a hero or a villain? Are you unsure? Why?

Sir James Douglas, governor of British Columbia

THINKING It Over

1. Look at the diagram of the political system in the Canadas on page H 17, and the text explaining it. In your own words, explain what is meant by the following statement: "The Crown, the nobility, and men of property all had a say in the running of the government."

2. Write a paragraph explaining why it was uncertain around 1860 that the British North American colonies could agree about their future. Use the information in the "My Thoughts" section of your chart.

The economy of British North America was becoming **industrialized**. Factories with steam-powered equipment were replacing small, hand-powered workshops. Goods such as stoves, coats, or wagon wheels could be produced more quickly than they had been in old-style workshops.

Effects of Industrialization

Industries did not appear everywhere across British North America at the same time. Factors such as geography, transportation, and population affected the growth of industries.

Canada East

One of the first places industry flourished was in Montréal in the late 1840s. The St. Lawrence River gave the city a good supply of water. Boilers were built to convert water into steam, which in turn ran pumps, lathes, drills, and other equipment. Factory owners hired workers from the city's poor to do the dreary and often dangerous work. These people were not well educated and were poorly paid. Many of them were recent immigrants to British North America, escaping even worse conditions in their homelands.

Much of the work in these factories was performed by women and children. Employers paid them less than they paid men. There were few laws to restrict child labour, and children as young as six years old sometimes worked in factories. Employers sometimes beat them if they made mistakes or fell asleep from exhaustion. This became a much larger issue in the 1890s as **capitalists** built many new factories in the expanding cities of the time. You will read more about this in Chapter 7.

During **READING**

Checkpoint
In your "My Thoughts" column, note what industrialization meant for the people of Canada. Why would some people think it was good, while others disliked it?

WORDS MATTER

industrialize develop industries, especially manufacturing industries

capitalists people who built and owned businesses

What effect would working in factories have had on the quality of life of a child, woman, and factory owner?

Factories in Canada East 1840s and 1850s

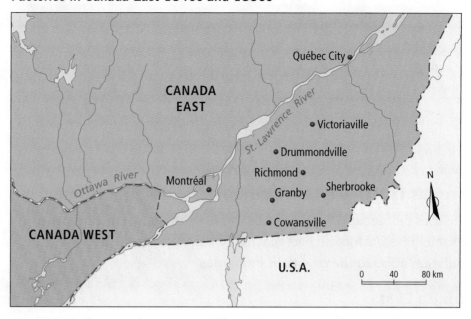

By the late 1850s, there were steam-powered factories in the suburbs of Montréal such as Hochelaga, Saint-Henri, Valleyfield, Saint-Hyacinthe, and Saint-Jean. As well, there were a few factories in the Eastern Townships and the Québec City region.

Montréal soon established itself as the most industrialized city in British North America. It held this position for about 100 years. Three industries dominated the city by the early 1860s. These are summarized in the organizer below.

Montréal was in its prime in 1872 as British North America's most industrialized city.

Leading Industries in Montréal, 1860s

Industry	Food	Footwear	Textiles
Examples	flour mills, sugar refineries, breweries, bakeries, butter and cheese factories	boot and shoe factories making footwear for all occasions	fabric factories making cotton bed blankets and sheets, clothing, curtains, etc.
Details	This was the largest industry at this time. Small and large operations existed in this industry, and there were many factories around the city.	This was the second-largest industry. Soon Canada East's footwear factories dominated all of eastern British North America.	The workforce comprised mainly women, assisted by children. Some of the work was still done in people's homes, so there tended to be a large number of small companies.

As Canada became industrialized, more and more people moved from rural to urban areas. In the large cities, factories sprang up. Working conditions were poor. Families had difficulty surviving on meagre wages.

PRINCE ALBERT'S STORY...

In 1860, large crowds welcomed Queen Victoria's son, Albert Edward, the Prince of Wales, when he visited British North America. The city of Montréal held a dinner for him with 3000 guests. The table was filled with offerings of oysters, lobster, beef, salmon, and duck.

The poor were forced to live in terrible conditions. Flea-ridden rats and mice spread typhus. Many children and their parents died from this disease.

xenopsylla cheopsis

In poor areas of the city, one in three children died before reaching the age of five.

In a time when the government provided little support for the poor, Montréal's religious order, the Sisters of Charity (the "Grey Nuns"), helped the sick and the disadvantaged. In 1867, the Grey Nuns took in 662 abandoned and orphaned children. Of these children, only 39 survived the year. The Grey Nuns continue their good work to this day.

Canada West

Industrialization began to flourish in Canada West in the 1870s. At mid-century, the largest industry there was textiles. Factories spun cotton into cloth for making items such as clothing, curtains, and tablecloths. The metalwork industry was growing quickly. Factories made stoves, pots and pans, beds, and other household goods.

Although Canada West got off to a slower start than Canada East, it soon caught up. By the 1880s, there were large industrial operations in what was by then called Ontario. In Chapter 7, you will learn how Ontario became the industrial centre of Canada's economy.

The Maritimes

Shipbuilding was an important craft in the Maritime colonies because fishing and overseas trade were so significant. Many of the workers were skilled carpenters, sailmakers, or wood turners. Shipyards eventually adapted to steam-powered cutting, shaping, and drilling methods. By the 1850s, the region's yards turned out an average of 374 ships a year.

Farming and logging were important in rural areas of the Maritime colonies where populations were low. Factories required large numbers of workers, so they were built in or near urban areas. The population was spread out in this region. As a result, by the 1860s, industrialization had only just begun in the Maritimes. Ever since, industrial production has been lower in this region than in Québec and Ontario.

Would you prefer working in a shipyard in the Maritimes, or working in a factory in Montréal? Explain your choice.

The West

The West was thinly populated and there was little industrialization there until the late 1800s. In the Prairies, the First Nations and Hudson's Bay Company employees ran the fur trade. Trapping, slaughtering, and skinning animals did not require industrial methods. The Hudson's Bay Company, which owned most of the Canadian Prairies, had banned settlers from moving into the region. The Hudson's Bay Company did not want agriculture or industry to disrupt the fur trade.

Like the Maritimes, the colonies of British Columbia and Vancouver's Island did not need factories; forestry and shipping were the leading economic activities. There was little industry in this region until the 1880s.

Environmental Milestones

The Rise in Global Temperatures

Scientists note that the gradual rise in world temperatures began around 1860. The growth of cities and factories led to the burning of fossil fuels—coal, oil, and gas—in ever-greater amounts. Fossil fuel consumption allows people to produce more and have higher living standards, but there is a cost to the environment. The global climate change experienced today has its origins in the mid-1800s.

As the forestry industry grew in the West, what kind of factories do you think would be needed?

Many "Little Countries"

WEB LINK •••••••••••••••
For more information on the European Union, visit our Web site.

In some ways, British North America was like the countries of Europe today. In Europe, more than twenty-five countries have formed an economic union to increase trade among themselves. They recognize that many of them are too small to develop large economies on their own, but together they can form one large trading bloc of almost 500 million people.

The British North American colonies had small populations and were distant from each other. If they formed their own economic union, they could increase trade among themselves. Goods could be traded between Sarnia and Halifax with ease because of the new railway. Talk of uniting the BNA colonies began in the 1860s. The colonies' economies were very different. How could such a union be successful, the politicians' critics asked?

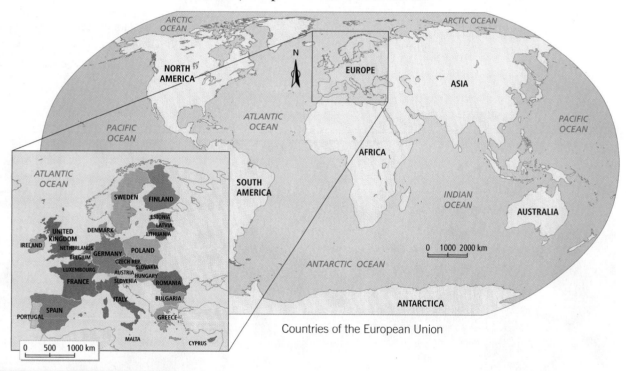

Countries of the European Union

THINKING It Over

1. In three sentences, explain a) what the main features of industrialization are, b) how it was different from the workshops that preceded it, and c) why the urban poor were so important in its development.

2. Think of the four regions examined in this section—Canada East, Canada West, the Maritimes, and the West. Create your own graphic organizer to summarize the main features of each of their economies.

3. Conduct research to find out what Canada's main industries are today.

4. Draw two more frames and provide captions for the Real People Making History feature on page H 25 that show what you would have done if you had been alive then and had the power to solve some of the issues.

PUTTING IT ALL TOGETHER

British North America was a collection of colonies spanning a vast geography. The colonies were very different from one another. Some, like Canada East and Canada West, had large populations, while others had small populations. Their economies were different. The Canadas were becoming industrialized, but the West and the Maritimes were not. The colonies also had similarities. They had similar political systems and faced similar political challenges. Could these colonies be united into a single nation?

After **READING**

Taking Notes to Compare and Contrast

Look carefully at the notes you have written in your graphic organizer. Which of the factors (physical features, political features, people, and economic features) do you think would have the most impact on whether or not the colonies could unite into a single nation? Discuss your opinion with a partner or small group.

Colony	Physical Features	Political Features	People	Economic Features	My Thoughts

THINKING It Through

1. a) Review the notes you made during reading. Use these to help create three Venn diagrams to illustrate the similarities and differences between the Canadas and the other British North American colonies at the time. Create one diagram for each of the following topics: (i) the people, (ii) the political structure, and (iii) the economies. **k t c**

   b) Pick one of your Venn diagrams and use it to write a paragraph about those similarities and differences. **c**

   c) Draw a picture, or describe a scene in words, to illustrate what you consider to be the most important similarity or difference in the topic you selected. In two sentences, explain what the picture or scene shows and why you chose it. **t c**

Factors that Drew the BNA Colonies Together

These paintings depict British North America in the mid-1800s.

Before *READING*

Making Connections
Photographs and art can tell us a lot about life during a time period, or era.
- What can you tell about life in British North America by looking at the images on these two pages? Brainstorm and compare your ideas with a partner.
- Using the images as reference, write a journal entry from the perspective of a 14-year-old living during that era.

What are three things that all Canadians can identify with today? Perhaps you thought of the flag, national anthem, currency, weather, or even the Trans-Canada Highway. In contrast, the colonies and territories of British North America in the mid-1800s had little in common with one another. It was not easy to get from one place to another, so contact was limited.

There were reasons that encouraged the colonies to work with each other, however. They needed to earn more money from the sale of resource products from their farms, oceans, mines, and forests, but it was difficult to trade with each other when each colony had different currency and rules, and weighed and measured things differently.

There were also external reasons why they needed to work more closely with each other. People were worried about being taken over by the United States. Around 1860, there was a general feeling that things had to change. How do you think your life might be different today if the colonies had not decided to cooperate and form a united country?

Questions to Consider as You Read this Chapter

You will explore these aspects of the Unit 1 Big Idea: **Why did some of the colonies put aside differences and create a new country—Canada?**

- What external factors threatened the future of British North America?

- What internal factors caused the colonies to work together?

- What were some conflicting points of view about issues facing the colonies?

- How does learning new terms improve your understanding of history?

CONSIDER BOTH SIDES: Should the Colonies Sign the BNA Act?				
Colony or Region	Evidence that Supports	Evidence that Opposes	Decision	Reasons

Around 1860, British North America's economy was weak. Economies need large populations in order to develop. Businesses need people to work for them and also to buy their products.

Intercolonial Trade

The populations of the colonies were still small and **intercolonial trade** was limited. It was hindered by the lack of efficient transportation systems to move the goods from one colony to another. In addition, the colonies used **duties**, or **tariffs**, to keep out goods from other colonies in order to protect their own goods. Some politicians realized that the colonies were missing out on an opportunity and should try to boost intercolonial trade.

External Trade

Up to this point, the colonies' economic development depended largely on **external trade**. These exports went mainly to Britain and the U.S.

To Britain

Britain had the largest economy in the world. It had a great demand for imported raw materials. British North America shipped wood, agricultural goods, and other raw products to Britain. British law allowed colonial products to be sold there free of tariffs.

The United States was developing rapidly, and it also exported goods to Britain; however, British law placed a tariff on American goods because they came from a foreign country. The cost of exporting goods was roughly the same in British North America and in the U.S. They included farm costs, transportation to a port, shipping across the Atlantic, and delivery to a seller in Britain. The tariff added an additional cost factor to American goods, which made them cost more than goods from British North America.

Because of this, British North American goods had an advantage over goods from the United States. This system was called **colonial preference** because it gave better treatment to goods from the colonies. It led to a healthy export trade from the colonies. Montréal became an important port as goods from the Canadas were shipped from there to Britain.

Montréal harbour, 1875. How might this scene appear today? What would be similar? What would be different?

Britain began to move away from colonial preference in 1846 when it **repealed** the **Corn Laws**. The Corn Laws governed the import and export of grain. These laws kept the price of imported wheat high. During the 1850s, Britain continued to change to a system of **free trade**. This meant that all imported goods were allowed in duty free, which lowered costs to consumers.

Britain was the largest producer of manufactured goods in the world. It believed that free trade in all products, both natural and manufactured, would give it a larger share of world trade. The move to free trade was a devastating development for British North American producers. They gradually lost their price advantage over American producers, and American producers took a larger share of the British market. How could British North American producers make up for the downturn in sales they were experiencing in Britain? You will revisit this question later.

During READING

Checkpoint
Why might the effects of free trade be a reason for signing the British North America Act? Note this in your organizer.

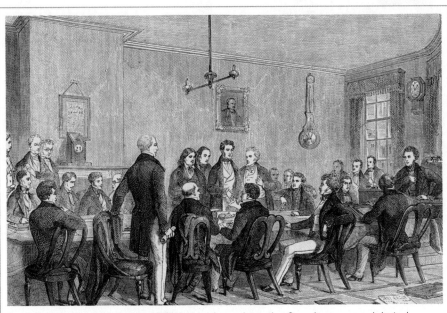

An anti-Corn Law meeting in 1841 in London, where the Corn Laws were debated before their repeal in 1846. In the 1900s, Canada signed free trade agreements with the United States and Mexico. Those were also debated. What are some advantages and disadvantages of free trade?

To the United States

The colonies also had a good export trade to the United States. Popular products there included lumber from New Brunswick, fish from Nova Scotia, and wheat from the Canadas. British North America and the United States signed the **Reciprocity** Treaty in 1854, which meant mutual reduction of tariffs. Britain signed the treaty on behalf of British North America because BNA did not have the authority to do so for itself.

The Reciprocity Treaty allowed free trade on natural products between the British North American colonies and the United States. Exports grew, and it looked as though the colonies had successfully found another market for their goods.

WEB LINKS •⸱⸱⸱⸱⸱⸱⸱⸱⸱⸱⸱⸱⸱⸱⸱⸱⸱
For more information on the repeal of the British Corn Laws and for more information on reciprocity, visit our Web site.

CANADIAN Illustrated News

Vol. XI—No. 7.   MONTREAL, SATURDAY, FEBRUARY 13, 1875.   SINGLE COPIES, TEN CENTS; $4 PER YEAR IN ADVANCE.

GEO. BROWN TINKER
GLOBE

CANADA; *by:* If you call that a good job, Ms. Brown, I don't; it won't hold water!
No amount of mending will fit it for use, now. And in future, Ms. Brown, you need not expect my custom.
SEND IN YOUR BILL.

This image was published on the cover of *Canadian Illustrated News* in 1875. Miss Canada returns a broken reciprocity pan to George Brown, telling him it does not hold water. What viewpoint does this illustration convey?

In 1865, the United States announced its intention to back out of the Reciprocity Treaty the next year because of three main reasons: it felt that British North America was benefiting more than it was from the Treaty; it disliked the tariffs that the Canadas placed on manufactured imports; and it wanted to punish Britain for supporting the South in the Civil War. This was the second damaging development for the colonies—first a sales loss in Britain, and now the same in the United States.

The Solution

Business leaders and politicians in the colonies began to wonder whether they could replace the declining export markets with a strong internal trade. Could they establish an East–West trading link? Could they, for example, sell Nova Scotia fish in Canada East, and wheat from Canada West in New Brunswick?

This was more easily said than done. They would need good railway systems to transport the goods. All the colonies had separate governments. How could businesses get politicians to agree on the best way to proceed?

For the first time, people began to think that it might be best to join all the colonies under a single government. For the Maritimes in particular, such a scheme had attractions. It would allow producers there to sell their goods to a large market in the Canadas. How might Canada East or Canada West benefit from uniting with other colonies?

THINKING It Over

1. Which of these terms are still used today—a) external trade, b) duties, c) tariffs, d) colonial preference, e) free trade, f) reciprocity, g) internal trade? How do you know? What issues are they used to discuss?

2. How did the loss of markets in Britain and the United States encourage some British North Americans to think that it might be a good idea to join the colonies together under a single government?

3. With a partner, choose one of the following and consider how that person or organization would have felt about the idea of joining the colonies together in 1866 (in favour, neutral, opposed). As a class, hold a town hall meeting to discuss the differing views between these groups: a) an American wheat producer, b) a Nova Scotia fishing company, c) a British importer of agricultural products, d) a tool-manufacturing company in Montréal. Use the notes in your Consider Both Sides chart to support your answers.

Conflicting Maritime Views on Joining the British North American Colonies

We now know that the British North American colonies were joined into a single country, Canada. Do you think everyone wanted this to happen? One of the important jobs of historians is to examine old documents to see how people felt about the great issues of the day.

When they examine records about joining the colonies, historians have found that there were great differences of opinion on the subject. They have also found that while some people argued in a reasonable tone, others took an emotional approach. Some were respectful of their opponents, while others could be discourteous. Look at the following extracts.

[Those who support joining the colonies] are a few ambitious individuals, who feel our legislature too small for their capacity, and its rewards too [small] for their acceptance... [They want to] enjoy fat salaries far away from the provinces whose best interests are to be shamefully voted away in return for [two weeks of] feasting and a few private promises.

Halifax Citizen, November 26, 1864

That... Canada [and] the Maritime Provinces can [only] ever attain real greatness... in such a combination as is now proposed, [can] be seen by anybody in the least acquainted with the position they occupy relatively to each other...

[W]here, I would ask can [opponents of joining the colonies] expect to find another Nova Scotian who would be content with a position of isolation so utterly fatal to [the colony's] progress... [to which... as the Atlantic frontage of British America, [it] may now look confidently forward?

Charles Tupper, 1866

THINKING It Over

1. Read the two extracts carefully. Note the position of each writer on the future of British North America and the reasons given. Think about the tone of each extract and identify wording that indicates the writer's bias. Answer the questions in an organizer like this one. 🅣 🅐

Comparison	Extract 1	Extract 2
In favour or opposed to joining		
Reasons given for this position		
My assessment on the arguments used. (Reasoned or emotional? Respectful or discourteous?)		

Among the people of the colonies, there was a wide range of attitudes about the best way forward. Some were concerned about religious freedom, others focused on land rights, and still others wanted to preserve historical ties. Consider the following groups. Do they share the same attitudes? Compare and contrast the differences between them.

Group	Location	Attitude
Mi'kmaq	Nova Scotia New Brunswick	Concerned about the significant loss of reserve lands to settlers who wanted the best lands for agriculture and water access.
Acadians	Nova Scotia New Brunswick	Not supportive of Britain after their expulsion from the region in the 1750s. Identified with North America. Most would be happy to be independent.
Loyalists	Nova Scotia New Brunswick Canada East Canada West	Ancestors came to the area from the United States in the 1780s. Wanted to preserve British ties for which their ancestors had risked their lives.
People of African descent	Nova Scotia Canada West	Were usually descended from Loyalists and escaped slaves. Wanted to preserve the British connection and not get taken over by the U.S.
People of British descent	Nova Scotia New Brunswick Canada East Canada West	The largest group in the colonies. Wanted to preserve ties with Britain either as colonies or as an independent nation.
Cree, Haudenosaunee, Ojibwe, and other First Nations	Canada East Canada West	Had fought for British against Americans in 1780s and 1810s. Were forced to leave the U.S. and settle in Canada. Hoped British would protect them, but had seen many of the best lands taken away from them.
French Canadians	Canada East	Had mixed opinions about British. Not particularly loyal to Britain. Would welcome independence, but fearful of being swamped by too many English-speaking people in a larger country.
Irish	All of British North America	Catholic Irish disliked British treatment of Ireland and wanted the colonies to be independent. Protestant Irish supported the British connection.

THINKING It Over

1. Which groups generally supported the British connection? Which groups generally opposed it?

2. Based on this evidence, how likely is it that the people of the colonies could be persuaded to support an independent Canada that retained some of its British connections? Share your ideas in a paragraph.

Transportation in British North America

Problems with the Existing Transportation System

How do you think colonists transported their goods for export? The existing transportation system consisted mainly of canals, lakes, rivers, and railways. There were a few roads, but these were of poor quality and were impassable for much of the year, as they were covered with snow in winter and coated with mud in the spring.

The canals and railways were designed to get goods to ports where they could be shipped to Britain and the United States. They were not designed to support internal trade among the colonies. If British North America was to establish an internal trade, it would need an efficient railway system to transport goods among the colonies. The timeline on page H 38 shows some of the highlights of railway building in British North America to this point.

During READING

Checkpoint
Why might effective transportation methods and routes be a reason to sign the British North America Act? Remember to write notes in your organizer.

WEB LINK •••••••••••••••••••••
For more information on the Intercolonial Railway, visit our Web site.

Difficulty in Completing the Intercolonial Railway

Large gaps in the railway system prevented East–West trade from growing. Some political leaders in the Canadas had ties to railway companies. George-Étienne Cartier from Canada East, and Alexander Galt from Canada West were examples of this. They were disappointed to see that the Grand Trunk Railway, which linked Toronto and Montréal, was not doing well financially. There did not seem to be enough passenger and freight traffic within the Canadas for the railway to make profits.

However, if the Intercolonial Railway were extended westward from the Maritimes to Montréal, they thought, traffic on the Grand Trunk would rise. Nova Scotia fish could be shipped all the way to Toronto and Sarnia for sale. Manufactured goods from the Canadas could be shipped to Saint John and Halifax for sale. Passenger traffic would go up, too. The Grand Trunk would make large profits.

Alexander Galt

First railway station in Niagara Falls, 1859

Grand Trunk Railway historic map, around 1900

Grand Trunk Railway train, Montréal, 1910

1818

- The first rail tracks are laid for a tram in Pictou, Nova Scotia. The tram cars, pulled by horses, are used to move coal from a mine.

1835

- Construction of the first steam-powered railway begins. The Champlain and St. Lawrence Railroad connects Lake Champlain in New York state with Montréal.

1839

- There are 16 km of horse-drawn railways around Niagara Falls.

1850

- There are 106 km of railway track in the Canadas.

1853

- The Grand Trunk Railway begins construction of a railway between Toronto and Montréal.

1854

- The Great Western Railway (registered in 1834) completed a line from Niagara Falls, through Hamilton and London, to Windsor.

1858

- The Intercolonial Railway begins in Nova Scotia, with a line from Halifax to Truro.

1859

- The Victoria Bridge over the St. Lawrence in Montréal opens, carrying trains across the river. The Mohawk nation helped build the bridge.

1860

- A section of the Intercolonial is built in New Brunswick from Saint John to Shediac. It is not extended farther because of a lack of money. There are 3200 km of railway track in the Canadas.

To complete the Intercolonial, investors would have to borrow large sums of money in London. The British banks were unwilling to lend the money unless they were certain the loans would be repaid. Baring Brothers, one of the largest British banks, thought that uniting the colonies would make them stronger and make repayment of the loans more certain. Barings stated that it would not lend any money for the Intercolonial as long as the colonies remained separate.

Manufacturers in the Canadas supported the Intercolonial. It would give them new markets in the Maritimes for their products. Food producers in the Maritimes were also in favour of the Intercolonial. They could see their goods selling in the larger markets of the Canadas. Many people's prosperity seemed to depend on completing the Intercolonial, and joining the colonies seemed to be a requirement for completing the Intercolonial.

THINKING It Over

1. What was it about the existing railway system in British North America that made it unsuitable for supporting an internal East-West trading system? *k t*

2. Which of the following would be likely to support completion of the Intercolonial Railway? Explain the reasons why each group you select would support it. *t c k*

   • the United States government

   • a lumber producer in New Brunswick

   • a stove manufacturing factory in Sarnia, Canada West

   • a store owner in Vancouver, B.C.

   • a British bank

   • a shareholder in the Grand Trunk Railway

3. Select one of the groups from question 2. Prepare either a letter to the editor or a short speech persuading others to agree with your view of the railway. *c a t*

4. Do you think First Nations supported the railway? Why or why not? *k a t*

Defence Issues

During *READING*

Checkpoint

How might the actions of the Fenians be a reason for or against signing the British North America Act? Record your ideas in your organizer.

During the War of 1812 (1812–1814), British North America successfully defended its colonies against the United States. For the next 50 years, the colonies were relatively secure from outside threats. Then a number of issues arose, forcing the colonies to re-examine their security.

Britain Begins to Withdraw Its Troops

Britain stationed troops all over the world to make its colonies secure. However, it was expensive to maintain these troops overseas. British politicians began to look for cheaper alternatives. With steam-powered ships, it was possible to send troops overseas more quickly than it had been a century earlier. They decided to maintain a skeleton defence force in the colonies and ship troops rapidly from Britain when needed. Do you think they were making a wise choice? Why or why not?

Britain became involved in a war with Russia, known as the Crimean War (1854–1856). The British used their strategy of lining soldiers in three ranks and not firing a shot until enemy troops advanced. This was a development of the strategy Wolfe used at Québec in 1759. It was now called the "Thin Red Line." The Crimean military effort drained troops from British North America, where Britain regarded the threat of war as slim.

How could the colonies defend themselves if they were invaded? British withdrawals made them feel less secure. There were too many colonies in British North America to develop a single defence strategy. Would joining the colonies into a single country allow them to better defend themselves?

This painting depicts the Charge of the British Light Cavalry Brigade, a group of allied troops from Britain and France who attacked the Russians at Balaclava during the Crimean War (1854–1856).

The Fenians

The Fenian Brotherhood was an Irish organization that used armed rebellion in their attempt to gain independence from Britain. Between 1847 and 1861, more than 2 million Irish people crossed the Atlantic to live in North America, especially the United States. This was part of the Great Migration that you read about in Chapter 1. The **Fenians** felt that Britain had treated Ireland very badly and brought misery to its people. What better way to gain revenge than to hurt British interests in the U.S. and British North America?

The Fenians began to organize local groups in the U.S., especially in northern states. The U.S. government did not try to stop the Fenians because some politicians thought they might be helpful in the event of an American invasion of British North America.

The people of British North America worried that the Fenians would invade. Some towns organized Committees of Safety to search for Fenian invaders. For example, Welland, in Canada West, organized such a group to protect the famous Welland Canal. The Six Nations chiefs were ready to provide men to defend the Crown's interests.

Few invasions occurred. In 1866, at Pigeon Hill, several hundred Fenians invaded Canada East from Vermont. They advanced 10 km but found no soldiers to fight. When they heard that colonial troops were on their way to intercept them, they retreated. Sixteen Fenians were captured and the rest were disarmed by American troops as they crossed back into Vermont.

WEB LINK • • • • • • • • • • • • • • • •
For more information on the Fenians, visit our Web site.

The military camp of the 60th Battalion at Pigeon Hill, Québec

Not all the Fenian attacks were so ineffective. They were prepared to use violence. In 1868, Thomas D'Arcy McGee was shot and killed in the streets of Ottawa. He was a politician of Irish origin who bitterly opposed the Fenians. The man convicted of his murder was believed to be a Fenian. Even before D'Arcy McGee's murder, politicians in the colonies had begun to wonder if a united country could better defend itself against threats like the Fenians.

Huge crowds turned out for the funeral procession of Thomas D'Arcy McGee, who was believed to have been killed by a Fenian.

Manifest Destiny

In 1861, the United States erupted into civil war. The North (known as the Union) fought the South (the Confederacy) over whether slavery should be legal in the U.S. Slavery had already been abolished in the British Empire in 1833.

The North was opposed to slavery for economic as well as moral reasons. Slavery allowed the South to produce agricultural goods at exceptionally low prices. The North **exploited** immigrant labour to keep its costs down. In the end, however, its production costs were still higher than those of the South.

The war increased tensions between the Union and British North America. In 1861, a naval incident almost brought Britain and the Union to war when an American warship stopped a British merchant ship and mail vessel (the *Trent*) on the high seas and captured two representatives of the Confederacy. For a time, war between Britain and the United States was a possibility. If this happened, British North America would inevitably be dragged into such a war. Later in the Civil War, agents of the Confederacy used Toronto and Montréal as bases to organize plots against the Union. The government in Washington demanded that the colonies should increase border security.

The Union was larger and more powerful than the Confederacy. By 1864, it had become obvious that the Union would win the war. When that happened, would the Union try to settle its scores against British North America? Some American politicians supported **Manifest Destiny**, the belief that the United States had a duty to take over all the land of North America. There was a feeling in the colonies that the Americans might use this principle as an excuse to invade the colonies at the end of the Civil War. This was just another factor that encouraged British North American politicians to consider joining the colonies into a larger organization—a single country.

WEB LINK •••••••••••••••••••
For more information on the U.S. Civil War or on Manifest Destiny, visit our Web site.

The American warship, the *San Jacinto* vessel stopping the *Trent*.

THINKING It Over

1. Complete an organizer like the one below, summarizing what you have learned in this section. *k c t*

2. In a paragraph, explain which of the three items examined in this section you think would have been the most important factor encouraging the colonies to work together. Explain the reasons for your choice. *t c*

Item	Important Facts	How It Encouraged British North America to Think About Creating a Single Country
Britain's withdrawal of colonial troops		
The Fenian raids		
The American Civil War		

Were the Fenians in North America Freedom Fighters or Terrorists?

Violence has sometimes been used for political gain. In Grade 7, you learned that Americans gained independence from Britain through armed revolution. Today, in many countries around the world, there are armed struggles for political purposes. Are the people involved in such struggles terrorists, using force illegally? Or are they freedom fighters, struggling for their cause or for the independence of their people?

The Fenians as Freedom Fighters

The Fenians justified their actions by saying that Britain had taken over Ireland by force around 1600. The British then imposed their way of life on the Irish. The British kept most of the wealth and all political control for themselves.

The only way to gain independence for the Irish people, the Fenians said, was to use force against the British, even if it meant attacking British North American colonies. Some innocent civilians in the colonies might die; that was the price to pay for the freedom of people in Ireland.

The Fenians saw themselves as freedom fighters. They felt they had just cause. They believed that this permitted them to use armed struggle to pursue their political goals.

The Fenians as Terrorists

Terrorism involves using illegal force to create terror in order to achieve a political goal. Many British North Americans believed the Fenians were terrorists. People in the colonies had nothing to do with the situation in Ireland, they said. Solving the problems that existed there should be a matter between the people of Ireland and the people of Britain. There was no justification for the Fenians to invade the BNA colonies from the U.S. Some innocent people died in the Fenian raids, critics pointed out. The invasions were illegal. For these reasons, many people felt that the Fenians were terrorists.

FREEDOM TO IRELAND.

The woman in this image symbolizes freedom to Ireland. Maidens wielding swords were historically used as symbols of liberty.

What Do YOU Think?

1. In point form, summarize the arguments for each side. **k**

2. Explain which view of the Fenians in North America you favour and why. **t** **a**

Political Issues Affecting the Canadas

When the Canadas were united in 1841, they established one legislature to pass laws for both colonies. The capital of the Canadas moved from place to place: Kingston, Montréal, Toronto, and Québec City. In 1857, Queen Victoria chose Ottawa as the permanent capital, and a new parliament building opened there in 1866. There were four major political parties in the new Parliament, as the organizer below shows. Which of these parties do you think were most likely to work together?

During READING

Checkpoint
Read the following section and add any relevant points to your Consider Both Sides organizer.

Name	Active in	Leader	Position on the political problems
Conservatives ("Tories")	Canada West	John A. Macdonald	Join BNA into a union based on representation by population
Liberals ("Grits")	Canada West	George Brown	Reform the union of the Canadas by adopting representation by population
Bleus	Canada East	George-Étienne Cartier	Work with Conservatives to join BNA if Canada East gets power over religion and family law
Rouges	Canada East	Antoine-Aimé Dorion	Join Canada East into the U.S. and reduce the power of the Church in political life

The Representation Issue

There was a flaw in the way the Canadas had been united. Each colony had the same number of seats in the legislature. This was called **equal representation**. It worked reasonably well until the population of Canada West began to rise much more quickly than that of Canada East. What does the following table show?

WEB LINK •••••••••••••••••••••••
For more information about political parties and leaders before Confederation, visit our Web site.

WORDS MATTER

equal representation each region has the same number of elected representatives

Colony	Population 1851 Census	Population 1861 Census	Seats in Legislature
Canada East	890 261	1 111 566	65
Canada West	952 004	1 396 091	65

The House of Commons, Ottawa, 2004

WORDS MATTER

representation by population
the number of elected
representatives is determined
by the size of the population in
the region represented

George Brown

    Some politicians from Canada West began to say that this was unfair. Their colony had more people than Canada East did, therefore it should have more seats in the legislature. This is called **representation by population**. These politicians began to press for representation by population. They calculated that if Canada East had 65 seats, Canada West should have 81 seats. They argued that Canada West should immediately get 16 additional seats. Three politicians became important as the debate raged. They were George Brown and John A. Macdonald from Canada West, and George-Étienne Cartier from Canada East.

George Brown ⊳ canada west.

The leading supporter of representation by population was George Brown. As owner of the *Globe*, Toronto's largest newspaper, he used its pages to write articles about the issue. In 1851, he entered politics, becoming a representative for the Toronto area in the legislature. He made fiery speeches there for representation by population.

George-Étienne Cartier

George-Étienne Cartier was a lawyer from Montréal who entered the legislature in 1848. When representation by population became a major issue, he became a strong enemy of the proposal. The **Canadiens** were already a minority in the Canadas and in the legislature, he said (because not all the Canada East citizens or representatives were of French extraction). Canada West was largely English-speaking. So giving it more seats would only increase the English majority in the legislature. English Canada might use its increased powers to push through the new laws that were harmful to French society. The Canadiens would never agree to this, Cartier said. Cartier and Brown became bitter political enemies as they fought over this issue.

George-Étienne Cartier

John A. Macdonald

John A. Macdonald was a lawyer from Kingston who had gained a reputation for fairness and political skill. He entered the legislature in 1844. Macdonald recognized that the fiery speeches of Brown and Cartier were not going to solve the representation by population issue. He realized that what Cartier really wanted was to ensure protection for the Canadiens, their language, and their customs, not to preserve the voting system. Macdonald eventually saw a better solution, one that might give both Brown and Cartier what each really wanted: representation by population for Brown, and protection for the Canadiens for Cartier. You will learn in the following chapter how Macdonald accomplished this.

WORDS MATTER

Canadiens Canadians of French descent

riding the area represented by an elected official

proportional representation a voting system in which a political party gets the same proportion of seats in government as the proportion of votes it received

referendum a vote by the citizens on a proposed government action

The Representation Issue Today

Under the traditional Canadian voting system, in each **riding**, the candidate who gets the most votes wins. This often leads to a political party getting the majority of seats even though it may not have the majority of votes. For example, if Candidate A gets 40 percent of the votes, Candidate B gets 25 percent, and Candidate C gets 35 percent, Candidate A wins even though 60 percent of the people who voted did not vote for her or him. Some reformers want to introduce **proportional representation**, under which a party getting, for example, 40 percent of the votes, gets that number of the seats. In 2007, a **referendum** was held and Ontario voters rejected a version of this system.

These voters are acting as "Doctors of Democracy," encouraging the reform of Ontario's electoral system. They support a mixed-member proportional (MMP) voting system, which is a form of proportional representation.

Stalemate in the Legislature

Politicians from Canada West wanted to improve transportation systems to increase trade between the Canadas. They wanted canals and railways expanded. Politicians from Canada East, however, did not feel that such improvements were necessary. Because Canada East and Canada West each had the same number of seats, the issue could not be properly solved. Every time a major bill came to debate in the legislature, politicians from the Canadas debated and voted each other into political deadlock.

Macdonald was trying to keep together a union that had been fragile ever since its controversial beginning with Lord Durham and his report, which you learned about in Grade 7. Macdonald desperately wanted all sides to work together—English and French, Canada West and Canada East. How could he find the solution?

Who Was Left Out of the Discussions?

Women were largely left out of all political life at this time. They were not allowed to vote, and could not hold government office. This lack of representation made it difficult for women to have their issues addressed by politicians. Many women were interested in political matters, however, and discussed issues with their husbands and friends. In this way, their ideas might have had indirect influence.

Similarly, Aboriginal people were left out of public life and political affairs. Traditional First Nations culture did not believe in individual property ownership, so they generally did not own land. Nor were they generally regarded as British subjects. Since both property ownership and citizenship were requirements for voting, many First Nations were excluded from this right. As a result, the views and hopes of many First Nations were largely ignored during the discussions about the future of British North America.

Things have since changed. During the 1980s, when Canada's Constitution was reformed, women and Aboriginal people were consulted. The new Constitution includes protection and consideration for both groups, as well as many others that had previously been ignored.

THINKING It Over

1. Imagine you are one of the following people: a) George Brown, b) George-Étienne Cartier, or c) John A. Macdonald. Write a speech to explain your position on the representation issue.

2. With a partner, discuss which politician had the best position on the representation issue.

3. Think about the representation of First Nations people in parliament. Even though First Nations were consulted during the constitution reform process in the 1980s, they do not have guaranteed representation in parliament. Why? Discuss your views in a small group.

Aboriginal People and Government

Then

Politicians regarded the First Nations as outsiders with no real interests in what was decided about the future of British North America. First Nations representatives did not take part in the decisions that were eventually made.

The federal government became responsible for the affairs of First Nations people and the lands reserved for them.

In unit 2, you will learn that the federal government used its powers to force First Nations to sign treaties. These treaties relocated First Nations onto reserves, often with poor land quality. For generations, First Nations people have struggled to regain the rights to their lands and for better representation. Though all Aboriginal rights have not yet been addressed, people remain hopeful with recent developments.

The men shown in this painting are often referred to as the "Fathers of Confederation." Analyze this image. How does it support the text above it?

Now

In 1999, the Northwest Territories was divided into two and the territory of Nunavut was created. Nunavut is the largest administrative area in Canada, but has a population of only about 31 000 people. More than 80 percent of the population is Inuit. "Nunavut" means "Our Land" in Inuktitut, the main language of the area. Nunavut elected its own territorial government, which delivers government programs to the people.

In 2007, the governments of Québec and Canada signed an agreement recognizing a new administrative region in northern Québec called Nunavik. It is home to about 10 000 Inuit in 14 remote communities.

Nunavik is not a separate territory, but it will have many of the same powers as a territory. It will receive provincial funding to deliver provincial services such as education and health care, just as Nunavut, Yukon, and the Northwest Territories receive federal funding to deliver such programs.

The creation of Nunavut and Nunavik shows that Canada is striving to find better ways to deliver services to First Nations. It more importantly acknowledges self-governance and shows that the North is becoming an increasingly important part of the nation's development.

The Inuit culture of the Nunavut government is reflected in details such as the ceremonial mace, made of a narwhal tusk.

What You Will Need

- a game board (provided by your teacher)
- one list of Key Developments (provided by your teacher)
- 2 counters of different colours
- 1 die
- a coloured pencil or marker of your choice

How to Play

A. Work with a partner. Imagine it is the mid-1860s. One of you represents George Brown, the other represents George-Étienne Cartier. You are competing to see who can win the political struggle over representation in the legislature.

B. On the game board, colour the squares as shown on the mini game board below.

C. Place your counters on START. Take turns rolling the dice and move your counter the number of squares you roll. If you roll a 6, you loose your turn.

D. If you land on a coloured square, look at the Key Developments item for that number. Follow the instructions given for that square.

How to Win

Play the game until someone reaches the YOU WIN! square. You do not need to roll the exact number to land on the YOU WIN! square. After the game, discuss the Thinking It Over questions with your partner.

								YOU WIN!
4	5	12	13	20	21	28	29	36
3	6	11	14	19	22	27	30	35
2	7	10	15	18	23	26	31	34
1	8	9	16	17	24	25	32	33

START

THINKING It Over

1. Why do you think players had to lose a turn if they rolled a 6?

2. Which Key Developments made Brown more likely to win? Cartier? Explain your choices.

3. What two additions would you make to the Key Developments so that they better illustrate the factors or events involved in the representation by population issue?

PUTTING IT ALL TOGETHER

You have learned that in the mid-1800s, some politicians began to think about uniting the BNA colonies into a single country. There were internal reasons, such as the desire to build a railway to increase trade and the challenge of political deadlock in the legislature. There were external factors as well. These included security issues. Another external factor was Britain's move to reduce the favoured treatment in colonial trade. Finally, you learned that people had different points of view about the best solution to the challenges faced by the colonies. It still was not known if political leaders could unite the colonies.

After **READING**

Synthesizing Information

Review your completed Consider Both Sides organizer. With a partner, have a mini-debate.

Debate the reasons for and against signing the British North America Act. Together, reach the best decision. Record the main reasons for your choice.

CONSIDER BOTH SIDES: Should the Colonies Sign the BNA Act?				
Colony or Region	Evidence that Supports	Evidence that Opposes	Decision	Reasons

THINKING It Through

Think of four questions that will help guide your inquiry about the two colonies' attitudes toward joining together. Use primary and secondary materials to research (see pages S 4 and S 5 in the Skills Tool Kit for help with primary and secondary sources). You are going to compare Canada West with one of the Maritime colonies. Select one of the following colonies.

- Prince Edward Island

- New Brunswick

- Nova Scotia

1. Locate and use some primary and secondary materials to research the two colonies' attitudes

toward joining the colonies together (see pages S 4 and S 5 in Skills Tool Kit for help with primary and secondary sources). Create a decision-making chart showing the advantages and disadvantages of joining for each colony. Consider both internal and external factors. **k** **t**

2. Create a display board in which you present the results of your findings. Include some visual items as well as text items. Some of these can be illustrations or extracts from primary materials. **c**

3. Use as many key terms as possible in your display. **c**

CHAPTER 3

The Events of Confederation

Every year, people celebrate Canada Day on Parliament Hill in Ottawa.

Before **READING**

Making Connections

Brainstorm some concerns you have about your neighbourhood, or think about how you could celebrate your neighbourhood.

- How would you get people together? What might get in the way of bringing them together? How might you solve your concerns?
- Create a poster to convince people to help you. Include a symbol that represents your neighbourhood and the issue being resolved.

Why do you think Canada celebrates its birthday on July 1? On that day in 1867, the country of Canada was created. Nova Scotia, New Brunswick, Québec, and Ontario merged when the leaders signed the British North America Act.

Considering what you have learned in chapters 1 and 2, why might this day never have happened? People in each colony could not always agree and had different ideas about issues, such as taxes and transportation. Another challenge was that people spoke different languages and had different beliefs and values. In order for the colonies to unite, political leaders had to convince the people that forming one country would be beneficial to everyone. Would you predict that the union came about with agreement and cooperation, or with disagreement and conflict? Why?

In 1867, crowds gathered in Market Square, Kingston, to hear the proclamation announcing Confederation.

Questions to Consider as You Read this Chapter

You will explore these aspects of the Unit 1 Big Idea: **Why did some of the colonies put aside differences and create a new country— Canada?**

- How were the politicians able to join the colonies together?

- How did the map of Canada change?

- How were the responsibilities of government divided between the federal and provincial governments? How is this organization reflected in our present-day government?

Title/Number	Page Number	Who/What?	How?	Where/When?	Important? Explain.	Interesting?

In 1820, five-year-old John A. Macdonald emigrated to Canada from Glasgow, Scotland. The family settled in Kingston Ontario.

TRAGEDY STRIKES

John experienced many personal tragedies in his life. When he was seven, he witnessed the traumatic killing of his younger brother.

James!

By the age of 15, John was apprenticing with a Kingston lawyer. Intelligent and driven, by age 21, he had his own law practice. As a teenager, John drank heavily. This was the beginning of a lifelong abuse of alcohol.

In 1837, John served in the volunteer militia and helped to put down William Lyon Mackenzie's rebels at the Battle of Montgomery's Tavern [also known as the Bar Fight on Yonge Street] during the Upper Canada Rebellion.

In 1843, the year John entered politics, he married Isabella Clark. They had two sons, but their first born, Alexander, died at 13 months. Sick most of their married life, Isabella became addicted to opium and died in 1857.

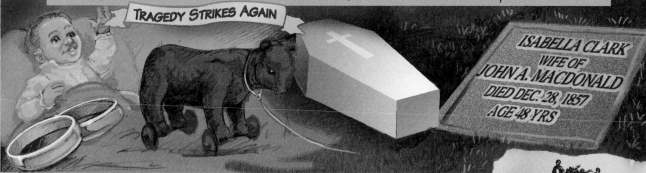

TRAGEDY STRIKES AGAIN

ISABELLA CLARK
WIFE OF
JOHN A. MACDONALD
DIED DEC. 28, 1857
AGE 48 YRS

John worked hard to build support for the idea of Confederation. In 1867, his dream came true.

CONFEDERATION!

John was knighted on July 1, 1867.

In the year of Confederation, John married Susan Agnes Bernard. Their daughter Mary was born with physical and mental disabilities. John doted on his daughter, reading to her every night before dinner, and even taking her to Parliament to listen to his speeches.

Baboo, shall we read this one again?

PROCLAMATION!

WHEREAS, THE
Honorable Thomas D'Arcy McGee
A Member of the House of Commons of the Dominion of Canada, was FOULLY ASSASSINATED IN THIS CITY, on the MORNING of the SEVENTH DAY of APRIL, 1868, in accordance with a Resolution of the CORPORATION of Ottawa, I, HENRY JAMES FRIEL, Mayor of the City of Ottawa, hereby offer a Reward of

REWARD
OF
$2000

For the Apprehension and Prosecution to Conviction of ...
I hereby also offer a further sum of
TWO T...

On April 7, 1868, John came home with blood on his clothes from carrying the body of his good friend D'Arcy McGee, murdered for his support of Confederation.

Macdonald championed a national policy of industrialization, railway building, and western settlement. He was accused of accepting bribes from contractors.

– and the fate of Canada will then, as a Dominion, be sealed.

Sir John A. Macdonald served as prime minister from 1867–1873 and 1878–1891.

CANADIAN PACIFIC SCANDAL

John sent this telegram to Hugh Allan, which revealed his part in the bribery scandal. The telegram read...

Ottawa, July 14th 1872

I must have another $10,000. Will be the last time of calling. Do not fail me. Answer today.

THE LAST SPIKE

Once the railroad was completed, the Macdonald cabinet imposed a head tax to limit Chinese immigration. In 2006, the Canadian government apologised for this policy.

When fortune empties her chamber pot on your head, smile and say 'we are going to have a summer shower.'

1875

James died Monday, 22 April at 20 minutes 6 o'clock p.m.

John's father had always refused to record John's little brother's death in the family book. Years later, John finally wrote these simple words about the brother whose death affected his life so greatly.

When John and his cabinet made the final decision to hang Louis Riel, John is known to have said...

"He shall hang though every dog in Québec bark in his favour."

John once told his private secretary, Joseph Pope...

I never had a childhood.

A man of great vision and many sorrows, Sir John A. Macdonald's accomplishments had a huge impact on Canada.

Creating a Nation

During **READING**

Checkpoint

Skimming means you are reading quickly across the lines, looking for main ideas and details. Scanning means that you are zigzagging up and down the page—most useful when you are looking for something specific, like a date, or a boldfaced word or name. Scan for visuals and subheadings to add information to your organizer.

In the early 1860s, the colonies of British North America were weak and isolated. Most colonists were keen to retain ties with Britain. They saw the United States as a threat, and were not sure how they could defend themselves without Britain. Then, in 1864, events relating to British North America's future began to move quickly toward unification. During the next three years, the structure of modern Canada began to emerge.

The Charlottetown Conference

In September 1864, the Maritime colonies held a **conference** in Charlottetown, Prince Edward Island, to discuss the idea of a Maritime union. British Columbia and Newfoundland were not invited. The Canadas were not Maritime colonies, but the leading politicians from the Canadas managed to get an invitation. Representatives from P.E.I., New Brunswick, and Nova Scotia met with representatives from the Canadas. The Canadians soon persuaded the Maritimers to give up their original plans. Instead, John A. Macdonald and his colleagues got them to consider a union with the Canadas.

The delegates at the conference agreed to support the idea of joining the Canadas and the Maritime colonies together. They also decided to meet again to discuss the plan further.

WORDS MATTER

conference a meeting for discussion of information or ideas

Women were not directly involved in the Confederation conferences. In the evenings, the wives and daughters of the delegates joined the men for dinners and dances, such as the one shown in this painting called *Ball at Legislature* by Dusan Kadlec. How might this kind of socializing help the men agree on important issues?

The Québec Conference

In October 1864, representatives of the colonies held a second conference in Québec City. This time Newfoundland attended as well, but British Columbia was too far away to be included. At Charlottetown, they had agreed to the principle of joining the colonies, but they had not discussed the details of how this would be done. In Québec City, they met for three weeks and worked out the rules for sharing power in the new country.

At the end of the conference, the delegates voted mostly in favour of the Québec Resolutions. These contained the details of how the new country would work. The following is a list of some of the features of Canada's government:

- A **federal** constitution. This meant there would be a government for the whole country, as well as for each province.

- Each level of government would be responsible for specific areas. For instance, **Indian** affairs were federal, whereas education was provincial, etc.

- In parliament, there would be a balance of representation by population and equal representation.

- There would be a balance between elected and appointed representatives.

John A. Macdonald was the main influence in the writing of these resolutions. In the parliament of the Canadas, he won support for the plan, with 91 votes in favour and 33 opposed.

Missing Voices

As had been the case in the Canadas in the 1850s, politicians paid no attention to First Nations' or black people's concerns. The politicians were men from Britain, Ireland, or France. They envisioned a Canada that would look very much like those countries. Parliament, the courts, the education system, and virtually everything else would be modelled after British and European examples.

Women were also ignored in the discussions, although they made up about half the population. Remember from Chapter 2 that women did not have any political representation. Although unfair, these groups were largely ignored in the discussions.

CANADA MINUTE

The Great Coalition
A coalition is a group of people, often political opponents, who agree to work together for a common goal. George Brown and John A. Macdonald, both Fathers of Confederation, disliked one another, but, in 1864, Brown put aside his personal feelings and offered to work together with Macdonald to find a solution to the colonies' problems. Later politicians have done the same thing. During times of war, political opponents have put aside their differences to work toward peace.

The resolutions that the Fathers of Confederation adopted laid the foundations for the way Canadian government is run to this day.

Opposition to the Québec Resolutions

Opinion was divided as to whether the Québec Resolutions were a good idea. Antoine-Aimé Dorion was the leader of Canada East's *Rouge* party. He believed that the proposals would lead to the destruction of the French culture in what would become Québec. Dorion wanted a referendum—vote by the people—on the plan for union, something Macdonald opposed. Dorion said:

> *If confederation should be adopted without the people of this province's sanction, the entire country will sorely learn to regret it.*

A young lawyer named Wilfrid Laurier wrote:

> *Twenty-five years ago the French nation… was more vigorous, more united, strongly French… Today it is… without strength, [and] divided… We must use all the influence we have left to obtain a free and separate government.*

Antoine-Aimé Dorion

In the Maritimes, there was even more opposition. Joseph Howe was a journalist and politician from Halifax. He helped Nova Scotia to win responsible government in 1848 and was premier of that province from 1860 to 1863. While the **Confederation** conferences were being held, he was leader of the opposition to Nova Scotia's joining Confederation. He argued that the population was not being fully consulted, and that Nova Scotia would be overwhelmed by the larger provinces of Ontario and Québec. Howe also felt that the Canadas were too far away from Halifax for the union to be successful. He wrote in the *Halifax Chronicle*:

> *Did anybody ever propose to unite Scotland with Poland or Hungary? [They are] [i]nland countries [1300 km] off in the very heart of Europe.*

Joseph Howe

Attitudes toward Confederation depended on the local concerns of each colony. Governments and people were often in conflict about the wisdom of the proposal. The following organizer summarizes the main issues in each of the colonies.

Colony	Government Leader	Attitude Toward Confederation
The Canadas	John A. Macdonald and George-Étienne Cartier	Strongly in favour. Saw it as a way to expand the domestic economy and provide better defence against the U.S.
Nova Scotia	Charles Tupper	In favour, but in the Nova Scotia assembly his opponents defeated his request for support of the Resolutions.
New Brunswick	Leonard Tilley	In favour. His party was defeated in the assembly in 1865 when it asked for a vote for Confederation. Tilley became premier again in 1866 and led New Brunswick into Confederation even though there was widespread opposition among voters.
Prince Edward Island	James Pope	In favour, if the new government would pay $800 000 to buy out the absentee landlords. The Liberal opposition called this bribery, and defeated Pope in 1867. The new government refused to join Confederation.
Newfoundland	Frederick Carter	In favour, but did not press the issue when civil disorder broke out over other issues in 1865. In 1869, he was defeated in an election by the Anti-Confederation party. Newfoundlanders feared that their traditional way of life would be undermined in Confederation.

The London Conference

In December 1866, representatives of Canada West, Canada East, New Brunswick, and Nova Scotia travelled to London, England. Newfoundland had dropped out of the discussions. The delegates took part in a conference with British officials about the future of the colonies. The colonial secretary, Lord Carnarvon, said of the conference's work

> *We are laying the foundation of a great State... perhaps one which at a future day may even overshadow [Britain]. But, come what may, we shall rejoice that we have shown neither indifference to their wishes nor jealousy of their aspirations.*

Lord Carnarvon. Predict reasons why you think he said the Canadas "may even overshadow [Britain]." How did you reach your conclusion?

Agreement was reached easily and Canada became Britain's first "self-governing Dominion." Canada retained the monarchy, and its membership in the British Empire. Since the king or queen had no real power in government, the monarchy remained a symbol and nothing more.

Canada had control over its internal affairs, but Britain would have control over foreign policy, meaning that Britain would negotiate with other countries on Canada's behalf. This situation continued until 1923. The conference delegates decided that Britain would continue to be responsible for any changes to the constitution of Canada, but only at the request of the Canadian parliament. It was not until 1982 that this power was officially handed over to Canada. As you can see, Canada was not entirely independent in 1867; however, it made some important steps in that direction.

Confederation

On July 1, 1867, a new country was born. The Dominion of Canada contained four provinces: Ontario, Québec, New Brunswick, and Nova Scotia. Queen Victoria had already chosen Ottawa as the capital of the Canadas, and a new parliament building had opened there in 1866. These now became the capital and parliament of the new nation.

Canada, 1867

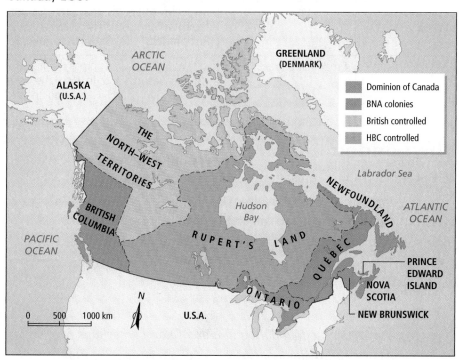

On that first "Canada Day," there were celebrations in many locations. Canons were fired, bands played, and fireworks exploded. The future looked bright. It would take much effort, however, to make Canada a prosperous and united nation. The rest of Sir John A. Macdonald's life, until he died in 1891, was dedicated to that goal.

THINKING It Over

1. Create and complete an organizer to show the dates, representatives attending, and key features of the Charlottetown Conference, the Québec Conference, and the London Conference. How does knowing this information help you better understand Canada's political landscape today?

2. Look at the quotations from Antoine-Aimé Dorion, Wilfrid Laurier, Joseph Howe, and Lord Carnarvon. Rewrite what each said in your own words. Whose opinion comes closest to your own opinion about the Confederation of Canada? Why?

The British North America Act, 1867

The **act** that made Canada independent was originally called the British North America Act (BNA Act). In 1982, it was renamed the Constitution Act, 1867. Historians still use the old name to describe the events of Confederation.

Features of Canada's New Government

The BNA Act set the government up in the following manner:

Item	Details
A federal system	There would be a parliament for the whole country, plus a legislature for each province.
Bilingual features	French and English would be the languages of parliament, plus the legislature of Québec.
A balance of representation by population and equal representation	Parliament would have two houses. There would be representation by population in the **House of Commons**. In the **Senate**, each region (Ontario, Québec, and the Maritimes) would have the same number of seats.
A balance between elected and appointed representatives	The House of Commons would be elected by voters; the Senate would be appointed by the prime minister.

Having two levels of government could be difficult unless each level understood which areas it was responsible for. Look at the chart on page H 62. Sections 91, 92, and 93 of the BNA Act clearly laid out what the various responsibilities were.

The provinces were given powers that were considered less important in 1867. However, two of these—health care and education—have become very significant. Why do you think Macdonald did not want to give the provinces too much power?

During READING

Checkpoint
Review the questions on page H 53. Look for answers as you skim and scan this chapter. Add the information to your organizer. Continue adding new sections to the organizer, using headings in addition to pictures.

WORDS MATTER

act a piece of legislation passed by parliament

House of Commons the house of parliament that is elected by voters and is based on representation by population

Senate the house of parliament that is appointed by the prime minister and is based on equal representation for various regions

THINKING It Over

1. Study the chart on page H 62. Which was the most powerful level of government in 1867? Today? Explain.

2. Some provincial governments today say that they should have more power. They say that they are closer to the people than the federal government is, and could therefore do a better job of dealing with matters such as telecommunications or protecting the environment. With a classmate, discuss which level of government you think can best deal with such areas of responsibility, and why.

John A. Macdonald looked at the government of the United States and decided Canada's government should be different. In the U.S., the states have many important powers. The federal government has only the leftover powers, and matters of foreign policy and national defence. This is why, for instance, criminal law is different in every state in the United States. Some states practise capital punishment for first-degree murder, while others have abolished executions altogether.

Macdonald believed that the Americans had not arranged things well. He thought that giving individual states too much power makes a nation less united. He believed that this had, in part, caused the American Civil War (1861–1865). Some states believed that they should have the right to practise slavery and refused to give up this right. This crisis nearly tore the country apart.

If the federal government had all the important powers, Macdonald believed, Canada could avoid having provinces leave the nation.

Not everything has gone to plan. Some powers that were considered unimportant and given to the provinces—such as health care and education—have since become important. Nova Scotia elected a separatist government in 1867. Québec held referendums on separation in 1980 and 1995. By and large, however, the division of powers has helped to keep Canada together.

Section	Clause	Item	Example
Section 91 (federal)	3	taxation	income tax, taxes on corporations, import duties
	7	national defence	the military
	24	Aboriginal affairs	Indian reserves and support (like health care and education)
	27	criminal law	making murder, smuggling, and theft illegal
	29	any item not specifically made a provincial power. (These are called residual powers.)	items that had not been invented in 1867, such as licensing of television stations or telecommunications networks
Section 92 (provincial)	2	limited powers of taxation	income tax, taxes on corporations, provincial sales tax
	7	health care	hospitals and licensing of doctors
	8	local government	the City of Toronto, Essex County (Windsor area)
	10	roads and bridges	maintaining highways that connect communities (whereas roads within communities are the responsibility of municipal governments)
Section 93 (provincial)	1	education	school boards, colleges, and universities

THINKING It Over

1. For one week, look through local and national newspapers and magazines. Listen to television and radio broadcasts. Find issues connected to government, such as health care, Aboriginal issues, revenues from oil and natural gas. Keep a list of the topics, note which government is responsible, and whether or not there is a conflict between the two levels of government. Share your findings in a small group. *t*

2. Do some research to find out about a recent dispute between the federal government and the provinces about one of the following areas: Aboriginal people, health care, the environment, trade, or telecommunications. Explain (a) the federal position in the disagreement, (b) the provincial position, and (c) which position you feel makes more sense, and why. *t* *a* *c*

HISTORICAL THINKING SKILL

Analyzing Cause and Consequence

In this chapter, you have been reading about Canada becoming a nation in 1867. When historians look at an "event" like Confederation they often ask why? and so what? questions. They want to know the causes of the event as well as the consequences of it.

Step 1 Analyze cause and consequence

The first stage in analyzing cause and consequence involves asking good questions about the event. Some of these questions for Confederation might be:

- Why did the colonies choose to come together at that particular time?
- Why did Confederation take the shape it did?
- What have been the long term results of the decisions made in the 1860s?

Step 2 Remember that answers can be complex

It is important to remember that answers to these kinds of questions are usually not simple, but quite complex. For example, causes usually include circumstances of the time as well as the actions of particular people. Most important events also have many consequences and some of these might be positive and others negative.

APPLY It

Using the material in this chapter and information from elsewhere, complete the following charts. Remember when thinking about the people that both supporters and opponents of Confederation helped to shape it.

Causes of Confederation

Cause	Impact on Confederation
Circumstances of The Time The United States was strong and united	Canadian colonies worried about invasion and so began to consider unifying.
People Antoine-Aimé Dorion	He and others were worried about the loss of provincial rights. He pushed the politicians to include strong provincial governments in the BNA Act.

Consequences of Confederation

Positive	Negative
Canada became a country that balances national and provincial concerns.	Aboriginal voices were left out. Aboriginal Peoples have had to fight for recognition and rights since 1867.

How Did the Map of Canada Change?

During **READING**

Checkpoint

Look again at the maps. What purposes do these visuals have? How do the maps help you to understand how Canada developed over time?

In 1867, Canada consisted of only four provinces (see map on page H 60). However, the new constitution allowed for the possibility that other provinces might join. On these maps, orange identifies Canadian provinces. The map of Canada underwent many changes between 1870 and 1871.

Canada, 1870–1871

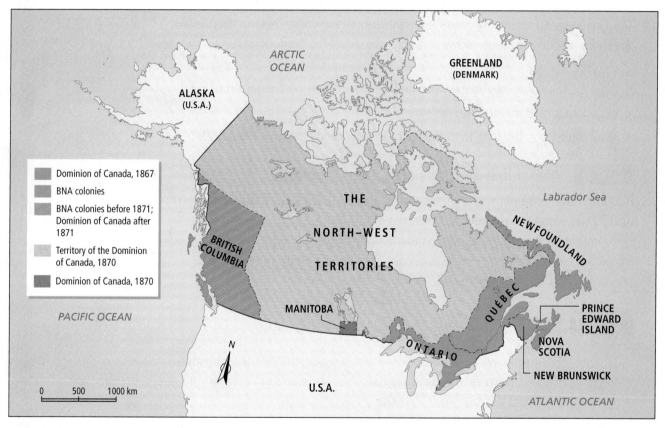

Legend:
- Dominion of Canada, 1867
- BNA colonies
- BNA colonies before 1871; Dominion of Canada after 1871
- Territory of the Dominion of Canada, 1870
- Dominion of Canada, 1870

0   500   1000 km

WORDS MATTER

hypothesis an educated guess or theory that has not been proven

If you look at a modern atlas, you will see that the map of Canada has changed again. In fact, the map has changed several times between 1871 and now. In later chapters, you will see how these changes occurred.

THINKING It Over

1. Compare this map to the map of Canada in 1867 on page H 60. Identify the changes you see between the two maps.

2. Why do you think these changes occurred? Make a **hypothesis** about each change. Record your hypotheses. You will return to them in later chapters.

PUTTING IT ALL TOGETHER

You have seen how the leaders of the colonies met and created a plan to join the colonies into an independent nation, Canada. You have examined the details of the plan that was developed by the politicians (the BNA Act). You have also studied the way in which the map of Canada changed in the years up to 1871.

After READING

Reading Visuals

Review your organizers.

How did the visuals and words in each section support each other? Were there any visuals you could have ignored and come back to later?

With a partner, discuss what would help you know when to focus on visuals and when to come back to them later.

Title/Number	Page Number	Who/What?	How?	Where/When?	Important? Explain.	Interesting?

THINKING It Through

1. You have seen how the map of Canada changed between 1867 and 1871. Now you are going to work with the changes that took place in 1873, 1898, and 1905. Using maps that your teacher will give you, examine how Canada grew during those years.

   a) Create your own copies of these maps. Be sure to show the boundaries of each of the provinces as they appear at each date. On each map, be sure to include all the map conventions you learned about in Grade 7 geography (title, legend, compass rose, and scale). In addition, on each map, indicate the date that each province entered Confederation. *k* *a*

   b) In a paragraph for each map, (i) identify the changes that have taken place in Canada since the previous map (between 1871 and 1873, 1873 and 1898, and 1898 and 1905), and (ii) predict how each set of changes would have helped to make Canada a stronger nation. *t* *c*

2. As an alternative, you could work in a group to organize a mock Confederation conference. Assign members of the group to represent the various leaders, each preparing a persuasive speech presenting that leader's point of view. Draft a set of six resolutions about how the proposed new country should be run. At the end of the conference, take a vote. *k* *t* *c*

3. Create a Word Power game. Choose five of the key terms from this chapter and write a multiple choice definition for each one. Include the correct definition using your own words and two incorrect ones. Trade games with a classmate and see how well you do at identifying the correct definitions. *k* *t* *c*

Back to the Big Idea

Why did some of the colonies put aside differences and create a new country—Canada?

Throughout this unit, you have

- looked at the main features of the colonies of British North America in the early 1860s

- examined the various factors that caused them to work together to solve their common problems

- followed the main events that took place as the political leaders worked to unite the colonies

- identified the various reasons the colonies thought they would be better off as an independent nation

Use the graphic organizers you completed while reading the chapter to review what you have learned. Create a graphic organizer to answer the question, **Why did some of the colonies put aside differences and create a new country—Canada?**

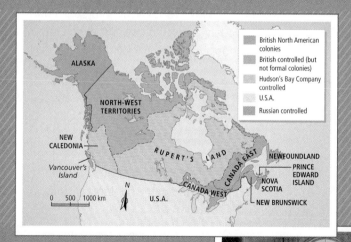

Show That You Know

Review the graphic organizer you created to answer the Big Idea question on the previous page. What do you think was the most important reason that the colonies decided to unite into a single nation? This will be the subject of your unit culminating activity.

Step 1 Ask questions

Create two questions for each inquiry word (who? what? when? where? why? how?) about your topic.

Tip: Review the material about asking questions. See page S 8.

Step 2 Identify primary and secondary sources

Make a short list of primary sources and secondary sources that could help you find information about your topic. Primary sources could include journals, letters, statistics, period documents, and maps. Secondary sources could include modern maps, illustrations, print materials, videos, CD-ROMS, and Internet sites. Create a bibliography containing at least two primary sources and two secondary sources that you will use.

Tip: Find sources in a library catalogue or on the Internet. See page S 2.

Tip:

- Include quotations from primary materials.
- Create any of the following visual items that apply: timeline, graph, map, model. See pages S 12– S 13.

Step 3 Summarize the information about your topic

Study your sources, making notes as you do so. Create short written summaries about different aspects of your topic.

Step 4 Arrange your material in an interesting and creative manner

Create your final copy, making sure that it contains all the elements listed in the various steps.

Tip:

- Create a written introduction and conclusion.
- Include your bibliography.

Step 5 Present your findings

Present your findings to a small group of students or to the whole class. Make sure that you have all of the following

- oral material
- visual material
- written material

Tip: Practise presenting your material to make sure it fits together properly.

The Development of Western Canada

> How and why did Canada expand so rapidly following Confederation?

Analyze this picture of Treaty negotiations. Who do you think took this photograph? Use three words to describe the atmosphere.

How might the building of the Canadian Pacific Railway influence your decision to settle in the West?

What effect do you think the Klondike gold rush had on western Canada?

What's the Big Idea?

Canada expanded rapidly after 1867. Newcomers moved into the Prairies and set up farms. Gold miners explored the mountains of what is now British Columbia and the Northwest Territories, looking for a lucky strike that would make them rich. The government approved of these developments. It arranged for the building of the Canadian Pacific Railway, which made the Prairies more easily accessible to settlers. The government made treaties with the First Nations and set up reserves. The Métis and First Nations did not always benefit from these changes.

Unit 2 tells the story of the development of western Canada and the lasting effects of this expansion.

Key Terms
treaties, Métis, Rupert's Land, provisional government, prospectors, panning for gold, staking a claim

What You Will Learn in this Unit

You will explore these aspects of the Unit 2 Big Idea:

- What factors contributed to the development of the Prairies, British Columbia, and the Yukon?
- What effects did the changes have on First Nations, Métis, and fur traders who lived there?
- How is the history of the West reflected in Canadian art, music, and institutions?
- How can I visually communicate the factors of Canada's expansion?

The Early Years of Independence

For centuries, First Nations lived off the land, often moving camp as they followed bison herds across the Prairies.

Before READING

Making Connections

Brainstorm times when you had a conflict or argument with an adult who had authority over you (parent, guardian, teacher) or with a peer.

- Write a paragraph or two explaining how you handled each situation, and which ones you were most successful at solving.
- Discuss with a partner: Were the conflicts you felt best about solved through discussion or through anger? Which situation allowed your opinions to be best understood?

Prime Minister Macdonald was keen to expand Canada westward. Why do you think this was? He wanted to ensure that the Prairies became Canadian, and was in a rush to claim them before the United States did. Many settlers in Ontario were keen to move westward and start farms on the rich lands of the Prairies. However, First Nations, Métis, and fur traders were already living in this region. How do you think their ways of life would change with the arrival of settlers?

Canada's early years of independence proved to be turbulent. The original inhabitants of the Prairies tried to defend their rights. This brought them into conflict with the government of Canada. This unit will explore the conflicts that arose regarding the future of the Prairies and how these issues were resolved.

Settlers arrived in the West and established homesteads on the land the First Nations lived and hunted on.

Questions to Consider as You Read this Chapter

You will explore these aspects of the Unit 2 Big Idea: **How and why did Canada expand so rapidly following Confederation?**

- Who were the people who had an interest in events in the West?

- What factors and people led to the settlement of the West?

- What were the causes and effects of the Red River Resistance?

- How does learning specific terms help to make inquiries and analyze historical information?

Thinking About Literacy

Asking Questions

Asking questions while you read can help you remember what you have read.

The following words are considered "question words": who, what, where, when, why, and how (5W + H). Use an organizer like the one shown below. When you encounter a new heading in the text, use the 5W + H to brainstorm other questions you may have. Record your answers in point form. What other resources could you use to locate information?

Subheading	Who?	What?	When?	Where?	Why?	How?	Possible Sources
Who first lived in the Prairie region?		What did they eat?		Where did they live?	Why did they live on the Prairies?		• encyclopedia • interview a historian

The First Nations lived in the Prairie region for thousands of years before the Europeans arrived. Their way of life was very different from Canadian culture in the East. Contact between First Nations and Europeans was limited. In 1867, the way of life for First Nations was about to undergo more change.

Who Are the First Nations People?

First Nations people share a deep connection with the land and respect for the natural world. Many of their oral legends involve the sacredness of wildlife and people's responsibility to preserve the environment.

Although "First Nations" is sometimes used to refer to all the First Peoples, the nations are all different, each with its own culture and language. Take the Blackfoot people as an example. The Blackfoot based their way of life on the bison, which provided food, shelter, and clothing. Other First Nations hunted wolf, caribou, and other wildlife. Some First Nations grew crops and lived in semi-permanent villages

What is now southern Alberta is just one part of the Prairies. In this area alone, there were three distinct groups of First Nations divided into several smaller subgroups. The map on page H 73 shows the traditional territories of some First Nations of the region.

WORDS MATTER

pemmican dried meat, pounded and flavoured with fat and local berries

First Nations Ways of Life

The First Nations did not live in fixed locations. They moved to wherever they could find the resources they needed: animal herds for food and clothing, stone for making tools, and berries during the summer months. As a result, they developed a keen knowledge of nature and animal life and this became a central feature of their culture. The land, water, and air that provided food were sacred to First Nations people.

This Stoney woman is drying meat. Why do think **pemmican** was such a useful food for First Nations?

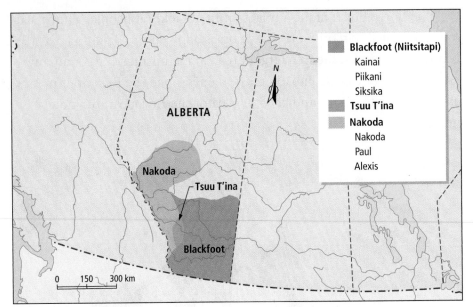

This map shows traditional locations of First Nations in southern Alberta. The idea of fixed territorial boundaries was not held by the First Nations. Traditional lands often overlapped.

Map legend:
- Blackfoot (Niitsitapi)
  - Kainai
  - Piikani
  - Siksika
- Tsuu T'ina
- Nakoda
  - Nakoda
  - Paul
  - Alexis

CANADA MINUTE

European Contact
The first recorded contact between Europeans and the Blackfoot people took place around 1754. Alexander Henday was an explorer for the Hudson's Bay Company (HBC). He tried unsuccessfully to get the Blackfoot to trade with the Company. At first, the Blackfoot did not need to trade with the Europeans; the Blackfoot felt they had everything they needed at home. They preferred traditional local trade among the First Nations. As the European fur traders moved farther inland, the Blackfoot entered into direct trade with them.

First Nations commonly assigned work based on gender. Men generally hunted and trapped wild animals. Women gathered roots and berries when they were in season. They also cut and dried animal meat, and made clothing and tents out of the hides.

The Blackfoot were particularly noted for their high-quality pemmican. They traded this food with First Nations farther north, where bison were not so common. In return, the Blackfoot received antelope and caribou hides, which were not very common in southern areas.

Especially during the summer, the various First Nations met to celebrate their culture. The Sundance is an example of such a festivity. People still take part in this celebration today to strengthen family relationships, arrange marriages, and give offerings to one another.

Introduction of the Horse

There were wild horses in North America until about 10 000 years ago. At that point they became extinct. When the Spanish began to explore Mexico in the 1520s, they brought horses with them. Some horses escaped or were traded with the Indigenous people of Mexico. The horses bred and ranged northward. When the horse came to the Canadian Prairies, First Nations captured and tamed some of them.

First Nations Terms for "Horse"

First Nation	Term	Meaning
Blackfoot	*ponokamita*	elk dog
Cree	*mistatim*	big dog

Why would the First Nations use the names of other animals to create a word meaning "horse"? What are some things we have had to create names for in modern times?

During READING

Checkpoint

Look at the photograph on this page. Which of this chapter's "Questions to Consider" (page H 71) does it help to answer? How do the image and caption help you to analyze historical information?

The horse had a major impact on the Blackfoot people. They used to follow the bison on foot. Now, horses allowed the Blackfoot to travel, hunt, and trade in a larger area. The Hudson's Bay Company and the North West Company tried to encourage the Blackfoot to expand their territory and become part of the European fur trade network.

The horse is pulling a frame called a travois. It is made of skins and poles from a teepee and is used to carry belongings. How is the travois an example of technology?

The Blackfoot Confederacy

The Blackfoot Confederacy was an alliance among the Piikani, Kainai, and Siksika peoples. The Tsuu T'ina people joined later. Primarily a military alliance, it was greatly feared by its enemies. Before contact, the Confederacy controlled much of the Prairie region of what are now Canada and the U.S.

The Cree and Assiniboine lived farther north, in rich fur-gathering territory, and became active trade partners with the French and British. They acquired firearms from their European trading partners in the process. They gradually began to push south into Confederacy territory. This led to the Battle of the Belly River between the Cree and the Confederacy in 1870, near what is now Lethbridge. This is considered to have been the last battle between First Nations in North America.

THINKING It Over

1. Review the questions you added to your 5W + H chart. Which of your questions were answered in this section?

2. Choose one of the following methods to share the answer to one of the questions you wrote: draw a picture, create an organizer, write a poem, make a diagram.

3. How were ways of life different for First Nations living on the Prairies compared to European ways of life in eastern Canada that you read about in Unit 1?

The First Nations were not the only people who lived on the Prairies before the settlers arrived. A second people had been living there since the 1700s. They were called the **Métis**. The name comes from an old French word meaning "mixed."

The Origins of the Métis

The French

The Métis were the descendants of European fur traders and First Nations. French fur traders married women from various First Nations. The children of these families married one another and had children. Over time, the Métis Nation was born.

By about 1750, there were enough Métis for them to be unofficially recognized as separate people. They were different from the First Nations and French people.

- They were often bilingual. They spoke French as well as First Nations languages such as Cree or Blackfoot.

- They engaged in a number of religious practices. Many were Roman Catholic but also practiced First Nations spirituality.

- They used European as well as First Nations methods of survival. They farmed. They were also excellent bison hunters.

WORDS MATTER

Métis people of mixed European and First Nations ancestry

WEB LINK

For more information on the Métis, visit our Web site.

Environmental Milestones

The Bison Hunt

Bison that lived on the Prairies provided food and clothing for the Métis and First Nations. Bison were hunted with bows and arrows or by stampeding them over cliffs. In the late 1800s, rifles became available in the Prairies. Now it required little skill to hunt bison. The millions of animals that existed in the 1830s were reduced to about 600 by 1890. A species was almost extinct, and the people who lived off them were left on the verge of starvation.

Examine the picture of a typical camp during a Métis bison hunt in the late 1800s. How are both European and First Nations ways of life represented? How do you know? See page S 12 for help with analyzing images.

Checkpoint

Go online and enter "HBC" in a search engine. What store do you find? Find HBC blankets on their site. What colours are they? What is the history of these blankets? Do some research to find out more.

WORDS MATTER

country-born people of mixed British and First Nations ancestry

The British

The Hudson's Bay Company began trading in 1670. After the Treaty of Utrecht, in 1713, Britain took over the French fur-trading posts in the interior. The king gave the HBC control over these posts. Many Cree men and women were living permanently in or near these posts. Many Scottish men worked for the HBC as fur traders. The HBC discouraged relationships between its employees and First Nations women, but such relationships were common. The children born from these relationships were called the **country-born**. In some ways the country-born were similar to the Métis, yet there were still some key differences.

- They took on some of the First Nations ways of their mothers and were often bilingual. They spoke English, not French.

- Many of them were Protestant, although they also practiced First Nations spirituality.

Over time, the term country-born died out. Today people of mixed First Nations and British heritage are also called Métis.

The Métis and Western Settlement

When settlers began to move into the Prairies, they introduced a way of life that was very different from that of the Métis. See the chart

Métis and Settler Perspectives

Item	Métis	Settlers
Bison	hunt only what was needed for survival and for limited trading purposes	hunt large numbers to sell meat and hides for money
Settlement	settle only a few areas, leaving the rest open for animal migration	settle larger areas, establishing farms to grow crops
The land	leave the land open to help the bison hunt	fence farms to keep wild animals, like bison, out

below to understand some of the differences.

THINKING It Over

1. Make a graphic organizer to illustrate the major characteristics of the Métis.

2. Review the questions you added to your 5W + H chart. Make a plan to answer one of the questions that was not addressed in this section. You may also want to develop another research question you have about the Métis. See page S 8 for help with forming research questions.

Métis Culture and Lifestyle

The Métis are a close-knit community with a strong identity. They have their own flag, shown above. Since 1983, the Métis National Council has represented the interests of the Métis in areas such as land, education, health, and socio-economic conditions.

The early Métis of the West developed a new language that was a combination of French and Cree, with some vocabulary from other First Nations languages. This is called Michif. Some Métis still speak this language. A similar language, called Bungee, combined mainly Cree and Scottish Gaelic. This dialect is now extinct.

The Métis have strong musical and culinary traditions. Métis people enjoy dancing to fiddle tunes that often mix Celtic and First Nations themes. The dancing is fast-paced and festive. Traditionally, they held dances regularly throughout the year, with the biggest one being held on New Year's Eve. Dancers feasted on fried bread, bannock, meatballs, and stew. What European and First Nations influences are reflected in the foods that were served?

Métis women have traditionally produced fine beadwork, porcupine quillwork, and embroidery. These works of art involve both First Nations patterns and French designs. Métis communities became famous for such artwork. Today, it is highly prized by art collectors

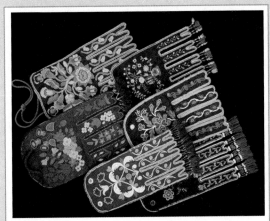

These Métis artifacts are called octopus pouches. How do you think they got this name?

Notice the Métis flags carried in this parade. Do some research to find out what the colours and the symbol represent.

THINKING It Over

1. Do further research to find out what aspects of Métis culture are still practised today. Prepare a brief oral report to share your findings. t c

2. What is the purpose of preserving ways of life, such as art, dance, music, and language? Discuss your thoughts in a small group. c a t

Why Was the Red River Resistance Significant?

In Grade 7, you learned about the rebellions of 1837–1838. In the first 18 years of Canada's existence, two more uprisings took place. The first of these was in Red River, in what is now Manitoba.

The Purchase of Rupert's Land

Canada West had been interested in gaining control of **Rupert's Land** since the 1850s. Canadians believed this area had economic potential. In 1867, the U.S. purchased Alaska from Russia. This fuelled Canada's longstanding fear that the U.S. would seek control of more territory north of its borders.

In 1869, the HBC agreed to sell Rupert's Land to the government of Canada. This area contained what is now northern Ontario and Québec, all of Manitoba, most of Saskatchewan, southern Alberta, parts of the Northwest Territories, and Nunavut. Canada paid $1 500 000 for this vast area. Prime Minister John A. Macdonald wanted to take control of the region as soon as possible. He appointed William McDougall as lieutenant-governor and sent him to Red River to establish a new government.

No one consulted the people living in the area about their wishes. When McDougall ordered land surveyors to go to Red River, the Métis residents objected. The Métis predicted that:

- The surveyors would divide the land into individual lots.
- The government would sell the lots to settlers.
- The settlers would start farms on their lots.
- Fences would be built to keep livestock in, and wild animals out.
- The fences would disrupt the bison hunt.
- The traditional Métis way of life would be destroyed.

The Métis were also concerned about the way the land would be divided. Traditional Métis farms on the Prairies were modelled on the seigneurial system of land division practised in New France as you learned in previous studies. Farms were long and narrow to let as many as possible have access to water and to woodlands that grew near the water. The shape of the farms was also good for the Métis social structure, as families on neighbouring farms were close and travel was easy.

The Canadian government, however, favoured the British grid method of land division, which divided the land into square sections (you will read more about this in Chapter 5). The surveying not only ignored Métis preferences, it also divided properties that were already in existence. In addition, the surveying began before the territory was turned over to Canada, and the surveyors arrived on occupied land without asking permission.

Another concern was that the new settlers would be English Protestants, not French Catholics. This would be another contrast to the Métis' existing way of life as the largest proportion of the community were Francophone Métis. What do you think the Métis could do to make their voices heard?

The Rise of Louis Riel

At this point, in 1869, 25-year-old Louis Riel became the leader of the Métis in Red River. He was well educated, religious, and a good speaker. Although he was born in Manitoba, he had lived in Québec for ten years while going to school. Riel returned to Manitoba when the transfer and surveying of Rupert's Land began to stir up controversy.

When Riel's cousin tried to stop surveyors from coming onto his land, Riel helped him. Soon after that, the Métis organized the National Committee of the Métis of Red River and elected Riel as secretary. The committee sent a note to Ottawa saying that the newly appointed lieutenant-governor, McDougall, should not try to come to Red River without special permission of the committee. When McDougall came, a group of Métis stopped him and escorted him to the U.S. border.

At the same time, however, Riel maintained that he was loyal to the Crown and wanted to negotiate with the government. He believed that the West had a right to have some say in the terms of joining Confederation. He tried to persuade the English-speaking residents of the settlement to join forces with the Métis and so deal with the Canadian government as a unified community.

When those efforts failed, Riel set up a **provisional government**. His plan was that the Métis and the Canadian government would co-operate to establish a permanent government that the Métis could support. Riel and the provisional government drew up a list of demands called the Métis List of Rights. Here are some of the things they demanded from Canada.

WEB LINK • • • • • • • • • • • • • • • •
For more information on Louis Riel and the Red River Resistance, visit our Web site. If you do further research on this event, also look under the term Red River Rebellion, as it was called historically.

Louis Riel, 1879

The Métis List of Rights

1. That the territory of the North-West enter into the Confederation of... Canada as a province...

7. That the schools be separate (based on religion) and that public money for schools be distributed among the different religious denominations in proportion to their respective population...

13. That treaties be concluded between Canada and the different Indian [nations] of the North-West...

16. That both the English and the French languages be common in the legislature, and in the courts... and [in] all public documents...

17. That the Lieutenant-Governor to be appointed for the Province of the North-West be familiar with both English and French languages.

18. That the Judge of the Supreme Court speak both the English and French languages.

Do you think the Canadian government would accept the Métis List of Rights? Riel appeared to be in a strong position. He had many supporters and the future looked promising for the people and the region. Then the situation quickly got out of hand.

During READING

Checkpoint
How did these demands influence the Canada we live in today?

Louis Riel (centre) and his associates formed the provisional government of the Métis Nation in 1869. Do you think the demands they listed were fair and realistic? Explain.

William McDougall (1822–1905) was a lawyer and politician from Ontario. He was a supporter of John A. Macdonald. In 1869, Macdonald appointed him the first lieutenant-governor of the North-West Territories. His orders were to bring the region under the control of the Canadian government and to prepare it for the arrival of settlers. He was not instructed to concern himself with the wishes of the First Nations and Métis people already living there.

Some people see McDougall as a loyal government servant who did what he was told. The government had given him his instructions, and he saw that they were carried out. Others see him as spineless. They say he should have realized that the government's instructions were flawed and acted accordingly, rather than remain silent. The result was the Red River Resistance of 1869.

What should be the role of the individual in dealing with instructions from superiors? When should orders be questioned? When should we carry them out, even if we may privately disagree with them? Think of a time when you were asked to do something you did not agree with. How did you decide what to do?

Did McDougall do what was right under the circumstances in 1869? Do you think William McDougall was a hero or a villain? Are you unsure? Why?

William McDougall

The Role of Thomas Scott

Thomas Scott was a Protestant from Ireland who had come to Ontario in 1863. He was among the first Canadians sent to Red River. He wanted Canada to expand and to be successful. He also wanted it to resist the pressures from the United States, where some politicians spoke about taking over all of Canada. Scott wanted Canada to remain part of the British Empire.

In Ireland at that time, Roman Catholics were permitted very few rights. Scott brought these views with him to Canada. He believed that Catholics should not be allowed to be part of government, and he told everyone about his views. This naturally made him unpopular with many people. In 1869, he drifted into Red River and began to tell people that the Métis were not fit to be part of a government. He said that Canada should simply ignore them and set up a government without consulting the Métis.

This illustration of the shooting of Thomas Scott was published in the *Canadian Illustrated News* on April 23, 1870. Based on what you have learned about the event, is this an accurate representation? Why or why not?

WORDS MATTER

treason an act of betrayal or disloyalty to one's country or government

Riel regarded Scott as a threat. Scott was a powerful symbol of opposition to the Métis. If more settlers came from Ontario, Scott might manage to organize them to resist Métis demands. With Riel's approval, the provisional government had Scott arrested and he was given a court martial. He was found guilty of **treason**. In March 1870, he was executed by firing squad.

The Future of the Métis

WEB LINK •••••••••••••••••
For more information on Thomas Scott, visit our Web site.

The execution of Scott caused hostility toward Riel. In the eyes of the Canadian government, Riel was a criminal. The government issued a warrant for his arrest. Riel and many of his followers knew it would be difficult to resist Canada and the settlers. Riel fled to the United States, and many of his followers went to what is now Saskatchewan. They hoped to escape from the pressures that settlement brought. However, the story of Riel and his followers was far from finished. You will read more about it in the next chapter.

Not all the Métis went west. Many remained in Red River. As they had predicted, their traditional way of life was eventually destroyed by settlement. The bison hunts died out. The Métis adapted to a new way of life. They retained many cultural traditions, but adopted the settled life of townspeople.

THINKING It Over

1. On page H 78, the Métis predicted what would happen in Red River when the land surveyors arrived. Draw a six-frame cartoon strip to illustrate each prediction described.

2. Read the Métis List of Rights and make a copy of the following organizer. Rewrite each of the six points in the list in your own words, then place it in the appropriate column of the organizer. To help you, one item has already been placed in the organizer.

3. In light of his views and behaviour, do you think Thomas Scott was disloyal to his country? Why or why not?

4. Do some research to find out whether execution for treason could happen in Canada today. Why do you think some laws change over time?

Government	People	Language and religion
• The Northwest Territories should become a province of Canada		

Three New Provinces and a Territory

By the end of 1869, Canada was made up of four provinces: Ontario, Québec, New Brunswick, and Nova Scotia. In the next four years, three more provinces joined the new nation.

Manitoba

In 1870, Canada passed the Manitoba Act, making Manitoba the fifth Canadian province. The Act came into effect on July 15, 1870. Here are some of the terms it contained. As you read these terms, think about how they compare to the rights that Riel had demanded.

- The province was confined to a small area around Red River and was only just over 39 000 km² in area. (Modern Manitoba occupies about 647 797 km².) The rest of the North-West Territories remained in the hands of the federal government.

- English and French were to be the languages of government and the courts.

- There were separate Protestant and Catholic schools paid for by the government.

- The right to English- or French-language education was not guaranteed. Only religious education was guaranteed.

- The federal government retained control over lands and resources, giving it great power in the development of the province.

  Manitoba was so small that it was nicknamed the "postage stamp province." The population census in 1871 recorded a mere 25 228 residents. Could the tiny province survive? There were many divisions among the people, as the following chart shows.

During **READING**

Checkpoint
Which of the "Questions to Consider" questions does this section help you to answer?

WEB LINK • • • • • • • • • • • • • • •
For more information on Manitoba becoming a province, visit our Web site.

Members of the Legislature of the province of Manitoba, 1893

Divisions in Manitoba, 1870

Issue	Divisions
Religion	Catholic, Protestant, Aboriginal spiritual beliefs
Language	French, English, Cree, and other Aboriginal languages
Economics	open land and hunting versus fenced farms

The Manitoba Act was the first federal Act to recognize the importance of bilingualism. When New Brunswick joined Confederation, French rights had not been recognized, even though much of its population spoke French. There were also pockets of French-speaking people across the Prairies, including the Métis. French was recognized as an official language of government and the courts in Manitoba. Canada's bilingual nature was reinforced.

WORDS MATTER

panning for gold searching for gold by collecting, then washing gold-bearing gravel in a pan

How could different groups learn to live alongside each other and solve their differences? In Chapters 5 and 6, you will see how some of these conflicts worked out.

North-West Territories

In 1870, Britain transferred control of the North-Western Territory to Canada. This was combined with Rupert's Land to become the Northwest Territories. The new region was governed directly by Ottawa, with no legislature of its own. It was not until 1876 that the federal government appointed a lieutenant-governor and a council for the Territories, and another 10 years before the Northwest Territories had seats in the federal government.

British Columbia

You learned in Unit 1 that there was another British North American colony on the Pacific coast. In 1858, gold had been discovered in the Fraser River, and prospectors flocked to the colony. As more gold was found, people continued to move to the region, many coming from California. When the future of the colony was discussed, some people wanted it to join the United States. Others felt its future lay with Canada.

Supporters of joining the U.S. believed that B.C. would expand and develop more quickly that way. It would be easy to build railway lines south to join the American lines in Washington State. This would allow people and freight to travel between B.C. and major cities in the U.S. However, this idea did not sit well with those who wanted to join Canada. It would take many years to establish a rail link with Canada, but becoming Canadian would allow British Columbians to retain their connections with Britain. In this way, they could still live under the monarchy; joining the U.S. would mean becoming part of a republic.

There were vigorous debates in the newspapers: the American solution offered speed of development; the Canadian solution placed more emphasis on tradition. In the end, the traditionalists won the debate, and British Columbia moved in the direction of joining Canada.

Panning for gold. What other natural resources might have encouraged settlers to move to the west?

Prime Minister Macdonald was anxious to expand Canada from sea to sea, so he reached an agreement with both the political leaders in B.C. and with the British government. The colony became Canada's sixth province in 1871.

However, British Columbia had a small population and was a long way away from the rest of Canada. In 1871, the population of the entire province was 36 247. The only rail link with the rest of Canada lay through the U.S. How could the new province trade with Ontario and Québec, given this situation?

Macdonald made one of his most reckless promises when he persuaded B.C. to join. The federal government promised that within ten years, by 1881, a railway would be built from Ontario to the Pacific Ocean. Macdonald's political enemies thought him foolish. Why do you think that was? Predict whether he was able to keep his promise. You will find out in Chapter 6.

WEB LINKS •••••••••••••••••
For more information on British Columbia becoming a province and for more information on Prince Edward Island becoming a province, visit our Web site.

Prince Edward Island

Prince Edward Island (P.E.I.) had been involved in early discussions about the creation of Canada. However, in 1867, the colony decided not to join the new nation. It soon realized that this was a mistake. Trade among the Maritime provinces (New Brunswick and Nova Scotia) and central Canada (Ontario and Québec) increased steadily after Confederation. P.E.I. did not share in this growth. The government of the colony tried to build a railway across the island, but it encountered huge costs.

Macdonald knew that P.E.I. was in poor shape. So he offered it a deal. The federal government would take over P.E.I.'s railway debts, and in return, P.E.I. would join Canada. This seemed like a good solution for everyone. In 1873, P.E.I. became the seventh province of Canada.

In 1997, the Confederation Bridge was opened, connecting P.E.I. to mainland Canada. How do you think the island was able to trade, grow, and prosper for 125 years, even though it was not physically linked to the mainland?

Canada's Population Distribution, 1873

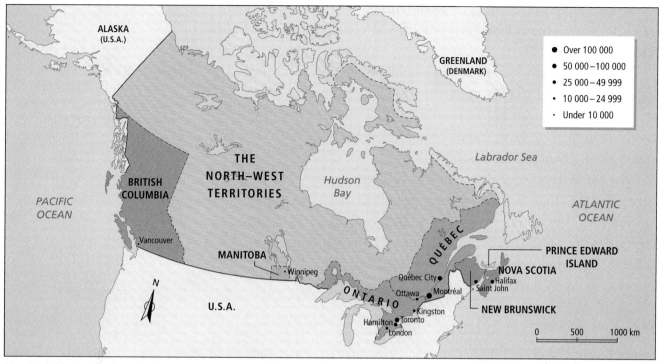

How far is Vancouver from Winnipeg and from Toronto?

A New Canada Emerges

By 1873, the map of Canada had begun to look more like its present form. From the Maritimes to British Columbia, all the land north of the United States was officially part of Canada. In the Prairies, Manitoba was tiny, and Alberta and Saskatchewan were not yet created. Newfoundland was still a separate colony, and would be for another 76 years. Nevertheless, Canada was emerging in its modern form. As its motto says, it ran "From Sea to Sea."

THINKING It Over

1. Create an organizer to show the details about the joining of Manitoba, British Columbia, and Prince Edward Island into Confederation. Make sure that your organizer contains key information such as date of joining, problems that existed prior to joining, how joining could help, and the effects of joining on Canada.

2. Reread the Canada Minute feature on page H 84. Why would having French as an official language in Manitoba be considered a breakthrough for French rights?

3. You have read that in 1870, the terms of Manitoba's becoming a province included government funding of Protestant and Roman Catholic schools. In 2007, government funding of faith-based schools was a controversial election issue in Ontario. Why do you think some people think it is important for religion to be part of education and other people do not?

PUTTING IT ALL TOGETHER

Canada was a divided and hesitant nation in 1867. In this chapter, you have seen how Canada made its first steps in growing larger and stronger. You learned how Canada expanded from four to seven provinces between 1867 and 1873. You also saw that, in Manitoba, this was achieved only after disagreements and conflict. The Métis and First Nations who lived on the Prairies felt that their way of life was threatened by the arrival of settlers from Canada. You have looked at some of the key individuals in the struggle and you have seen what they wanted for the region.

After READING

Asking Questions

We study history because it has an impact on life today. Choose one topic from this chapter: First Nations, Métis, Catholic and Protestant schools, official languages, new provinces. You have historical information in the chart you completed in this chapter. Look for information about the same topic in Canada today. Try magazines, newspapers, and Web sites. Write one paragraph about the topic in the 1800s, and one paragraph telling how the topic concern appears today. In your concluding paragraph, answer the question, "Is Canada still a divided and hesitant nation?" Support your answer with what you have learned.

Subheading	Who?	What?	When?	Where?	Why?	How?	Possible Sources
Who first lived in the Prairie region?		What did they eat?		Where did they live?	Why did they live on the Prairies?		• encyclopedia • interview a historian

THINKING It Through

Use your 5W + H chart to review the information in this chapter. Then conduct research of your own to complete the following tasks. See pages S 6 and S 7 for help with research.

1. Create a Venn diagram to illustrate the similarities and differences between the Métis and the settlers from Ontario who were beginning to drift into Red River in the 1860s. **k c**

2. a) Draw a picture of a scene, or describe the scene in words, to illustrate what you consider the most important similarity or difference that you identified in your Venn diagram. b) In two sentences, explain what the picture or scene shows, and why you chose it. **t c**

3. Pick one of the provinces examined in this chapter. (Manitoba, P.E.I., B.C.) Do some research on the population, economy, and lifestyle of the province you choose. Create a visual display to illustrate how it has changed since it joined Canada. Answer the following question: Has belonging to Canada benefited the province? **t c a**

4. Create a Jeopardy-style game with the key terms in this chapter. For each term, write the answer in your own words. Then with a partner or in a small group, read your answers and have your classmates come up with the right questions. For example, Answer: the first interaction between First Nations and Europeans. Question: What is "contact"? **k t c**

The Expansion of Settlement

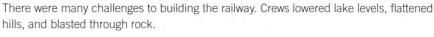
There were many challenges to building the railway. Crews lowered lake levels, flattened hills, and blasted through rock.

Before READING

Making Connections
Imagine you have been hired to plan the development of a 5-km wheelchair-accessible path through a local park in your community.

· How will you decide what route your path will take? Where will you get building supplies? How will you clear trees and bushes? What happens if there are water sources and steep hills?

These are just a few of the questions the Canadian government had to face as they planned to lay approximately 5000 km of railway tracks across Canada.

The Canadian government wanted to expand settlement in the Prairies, but there was no efficient way to get families there. It was also difficult to get supplies into the region and farm products out. With a railway, settlers would be able to reach the Prairie region more quickly and easily than they did by horse and wagon. Trains could deliver supplies and farm products.

The railway linking all the provinces would become a symbol of Canada's unity. It would show the United States that the Prairies were Canadian territory. How else was the railway project critical in the development and expansion of our country?

While encouraging new settlement in the Prairies, the government had to consider the First Nations who were already living there. It signed a series of treaties with the First Nations. Meanwhile, the Métis who had fled from Manitoba after the Red River Resistance were sending petitions to the government without getting much response. What do you predict their dissatisfaction might lead to?

Why have railways always been important in expanding population and trade?

Questions to Consider as You Read this Chapter

You will explore these aspects of the Unit 2 Big Idea: **How and why did Canada expand so rapidly following Confederation?**

- How did building the railway lead to an increased population in the West?

- How did settlers and railway workers affect the ways of life of First Nations?

- What were the causes and effects of the Northwest Rebellion?

- How can artists and writers help us understand history?

Predicting

The 5W + H can help you make predictions and conclusions based on what you read.

Use an organizer to make predictions and conclusions about each main idea. To create a question, use one question word, plus the word in the second column. Try to create one question in each area: prediction, probability, possibility, and thinking. One example is filled out for you below.

Purpose	One 5W + H	Add On	Question	Answer/Notes
Prediction (before reading)	Who?	+ will	Who will sign the treaties?	
Probability		+ would		
Possibility		+ can		
Thinking		+ might		

Canada wanted to settle the Prairies with Europeans, but the First Nations were already living there. They had lived on the Prairies for thousands of years. How could the government meet its goal of expanding and developing the West when its view of the land and resources was so different from that of the First Nations people?

Different Perspectives on the Land

First Nations' View

First Nations people believed that they did not own the land, but had been entrusted by the Great Spirit to take care of it. In return, the Great Spirit allowed them to live off the land's resources. Humans were to take only what they needed for their survival so that the land could exist forever.

Settlers' View

The settlers and the government believed that people could own individual plots of land. They could put fences around their plots to keep people and wild animals out, and keep farm animals in. The settlers also believed that they, because they owned the land, had the right to use it for whatever purposes they liked.

Treaties with First Nations

While Canada was still a collection of colonies, the French and British governments had relied on **treaties** to deal with land-use conflicts. In the Maritimes, treaties did not deal with land ownership, but in other regions they did. In these treaties, First Nations agreed to give up their rights to lands upon which they had lived for centuries. In return, the government promised to

- recognize First Nations' rights to live on individual **reserves**
- recognize First Nations' rights to hunt and fish on their reserves according to their ancient customs
- provide annual payments to reserves to compensate First Nations for the lands they had given up
- supply farming implements, seeds, and livestock, as well as instruction in new farming techniques
- build schools on reserves

During **READING**

Checkpoint

Can you create a new "Probability" question for your chart?

WORDS MATTER

treaties legal documents outlining agreements between nations

reserves land set aside for exclusive use by First Nations people

Looking back today, it is fair to say that the First Nations did not imagine how drastically their lives would change as a result of the treaties. First Nations had long been making treaties among themselves. To the First Nations, treaties are solemn and sacred agreements. However, because their traditions transmitted laws orally, First Nations had no experience with written documents. In addition, the treaties were in French or English, not First Nations languages.

The Crown representatives told the First Nations chiefs that this was the best deal they could expect, and if they refused to sign the treaties, they might end up with nothing. How could you go about finding out whether or not the information the representatives gave the First Nations was true?

WEB LINK • · · · · · · · · · · · · · · · · · · ·

For more information on First Nations treaties, visit our Web site.

The Numbered Treaties

The numbered treaties dealt with northwestern Ontario and the Prairies. They were called "numbered" because they did not have names, merely numbers to distinguish one from the other. Treaties 1 to 7 dealt with what are now Manitoba, Saskatchewan, and Alberta. The map below shows the territory covered by each treaty.

Treaties One to Seven, 1871–1908

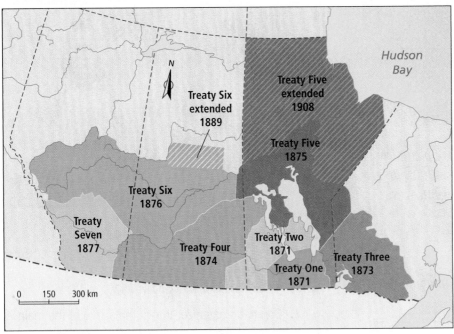

As you can see from the map, the First Nations gave up their rights to most of the Prairie region in these treaties. Would you have signed a treaty? Why or why not?

Treaty 6 covered a huge area—about 300 000 km², more than twice the area of the Maritimes. Alexander Morris was the government's representative. During the negotiations with the Cree people of the area, he painted a rosy picture of life on the reserve.

Alexander Morris' View

All along that road I see Indians gathering, I see gardens growing and houses building; I see them receiving money from the Queen's Commissioners to purchase clothing for their children; at the same time I see them enjoying their hunting and fishing as before, I see them retaining their old mode of living with the Queen's gift in addition.

The Cree were divided on whether or not to sign the treaty.

Chief Poundmaker's View

This is our land! It isn't a piece of pemmican to be cut off and given back to us. It is our land and we will take what we want.

Chief Star Blanket's View

Can we stop the power of the white man from spreading over the land like the grasshoppers that cloud the sky and then fall to consume every blade of grass and every leaf on the trees in their path? I think not.

The Cree suffered greatly after signing Treaty 6. In the winter of 1883–1884, about 10 percent of all First Nations on the Prairies, including the Cree, died of starvation. Fur traders and hunters slaughtered the bison herds, and there was not enough food for the First Nations.

Chief Mistahimaskwa's (Big Bear's) Observation

Our big game is no more. You now own millions of acres... We have no food...We cannot work. We are tired. Feed us until we recoup our wasted bodies... We are hungry.

Treaty 6 had a destructive effect on the Cree. They were cut off from their ancient hunting and trapping ways; as a result, they did not have enough food. The federal government never lived up to its promises. A proud people entered a long period of despair.

Chief Poundmaker and his wife, 1884

Chief Mistahimaskwa (Big Bear), 1888

THINKING It Over

1. Create an organizer that summarizes a) the main terms of Treaty 6, and b) its effects on the First Nations. Ⓚ Ⓣ Ⓒ

2. Visit the Web site of the Confederacy of Treaty 6 First Nations. Create a visual or a series of visuals to summarize the initiatives that these nations are making today in fields such as health, education, and economic development.

The Indian Act

In 1876, the government passed the Indian Act. The Act created the principle of **Indian status**—the term that identified people as First Nations. Here are some of the things the Act said:

- Only "full-blooded" First Nations people could have Indian status. This meant the Métis were not eligible.

- First Nations people on reserves became **wards of the state**. They were forbidden to vote or drink alcohol. First Nations people who lived off the reserves were not considered wards of the state and were not entitled to the same benefits.

- First Nations women who married non-First Nations men lost their Indian status and the right to live on the reserve. Non–First Nations women who married First Nations men gained Indian status.

- The federal government could license companies to take timber from reserves. None of the money from this went to the reserves.

- First Nations people who committed crimes could be tried in the courts of Canada. This took away the traditional right of First Nations Elders to deal with lawbreakers among their people.

- First Nations people could have full Canadian citizenship, including the right to vote, only by giving up their Indian status.

To this day, many people regard the passing of the Indian Act as one of the worst things the government did to First Nations people. Some of these policies changed many years later. For example, in 1985, First Nations women who married non-First Nations men won the right to remain on reserves and retain their status. In 2003, the Supreme Court ruled that Métis are entitled to benefits under the Indian Act.

WORDS MATTER

Indian status the term that identified people for recognition as "Indians"

wards of the state people who are under the care of the government; usually children or people who are unable to be responsible for themselves

WEB LINK •••••••••••••••••••••
For more information on the Indian Act, visit our Web site.

THINKING It Over

1. a) In your own words, summarize the differences between the First Nations' and the settlers' view of the land. b) Think of your own community. Which view seems to have survived? In your opinion, why is this?

2. Research one of Treaties 1–5 or 7. Create an organizer to summarize and compare its terms with Treaty 6.

Developing the West

During READING

Checkpoint

What does this tell you about conditions on the ships? Can you create a "Thinking" question for your chart?

The government of Canada had a problem. How could it fill the West with settlers? The 1871 census showed that Canada had a total population of 3 737 257; however, the West's population was small, as the following table shows.

Population of the West, 1871

Province/Territory	Population	Percentage of Total Population of Canada
Manitoba	25 228	0.67%
Northwest Territories*	48 000	1.28%
British Columbia	36 247	0.97%
Total	109 475	2.92%

* At this time, the Northwest Territories included what is now Alberta, Saskatchewan, and most of Manitoba.

WORDS MATTER

quarantine to keep people in isolation from others to prevent the spread of disease

How would you describe the conditions on this immigrant ship?

How do you think new immigrants would have felt when they landed at Grosse Île and found they had to stay in this quarantine station?

How could the government increase the number of settlers? There were not enough people living in Canada to expand into the region, so the government would have to consider new ways to boost the population. The government set up a system to make it easier for immigrants to enter Canada and settle in the Prairies. As a result, thousands of immigrants arrived from overseas.

The Immigration Act

The Immigration Act of 1869 was the first of a number of acts passed to manage the flow of immigrants to Canada. Its main purpose was to keep people with contagious diseases out of the country. Limits were placed on the number of passengers that could be carried on immigrant ships. The Act also required ships to show passenger lists to officers of the government upon their arrival. These officers would place seriously ill passengers in **quarantine** until they either got better or died.

The Dominion Lands Act

You may remember from Chapter 4 that in 1869, the federal government bought Rupert's Land from the Hudson's Bay Company. In 1872, the Dominion Lands Act set up rules about how this land was to be used.

Land Distribution

The Prairies were divided into townships, blocks of land almost 10 km square. Each township was divided into 36 sections. Two sections were set aside for the Hudson's Bay Company and two were set aside for school use. (A school would be built on part of one section, and the remaining land was sold or rented to provide revenue.) Sixteen blocks of land were for sale or rent to help pay for railway construction. The remaining sixteen were designated as **homesteads**, lands turned over to people for farming.

A family could acquire a homestead quarter section for a $10 registration fee if they built a house or they turned some land into a farm within three years. Failure to meet these conditions meant the land had to be given back to the government.

The "Road Allowance People"

The Métis did not fare well under the Dominion Lands Act. Many tried to homestead, but found it difficult. The Métis were not treated the same as immigrant settlers. Among other things, they could not get modern steam-driven farm equipment and had to rely on hand tools. Métis author Maria Campbell wrote about what happened to Métis families in Saskatchewan under the Dominion Lands Act:

> *Fearless men who could brave sub-zero temperatures and all the dangers associated with living in the bush gave up, frustrated and discouraged.*
>
> *Gradually the [Métis] homesteads were reclaimed by the authorities and offered to the immigrants. The [Métis] then became squatters on their land and were eventually run off by the new owners. One by one they drifted back to the road lines and Crown lands where they build cabins and barns and from then on were known as "Road Allowance People."*

How might this situation influence the relationship between the Métis and the government?

WORDS MATTER

homesteads lands turned over to settlers for the purpose of farming

What do you think was the purpose of this poster, produced in the early 1900s in Ontario? Who do you think was the intended audience?

Métis author and activist Maria Campbell

The Arrival of the Settlers and Immigrants

Free land was very appealing to people at this time. For starters, they could grow their own food and would not have to fear starvation. However, there was no railway, and it was still very difficult to get to the Prairies. Most settlers ended up walking great distances to get to their homesteads. As a result, the population of the Northwest Territories increased slowly during the 1870s. The table below illustrates this slow growth.

Population of the West, 1881

Province/Territory	Population	Increase from 1871
Manitoba	62 260	37 032
Northwest Territories	56 446	8446
British Columbia	49 459	13 212
Total	168 165	58 690

Settlers were increasing the population of the West, but the government was impatient. It became obvious that if the government was to increase the population of the Prairies, it would have to complete a railway through the region. It increasingly turned its attention to this matter.

THINKING It Over

1. For each region in the population table above, calculate what percentage of the 1881 population arrived since 1871. Make a bar graph with 2 bars side-by-side for each region. One of the bars will represent the 1881 population of the region. The other bar will represent the percentage of the population that arrived in the region since 1871. There are two vertical axes for this graph: one on the left for population in 1881, and one on the right for the percentage of new arrivals. Colour the two kinds of bars different colours and include a legend. Write two conclusions you can draw from your graph. See pages S 16 to S 18 for help with graphs.

2. In your own words, explain the difficulty the government had in filling the Prairies with settlers. How would building a railway help to solve this problem?

3. Canada still has vast open spaces, with more than half of its population living between Montréal and Windsor. In a small group, discuss why that is. Should the government encourage people to migrate to the underpopulated areas today? Why or why not?

4. Revisit the predictions of the Métis on page H 78. Make a chart showing which predictions came true.

Immigration

Then

Canada had a small population in the late 1800s. Although the number of immigrants coming to Canada was small, they made up a significant percentage of the population. At that time, Canada actively encouraged immigration, publishing pamphlets and posters in various languages, and distributing them in European countries. Why do you think Canada focused on Europe to attract immigrants?

Now

The number of immigrants coming to Canada is much larger today. So, too, is the existing population. As a result, the percentage figures are generally lower than they were in the late 1800s (see the chart below).

Canada has always relied on immigrants to increase its population. Apart from First Nations people, everyone in Canada is an immigrant or is descended from immigrants. To this day, people continue to come to live in Canada from all over the world. This is a key factor in giving Canada its diverse nature.

Year	Immigrants	% of Total Population
1870	24 706	0.67%
1875	27 382	0.74%
1880	38 505	1.04%
1885	79 169	1.83%
1890	75 067	1.73%

Year	Immigrants	% of Total Population
1986	88 657	0.35%
1991	230 781	0.82%
1996	217 478	0.75%
2001	250 600	0.83%
2006	254 359	0.8%

In what ways might immigrants' reasons for coming to Canada today be the same, or different from their reasons in the 1800s?

As you learned in Chapter 2, British Columbia joined Confederation in 1871. At that time, Prime Minister John A. Macdonald promised to build a railway from Ontario to the West Coast within ten years. At first, the results were disappointing. Private companies could not see how such a railway would make a profit, and they did not want to invest in it. To make it more attractive for companies, Macdonald was prepared to offer them financial help and free land. How might this offer change how and when the railway was built?

A railway company could become rich because of the massive amounts of free land it would get. Soon fierce competition arose between groups to get the contract. However, before construction of the railway really got going, Macdonald became involved in a political crisis.

The Pacific Scandal

It was election time in 1872, and Macdonald needed money to pay for the Conservative Party's campaign. Sir Hugh Allan was a rich ship owner, and he donated $360 000 (equivalent to more than $7 million today) for the party to cover its campaign expenses. Allan was a member of a group that was trying to win the contract to build the railway. The $360 000 looked like a bribe to make sure that Allan's group had an advantage over its opponents. People who knew about it tried to keep the matter quiet.

The Conservatives barely won the election over the Liberals (103 seats to 97). Macdonald's government awarded the contract to build the railway to Allan's group. Then word began to leak out about the money Allan had given to the Conservatives. Two views emerged on the subject.

Support for Macdonald

At that time, it was legal for companies to give political parties money for their expenses. However, it was not legal to bribe politicians to take certain actions. Supporters claimed there was no evidence that Macdonald had agreed to give Allan's group the contract to build the railway in return for the money. So the money was not technically a bribe. Therefore, Macdonald's actions were proper, said his supporters.

Sir Hugh Allan

Criticism of Macdonald

It is important that politicians obey the law. It is also important that they appear to obey the law. Allan gave the money to Macdonald, who awarded Allan's group the contract. This created the appearance of improper conduct. For this reason, Macdonald's actions were wrong, said his critics.

Macdonald's Defeat

As a result of the scandal, Macdonald and his Conservative government were defeated in the House of Commons in 1874. Another election was called. This time, the Liberals defeated the Conservatives by 133 to 73 seats. The Liberal Party leader, Alexander Mackenzie, became prime minister.

Macdonald's Return

In 1878, Macdonald returned to power when the Conservatives defeated the Liberals by 137 to 69 seats. Macdonald won that election by coming out with a new economic policy. It was known as the National Policy and it did the following

- Raised tariffs on foreign manufactured goods. This helped Canadian manufacturers by making imports more expensive.

Examine this election campaign poster from the 1800s. What can you infer from it? What features can you identify that serve as symbols representing something else?

- Reduced tariffs on imported raw materials. This also helped manufacturers by allowing them to get cheaper materials.

The National Policy was very popular among Canadian industries. It provided many jobs in Canadian factories. It also allowed Macdonald to win three more elections (in 1882, 1887, and 1891).

The term "National Policy" died with Macdonald in 1891. For the next century, Canada maintained import duties on manufactured goods. In the 1990s, Canada moved toward free trade. Since the North American Free Trade Agreement came into effect in 1994, all goods manufactured in Mexico or the U.S. enter Canada duty-free. Duties on goods from many other countries have also been lowered.

The Canadian Pacific Railway

The scandal and the Liberal government ended Sir Hugh Allan's involvement in the railway. The Liberals were less committed to building the railway. By 1878, they had made only a few attempts at starting construction in Ontario and Manitoba.

The government was running out of time on its ten-year promise to British Columbia. In 1881, Macdonald awarded a new contract to build the railway to a Montréal company, the Canadian Pacific Railway (CPR). Its supporters included rich merchants and bank owners like Donald A. Smith, J.J. Hill, and George Stephen. In return for building and running the railway, the government agreed to give

- $25 million in cash

- about 10 million hectares of free land

- a guarantee of freedom from competition for 20 years

The company rushed to build the railway and completed it in just over four years.

Railway Construction

For five summers, workers toiled to lay track from Callander, Ontario, to Port Moody, British Columbia. It was relatively simple work through the Prairies, but the rock and muskeg in northern Ontario and the Rocky Mountains in the West presented huge obstacles. Fortunately, the CPR had a competent general manager.

WEB LINK •
For more information on the building of the CPR, visit our Web site.

Think about clearing a route for the railway through the Rocky Mountains. What would have to be done? Remember that there were no trucks or bulldozers at that time.

William Van Horne

William Van Horne was born in the U.S. in 1843. By 1880, he was general superintendent for a railway based in Milwaukee, Wisconsin. On January 1, 1882, he was appointed general manager of the CPR. His first duty was to supervise the building of the line. By 1883, it was complete from Winnipeg to Calgary.

He had his own private railcar and was deeply involved in the daily running of the line. He personally oversaw the hiring of **navvies** (labourers). He supervised the purchase of materials, and decisions regarding the line's route. When Van Horne's work was done, the CPR would act as a powerful symbol of Canada's expansion and nationhood. In 1888, Van Horne became president of the CPR. By the time he retired in 1899, he had made a huge impact on Canada.

William Van Horne

Chinese Labour

Andrew Onderdonk also supervised the building of the line eastward from Port Moody to Craigellachie, in British Columbia. Laying a route along the Fraser River was difficult work. There was a shortage of labourers in B.C., so the CPR imported workers from China. About two-thirds of the workers on this section were of Chinese origin.

The Chinese workers did the most dangerous work. They often blasted rocks with nitroglycerine, an extremely dangerous explosive. Many workers died in accidents involving these explosives. Many were also killed by falling rock blasts. Crowded living conditions, poor diet, cold weather, and lack of medical care also caused hundreds of workers to die. It is estimated that 600 to 700 Chinese workers died during construction of the railway. In addition to this, while white railway workers earned $1.50 to $2.50 a day, Chinese labourers were only paid $1 a day.

When construction was finished, the government wanted the Chinese to return to China. To encourage this, the government made it extremely difficult for the Chinese workers to bring in other members of their families. In 1885, the government imposed a "head tax" of $50 on every Chinese person coming to Canada. In 1900, the tax was increased to $100, and to $500 in 1902.

WORDS MATTER

navvies labourers; it is an abbreviation of the word "navigator" in the old-fashioned sense of a canal builder

During READING

Checkpoint
How fairly were the Chinese workers treated? Can you create a "Possibility" question for your chart?

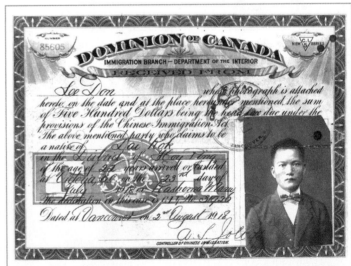

You read that Canada was encouraging immigration, but then it discouraged Chinese people from coming to Canada. Imagine you are a Chinese railroad worker. Write a letter to your family in China explaining why you cannot send for them to join you in Canada.

During the railway construction, some of the Chinese workers discovered jade deposits in the rocks of British Columbia. Jade has special value in Chinese tradition, as it is believed to bring health, wealth, and happiness. These workers supplemented their wages by mining jade and shipping it to China.

Completion of the Line

Donald Smith, Lord Strathcona, was president of the Bank of Montréal and provided much of the money to build the line. For this reason, he was given the honour of driving in the last spike at Craigellachie, B.C., on November 7, 1885. This spike joined the lines from the East and West together. The first passenger train left Montréal on June 28, 1886, and arrived at Port Moody six days later. In May, 1887, the line was completed from Port Moody to Vancouver. Finally, the transcontinental railway was completed.

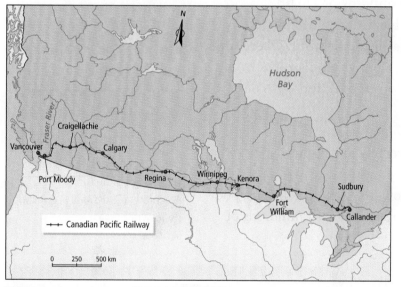

This map shows the new CPR line. Railway lines had been established east of Callander for some time.

The Impact of the CPR

The CPR ensured the survival of Canada. It made it possible to transport people and products right across the land from Nova Scotia to British Columbia. Settlement of the Prairies was also made possible. It acted as a visible symbol to the U.S. that all lands north of the 49th parallel were Canadian territory. It was one of the greatest achievements of the time.

THINKING It Over

1. a) Identify three challenges to building the railway and describe how each was overcome. b) Did the people involved with the railway project make the best decisions to overcome these challenges? Why or why not?

2. Obtain from your teacher the words to Gordon Lightfoot's song, "Canadian Railroad Trilogy." Your teacher can give you a copy of the words to follow as you listen. Draw a picture or write a poem to describe three things you found interesting in Lightfoot's song. Explain the reasons for your choices. Share and discuss your work with a partner.

3. In 2006, the Canadian government formally apologized to Chinese Canadians for unjust treatment in the past. With a partner, discuss the value of an apology more than 100 years after the injustice took place. What else, if anything, could the government do to correct the injustice today?

By 1885, settlers had begun to arrive in what is now Saskatchewan. Many Métis who had left Manitoba after the 1869 Resistance had settled in Saskatchewan, and they foresaw that they might lose their lands as they had in Red River. Earlier you read about the difficulties the Métis faced under the Dominion Lands Act. Over the years, their situation became more serious. The bison were disappearing and food was scarce. Many Métis faced starvation. How could the Prairies support more settlers?

During **READING**

Checkpoint
Earlier you learned about the different attitudes people had toward the land and the wildlife. Review and note whose interests must have won out if the bison were disappearing.

A Rebellion in the Making

The Métis began to send petitions to Ottawa, asking for secure title to their lands, agricultural aid, schools, and a local police force. When Ottawa ignored their demands, dissatisfaction grew.

Riel's Return

Louis Riel had been living in the United States. He was persuaded to return to lead the Métis a second time. On March 19, 1885, Riel seized the parish church at Batoche and formed a second provisional government. It was a repeat of the strategy he had used at Red River in 1869. First Nations chiefs supported this move. Cree chief Big Bear and Blackfoot chief Crowfoot were prepared to support Riel.

Macdonald's Advantages

There were some key differences between the first situation in 1869 and the second one in 1885. This time, Macdonald had some important advantages.

- He did not delay, and decided at once to fight Riel and his supporters.

- The North-West Mounted Police had been formed in 1873 (you will read more about this in the next chapter). Officers were in the area, available to fight. On March 25, the government began to assemble troops.

North-West Mounted Police barracks and parade square, 1885

- The CPR was almost complete. Soldiers could be mobilized quickly and sent from the East to resist Riel's troops. By April 10, 3000 troops had assembled at Qu'Appelle, near Batoche.

Major Events

Riel realized that war was afoot. He appointed Gabriel Dumont as his military commander. Dumont adopted **guerrilla tactics** to great advantage against the government troops. Instead of fighting the army head-on, Dumont's troops used ambushes. This worked well against the superior numbers and weapons of the army.

WORDS MATTER

guerrilla tactics fighting by means of ambush and surprise attacks

Battle of Duck Lake

Dumont won some early victories before the full force of the government could be assembled. At Duck Lake on March 26, 1885, Cree and Métis fighters forced the police and the army to retreat to safety. Guerrilla tactics were working.

Massacre at Frog Lake

On April 2, a breakaway band of Plains Cree warriors attacked Frog Lake. The focus of the attack was Thomas Quinn, an Indian agent who had treated the Cree badly. When he refused to go with his captors, he was shot. In the chaos that followed, eight other white men were killed.

In November, six Cree men were tried and hanged for their roles in the Frog Lake Massacre.

This incident was different from the battles of the Northwest Rebellion in that it was not Métis military forces fighting the Canadian army, but an independent band of warriors, motivated by hunger and mistreatment. As such, it influenced the reaction of settlers and the NWMP toward the rebellion, and it compelled the government to pay attention to the growing unrest.

Graves of the victims of the Frog Lake Massacre are marked with crosses.

Battle of Fish Creek

On April 24, Dumont organized about 150 First Nations and Métis fighters to ambush government soldiers at Fish Creek, about 20 km from Batoche. The government troops were taken by surprise. They suffered casualties before additional soldiers arrived as reinforcements. Both sides withdrew from the area.

Battle of Cut Knife

On May 1, War Chief Fine Day, with a force of Cree and Assiniboine fighters, encountered a government military force at Cut Knife. The army was almost surrounded by the warriors. Poundmaker, the Cree chief, persuaded the fighters not to pursue the army. They retreated, and casualties were fewer than they might have been.

Battle of Batoche

Riel was unhappy with Dumont's progress. He ordered Dumont to stop his guerrilla campaign and organize his followers to defend Batoche. This proved to be a military error. The army could now concentrate their efforts on one spot. Government troops marched on Batoche, taking all their equipment with them. The force of 900 soldiers attacked the 300 Métis, Cree, and Dakota defenders of Batoche from May 9 to 12. The defenders resisted at first, but government troops eventually captured the stronghold. Riel surrendered and was arrested. Dumont fled to the United States.

Chief Fine Day

From what you know about the Battle of Batoche, what moment has the artist captured in this image? Whose point of view is represented?

No figure in Canadian history has stirred as much controversy as Louis Riel. His fight for the rights of the Red River Métis has become an iconic piece of Canadian history. Passions still run high around this man whose impact on Canada was monumental.

HERO?

FREEDOM FIGHTER?

MURDERER?

FATHER OF CONFEDERATION?

TRAITOR?

MARTYR?

MADMAN?

PROPHET?

Born in Red River in 1844 Riel was a bright and well-educated child. At age 14 he was sent to Montréal and studied for ten years to be a Catholic priest. Four months shy of becoming a priest, he left his studies when he fell in love. The woman's family would not agree to the marriage because he was Métis, and he returned to Red River. By age 25 he was politically involved in the rights of the peoples of the North-West.

In 1869, the Hudson's Bay Company sold Rupert's Land to the Canadian government. Without consultation, Canada sent surveyors to the Red River Valley—home to the Métis—to claim the land for Protestant and English-speaking settlers. The Métis, fearing the threat to their way of life, named Louis Riel their leader and formed a provisional government.

MÉTIS PROVISIONAL GOVERNMENT 1869

The Métis believed the settlers would fence the land and disrupt the bison hunt on which they depended.

Thomas Scott belonged to a Protestant, anglophone group that tried to attack Fort Garry. He was jailed and then executed by order of the provisional government. His death fired up religious, political and racial tensions.

This land belongs to Canada. They will not dare to shoot me!"

IN ONTARIO

...we call upon the government to avenge [Scott's] death, pledging ourselves to assist in rescuing Red River territory from those who have turned it over to popery, and bring to justice the murderers of our countrymen.

MEANWHILE, IN QUÉBEC...

We pass a unanimous resolution asking the governor general to grant amnesty to Riel.

Riel escaped before Canadian troops arrived to arrest him for the "murder" of Thomas Scott.

Riel was disliked in Ontario, and admired and supported in Québec.

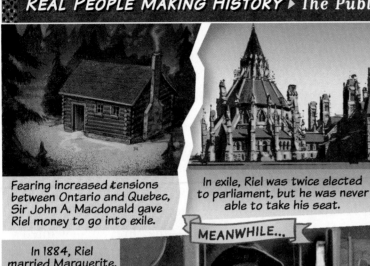

Fearing increased tensions between Ontario and Quebec, Sir John A. Macdonald gave Riel money to go into exile.

In exile, Riel was twice elected to parliament, but he was never able to take his seat.

Riel hid from the law for many years. He suffered a nervous breakdown, displayed erratic behaviour, and held religious ideas that were considered unconventional. He was committed to a mental institution in Québec in 1876. After his release in 1878, his growing appeal as a leader was based not only on his political aims, but also on his religious vision.

In 1884, Riel married Marguerite, a Métis woman.

MEANWHILE...

Many Métis moved westward, Gabriel Dumont went to the United States to ask Riel to present the Métis' grievances to the government.

I am the prophet of the New World.

THE NORTH-WEST REBELLION, 1885

Village of Batoche

Métis Forces

Saskatchewan River

Middleton's Army

Riel and his supporters set up a provisional government in March, 1885, hoping to make their demands heard. Within weeks however, Macdonald had assembled 3000 troops near Batoche. While Riel prayed, Gabriel Dumont used guerrilla tactics and won some early victories. Resistance forces were outnumbered and by June 3, it was all over. Dumont escaped to the U.S. and Riel was arrested and charged with treason.

Your Honour, Mr. Riel is insane.

TRIAL FOR TREASON

I worked at the risk of my life, to better the condition of the people of the North-West. What you will do in justice to me, in justice to my family, in justice to my friends, in justice to the North-West, will be rendered a hundred times to you in this world, and to use a sacred expression, life everlasting in the other.

A LINE OF RIEL'S POETRY...

How many who, with good desires, have died and lost their souls to fires.

Riel remains a hero to the Métis. The fight to pardon him continues to this day.

WEB LINK •••••••••••••••••••••••

For more information on the Northwest Rebellion, visit our Web site.

The Final Battles

The Cree fighters continued their resistance for a few days, but the fighting ended after skirmishes at Frenchman's Butte on May 28 and Loon Lake on June 3. The Northwest Rebellion was over.

Aftermath of the Rebellion

The Northwest Rebellion was the final resistance of the Métis and First Nations to the advance of the settlers. Riel was tried for treason and executed (see Real People Making History, pages H 106–H 107).

English–French tensions exploded across the country. People of British background—the "English"—wanted Riel to be dealt with harshly. The majority of people in Québec—the "French"—wanted him to be regarded as a hero because he had defended Roman Catholic and French language rights. Macdonald did not try to find a middle ground. When Riel was convicted of treason, Macdonald allowed the death sentence to be carried out. This infuriated the French. Support for the Conservative party in Québec plummeted.

In 1992, the government of Canada proposed a bill that reversed Riel's conviction for treason, recognized him as the founder of Manitoba, and acknowledged his contribution to the advancement of Confederation and of Métis rights. How do you think such a drastic change of public opinion comes about?

Why do you think Gabriel Dumont is on a Canadian stamp issued in 1985?

THINKING It Over

1. Make a timeline of the major events of the Northwest Rebellion. Include the dates, names of events, and a short summary.

2. Create a cause-effect-results chain web for the Northwest Rebellion. List each event and identify it as a) cause, b) effect, or c) result. See page S 19 for help with cause and effect.

3. a) Work with a partner. It is 1885. One of you prepares a short, one-minute speech to the judge, saying why Louis Riel should be executed. The other argues that he should be found insane. Do some research to find arguments for the two speeches. b) Deliver your speeches to each other. c) Now step out of your roles. Discuss whether you think he should have been executed, and why.

HISTORICAL THINKING SKILL

Developing Historical Perspective

"Louis Riel, you have been found guilty of the most pernicious crime a man can commit; you have been found guilty of High Treason. For what you did, your remarks form no excuse whatever, and the law requires you to answer for it."

Judge Hugh Richardson, 1885.

"In 1992, the Parliament of Canada and the Legislative Assembly of Manitoba formally recognized Riel's contribution to the development of the Canadian Confederation and his role, and that of the Métis, as founders of Manitoba."

Plaque on a statue of Louis Riel near the Manitoba Legislature.

Why do you think these views of Louis Riel and his actions are so different? Is one view simply wrong or misguided, and the other one right? Part of the reason for the difference is because they were written at different times in history. People who live at different times often develop different perspectives on events or issues. Part of understanding history is considering differences in perspective.

Step 1 Identify your own perspective

Before you can recognize other perspectives, you have to realize that your perspective comes partly from the time and culture in which you live, and is not shared by everyone. Consider an issue and ask yourself the following questions:

* What do I think about the issue and the best way to resolve it?

* What are my reasons for holding these views?

* What about my circumstances, culture, or time period might have influenced my positions?

Step 2 Identify other perspectives

People from different cultural groups develop different perspectives. Page H 90 of this chapter, for example, describes the different perspectives First Nations and settlers had of the land. One historian wrote a book titled *The Past Is a Foreign Country* to point out that perspectives are often different over time, just as they are across cultures. For the issue you identified above, ask yourself the following questions:

* What perspectives different from mine exist on this issue? (These might be in our time or in other historical periods.)

* Who holds these perspectives?

* What about their circumstances, culture, or time period might have influenced their decisions?

APPLY It

Review the section of the chapter on the Northwest Rebellion (pages H 103–H 108) and complete the following chart.

Who were the individuals or groups involved?	What was their perspective on the Rebellion and trial of Louis Riel?	What were the common living conditions, experiences, or historical circumstances that might explain why they held that perspective?

What You Will Need

- a game board
- one die
- six counters in two colours (e.g., three red and three green)

How to Play

A. Work with another person. It is 1880. Macdonald is desperately trying to get a private company to build the CPR from Ontario to British Columbia. Can your company be the first to reach an agreement with the government? To make the scheme possible, you will need

- $25 million
- about 10 million hectares of free land
- a guarantee of freedom from competition for 20 years

B. Place your counters on the START squares. Each player uses one colour.

C. Player A rolls the die and moves the "money" counter ahead by the number rolled. Then Player B takes a turn. If a roll lands on 3 or a 6, move the counter backward, but do not go below START.

D. In turn, the players roll the die and move their "hectares" counter forward.

E. In turn, the players roll the die and move their "years" counter forward.

How to Win

Repeat steps C to E until one player has moved all three counters into the highest squares and has persuaded the government to grant these terms to build the CPR. (Players do not have to roll the exact number to move into the highest squares.) When one of your counters is finished, you may have two die rolls in another turn to help you along.

$25 m	10 m ha	20 yr	$25 m	10 m ha	20 yr
$24 m	9.5 m ha	19 yr	$24 m	9.5 m ha	19 yr
$23 m	9 m ha	18 yr	$23 m	9 m ha	18 yr
$22 m	8.5 m ha	17 yr	$22 m	8.5 m ha	17 yr
$21 m	8 m ha	16 yr	$21 m	8 m ha	16 yr
$20 m	7.5 m ha	15 yr	$20 m	7.5 m ha	15 yr
$19 m	7 m ha	14 yr	$19 m	7 m ha	14 yr
$18 m	6.5 m ha	13 yr	$18 m	6.5 m ha	13 yr
$17 m	6 m ha	12 yr	$17 m	6 m ha	12 yr
$16 m	5.5 m ha	11 yr	$16 m	5.5 m ha	11 yr
$15 m	5 m ha	10 yr	$15 m	5 m ha	10 yr
$14 m	4.5 m ha	9 yr	$14 m	4.5 m ha	9 yr
$13 m	4 m ha	8 yr	$13 m	4 m ha	8 yr
$12 m	3.5 m ha	7 yr	$12 m	3.5 m ha	7 yr
$11 m	3 m ha	6 yr	$11 m	3 m ha	6 yr
$9 m	2.5 m ha	5 yr	$9 m	2.5 m ha	5 yr
$7 m	2 m ha	4 yr	$7 m	2 m ha	4 yr
$5 m	1.5 m ha	3 yr	$5 m	1.5 m ha	3 yr
$3 m	1 m ha	2 yr	$3 m	1 m ha	2 yr
$1 m	0.5 m ha	1 yr	$1 m	0.5 m ha	1 yr
START	START	START	START	START	START

THINKING It Over

1. Was the winner generally ahead throughout the game, or did he or she only start to move ahead in the final rounds? Why do you think this occurred?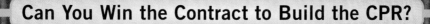

2. How did a player have an advantage when one of the counters was finished?

3. Do you think this game illustrates some of the advantages and disadvantages a company might have trying to win the contract to build the railway? Explain your answer.

PUTTING IT ALL TOGETHER

You have looked at a few more factors of how Canada expanded. You have seen how the expansion of the West became the focus of Macdonald's attention from 1869 onward. You have learned that treaties and the Indian Act changed life of the Prairies forever. Another rebellion, in 1885, proved unsuccessful and failed to keep the settlers out. The First Nations and Métis had to adapt to a new way of life, one that was harsh and restricted compared to their traditional way of life. The completion of the CPR, in 1885, was a major development in the expansion of Canada and an important symbol.

After READING

Predicting

Return to the chart you created and completed as you read this chapter. Which of your predictions were correct and why? Which of your questions were most useful in getting information and why? Discuss with a partner.

With your partner, use the most useful questions from your chart to create an organizer that might help a student who has a tough time with History. To help choose an organizer, skim through this book to see various organizers.

Purpose	One 5W + H	Add On	Question	Answer/Notes
Prediction (before reading)	Who?	+ will	Who will sign the treaties?	
Probability		+ would		
Possibility		+ can		
Thinking		+ might		

THINKING It Through

1. In a small group, write the key terms on a slip of paper. Divide the group into two teams and appoint a game leader. The leader will draw a slip of paper and show the word to one student in each team. Those two take turns giving one-word clues to their team and the first team to identify the word first earns a point. The game leader is the final judge. Teams can alternate who gives clues and who guesses. *k t c*

2. The development of the West and the Northwest has inspired many creative people to try to capture its spirit. These include
   - Emily Carr (painter)
   - Mungo Martin (artist)
   - Paul Yee (writer)
   - Robert Service (poet)

Do some preliminary research to find which one of these interests you the most and about whom you can find sufficient material for this Performance Task. For the person you have chosen

a) Locate primary and secondary source material that describes the person's life and illustrates the person's work. *k t*

b) Create a display with details of the person's life and examples of the person's work. *t a c*

c) Create a conclusion in which you summarize the importance of the person's contribution to recording history. *k t a*

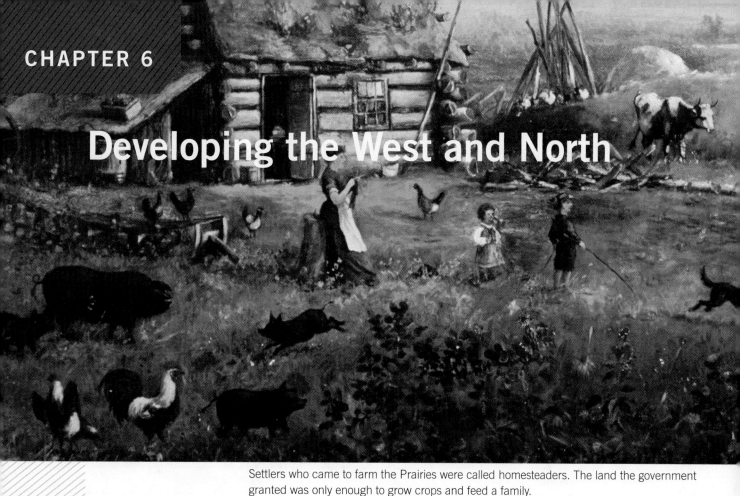

Developing the West and North

Settlers who came to farm the Prairies were called homesteaders. The land the government granted was only enough to grow crops and feed a family.

Before **READING**

Making Connections
- What do you picture when you hear the phrase "Wild West"? Turn to a partner and discuss your image. Then try to figure out why you have that picture in your mind. What things outside of school created that image for you?

As settlers moved to the Prairies, small communities began to develop where they could buy the goods they needed and sell their produce. The railway system grew, with lines branching out from the main line. This process determined where towns and villages would develop. The process was slow, steady, and permanent, but the Canadian government wanted to populate the region even more. What would you tell people to convince them to settle in the West in the late 1800s?

Areas north of the Prairies were not well-suited to farming. During the gold rushes, thousands of prospectors travelled to the North, worked their claims, and moved on. Nevertheless, the gold rushes led to further settlements, as well as the creation of the Yukon Territory in 1898. How do you think these communities, such as Dawson City, look today? How might they differ from the early days of settlement?

Many prospectors spent all their money travelling to the isolated northern region. Their hopes of finding gold were short lived.

Questions to Consider as You Read this Chapter

You will explore these aspects of the Unit 2 Big Idea: **How and why did Canada expand so rapidly following Confederation?**

- How did the settlers develop agriculture in the West?

- Why did communities develop in certain locations and not in others?

- How did the gold rush era affect the development of the West?

- How was law and order maintained in the "Wild West?"

- How can I describe the experiences of a person living in this time period?

Thinking About Literacy

Recognizing Signal Words

Signal words, or transition words, help to link ideas. Transition words can define (*is, means*), give examples (*such as, including, as illustrated*), compare (*like, similar*) or show cause and effect (*as a result, consequently*). Signal words can also suggest an opinion. Some opinion words are *fortunately, disagree, likely*.

As you read this chapter, note signal words as you find them. Write down why that word is being used. You can use an organizer like this one.

Page	Signal Word	Purpose of Signal Word

As you read in the previous chapter, there was a need for a police force to help peaceful development of the Prairies, maintain law and order on the frontier, and establish Canadian authority in the North.

The North West Mounted Police

The government created the North West Mounted Police (NWMP) in 1873. South of the border, the U.S. cavalry wore blue uniforms. To distinguish NWMP officers in Canada from their American counterparts, the force wore bright red uniforms. In 1874, hundreds of NWMP officers left Fort Dufferin, Manitoba, and headed west. They fanned out into different parts of the region and built a number of forts in which they lived.

WEB LINK ●·····························
For more information on the NWMP and the RCMP, visit our Web site.

The Whisky Trade

One of the first things that the NWMP officers had to do was to control the illegal whisky trade. Unscrupulous merchants were supplying low-quality alcohol. Liquor consumption led to increased violence, adding to the West's reputation as a wild, lawless place.

The whisky trade was particularly harmful to First Nations. Until Europeans arrived, First Nations people had not had access to alcohol. The whisky trade had devastating effects on their lives.

Promises to the Blackfoot

Reverend John McDougall, a Methodist minister, was sent into Blackfoot territory. He promised that the NWMP would end crime, such as whisky trading and horse stealing. He told them that everyone would be equal in the eyes of the law. Chief Crowfoot told him:

Reverend John McDougall leads the First Nations contingency at the Calgary Stampede Parade in 1912.

My brother, your words make me glad... We want peace. What you tell us about this strong power which will govern with good law and treat the Indian the same as the Whiteman makes us glad to hear. My brother I believe you and am thankful.

Preventing "Indian Wars"

In the late 1800s, the western U.S. experienced a great deal of conflict between the settlers and Native Americans. These battles were known as the "Indian Wars." Although Canada experienced some conflict, it was nowhere near the scale of that in the U.S. The NWMP were credited with preventing large-scale violence. The NWMP established forts and controlled the whisky trade. They developed friendships with First Nations people, which helped in the treaty negotiations. As you read about in Chapter 5, the treaties had their own challenges.

During **READING**

Checkpoint
Think about what the letters NWMP and RCMP stand for. What does the change from NWMP to RCMP say about how Canada has changed?

The Royal Canadian Mounted Police

The NWMP was the forerunner of the Royal Canadian Mounted Police (RCMP). In 1920, the force adopted its present name. Today, the RCMP is the largest police force in Canada, with about 26 000 officers and civilian employees. It is responsible for enforcing federal laws throughout Canada.

NWMP Forts in the Prairies, with Founding Dates

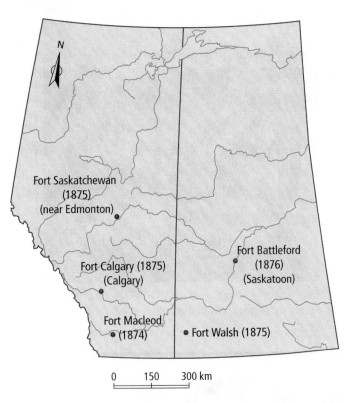

Why do you think forts were located in these spots?

For ceremonial occasions, the RCMP still wear the traditional red tunic the NWMP were known for. Why do you think that is?

THINKING It Over

Do some research to find out more about the NWMP and the RCMP. Create a Venn diagram to compare the duties of the NWMP in the 1880s and the RCMP today.

Changing Faces in the Police Force

Then

In 1874, the first NWMP officers left Manitoba to establish order in the West. The government wanted strong, able-bodied men who could ride horses well, and read and write in either English or French. The NWMP and the RCMP continued to only hire men who met height and weight criteria, and adhered to the strict dress code. Unofficially, women helped the police force by dealing with female offenders. Later, women were sometimes hired as civilian members to work as lab technicians or to fulfill office duties.

Now

The RCMP has since changed its hiring policies. Recruits no longer have to meet certain restrictions, but they have to complete a timed physical task they might face while on duty. Women can apply to the force. In 1975, the first all-female troop graduated wearing the traditional red serge.

In 1990, the uniform dress code was examined when Baltej Singh Dillion, a Sikh, was accepted into the RCMP. He fought for his right to wear a turban. Dillion won his case and Sikhs have since been permitted to wear turbans in the police force. One year later, the first all-Aboriginal troop completed their RCMP training. More than 190 First Nations now work with the RCMP.

This image shows a typical early NWMP troop of the late 1800s. What are some of the traits these men share?

Why do you think steps were taken to increase the presence of women and visible minorities in the RCMP?

THINKING It Over

1. Decide what criteria should be used to hire officers today. With a partner, discuss what you based your decisions on.

2. What is the importance of a uniform? Does dress interfere with a person's ability to do a job? Why or why not?

3. Using your research from page H 115, what role do you think the RCMP should have in the future?

The railway was completed and a new police force had been established to ensure a safe passage westwards. The Prairies were ready for settlers.

The Settlers Pour In

Before the completion of the CPR in 1885, settlers had to travel west by horse and wagon. It was a difficult and dangerous journey. Most settler families began their final westward trek in Winnipeg. Many of them would not survive the journey to their new homestead. If they did, they had to build shelters and find food before the long and cold winter set in. Who might be able to help the homesteaders adapt to life on the Prairies?

The Plaxtons were a family who headed west from Ontario to take up a homestead in Prince Albert, in what is now Saskatchewan. Mud and mosquitoes made the journey a nightmare. Jennie Plaxton wrote:

> *We travelled quite a distance when we met another couple— also a bride and bridegroom. The bride was in torment with mosquitoes just nearly crazed with them... [O]ne morning while he was hunting his horses, the young wife found his revolver and shot herself. The poor woman was buried on the top of a hill where a wooden cross marks her grave.*

What would you advise the homesteaders to bring on their journey to survive temperatures as low as -40°C?

After completion of the Canadian Pacific Railway (CPR), the number of settlers increased rapidly. In 1891, Ontario had a population of more than 2.1 million people, and Québec had under 1.5 million. The West and Northwest had small populations by comparison, but they were growing steadily.

Population in the Northwest, 1871, 1881, 1891

Year	Manitoba	Northwest Territories	British Columbia	Total
1871	25 228	48 000	36 247	109 475
1881	62 260	56 446	49 459	168 165
1891	152 506	98 627	98 173	349 306

Experimenting with Wheat

In the Prairies, the growing season can be as short as 90 days. Many crops that grew well in the East needed a longer growing season on the Prairies. Farmers began to experiment with different wheat strains to see if they could develop new varieties that were better suited to the Prairie climate.

By the 1890s, the government recognized that developing suitable grain varieties was a key requirement to populating the Prairies with farms and settlers. By the turn of the century, scientists at the Department of Agriculture had developed a new variety of wheat called Marquis. It was ideal for the Prairies because it ripened early and could take heavy winds. How could Marquis wheat allow settlers to extend the agricultural belt in the Prairies?

WEB LINK ● ● ● ● ● ● ● ● ● ● ● ● ● ● ●
For more information on Canada's development of wheat, visit our Web site.

This grain harvesting machine called a binder was invented in the 1880s. Why do you think the Prairie region became known as "the breadbasket of Canada"?

The Diaries of Captain John Palliser

Captain John Palliser was an Irish landowner who spent from 1857 to 1860 investigating the land in the Prairies. He was sent there by the British government to report on the area's possibilities for the future. His diaries of the expedition give us a good idea of what the area was like before settlement began. Here is how he described what is now the southern limit of Calgary.

We started at noon to-day... At the same time the whole camp started, and as the long straggling train of [Stoney First Nation] men, women, and children... wound up the zigzag trail that leads from this pretty little valley to the level of the plain above, the scene was very picturesque... The pasture is now very fine everywhere, and timber plentiful in many places, as we have now entered the belt of fine country that skirts the base of the mountains.

The view, including a humanized foreground, [varying levels of land]... vertical vegetation offering shade as well as signposts for [judging] distance, and (at this point in its course and at this time of year) a meandering river, seems to welcome [us] back to [this pleasing region].

Palliser described the landscape, but not the weather. How might his report have been different if it had been a cold winter day?

THINKING It Over

1. In your own words, identify three positive things that Palliser notes about the region. **K**

2. Imagine you are a member of the British government who is reading Palliser's report of his journey. Would you regard the region he describes in this extract as suitable for settlement? Explain your reasons to a partner. **t C**

The Growth of Winnipeg

WORDS MATTER

incorporated formally organized as a community with its own local government

land speculators people who buy cheap property hoping its price will rise

scrip a coupon that could be exchanged for land

Before 1880, Winnipeg had been a collection of ramshackle buildings, wooden sidewalks, and dusty streets. It was **incorporated** in 1873, but it did not appear to have a real future. Then, in 1881, word leaked out that the CPR would be routed through Winnipeg. How would this development change the value of the land?

People from the East began to flood in, trying to make fast money. In the next few months, 3000 **land speculators** hit town. They planned to buy land cheaply, hold it for a while, and sell it for a huge profit. They preyed on people who did not know how valuable their land could become.

The Métis were entitled to more than 600 000 hectares of land under the deal that brought Manitoba into Canada in 1870. Each Métis family got a coupon, called **scrip**, that could be exchanged for a designated amount of land. Many had never claimed their land and still possessed their scrip. Land speculators often bought up the scrip for virtually nothing. Of the 15 000 or so scrips handed to the Métis, about 12 800 ended up in the hands of speculators. What effect would this have had on Métis land ownership?

Soon Winnipeg was a bustling town. The railway made the city a gateway to the West as immigrants crowded through it on their journeys to claim a homestead. By 1900, its population was 52 000, and it was on its way to becoming an important city. In 2006, Winnipeg's population was 694 668.

Winnipeg was a "gateway to the West." How would that help its economy?

The Rise of Prairie Towns

A similar pattern developed across the Prairies. The railway added value to the land it passed through, and towns sprang up along the main line. Homesteads without railway access were less valuable as they remained isolated and spread out. What patterns do you see in the following three case studies?

Portage la Prairie

Portage la Prairie was established as a site for fur-trading posts. Until 1880, its population was small. The land in the region was fertile and therefore well-suited for farming, but the only way into the community was by canoe along the river. In 1880, it was announced that the CPR would come through the community. Soon access would be easy. The settlement grew rapidly. By 1907, there were enough people for it to incorporate as a town. In 2006, Portage la Prairie's population was 20 494. It has become a regional centre for western Manitoba.

Lumsden

Lumsden was originally a village called Happy Hollow. It was situated 26 km northwest of Regina and the CPR main line. The land there was fertile and ideal for growing wheat; however, there was no simple way to get materials in and out of the area. In 1890, another company opened a railway line near Regina, running north through Lumsden. Happy Hollow changed its name to honour Hugh Lumsden, a senior engineer for the rail company. It was incorporated as a town in 1905 and has been an economic centre for farms in the area for more than a century.

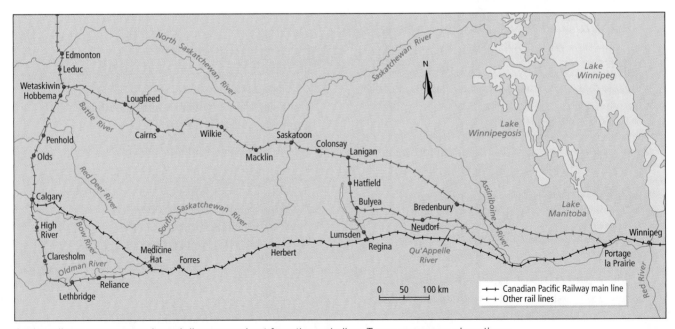

As the railway system grew, branch lines spread out from the main line. Towns sprang up along these routes, as this map shows. What effect did this have on the development of the West?

The communities of the Prairies developed as they did because railway companies planned station stops approximately every 16 km. A horse could haul a loaded cart 8 km to a grain elevator and home again in a day. The grain was loaded from the elevator onto a train and hauled away to market. With stations 16 km apart, all farms on the line were within a day's journey of an elevator and railway station.

Olds

Olds lies 89 km north of Calgary. There was little settlement in the area. The land is ideal for cattle ranching, but unless farmers could easily get their animals out to market, they would not establish operations here. The coming of the railway changed all that.

Many old wooden grain elevators have been taken down and replaced with concrete and steel versions. What are the benefits of preserving historic grain elevators?

The CPR came through Calgary and settlers began to arrive to take up homesteads. However, it was not until the opening of the Calgary–Edmonton Railway in 1891 that settlers could easily travel north of Calgary. The village of Olds developed at this time, and it was incorporated as a town in 1905. It was named after George Olds, who was a traffic manager for the CPR. It quickly developed into a cattle ranching centre. Olds has become a bustling town, offering a variety of services to the area. In 2006, its population was 7248.

THINKING It Over

1. Summarize the key difficulties that settlers faced in trying to establish a new life for themselves in the Prairies. Do you think you would have been able to deal with these conditions? What are your reasons?

2. In your own words, explain how the following things are linked to the development of the Prairies:
   • fertile land
   • settlement
   • railways

3. With a partner, discuss what effects the exploding settler population was likely to have on the Métis and First Nations populations.

4. Research the work of William Saunders (1836–1914) and Sir Charles Saunders (1867–1937), who developed Marquis wheat. In a table, graph, or chart, illustrate a particular aspect of their importance.

5. Do some research on the history of one of the settlements shown in the map of new towns on page H 121. Does the settlement you chose follow the same patterns as those shown in any of the three communities examined in this section— Portage la Prairie, Lumsden, and Olds? In a small group, explain any similarities and differences you found.

For help with research activities, see pages S 6 and S 7.

In this chapter, you have been learning about the settlement of the Prairies. This was a planned and orderly movement of people, regulated by the government. There was another movement of people in the West, and it was wild and uncontrolled. This movement was caused by gold fever.

Donald McLean was a trader for the Hudson's Bay Company in B.C. He bought gold dust from the First Nations people in the Kamloops area in the 1850s. He knew that when word got out about the presence of gold in the region, prospectors would flock to the area. He wrote:

Checkpoint
You thought about the Wild West when you started reading this chapter. How does the phrase "wild and uncontrolled" contribute to that image?

> *The reputed wealth of the [area] is causing much excitement amongst the population of the United States of Washington and Oregon, and I have no doubt that a great number of people from those territories will be attracted [there] in the spring.*

The Fraser River Gold Rush

Since 1849, **prospectors** had been panning for gold in California. They sifted the sludge in sandbanks, looking for small pieces of gold that had been washed out of the ground by the river's action. However, California was becoming worked out, and prospectors began to look for gold elsewhere.

In 1858, prospectors found gold in the Fraser River valley, near Lillooet, B.C. This set off a wave of people who made their way north, hoping to make their fortune. Dr. J.S. Helmcken described the morning of April 25, 1858, in Vancouver harbour.

WORDS MATTER

prospectors people seeking valuable minerals, especially gold

> *One [S]unday morning we were astonished to find a steamer entering the Harbour from San Francisco... [The miners]... built tents of grey cotton: hundreds of these tents dotted the land from Government Street almost as far as Spring Ridge... The town thus grew and grew... Everyone wanted to get to Frazer's [sic] River.*

CANADA MINUTE

The First Gold Strike
The first gold discovery in Canada was made in 1823. It was along the shores of Rivière Chaudière in the Eastern townships of Lower Canada (Québec).

WEB LINK •••••••••••••••••••

For more information on the gold rushes, visit our Web site.

Within a year, about 30 000 people had made their way to the Fraser River in search of gold. Most were Americans who had sailed up the coast to Vancouver. There was no railway from Montréal or Toronto to British Columbia, so Canadians had great difficulty getting there. The town of Yale quickly became the centre of activities in the valley.

Cariboo Wagon Road above Yale River

Cariboo Gold Rush

There was a second gold rush from 1860 to 1863. Prospectors found gold farther north, on the Horsefly River. A new community— Barkerville—sprang up. This site contained deep **placers**. The hillsides also contained deep **veins** of gold. The prospectors first **staked a claim**. Then they dug mines and hacked out the gold-bearing rock. Before Barkerville ran out of gold in the 1930s, it produced about 37 500 ounces (more than 1100 kg) of pure gold.

Compared with the settlement of the Prairies, this movement of people was mayhem. People raced to get to promising sites. There were no police to maintain order. People stole each other's stashes of gold. Miners got swindled out of their money in crooked card games or spent it in bars.

Getting supplies in and out of the gold rush area proved to be a big challenge. The Cariboo Wagon Road was built from Yale to Barkerville just for this. Wagons pulled by teams of strong horses could carry several tonnes of freight. You could get a ride in a stagecoach between the two towns. The journey took about six and a half days. Today, the Trans-Canada Highway follows much of the original Cariboo Wagon Road. One ambitious company brought in camels because they could carry heavier loads and travel farther in a day than mules could. The camels were not well-suited to the terrain, however, and the experiment failed.

You could ride a stagecoach between the towns that grew around the gold rush.

Why would camels not be well-suited to the Cariboo gold rush?

In June of 1862, a group of about 150 men, one woman, and three children left Fort Garry (Winnipeg) heading for the British Columbia goldfields. They were known as the Overlanders.

Augustus Schubert, a German immigrant was age 30 when they set out.

Catherine O'Hare Schubert, a 27-year-old Irish immigrant was 4 months pregnant.

Their children were ages 5, 3, and 1.

The sisters at St. Ann's Mission, near Fort Edmonton, tried to persuade Catherine to stay with them until the baby was born. Catherine refused.

Thank you, but I want my family to stay together.

As the Overlanders crossed the mountains, they were forced to abandon horses, cattle, and everything but necessities. Catherine watched fellow travellers die due to the grueling hardships.

In northern B.C. some of the Overlanders built rafts to travel down the Thompson River toward Quesnel.

Come, my boy!

It is said that that Catherine went into labour while still on the raft. On shore, in wintry conditions and with the help of First Nations women, Catherine gave birth to a healthy baby girl named Rose.

SAFE ARRIVAL

After nearly twenty years of unsuccessful gold prospecting the Schuberts settled on a farm in B.C.'s Okanagan Valley. Catherine died in 1918 at the age of 83. She was a true pioneer and the first European woman to cross overland to B.C.

The Effects of Prospectors

The arrival of the gold prospectors was destructive to the First Nations. Prospectors damaged the land in their attempts to find gold. They sometimes burned off forest areas to get to gold-bearing rock. The chemicals they used sometimes got into the water system. They did not consult the First Nations or seem to care about the effects of these chemicals on these people.

Before the gold rush, the government had not signed treaties with First Nations living in the area. Prospectors took over the land and started mining. First Nations are currently negotiating with the government for compensation for the damage done to their societies and the land by the gold prospectors.

This is a modern gold mining operation. How do you think the environmental impact of modern gold mining is different from the impact of the gold rush?

THINKING It Over

1. In point form, summarize five events described in this section. Identify which one you would most like to have witnessed. Explain your reasons.

2. Research more information about the gold rush communities of Yale and Barkerville. With a partner, discuss which aspect of gold rush life you find interesting.

3. Imagine you are Catherine Schubert in 1918, looking back over your life. Write a journal entry or a poem expressing how you feel about your life. Or write and present a short monologue as though you are Catherine telling her grandchildren stories about "the old days."

Determining Historical Significance

What is history? You might think that is a simple question that can be easily answered with something like, "History is the story of everything that has happened in the past." That answer is not truly correct, however. The past and history are different things. The chart below illustrates some of the differences.

The Past	History
The past is everything that ever happened.	The past is past; it no longer exists.
There is no organized story to the past, only evidence that survives to give us clues about what happened.	History only deals with a small part of what happened in the past.
History is a present account or story of the past.	History uses evidence of the past to tell stories about it.

Step 1   Make decisions

One challenge that historians encounter is making decisions about what parts of the past are significant enough to include in their accounts. Various historians make different decisions about this. The chart below contains tables of contents from two books used to teach Canadian history in Canadian schools.

From *Canada's Heritage* by A.A. Cameron 1955, revised 1967	From *Canada Through Time* by Angus Scully, John Bennington, Rosemary Evans, and Carol Wilson, 1992
Unit 1–Our British Background	Unit 1–You and Your Community
Unit 2–Our French Background	Unit 2–The Native Peoples of Canada
Unit 3–Our American Neighbour	Unit 3–The Community of New France
Unit 4–Canadians Help to Build Their Heritage	Unit 4–Building a New Society

Make your own chart outlining the similarities and differences between these two tables of contents. Since the period of history covered is basically the same, what do you think explains the differences? Why did these historians select some very different things to include in their books?

Determine significance

Historians cannot tell about the whole past, so they must select parts of it that they think are particularly important. To do this, they consider several criteria such as

- Was the event important at the time it happened? Did people notice it?
- What consequences did it have? How many people did it affect? For how long? Over what area? How long did the consequences last? Are we still experiencing the consequences?
- Is it symbolic of some important period or movement in history?
- Has it been memorialized and remembered? If so, how? In books? Museums? Monuments? Historic sites?
- Does it help explain important things about the present?

APPLY It

Use the questions above to try to explain the differences in the tables of contents. Why, for example, does the book written in 1992 include a whole unit on Native Peoples while the other table of contents does not mention them?

Pick out five historical events or people from your textbook. Use the questions above to help you decide which are the most significant.

Take a look at other textbooks that cover the same period as yours and chart the similarities and differences. What do they show about what the different historians consider significant?

Why Was the Yukon Territory Created?

During READING

Checkpoint

"Until" is a signal word. What does it help you to understand here? Add it to your list.

In August 1896, prospectors discovered placer gold on a river that flowed into the Klondike River, in the Northwest Territories. Things remained calm until word leaked out. In July 1897, two ships reached Seattle and San Francisco with gold from this strike. A Seattle newspaper published a report saying that there was "a ton of gold" in the Klondike. Soon 100 000 **stampeders** were on their way to the remote location. About 30 000 successfully got there.

Getting to the Klondike

The quickest, yet most expensive, way to the Klondike was by boat to Alaska. The stampeders then had to cross the mountains.

The Mountain Passes

The Dalton Trail was one of the easier and less dangerous routes, but it was the longest. The Chilkoot Pass route was steep and hazardous. If they could afford it, stampeders could hire packhorses to ferry their supplies up the pass. The last 800 m to the summit rose 300 m, however, and this was too steep for pack animals. The stampeders had to cache their supplies at the top, as they carried them up, load by load, on their backs.

White Pass was even more difficult. More than 3000 pack animals died on it. It was nicknamed "Dead Horse Trail." Once the stampeders reached Whitehorse, they had to go by boat along the Yukon River to Dawson City, about 800 km away.

The "All-Canadian" Route

The route through Alaska was expensive. Some stampeders tried to make their way to the Klondike by "all-Canadian" routes from Edmonton, Alberta, or from Prince George, British Columbia. These routes were slow, however; the trip could take as long as two years.

Ferrying Supplies

The stampeders could buy almost nothing along the way. There were no suppliers, so they had to take supplies with them. This meant that they had to go back and forth along this route, ferrying some of their supplies each time. NWMP officers stationed themselves at the top of the Chilkoot Pass and White Pass. If stampeders did not have enough supplies to last them for a year, the police turned them back. Otherwise stampeders risked starvation. Here is a list of the food items considered necessary for one year.

Stampeders climbing the Chilkoot Pass, 1897. At the top, 1500 steps had been carved out of the snow and ice for the people climbing up.

WORDS MATTER

stampeders people who rushed to gold strikes

45 kg navy beans	4.5 kg tea	115 g vinegar
68 kg bacon	9 kg coffee	2 dozen tins condensed milk
180 kg flour	4.5 kg baking powder	9 kg dried potatoes
18 kg rolled oats	9 kg salt	2 kg dried onions
9 kg corn meal	450 g pepper	6 tins/110 g beef extract
4.5 kg rice	900 g baking soda	34 kg dried fruits
11 kg sugar	225 g mustard	

In addition, stampeders had to haul their clothing and their camping and prospecting equipment.

Women in the Klondike

Difficult as the trek was for men, it was even more challenging for women. Customs of the day required that women wear corsets, ankle-length skirts, and high-heeled boots. Women who discarded these in favour of more practical men's clothing were considered immoral. Some women also had children to care for in the harsh conditions.

Dawson City

The Klondike River had always had rich stocks of salmon. First Nations people traditionally met there every summer to catch fish and to dry them on the flat land where the Klondike and Yukon Rivers met. When gold was found in 1896, a surveyor staked the flatland for the town he knew would soon spring up. Soon, about 16 000 people were living there as gold fever reached its peak. The First Nations had lost their fishing grounds. Between 1897 and 1904, stampeders are estimated to have taken out more than $100 million in gold.

Many of those who made it to Dawson City were disappointed. Early arrivals had staked the best claims. The claims that remained required an awful lot of work. Most of the gold lay at a depth of about 3 m. In winter, the ground was frozen and impossible to dig. Once the ground had thawed in spring, stampeders had to dig up loads of muck and sluice the gold from it—a dirty and unhealthy job.

The End of the Gold Rush

The gold deposits were soon worked out. In 1899, gold was found in Nome, Alaska. Many stampeders moved on. The Klondike gold rush was over, and Dawson City grew smaller. Today, tourism is its largest industry.

Skookum Jim Mason, a member of the Tagish First Nation, became very rich from mining gold on Bonanza Creek. He later left money to support other First Nations people living in the Yukon.

Dawson City was founded in 1896. By 1898, it was the largest city west of Winnipeg, with about 40 000 people in the area.

The Creation of Yukon Territory

The Klondike was part of the Northwest Territories. The gold rush showed that the region was rich in natural resources. People pressured the federal government to divide the territory in two. The government agreed, and in 1898, the Yukon Territory was created. It took its name from the Loucheux First Nations name *Yu-kun-ah*, or "great river." Dawson City was its first capital, but years later, in 1953, the capital was transferred to Whitehorse.

WEB LINK • • • • • • • • • • • • • • • • • • •
For the remainder of this Robert Service poem, and more information on Service, visit our Web site.

Robert Service: A Poet's View of the Klondike

Nothing captures the essence of life during the Klondike gold rush as does the poetry of Robert Service (1874–1958). He worked for the Canadian Bank of Commerce at Whitehorse and Dawson City. He wrote poetry in his spare time, and published his first poems in 1907.

Robert Service in a canoe, Northwest Territories, 1911

Service's poems deal with the wild characters he observed in the gold rush towns of the Yukon. There were thieves, card sharks, and people out for a good time. Service wrote poems that made his characters leap off the page. He was important as one of the first writers who established an international reputation for storytelling for Canada. This is part of Service's poem "The Spell of the Yukon."

I wanted the gold, and I sought it;
I scrabbled and mucked like a slave.
Was it famine or scurvy, I fought it;
I hurled my youth into a grave.
I wanted the gold, and I got it—
Came out with a fortune last fall,
Yet somehow life's not what I thought it,
And somehow the gold isn't all.

No! There's the land. (Have you seen it?)
It's the cussedest land that I know,
From the big, dizzy mountains that screen it
To the deep, deathlike valleys below.
Some say God was tired when He made it;
Some say it's a fine land to shun;
Maybe; but there's some as would trade it
For no land on earth—and I'm one.

THINKING It Over

1. Create a mind map or other organizer to identify some of the hardships the stampeders experienced getting to the Klondike, and surviving once they got there. 🄚 🄣

2. Your teacher will hand out the Robert Service poems "The Shooting of Dan McGrew" and "The Cremation of Sam McGee." With a partner, take turns reading aloud verses from the poems. With a partner, present 1–2 of your favourite verses to the class. Explain how the poem is connected to Canadian history. 🄣 🄒 🄐

PUTTING IT ALL TOGETHER

You have learned about the settlement and development of Canada as it expanded westward after Confederation. Settlers and agricultural methods spread to the Prairies. Towns developed along the railway. Gold rushes occurred in British Columbia and the Klondike. The Klondike rush was so powerful and sudden that the federal government created a new territory—the Yukon Territory—out of the Northwest Territories. Throughout the period, the red uniforms of the North West Mounted Police became a symbol of Canadian law and order in the West and the North. The era examined in this chapter set the way for Canada to become a strong and united country.

After READING

Recognizing Signal Words

Write a cause-and-effect paragraph to show what caused an area of the West to be settled. Use your signal words when writing.

Page	Signal Word	Purpose of Signal Word

THINKING It Through

1. In a group of three, each student researches the roles and reactions of one of the following to the expansion of Canada:
   - a settler family developing a homestead in the Prairies
   - a First Nations or Métis person living in the West
   - Captain John Palliser on his expedition through the Prairies
   - a stampeder during the Klondike gold rush
   - a NWMP officer stationed in either the Prairies or the Klondike region

   For help with creating questions to guide your research, see page S 8.

2. a) Use your research to make a visual and written display. b) Create a one-page graphic novel, similar to the one on page H 126, about your person. Include appropriate vocabulary used during the time period. Add the graphic novel to your display. c) Combine each group member's display to create a mini-museum. Guide other students through your exhibit.
   Ⓚ Ⓣ Ⓒ

Back to the Big Idea

How and why did Canada expand so rapidly following Confederation?

Throughout this unit, you have

- looked at how settlers and immigrants have helped develop Canada
- examined the effects of treaties and settlement on First Nations people
- identified the role of the North West Mounted Police
- learned why and where communities developed

Use a graphic organizer to answer the question, **How and why did Canada expand so rapidly following Confederation?**

Show That You Know

Historians look to the past to find out how and why a major change took place over a period of time. They identify different factors that contributed to the overall change, explaining the contribution of each factor. Review what you have written to answer the Big Idea question on the previous page. With one or two partners, identify three factors that contributed to the rapid expansion of Canada after Confederation. You will create a display, incorporating text and visuals, to show how and why Canada expanded so quickly.

Tip: Make sure that you fully understand the different components (such as title, subheadings, text, pictures, cartoons, or other visuals) that your teacher expects you to use in your display.

Step 1 Research each reason

Use a variety of primary and secondary sources to find information about the three reasons you have selected. Make sure you assemble a variety of visual and text items.

Tip: To understand primary and secondary sources, see page S 4.

Step 2 Create a rough outline of your display

Select the key items you wish to include in your display, and draw up a rough plan for where each one will go in the display. Try to make your display visually attractive as well as historically accurate.

Tip: You may find it easier to have correctly sized roughs of the various items and physically move them around a display rough until you get the best results.

Step 3 Create the final copy of your display

Arrange your material in an interesting and creative manner. Create your final copy, making sure that it contains all the elements listed in the various steps.

Tip: You may find it easier to cut out the various items you are going to include and to paste them onto a cardboard backing.

Step 4 Present your findings

Present your display to a small group of students or to the whole class. Depending on how much time you have, explain each item or select a few key ones. Allow time for your audience to ask questions after your presentation.

Tip: Practise presenting your material to make sure that you know exactly what you are going to say about the items you have included in your display.

Canada: A Changing Society

> How did social and economic factors, technology, and people promote change in Canada?

Why do you think almost 4000 First Nations men served in the Canadian army in the First World War?

In the early 1900s, Canadian cities were growing very rapidly. Why do you think that might have been?

Why was getting the vote important to women?

What's the Big Idea?

In 1904, Sir Wilfrid Laurier said, "Let me tell you, my fellow Canadians, that all the signs point this way, that the twentieth century shall be the century of Canada... Canada shall be the star towards which all men who love progress and freedom shall come." Why might Laurier have made this statement? Who do you think would agree, or disagree, with his ideas?

Unit 3 will help you examine the opportunities, challenges, and changes faced in Canada between 1885 and 1914. You will use graphic organizers to review what you have learned.

Key Terms
advocate, movement, temperance, reciprocity, entrepreneurs, multiculturalism, alliance, entente

What You Will Learn in this Unit

You will explore these aspects of the Unit 3 Big Idea:

- What were the key features of Canada between 1885 and 1914?
- What contributions did different people and groups make to its development?
- What were the social and economic conditions in Canada?
- What internal and external pressures for change existed?
- How did Canadians respond to these pressures?
- How can I use the inquiry process to evaluate and present my research?

CHAPTER 7

Growth and Change

This industrial section of Chaudière, Ontario, is typical of the growth of factories in Canadian cities in the early 1900s.

Before *READING*

Making Connections

Look at the labels on your clothes. Make a list of the countries where they were made. Find out whether any of those countries use child labour.

- What labour laws exist for children in Canada? Consider age requirements, hours, pay, health, and safety. This chapter will help you see why these laws are important, and how they came to be.

What do you think your first job will be out of school? How will your career be similar to that of someone living in Canada before the 20th century? Up to the late 1800s, Canada's economy had been based almost entirely on natural resources—the fur trade, farming, fishing, and forestry. The period between 1890–1914 witnessed the rapid growth of Canadian mining and manufacturing.

New communities, like Lethbridge, Alberta, and Sudbury, Ontario, developed to take advantage of local resources. Older cities, such as Montréal, Québec, or Toronto, Ontario, continued to grow into large manufacturing centres. Factories were built there to take advantage of the large supply of cheap labour. The growth of cities brought new challenges, however. Many factory workers, including women and children, worked long hours in terrible conditions for very little pay. What could be done to improve their quality of life?

These women, demonstrating in New York City in 1912, show that Canadian women were not alone in their fight for the right to vote. What does this tell you about the importance of this struggle?

Questions to Consider as You Read this Chapter

You will explore these aspects of the Unit 3 Big Idea: **How did social and economic factors, technology, and people promote change in Canada?**

- When and how did mining and manufacturing become important?

- What factors contributed to the growth of industries and cities?

- What effect did inventions and technology have on Canadians?

- How would my life be different if there had not been pressure to change the position of women and children in Canada?

- How can I compare the challenges facing farmers and workers around 1900 with their challenges today?

Thinking About Literacy

Finding the Main Ideas

A concept map is similar to a web, but is organized into specific subtopics.

Your purpose is to determine what changes took place and how these affected Canada. Use the subheadings or questions in this chapter as subtopics. Add details under each subtopic.

Subtopic
-
-
-

Subtopic
-
-
-

Change in Canada

Subtopic
-
-
-

A Study of Two Towns: Lethbridge and Sudbury

During READING

Checkpoint

When you compare something, you examine similarities and differences. Create a T-chart or Venn diagram to compare Lethbridge and Sudbury. How do these two cities reflect change in Canada? Add that information to your concept web.

In previous chapters, you have learned about the expansion of agriculture that took place in the 1880s and 1890s. This trend continued into the 1900s. There was a strong demand in the United States and Europe for wheat, Canada's main export. In 1901, wheat exports amounted to 2 000 000 tonnes. By 1913, they had climbed to 7 700 000 tonnes. Farmers could sell all the wheat they could produce.

There was another kind of economic expansion going on at this time. Canada is rich in natural resources such as coal, iron, copper, and nickel. These were not as valuable as gold, but there were large deposits of these minerals across the country. Once prospectors found the deposits, businesses quickly took over to develop them. In this section, you will learn about how fuel and mineral resources were responsible for the start of two towns that are now cities.

WEB LINK •
For more information on Lethbridge, Alberta, visit our Web site.

Wheat became "king" in the Prairies. Why do you think that was?

Predict what you think Lethbridge's population will be in 50 years. What did you base your prediction on?

Lethbridge, Alberta

The area that eventually became Lethbridge lay in the extreme southwestern part of the Northwest Territories, about 200 km southeast of Calgary. It is rich in coal deposits. It became the first industrial town in western Canada. Lethbridge showed that the West's economy would not be based just on agriculture. Mining was going to be important to the region. Today oil and natural gas have replaced coal as Alberta's most valuable fossil fuels. Lethbridge's population in 2006 was 95 196.

1874

- Nicholas Sheran, a New Yorker who originally came to Canada as a gold prospector, opened the first coal mine digging horizontally into the side of a river valley to create a drift mine. He supplied coal to the NWMP post at Fort Macleod. He soon sold his coal across the border in Montana, where it was very popular at $25 a tonne.

1882

- The North Western Coal and Navigation Company established the first large-scale operation in the area. Miners used hard labour and some mechanical aids to dig the coal. Horses and mules dragged the coal out in cars on railway track. The miners eventually dug a drift mine about 300 m into the side of the valley. This was as far as they could go without proper ventilation methods.

1883

- There were four drift mines dug into the valley, and a dock on the Oldman River was used to ship the coal to the CPR main line.

1884

- The town was known as Coalbanks and had a population of about 250 people.

1885

- The company built a 175-km railway line from Coalbanks to Dunmore, near Medicine Hat, to join the CPR main line.
- A new town, called Lethbridge, was surveyed to replace Coalbanks. It had six stores, five hotels, 19 saloons, four billiard rooms, two barber shops, and a stable. Its population was about 1000.

1892

- The first shaft mine was dug. Shaft mines contain a vertical shaft, with horizontal galleries coming off it into the coal seams.

1908

- Coal production reached 1634 tonnes/day

1914

- The outbreak of the First World War further boosted demand for coal.

1884

- Thomas Froode and James Cockburn founded the McAllister and Lady MacDonald Mines in Sudbury in 1884, mining copper and other minerals.

1885

- Samuel Ritchie, from Akron, Ohio, began prospecting in the area for copper deposits.

1886

- Ritchie's Canadian Copper Company began mining in the area, with a workforce of 25 miners. The rock contained large amounts of nickel, but it had no commercial use at the time. British and French scientists later developed a way of using nickel to harden steel and the demand for nickel took off.

1893

- Thomas Baycroft, a Scotsman, founded the Tam O'Shanter mine property in Snider Township. Legend has it that Baycroft had such a keen prospecting instinct that he could literally smell mineral deposits. He later sold the mine to the Canadian Copper Company.

1898

- Aeneas McCharles, a prospector from Cape Breton, Nova Scotia, founded the North Star Mine near Creighton. He sold it to Mond Nickel Company in 1902.

1902

- Ritchie merged the Canadian Copper Company with six others to form the International Nickel Company—Inco.

1907

- John Frawley, one of Sudbury's first merchants, and Luc Potvin established a gold mine in Long Lake, near Sudbury. It operated from 1909 to 1916, employing about 600 miners. By 1910, it was producing about 25 percent of Ontario's gold.

1914

- The outbreak of the First World War further boosted demand for nickel and the other minerals that came from Sudbury.

Sudbury, Ontario

There was no settlement in the Sudbury area until the CPR line came through in the early 1880s. In building the line, labourers uncovered rocks that contained a valuable mineral, copper. Prospectors soon moved in to look for rich sites. They could quickly become rich by discovering deposits and later selling the sites to businesses that could mine them. Copper—and later nickel—became the basis of Sudbury's wealth. These minerals were exported all over the world. In 2006, Sudbury's population was 157 857.

WEB LINK • • • • • • • • • • • • • • • • • • •

For more information on Sudbury, Ontario, visit our Web site.

What reasons would a family have to relocate to Sudbury, Ontario?

Canada's wealth began with its agriculture, but mineral and fossil fuel production developed and expanded rapidly in the late 1800s and early 1900s. These two industries showed what a promising future Canada had. Immigrants began to flock to the new nation to find work, not only on its farms, but also in its mines. Soon, the Canada of 1867 was unrecognizable in the rapid economic expansion that took place.

THINKING It Over

1. a) Identify two events in the history of i) Lethbridge and ii) Sudbury that you find significant. Create two newspaper headlines that could be used to introduce a report about each event. b) Explain why you find the events you chose significant.

2. In a small group, discuss how other groups, such as First Nations or farmers, might feel about the events you chose in question 1.

3. a) Do some research into the size and economic structure of your own community around 1900. What was its size then, and now? What were/are its main industries? b) Create a Venn diagram to compare the development of your community with that of Lethbridge or Sudbury.

In the 1890s and the early 1900s, Canadian cities grew, factories were built, and the demand for workers increased. Mine and factory owners turned to children as sources of cheap labour.

POOR CONDITIONS

LOW WAGES LONG HOURS

There were no health and safety standards in the workplace. Children were abused. They were often fined for talking or being late, and as a result, sometimes ended up owing the company money. Workdays were often 12 hours or more. Children as young as eight worked under these conditions.

Whether they worked in a rural mine or an urban factory, these children and their families had very little money, and lived in poor conditions.

AT THE ROYAL COMMISSION ON THE RELATIONS OF CAPITAL AND LABOUR 1889

I think that by age 12, a child should be able to work.

He struck her several times on the body... When the overseer let her go, she was so weak she had a hard time getting up.

Human needs before property rights!

VOTES FOR WOMEN!

THE LAW CONCERNS WOMEN

END CHILD LABOUR

VOTES FOR WOMEN

PROGRESS WAS SLOW

At the turn of the century, the Social Gospel movement brought together reformers who spoke out against the injustices of child labour, inequality, poverty, and for women's suffrage. A prominent reformer, J.S. Woodsworth, worked with the poor at the All People's Mission in Winnipeg. Many women's groups were dedicated to ending child exploitation and fought for better living and working conditions.

How Did Cities and Factories Grow?

Canada experienced rapid expansion between 1881 and 1911. In 1881, about 25 percent of the population lived in cities. By 1911, this percentage had almost doubled. At the same time, there was a rapid increase in the number of factories manufacturing goods. **Entrepreneurs** opened factories in cities that had access to raw materials and transportation. The growth of cities and the growth of factories were related to each other.

The Snowball Effect of Factory and City Growth

The growth of cities and industries created a snowball effect. They grew together, getting larger all the time. The process worked like this.

The Snowball Effect of Canada's Population

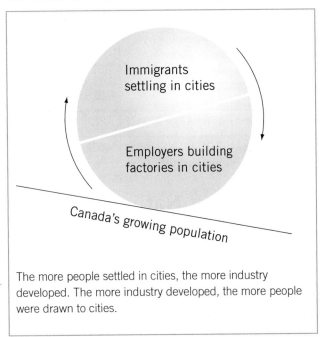

The more people settled in cities, the more industry developed. The more industry developed, the more people were drawn to cities.

Immigration

Immigration was the most important factor in population growth at this time. The number of immigrants varied depending on how well the economy was doing. If the economy was doing well, the government opened the immigration tap. If it was performing badly, the government slowed immigration to a trickle. You can see the variation in immigration rates in the table on the next page.

During **READING**

Checkpoint

What main idea about change is discussed in this section? Add it to your concept map.

WORDS MATTER

entrepreneurs people who start or organize businesses

Environmental Milestones

The Creation of National and Provincial Parks

Despite the growth of cities and factories, there were also efforts to preserve the environment. Banff National Park, west of Calgary, was founded in 1885. It is Canada's oldest National Park. Algonquin Provincial Park, in eastern Ontario, was founded in 1893. It is the oldest provincial park in Canada. This was an era of rapidly expanding population and settlement. Such parks were set aside to preserve the natural beauty and ecology of the areas.

Immigration to Canada, 1880s–1910s

Decade	Immigrants
1881–1890	866 177
1891–1900	339 268
1901–1910	1 644 347
1911–1920	7 712 624

WORDS MATTER

expropriate legally take property from its owner

cottage system the manufacture of goods made by many people working individually in their homes

factory system the manufacture of goods made by many people working together in a large building

Immigration reached its peak in 1910 and the years immediately following it. In 1913—the last full year before the outbreak of the First World War—400 870 immigrants streamed into Canada. Most were escaping terrible conditions in their home countries and hoped for a better life for themselves and their families. Some came in search of land to homestead; some were recruited for mining; others took factory work.

The Growth of Cities

Cities seemed to be a natural place for many immigrants to settle and search for work. The following table shows how quickly Canadian cities developed during this era. The country was on its way to becoming an urban society.

Population Growth in Canadian Cities, 1891–1911

Place	1891	1911	Increase
Halifax	38 437	46 619	22%
Montréal	219 616	528 000	140%
Toronto	181 215	381 833	111%
Winnipeg	25 639	136 035	431%
Calgary	3876	43 704	1028%
Vancouver	13 709	120 847	782%
Canada	**4 833 000**	**7 207 000**	**49%**

Industrialization and First Nations

Some First Nations people took construction jobs in the growing cities or worked in mines, lumber mills, or canneries. Some Aboriginal women were hired for cleaning or laundry. On the whole, however, First Nations people were marginalized by industrialization, especially as immigrants became more numerous.

This was not the case for all Aboriginal people. Some who stayed on reserves prospered if they had good land. In Saskatchewan, for example, the Assiniboine reserve successfully practised mixed farming, growing vegetables, grain, and raising cattle and sheep. However, Aboriginal lands were in demand by growing towns and industry. In 1908, the federal government made it possible for Aboriginal people to be moved from any reserve that was close to a town of more than 8000 citizens. In 1911, a change to the Indian Act allowed municipalities or companies to **expropriate** reserve land for certain uses, such as roads or railways.

Factories Changed the Way People Worked

John A. Macdonald's National Policy increased tariffs on imported manufactured goods. This encouraged businesses to build factories at home to supply the expanding Canadian market. The period from the 1880s onwards saw a huge growth in factories that manufactured clothing, household goods, and many other products. Factories changed the way goods were produced. Up until the appearance of factories, textiles had been made in the **cottage system**. Look at the following table and note some of the differences between the cottage system and the **factory system**.

Woman in a sewing factory, around 1912

How a Shirt Was Made

The Cottage System—1800	The Factory System—1900
1. Farmers grew and harvested flax. They then sent the flax to individual families in their cottages.	1. Cotton fibre was imported from the U.S. to a factory in the city.
2. Children separated the fibre from the rest of the plant.	2. Various machines spun, wove, dyed, cut, and sewed the cloth to produce a finished shirt.
3. Women used spinning wheels to spin the fibre into thread.	3. Unskilled workers fed materials into the machines, removed finished products from them, and kept them clean. Skilled workers maintained the machines.
4. Men wove the thread into linen cloth.	
5. The cloth was then sent to another family cottage.	4. The shirt was then sent to the store for sale.
6. Children dyed the cloth.	
7. Adults cut and sewed the cloth to produce a finished shirt.	
8. The shirt was then sent to a shop to be sold.	

Spinning, weaving, cutting, and sewing required much skill. Families worked together to produce goods.

Women and children performed much of the work. Families did not work as a unit.

Working Conditions in Factories

Factories were dangerous places to work. Today, most factory machines are powered by electricity. They draw power through protected electrical cables. In the 1890s, access to electricity was not common. Factory machines were often powered by open belts running from pulleys in the ceiling. These were, in turn, powered by belts running from a pulley attached to a steam-powered boiler. With all these open belts so close to workers, accidents were inevitable. Hair, arms, and clothing could easily get caught up in the belts, so workers had to be very careful. In the cramped working conditions, mistakes were easy to make.

Although factory work generally paid poorly, women and children earned less than men did. In 1911, in Québec textile factories, female spinners were paid on average 12.8 cents an hour. Men earned 19.6 cents for similar work. Factory wages did not go far.

Rising Voices Demanding Change

How would you describe the working conditions in this factory?

These social injustices did not go completely unnoticed. Various groups began to **advocate** for reform in the factories. Religious organizations, social reform groups, and trade unions were prominent in the struggle for social change.

The Social Gospel

James S. Woodsworth was a Methodist minister in Winnipeg. He supported an interpretation of the Bible that was known as the **Social Gospel**. Religious people had a duty to improve their communities, he said. Woodsworth and others organized charities to help the poor and pressured the government to pass laws to protect workers. The Social Gospel **movement** became an important force in the early 1900s.

The Temperance Movement

The Woman's Christian **Temperance** Union (WCTU) was founded in the 1870s. It supported **prohibition**. Temperance literally means "moderation." To the WCTU, it meant banning alcohol entirely. The movement saw alcohol as a social evil. In their opinion, alcohol caused drunkenness, crime, family violence, and consequently ruined many lives. The WCTU organized factory workers into groups to "take the pledge"—vow to refrain from alcohol consumption.

The WCTU also demanded that the government introduce laws to protect workers from the worst evils of the workplace, such as child labour. They campaigned against the use of tobacco and actively promoted education and women's rights. The WCTU continues its work to this day.

James S. Woodsworth

Woman's Christian Temperance Union convention in Calgary, 1911

CANADA MINUTE

Women and the Vote

There was much resistance to women's suffrage (the right to vote in elections). In Ontario, women who owned property could vote in local elections from the 1850s onward, but the fight to vote in provincial and national elections continued. In 1916, Manitoba became the first province to allow women to vote in provincial elections. In 1917, some women got the vote in federal elections. The following year, most women got the federal vote.

WEB LINK • • • • • • • • • • • • • •
For more information on the Woman's Christian Temperance Union, visit our Web site.

WEB LINK • · · · · · · · · · · · · · · · · ·

For more information on the history of labour unions, visit our Web site.

Labour Unions

The terrible conditions in many Canadian factories led many workers to join labour unions affiliated with workers' unions in the U.S. Unions worked to improve conditions through negotiations with employers, and strikes, if necessary. Unions in Canada made only limited progress at this time, for the following reasons:

- The federal and provincial governments were hostile to unions. They saw unions as conspiracies to hurt employers.

- Unions were generally interested only in male workers. The Knights of Labor was one of the first unions to concern themselves with women, as well as men.

- Early unions were formed by skilled workers, such as boiler makers or carpenters. They were generally not concerned with unskilled labourers.

Year	Number of Employed People	Number of Unionized Workers	Percentage
1911	2 723 634	133 100	4.9%
2004	13 400 000	4 100 000	30.6%

Why might unions enter a float in a parade, such as this Teamsters Union float in a Lethbridge parade in 1912?

As the chart shows, more than 95 percent of workers in Canada were not union members in 1911, so unions had very limited influence. As the number of immigrants continued to rise, and cities and factories grew, union membership also increased. Still, factory wages remained low and working conditions poor for many years. The hard work and dedication of unions and the various other groups that tried to improve the situation ensured progress, but it was slow.

THINKING It Over

1. Look at the table on page H 147 showing how a shirt was made in the old cottage system and in the factory system. Use illustrations to create a timeline to show the various stages of production in both systems. Which system do you prefer? Why?

2. Much has been accomplished in terms of the conditions these women worked to improve upon, but there are still areas in the world where those conditions are still serious concerns. Choose one issue, such as child labour, women's right to education, factory conditions, or health care, and write a persuasive letter to the editor expressing your point of view on the matter. Remember to explain your reasons for your opinion.

Using Historical Novels

You can learn a lot about history by reading historical novels. The following is an extract from *L'enfant cigarier* (*The Child Cigar Maker*), written by Marie-Paule Villeneuve. It tells the story of Jos, an 11-year-old boy employed in a cigar factory.

How would you feel about having to work in a cigar factory instead of going to school?

The Queen Cigar Factory waited for him... Whenever he saw it, Jos always felt his heart flutter. A dungeon. From seven in the morning to six at night... he was held prisoner there, six days a week...

Jos had been employed at Queen's since September 6, 1885, his ninth birthday. That year, the Québec government passed a law preventing manufacturers from employing boys less than 12 years old, or girls less than 14...

As the morning passed, Jos placed the cigars in piles. The supervisor passed by regularly, collecting each batch of 50, eliminating at least five that were too long, too ripped, too fat, or too thin. Jos didn't hear his criticisms any more. He knew that the darned cigars wouldn't get thrown out. Subtracted from his pay, that was all...

Jos had worked at Queen's for two and a half years. His work contract, which his father had signed with an X at lawyer Archambault's office, stated that he would get a dollar a week the first year, two the

second and three the third. After two and a half years, he never earned more than a dollar, his wages always being cheated by fines that he thought were unjustified...

[At the end of the week, Jos's fines are greater than his wages. He owes the factory 15 cents. His father complains to the manager. The manager explains,] "It's very simple. He's made 500 cigars, of which 200 were ruined. He talked to his work companions ten times and was late for work once. In future, when he's not on time, he must report to the police station, as stipulated in his contract. The company has agreed to teach him the trade of a cigar maker. It's a chance for him. Do you want him to be a packer like you all his life? It's for his own good. He's only an apprentice."

THINKING It Over

1. Think of three words that describe your feelings about the working conditions the author describes in the factory. Discuss the reasons for your word choice with a partner. **t c**

2. With a classmate, discuss what strategies the author has used to inform her audience about the topic. How effectively has she done this? What would you do differently? **t c a**

During READING

Checkpoint

Write the name of each person in this section and note if and how that person's contribution relates to your life.

The late 1800s and early 1900s was a period when many inventors and pioneers had an influence on the development of Canada. Some made inventions that directly helped businesses to expand, or people to live easier lives. Others pioneered new roles for women or better schools for children. The work of the inventors and pioneers was amazing and has had a lasting impact.

George Ross (1841–1914)

George Ross was Ontario's Minister of Education (1883–1896) and Premier (1899–1905). As Minister of Education, he improved the education system in the province, building many new schools to house the rapidly expanding population. At that time, there were lots of disputes over language and religion. (For example, Should French be allowed as a language of instruction? Should the government fund Roman Catholic schools?) Ross managed to reduce tensions over these issues and to give more children a chance at an education. Businesses benefited by having employees who could read and write. They could read and understand instructions for operating machinery and also safety warnings.

Alexander Graham Bell (1847–1922)

Alexander Graham Bell, a Scottish immigrant, was an inventor with many different interests. He worked with his father as a speech therapist for hearing impaired people. He was especially interested in how sounds are transmitted. He began to experiment with different ways of transmitting sounds—such as the human voice—by electrical connections. He is most famous for developing the first telephone system in 1876. With his assistant, he was able to transmit understandable sounds by wire in a demonstration in Brantford, Ontario. This led to the development of the first telephone, which gained popularity in the 1890s. The telephone helped businesses to communicate more easily with one another. Today, it is a part of everyday life.

John A.D. McCurdy (1886–1961)

John A. D. McCurdy was a partner in the Aerial Experimental Association, at Baddeck, Nova Scotia. McCurdy worked with Alexander Graham Bell and Bell's wife, Mabel Hubbard, to develop a "flying machine." They successfully launched more than 200 short flights before their greatest success, in 1909. The "Silver Dart" was the first powered airplane to take flight in the British Empire. McCurdy spent the rest of his life helping to develop airplanes. Very expensive at first, air travel allowed business people to travel greater distances to supervise their companies.

Adam Beck (1857–1925)

Adam Beck was first a business person in London, Ontario, and was later elected mayor. He saw that electricity could make people's lives easier. In 1905, he persuaded the Ontario government to develop a hydroelectric plant in Niagara Falls. It began operations in 1910, supplying cheap power to homes and businesses in the area. He worked tirelessly to persuade cities and towns to hook into the hydroelectric system. Electrical machines replaced steam-powered ones in factories. This eliminated many of the open belts and pulleys, and greatly reduced worker accidents.

Martha Black (1866–1957)

Martha Munger came from Chicago, but spent most of her life in the Yukon. She prospected for gold during the Klondike Gold Rush of the 1890s, and later ran a sawmill. In 1904, she married George Black, Commissioner of the Yukon, and she later became a member of parliament. She gave lectures on the Yukon in Britain, and was made a member of the Royal Geographical Society in 1917—a rare honour for a woman at this time. In 1935, she was elected to parliament as the member for the Yukon—only the second woman to be elected to the House of Commons. Her book, *My Seventy Years*, tells of her adventurous life, from the gold rush to parliament.

Robert Samuel McLaughlin (1871–1972)

Robert Samuel McLaughlin worked with his father and brother in a carriage-building business in Oshawa, Ontario. In 1908, he expanded the business to include automobile production. The company built Buicks and Chevrolets in Oshawa for an American company. In 1918, General Motors of Detroit bought the business, but retained McLaughlin as its president. Oshawa became a major automobile-producing centre. By the mid-1920s, the plant employed more than 3000 people. Trucks and other automobiles made it easier to ship raw materials to factories and finished goods out of them. This helped businesses become more efficient.

Guglielmo Marconi (1874–1937)

Guglielmo Marconi was born in Italy. He was interested in electricity and radio waves. Around 1900, he began to investigate long-distance radio waves. He believed that it was possible to send signals across the Atlantic. In this way, a radio company could compete with telegraph cables connecting Europe and North America. In 1901, he launched a kite containing a radio antenna into the air at Signal Hill in St. John's, Newfoundland. He successfully received radio signals transmitted from a tower in Cornwall, England, 3500 km away. These experiments were important in helping to develop regular trans-Atlantic radio contact.

Mabel Hubbard Bell (1857–1923)

Mabel Hubbard was born in Boston, Massachusetts. She became deaf at the age of five, from Scarlet fever. Mabel Hubbard was highly intelligent, with a special talent for science. She married Alexander Graham Bell in 1877. Mabel and Alexander were the first editors of a magazine published by the National Geographical Society, which was founded by Mabel's father in 1888. It has since become one of the world's leading monthly magazines. She ably assisted Alexander in many of his experiments. She also assisted their friend, J.A.D. McCurdy, as he developed his "Silver Dart" airplane. She developed a strong interest in women's rights. She helped women to get appointed to teaching positions in Boston in the 1870s. She also played a prominent role in efforts to win women's suffrage in the U.S. She was a pioneer who did not let any obstacle stand in her way to achieve success.

These pioneers and inventors helped to create change in Canada. Life in cities and factories began to improve. Transportation improved. Women and children started to get fairer treatment. What would life be like today if it were not for the achievements of these pioneers and inventors?

THINKING It Over

1. Why were these inventors and pioneers significant? With a partner, discuss how their contributions are significant to your life today.

2. Choose four of the people in this section. What effect did their work have on business and industry in the past and today?

3. Plot these people and their contributions on a timeline. With a partner, discuss how some of their contributions might have helped others to make their contributions.

How Did Women's Roles Change?

The role of women in society was severely restricted in the late 1800s. Married women were expected to devote their lives to their family. It was extremely rare to find women involved in business or politics. This situation began to change as some women and organizations started to challenge the limitations placed on them.

During **READING**

Checkpoint
Note how each woman contributed to change in Canadian society.

Dr. Emily Stowe (1831–1903)

In 1854, Emily Jennings became the first female principal of a public school in Canada West. She was principal of Brantford Central School until she married John Stowe in 1856. As expected of middle class women at the time, she resigned from her job and devoted her life to her family.

After raising three children, she decided to become a doctor. No medical school in Canada would accept a female student, so she enrolled in a school in New York. She graduated in 1867, and decided to open a medical practice in Toronto. However, the body that licensed doctors in Ontario refused to accept her application. She then opened a medical clinic, specializing in the nursing care of women and children. After 13 years, in 1880, she finally obtained a licence to practise medicine. In 1883, Dr. Stowe's daughter, Dr. Augusta Stowe-Gullen, became the first woman to graduate from a Canadian medical school.

In 1981, a Canadian postage stamp honoured Emily Stowe.

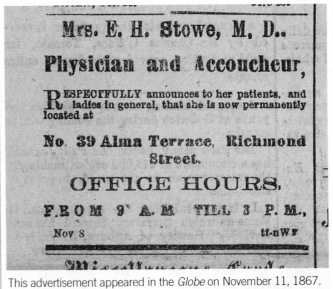

This advertisement appeared in the *Globe* on November 11, 1867.

Ishbel Maria Gordon, Lady Aberdeen (1857–1939)

Ishbel Maria Gordon's husband, Lord Aberdeen, was governor general of Canada from 1893 to 1898. Ishbel, though, refused to play the quiet life expected of the wife of the queen's representative. Lady Aberdeen opposed the working conditions that women faced in factories; she also opposed the many limits society placed on all women. She believed that women could help to make society more civilized if they were allowed to play a larger role in it.

How do you think politicians or factory owners would have reacted to Lady Aberdeen's views at this time? How would women have reacted? Explain.

WEB LINK ●·····················

For more information on women who influenced change in Canada, visit our Web site.

She served on committees and was important in the founding of the National Council of Women of Canada (1893) and the Victorian Order of Nurses (1897). Queen's University recognized Lady Aberdeen's accomplishments by granting her an honorary degree. She was the first woman in Canada to receive such a degree. Her commitment to women's issues made her an important force of change at this time. Her work resulted in many benefits for women.

The National Council of Women of Canada (1893)

The NCWC was one of the first groups founded to pressure politicians and business leaders to address women's issues. Its first president was Lady Aberdeen. The NCWC worked for the expansion of education for women. It supported women's rights to vote and become involved in public affairs. Today, the organization is still a powerful supporter of women's causes.

The Victorian Order of Nurses (1897)

To celebrate Queen Victoria's sixty years on the throne, Lady Aberdeen helped to establish the Victorian Order of Nurses (VON). Its mission was to provide community health care by going into people's homes to give nursing assistance. The people who benefited most were the elderly or chronically ill. The VON built 44 hospitals, but eventually handed them over to other organizations to run. It felt it would be better to focus on home nursing than to diversify.

Two women cyclists. Bicycles liberated women from restrictive clothing and from chaperones.

VON nurses leaving the Montréal branch building to go out into the district, 1910. Why is public health nursing still important today?

Adelaide Hoodless (1857–1910)

Adelaide Hoodless lived a comfortable married life until her infant son died after drinking non-pasteurized milk. She realized that many women needed better education. They particularly needed to know more about household management. She pushed for domestic science classes in schools. She also worked with Lady Aberdeen to found the NCWC and the VON. She founded the Women's Institute (WI) movement to educate and support fairness for women in society. In 1897, she opened its first chapter at Stoney Creek, Ontario. From these small beginnings, the WI grew into an international organization.

Adelaide Hoodless

Nellie McClung (1873–1951)

Nellie McClung became a member of the Woman's Christian Temperance Union and supported its efforts to prohibit the sale of alcohol, obtain better labour laws, and allow women to vote. From 1921 to 1926, she was a Liberal member of the Alberta Legislature for a district in Edmonton. She became a prominent speaker and writer across western Canada. Today, she is regarded as an important part of the movement to obtain fair treatment for women in Canadian society.

Emily Murphy (1868–1933)

Emily Murphy was born in Ontario, but spent most of her adult life in Manitoba and then the Edmonton area. She became a self-taught legal expert and lobbied governments to improve the legal rights of women. In 1911, she persuaded the Alberta government to pass an act guaranteeing widows one-third of their husband's wealth. In 1916, she was the first woman in the British Empire to be appointed as a magistrate. In this position, she could act as a judge in some court cases.

Emily Murphy

On her first day as a magistrate, a lawyer challenged her right to hold the position as she was not considered a "person" in the legal sense of the term. She denied the lawyer's motion that she should step down from the case. She began to work with others in a series of court actions to have the law changed to ensure that women were legal persons. At this time, the law did not allow women to be appointed to the Senate. In 1929, the law was changed to allow women to be members of the Senate.

THINKING It Over

Research the roles and status of First Nations women in the late 1800s and early 1900s. Record your findings in a chart. Watch for bias in your sources and distinguish between fact and opinion. See page S 10 for help with detecting bias.

Understanding Historical Evidence

You learned in Chapter 6 that some parts of the past are left out of history books because historians do not think they are particularly significant. Other parts are left out because there is no evidence left for historians to use to develop their stories. Historians must have evidence in order to write history. Two kinds of evidence historians use are accounts and traces.

Accounts describe or explain events—they tell stories. They can be primary sources, such as diaries or letters from the time of the events, or secondary sources written later. Your history book is a secondary source account.

Traces are items from the past that do not tell a story by themselves, but offer clues about what life was like or what happened. They are usually primary sources such as artifacts, photographs, and buildings. Historians try to read the clues in traces to help them develop accounts of the past. The tag pictured below is a trace from around the time of Confederation.

It is a trace because it does not tell a story of what happened, but it does offer lots of information or clues about what life was like. When historians find a trace, they ask some questions like the ones below. Try these with this trace.

Step 1 Questions for artifacts

- What is the object?
- What might it be used for?
- Who would use it?
- When or in what period was it used?
- What clues or information does it give about the time or about the people who made it and used it?

Photographs are also traces. Historians often use them to gather evidence to help tell stories. On page H 57 of your textbook, there is a photograph of the people who participated in the Québec Conference in 1864. It is a trace. Look at it carefully and consider the following questions.

Step 2 Questions for images

- Who is in the image? (You might also ask who is not in the image?)
- What are the people in the image doing?
- Who might have taken the picture?
- Why was the picture taken?
- When was it taken?
- What does the picture tell you about the time period, Confederation, and the people responsible for it?

APPLY It

Your textbook includes images of artifacts, buildings, and people engaged in various activities. These are all traces that provide evidence of what happened in the past. Examine some of these, asking the kinds of questions outlined above, and develop a list of things you can say about Canada in the 1800s.

PUTTING IT ALL TOGETHER

Between 1890 and 1914, social and economic factors, technology, and people promoted change in Canada. The mining boom led to the creation of new towns. In established towns, the population grew rapidly. Immigrants poured in, many of them settling in Montréal, Toronto, Winnipeg, and Vancouver. Companies located factories in cities to take advantage of the population growth. Working conditions were poor, especially for women and children. New inventions sometimes improved working conditions. There were many movements to improve people's lives. Although change did not happen immediately, this period is still marked by steady growth.

After READING

Finding the Main Ideas

Use the information in your concept map to answer the question, What significant changes occurred in Canadian society during this period?

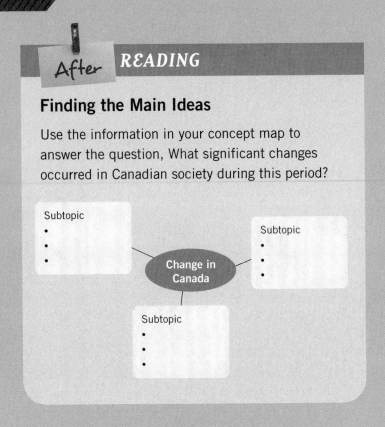

THINKING It Through

1. Research the working conditions of a) farmers, and b) labourers in 1900 compared with today. Create two Venn diagrams—one for farmers and one for labourers—to compare working conditions around 1900 with working conditions today. Include key points that apply in the appropriate parts of the diagrams. k t c a

2. Use the information contained in your Venn diagrams to write two paragraphs—one about farmers and the other about workers. What are the differences and similarities in the challenges they faced around 1900 and today? c a t

3. Draw a picture or describe a scene in words to illustrate the biggest challenge the farmers or workers have ever faced. In two sentences, explain what the picture or scene shows, and why you chose it. c a t

4. Create a "cloze," or fill-in-the-blank, test for your classmates. For each key term in this chapter, write a sentence using the term, but leave a blank space where the key term belongs. Swap papers with a partner and see if you can correctly fill in the spaces on each other's tests. k t c a

CHAPTER 8

The Laurier Era

Homesteaders transformed raw Prairies into farms.

Before **READING**

Making Connections

Art tells us a lot about a time period. Look closely at the painting above.

- What do you see? What other things could the artist have added to the painting? Discuss your observations with a partner.

On July 29, 1910, Prime Minister Wilfrid Laurier bought a newspaper from a 15-year-old boy on the platform of a Saskatoon train station. The two spoke about the news. Then the newsboy said, "Well, Prime Minister, I can't waste any more time on you. I must get back to work."

Wilfrid Laurier served as Canada's prime minister for fifteen consecutive years. He led the country during a time of great social and economic change. What effects did his political policies have on our nation?

Forty-seven years later, that same newsboy from Saskatoon became prime minister of Canada. His name was John Diefenbaker. How do you think this chance encounter might have influenced him?

Poster encouraging immigration to Canada, circa late 1800s

Questions to Consider as You Read this Chapter

You will explore these aspects of the Unit 3 Big Idea: **How did social and economic factors, technology, and people promote change in Canada?**

- How did Laurier address the challenge of boosting Canadian immigration?

- How and why did English–French tensions further develop during this period?

- How did the public react to Laurier's wish for closer economic ties with the United States?

- What factors led to Laurier's defeat in the 1911 election?

- How have Canada's campaigns to attract immigrants changed in the past century?

Thinking About Literacy

Identifying Points of View

In this chapter, you will learn about people and groups who sometimes wanted opposing things.

As you read, use an organizer like the one below. Write the name of the person or group in the "somebody" column, what they wanted in the "wanted" column, any obstacles or what others thought in the "but" column, and the result (positive or negative) in the "so" column.

Somebody	Wanted	But	So

In 1896, Wilfrid Laurier led the Liberals to power when they defeated the Conservatives in a national election. John A. Macdonald had died in 1891, and the government had since lacked direction. Laurier was determined to deal with what he saw as important issues for Canada's future.

The Population Challenge

The first challenge Laurier faced was the issue of Canada's small population. Despite the country's huge size, Canada had only grown from about 3.5 million people in 1867 to about 4.9 million in 1891. There was another problem as well: the population was divided unequally amongst the provinces and territories. Look closely at the map below. Where did more than 90 percent of the population live?

Population Distribution in Canada, 1891

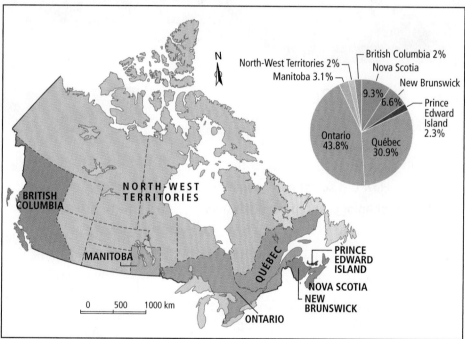

Which would be the most convenient trading partners for each province? Why might Canada still view the U.S. as a threat?

Almost 93 percent of the population lived east of the Manitoba–Ontario border. As you have learned, the Canadian government was eager to populate the West. Although immigrants had arrived, few had the skills necessary to start and maintain homesteads. What might Laurier's next plan of action be to attract more immigrants?

Clifford Sifton's Immigration Plan

Clifford Sifton (1861–1929) was a lawyer and politician in Manitoba. Laurier appointed him minister of the interior in 1896. Most of the people settling in the West were of British and Irish origin. Sifton realized that Canada needed to change its immigration policy. He thought that people from other areas might be better suited for the hardships of farming on the Prairies. To him, the ideal Prairie farmer was

> A stalwart peasant in a sheepskin coat, born on the soil, whose forefathers have been farmers for ten generations, and a stout wife and half-a-dozen children…

Immigration Campaigns

Sifton organized immigration campaigns in many European languages to attract the settlers he was looking for. The government prepared pamphlets telling immigrants of the advantages of what it called "The Last Best West." These included free land, rich soil, government assistance to get started, a healthy climate, and freedom from oppression for themselves and their families.

Sifton's immigration plan also actively recruited American farming families, as these people were experienced in prairie farming. They also brought with them equipment and capital. There was an exception to this welcome, however: no black farmers were recruited. Even though Canada already had numbers of black immigrants, especially Loyalists and slaves who had arrived on the Underground Railroad, there was still a prevailing anti-black sentiment. Social views at the time were often **prejudiced** and **racist** and many people were considered undesirable as immigrants.

During **READING**

Checkpoint
Remember to add this to your chart. Think about what Sifton wanted.

WORDS MATTER

prejudice unfavourable feelings, opinions, or attitudes toward a racial, religious, or national group

racist intolerance of other races or the belief in the superiority of one race over another

Compare these images of the Canadian Prairies (left) and the Roztocze region in southeast Poland (right). Why might Canada encourage immigrants from agricultural areas in other countries?

Where Did They Come From? Immigration in 1903

Country of Origin	Number of Immigrants
Britain	41 775
Poland	8656
Russia	5505
Scandinavia	5448
The Balkans	4273
Italy	3371
Other countries	9783
Total	78 811

A Typical Immigrant Family

Here is what one Canadian has written about his ancestors:

[Around 1900], Nicholas Kitzan came to Canada from Bukovyna, now part of Ukraine, to make enough money to bring his family to the New World. In 1911, his wife Nettie and their children followed. Together, they settled a homestead in Saskatchewan that was near friends and family and in a setting that reminded them of home. Eking out a living, however, was never easy. They arrived with little money, few possessions and no ability to speak English. The land they chose was marginal, and the Canadian environment unpredictable. Despite these challenges they persevered.

Nicholas and Nettie were… just two out of hundreds of thousands of immigrants… who arrived in the Canadian West between 1896 and 1914.

Together these men and women from different countries and cultures played an important role in developing the Prairie West and its unique identity. In so doing, they also contributed to the development of the country as a whole.

WEB LINK • • • • • • • • • • • • • • • • • •
For more information on Canada's immigration policies, visit our Web site.

Write a caption that captures what you think these immigrants were feeling.

Why the Immigrants Came

Immigrants came because of two sets of factors. "Push" factors encouraged them to leave their homelands. "Pull" factors encouraged them to choose Canada.

Push Factors	Pull Factors
People left their homelands for the following reasons: • **Lack of land:** There was a shortage of good farmland. Industrialization was spreading rapidly throughout Europe, forcing many to work in dangerous and unhealthy factories. • **Lack of personal freedoms:** Many people were persecuted for religious or political beliefs in their countries of birth. Above all else, people want to ensure a safe life for their families. • **Threat of war:** The first half of the 20th century saw European nations embroiled in two World Wars. War brings death and destruction to all in its path.	Many immigrants chose Canada for the following reasons: • **Free land:** Families could get homesteads of 65 hectares for free. They could buy another 65 hectares for $480 once they developed their homestead. • **Good farming conditions:** Rich soil and the development of wheat strains especially suited to the Prairies, such as Marquis wheat, ensured successful crops for farmers. • **Ethnic communities:** Immigrants of particular ethnic groups tended to congregate in similar regions. There, they could live as they had in their homelands, surrounded by people who spoke their language and shared their customs.

The Growth of the Prairies

These immigration campaigns were successful. Within 10 years, the population of the Prairies rose by 195 percent.

Population of the Prairies, 1901 and 1911

Province	1901 population	1911 population
Manitoba	255 211	461 394
Saskatchewan*	91 279	492 342
Alberta*	73 022	374 295
Total	419 512	1 328 121

*Officially part of the Northwest Territories until 1905

During the Laurier years, Canada's population expanded rapidly through immigration. Immigrants came from a variety of countries. Many did not speak English or French when they arrived. These people brought with them new languages, customs, and cultures. This was the point when Canada started to become a more **multicultural** nation.

WORDS MATTER

multiculturalism *many culturally distinct groups living within a society*

Dispersal of the Métis virginia

WEB LINK •·············
For more information on Métis farming, visit our Web site.

The increasing flow of immigrant settlers to the Prairies further disrupted the lives of the Métis. Waves of settlers moved into an area, established farms, and developed large towns and cities. The Métis moved out in search of land where they could hunt, fish, and trap. The Métis population became dispersed across the Prairies. At the same time, however, some Métis people were settling and farming or working as ranch hands. The Métis of Saskatchewan were known for their skill in breeding livestock.

By 1900, although the scrip system was still in use, its failure was becoming apparent. Many Métis sold their scrip because their land was far from family and friends or because it was poor land without access to water. Others were cheated out of their scrip by land speculators. This left Métis people without much of a land base and contributed to the disruption and scattering of Métis communities.

Schoolchildren on a Métis farm in Saskatchewan. Some Métis families remained on their homesteads and became successful farmers.

THINKING It Over

1. Review the "push" and "pull" factors that led to the settlement of the Prairies. Which single factor do you think would most encourage you to immigrate to Canada around 1900? Explain the reasons for your choice. *k t a*

2. In a small group, compare the attractions of the Prairies with those of your community around the 1900s. Which location do you think would be more attractive to immigrants? Why? *k t*

3. What features of your community would attract immigrants today? Write a short speech you might give if you were sent on tour as a recruiting agent for your community. *t c a*

4. Select what you think was the most important cause of the dispersal of the Métis. It may help to make a cause-and-effect chain. See page S 19. Do you think the Métis could have done anything to resist this cause? Explain your reasons. *k t*

PAU.

English–French tensions have been an issue throughout Canada's history. You will recall the disputes between the early fur-trading companies and the Seven Years' War. You have examined the disputes between Canada East and Canada West over representation. You have seen the tensions following the Métis resistance and the execution of Louis Riel. Laurier saw that English–French issues could divide Canadians. He wanted to prevent those issues from destroying the Liberal party. So he always sought to find a compromise when these tensions mounted.

During **READING**

Checkpoint
Look for points to add to your chart. List each person and group of people (French and English) in your chart, then continue to look for what they wanted and what got in their way.

The Manitoba Schools Crisis

The most serious English–French crisis of the time erupted in Manitoba.

The Manitoba Act

The Manitoba Act of 1870 gave guarantees to both English- and French-speaking people. The province, it stated, would be bilingual. In education, too, guarantees were made to both sides.

- English- and French-language rights were guaranteed in the legislature and courts.

- There would be religious schools—Protestant and Roman Catholic.

Although language rights were not guaranteed in schools, a system evolved in which schools were either English and Protestant or French and Catholic. This seemed to satisfy both populations.

Manitoba Schools

Manitoba received many immigrants during the 1880s, most of whom were English speaking and Protestant. By 1890, there was a large English-speaking majority. Anglophones began to press for Manitoba to review its language laws. In 1890, the provincial government passed laws that changed the rules.

- It abolished French as an official language. Debates in the legislature and proceedings in courts had to be in English only.

- It passed an act that removed government support from Roman Catholic schools. Now they would run as private schools and parents would have to pay fees for their children to attend.

Comment on what this political cartoon says about Laurier's role in the Manitoba schools crisis.

pdu.

Sir Wilfrid Laurier was the first bilingual Canadian prime minister whose first language was French. He showed Canadians that speaking both languages is an important asset in Canadian politics. Other Francophone prime ministers have been Louis St. Laurent, Pierre Trudeau, and Jean Chrétien. All recent prime ministers have been bilingual.

The Legal Ruling

Opinions tended to run along language lines. English speakers across Canada supported Manitoba's reforms. French speakers were strongly opposed. The legal system could not offer a clear solution. In 1895, a ruling in the courts stated that Manitoba had the power to make these changes, but the federal government had the power to step in and overrule them if it wished.

The Political Situation

The Conservative government in Ottawa decided to introduce legislation to restore the old system in Manitoba; however, Laurier, the Liberal opposition leader, was opposed to it. You might think that because of his background, he would support the reintroduction of French and Catholic rights, but Laurier was also a politician. He wanted to become prime minister. He recognized that if he opposed the government, the French would call him a traitor to their cause. If he supported the government, the Liberals would not win many English votes in the next election.

Laurier's Compromise

In the House of Commons, he offered another solution. It had two parts. If elected to government, the Liberals would

- not restore government support for separate schools in Manitoba

- pass a law allowing French instruction in any school if there were at least ten children requiring it

- allow for religious instruction of Catholic children by priests at the end of the school day

This was an effective compromise. Each side felt that it was getting enough of what it wanted to support the position. Laurier's opposition forced the government to withdraw its bill from parliament and to call an election. Laurier's compromise was hard on Francophone groups such as the Métis, however, because nearly all of them were Roman Catholic. It weakened the identity of such groups who had previously enjoyed separate schools.

In your opinion, what was Wilfrid Laurier's most significant accomplishment? Explain.

The Election of 1896

The most important issue in the campaign was the Manitoba schools situation. Support for Laurier's compromise grew. The Conservatives seemed confused and divided. If you compare the results of the elections of 1891 and 1896, you can see how large the Liberal victory was.

Election	Liberals	Conservatives	Others	Total
1891	92	123	0	215
1896	117	89	7	213

The Laurier–Greenway Compromise

In 1897, Laurier worked out a compromise with Thomas Greenway, Premier of Manitoba. The law would be changed along the lines of Laurier's solution. Anglophones and Francophones would get some of what they wanted, but not everything. Similar laws had been passed in New Brunswick (1871), Prince Edward Island (1877), the Northwest Territories (1892), and Saskatchewan and Alberta (1905).

Reactions

Not everyone agreed with Laurier's compromise. Archbishop Adélard Langevin of St. Boniface, a Catholic church near Winnipeg, lamented

Thomas Greenway

> *Today is the saddest day of my career as a Bishop. It is with a broken heart that I stand before you. I protest with all my strength against the use of that word: Agreement… Instead of negotiating with us, the government dealt with those that oppressed us.*

Others thought the issue had been blown out of proportion. *Grip* magazine had earlier carried a cartoon about the same issues in the North-West Territories (see page H 170). Language and religion play powerful roles in politics. Laurier managed to find compromise on these issues, even though he had a great deal of opposition. This ability to find the middle ground was one of the reasons he remained prime minister for 15 years (1896–1911).

Bilingualism in Canada

Then

In 1881, 58.9% of Canada's population was of British origin, and 30% was of French origin*. Bilingualism was limited. Both languages could be used in the parliament in Ottawa and in the New Brunswick and Manitoba legislatures. The use of French was discouraged outside of Québec and Acadian parts of New Brunswick, and most Canadians did not have a right to government services in French.

*At that time, the census did not track first language.

Now

In 2001, 59.2% of the population spoke English as their first language, and 22.7% spoke French as their first language. The use of both languages is guaranteed in dealing with the federal, Québec, New Brunswick, and Manitoba governments. The use of French is encouraged in English-speaking areas. For example, in Prince Edward Island in 2000, 20% of students were enrolled in French immersion.

Analyze this illustration. What perspective does the artist have on bilingualism?

THINKING It Over

1. Make a copy of the following organizer and fill it in with information from this section.

2. Look at the cartoon above. What is the cartoonist trying to say about the issues? See page S 12 for help in analyzing images. Draw your own cartoon to illustrate your view about the issue. Compare cartoons with a classmate and discuss the issues they raise.

Group	What They Wanted	Why They Might Support Laurier's Compromise	My Reactions to Their Position
English			
French			

How Important Was International Trade?

As a new country with a growing population, Canada had a small economy. It needed strong economic partners in order to increase its prosperity. Who should be Canada's main trading partner?

Canada's Economic Patterns

If you examine Canada's trade patterns, you will see how important the United States and Britain were to Canada's economy.

Exports and Imports

In Canada, there was divided opinion on whether Canada's economic future lay with Britain or the United States. The debate had a lot to do with the nation's existing patterns of exports and imports. The table below illustrates Canada's trade patterns with these two countries. The **balance of trade** column refers to the difference between exports and imports. A positive balance means Canada exported more than it imported. A negative balance is the reverse.

WORDS MATTER

balance of trade the difference between a country's imports and exports

foreign investments money invested in companies in a country other than one's own

Canada's International Trade, 1910

Country	Exports To	Imports From	Balance of Trade
Britain	$140 500 000	$107 722 000	$32 778 000
U.S.	$108 198 000	$262 142 000	- $153 944 000

International Investments

Economics involves more than just trade between two countries. Nations need money to build their economies. **Foreign investments** are a highly important part of economic relationships. The following table shows you the major sources of foreign investment in Canada.

Where Did Canada's Future Lie?

Britain was the richest country in the world, but the U.S. was not far behind and was growing quickly. The U.S. and Canada share a long border, so trading was quick and easy. Trading with Britain required a long Atlantic voyage. Some people in Canada began to recommend closer economic ties with the U.S.

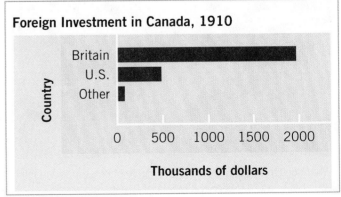

Foreign Investment in Canada, 1910

Laurier and Reciprocity

By 1911, Laurier was convinced that Canada's economic future lay with the United States. Although Britain was still a more important economic partner, the U.S. was growing much more quickly. It would soon be Canada's most important partner. Laurier wanted closer economic links between the two nations. His representatives reached a reciprocity agreement with the Americans. This would allow natural products to cross the border duty-free. Duties on manufactured goods would be reduced. The agreement had to be approved by both governments before it came into effect. The U.S. welcomed the agreement. Its government quickly accepted the treaty. In Canada, however, there was a sharp division of opinion on the subject. Many people thought Britain should remain Canada's main economic partner. A battle soon erupted in the House of Commons.

Trade with Britain and the U.S. Today

Exports to Britain	$11 559 900 000
Imports from Britain	$9 543 000 000
Exports to the U.S.	$360 963 300 000
Imports from the U.S.	$264 889 200 000

What does this lineup of trucks waiting at a border crossing tell you about trade between the U.S. and Canada today?

What elements of a political cartoon help convey a message better than a paragraph might? What do the people in this cartoon represent?

Laurier's Position

Laurier realized that he could not find a compromise on reciprocity, so he took the treaty to the House of Commons to get the House's approval. On March 7, 1911, he told the House of Commons,

During **READING**

Checkpoint
Add each of the positions taken to your chart. At the end, consider why reciprocity was a controversial issue for Canadians.

> *If my voice could be heard that far, I would presume to say to our American friends: There may be a spectacle perhaps nobler yet than the spectacle of a united continent, a spectacle which would astound the world by its novelty and grandeur, the spectacle of two peoples living… along a frontier nearly [6400 km] long, with not a cannon, with not a gun frowning across it, with not a fortress on either side, with no armament one against the other, but living in harmony, in mutual confidence, and with no other rivalry than a generous emulation in commerce and the arts of peace.*

Borden's Position

Conservative leader Robert Borden launched a savage attack on the idea of a trade agreement with the U.S. He accused Laurier of abandoning Britain, which, he said, had done much to develop and assist Canada. All the Conservatives and some of the Liberals supported Borden's position. It looked unlikely that the House would approve the treaty if the members voted on it.

Sir Robert Borden

The Election of 1911

Laurier decided that the best tactic was to call an election and make reciprocity the issue. If the voters returned the Liberals to office, he would be able to get the House's approval for the treaty. Laurier no longer wanted compromise on the issue. He was going for victory. However, the voters showed a great deal of support for Britain and suspicion of the U.S. People of British origin were by far the largest group in Canada. They voted to maintain traditional ties with Britain. In Québec, Francophone voters did not particularly like the U.S. either. They feared that reciprocity would lead to a U.S. takeover of Canada. Francophones would be such a small minority in the larger country that their culture and language would be further threatened. So they did not support Laurier either. The election was held on September 21, 1911. Its results were eagerly awaited by the voters and politicians.

William Lyon Mackenzie King, who would later become prime minister, speaking at a Liberal Party rally during the 1911 election campaign

Would Reciprocity Benefit Canada?

The reciprocity issue had been around for many years when Laurier raised it as a political issue for the election of 1911. The following extracts from the 1880s and 1890s summarize the key differences of opinion that still existed in the 1910s. It had stirred up political debate for a generation and there was still no general agreement on the subject.

J.W. Longley, a journalist and author from Nova Scotia

The proposition to take down the custom houses between the United States and Canada... is the most wide-reaching... political matter demanding the consideration of... North America...

[N]o one can honestly say that there is any natural commercial relationship between [Canada's provinces]. Between the Maritime Provinces and Ontario there is but little trade. Between British Columbia and the rest of the [provinces] there is scarcely any trade at all.

On the other hand, between the Maritime Provinces and the New England States there is the most natural... commercial relationship... British Columbia finds its [best market] in California and Oregon...

Sensible Canadians recognize plainly enough that unrestricted trade with the United States would be of immense value, and they are anxious to secure it.

Letter from J.W. Longley to Erastus Wiman, 1887

Louis-Georges Desjardins, a politician from the Québec City area,

In my opinion, the most complete evidence shows that... unrestricted reciprocity [between Canada and the United States]... would surely lead to commercial union...

All those in the [United States] who declared themselves... in favour of... unrestricted reciprocity... expressed the opinion that [it] would result in [an American takeover of Canada].

I can [confirm]... that nearly all of those in Canada who fought [it] did so because they were convinced it would quickly pave the way to political union...

[If Canada became part of the United States], it is said that Québec would have a population of three or four million because of European immigration, but would it be more French?

There is no mistake. [Being part of the United States] would give [Québec] a much inferior political situation than we now have in [Canada]. We now make up one-quarter of the population. We would scarcely make up a fortieth after union with the United States.

**Louis-Georges Desjardins,
Considérations sur l'annexation, 1891**

What Do YOU Think?

1. Which writer favoured reciprocity? Which one was opposed? What reasons did each writer give for his position? **k** **t**

2. If the same arguments were being made today, which writer's position would come closest to your own? Why? **k** **t**

Voting Patterns in the Elections of 1904 and 1911

When historians compare the elections of 1904 and 1911, they can observe changes in the voting patterns. Each pie graph below represents the percentage vote for the parties in the provinces shown.

The Election of 1904

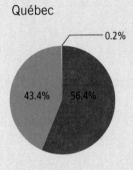
Québec
0.2%
43.4% 56.4%

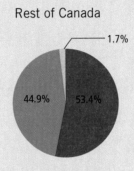
Ontario
0.2%
50.3% 49.5%

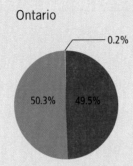
Rest of Canada
1.7%
44.9% 53.4%

The Election of 1911

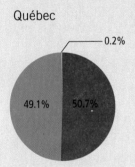
Québec
0.2%
49.1% 50.7%

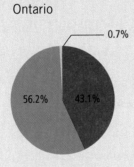
Ontario
0.7%
56.2% 43.1%

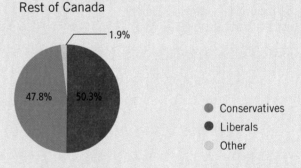
Rest of Canada
1.9%
47.8% 50.3%

● Conservatives
● Liberals
○ Other

THINKING It Over

1. In which part of Canada did a) the Liberals and b) the Conservatives win the highest percentage of votes in 1904? Now do the same for 1911. **k**

2. a) In which part of Canada did the Liberals' percentage fall the most from 1904 to 1911?
b) In which part did the Conservatives' percentage rise the most from 1904 to 1911? **k**

3. Examine the voting patterns shown above for the election of 1911. Which party do you think won the election? Give reasons for your answer. Keep this information, as you will need it later in the chapter. **t**

The Results of the Election of 1911

On page H 175, you learned how voting patterns changed between 1904 and 1911. Canadian elections are decided by the number of seats each party wins, not the percentage of votes each party gets. Here is what the numbers showed.

Party	Number of Seats (1904)	Number of Seats (1911)
Conservatives	75	133
Liberals	139	86
Independents	0	2
Total	214	221

Laurier had won victories in 1896, 1900, 1904, and 1908. He had been prime minister for 15 years. This time he was defeated. He was 69 years old. Many thought he was finished as a politician, but he remained leader of the Liberals for almost eight more years until his death in 1919.

Reciprocity had no future in Canada. The voters had returned the Conservatives to power, and they were opposed to the issue. For the immediate future, Canada would still be economically tied to Britain. The election of 1911 was critical in Canadian history. Voters chose British ties over American ones. Within three years, Canada was at war on the side of Britain against Germany.

WEB LINK ● ·

For more information on reciprocity and free trade, visit our Web site.

THINKING It Over

1. Which country—Britain or the U.S.—do you think was more important to Canada in this period a) as a market and b) for foreign investment? Explain your reasoning.

2. a) Which party won the election of 1911? What was the main issue?
   b) Return to the prediction you made earlier in the chapter about the election's result on page H 175. How accurate was your answer? Explain.

3. Create an organizer, picture, mind map, or another visual to illustrate the differences between the Liberals and Conservatives on the subject of reciprocity. Show your work to a classmate. Discuss how effectively both pieces of work show the differences.

PUTTING IT ALL TOGETHER

In this chapter, you have looked at social and economic factors, and people that promoted change in Canada. You have examined some of Sir Wilfrid Laurier's major political decisions and their effect on Canada's development. These included boosting immigration, trying to calm tensions between English and French speakers, and promoting economic reciprocity with the United States. You have also learned that Laurier generally sought political compromise.

The years from 1896 to 1911, when Laurier was in power, saw the growth of Canada's population, cities, and international trade. Canada's role in the international arena became more prominent. As global tensions mounted, Canada had to make some tough decisions.

After READING

Identifying Points of View

Use your notes in your organizer (below) to write a news article about one event from this period. Also review the organizer to see whether it helps you answer the Big Idea question posed at the beginning of this unit.

Somebody	Wanted	But	So

THINKING It Through

1. a) Do some research into i) the type of immigration campaigns that Canada operated around 1900 to attract immigrants to settle here, and ii) the types of campaigns that Canada organizes today to attract immigrants. Pay particular attention to the following points.
    *   the region(s) of the world on which the campaign is focused
    *   the nationalities of the people that the campaign is trying to attract
    *   the types of people (farmers, tradespeople, city workers, business owners, professionals, etc.) that the campaign is trying to attract
    *   the images of Canada the campaign contains and its possible impact on the groups being targeted
    *   the design and presentation of the campaign
    k *t*

    b) Create your own immigration campaign for i) around 1900, and ii) today. Select media that are appropriate for each period. For 1900, a poster or pamphlet is appropriate. For today, television advertisements or computer-generated graphics are also appropriate. Be sure to address all the points in the bulleted list above. *k* *t* *a*

    For help with the research, see page S 6.

2. Engage in a classroom discussion about how immigration campaigns have changed in the past century. Use key terms from the chapter to illustrate your ideas. *a* *c*

Canada and the Coming of the First World War

Canadian volunteer soldiers served in the Boer War. Why would Canadians be involved in a war in southern Africa?

Before READING

Making Connections

In the last chapter we learned that Canada had to think about its ties with Britain and the U.S. in terms of trading. During the First World War, Canada had to decide whether to support Britain. Consider what you have learned about the role of Britain in the development of Canada and discuss the following questions:

- Should Canadians fight in the war? Why or why not? How would other groups, such as Francophones and First Nations, respond? What might influence their views?

In the early years following Confederation, Canada was able to grow, free from external conflict. From time to time, there were disagreements with the United States, but there was little threat of a full-scale war. In the 1890s, tensions within Europe grew, especially between Britain and Germany. These tensions threatened to lead European nations to war. Would Canada be dragged into this foreign dispute?

From the early 1890s to 1914, a constant threat of war was looming. Britain asked Canada to play a larger role in defending the British Empire. English- and French-Canadian voters showed different opinions on the subject throughout the period. Canadian politicians and journalists debated the extent of the nation's involvement. What role did Canada end up playing during times of international conflict?

At the start of the war, crowds gathered to cheer the soldiers on their way. What do you think the public attitude was after a few years of war?

Questions to Consider as You Read this Chapter

You will explore these aspects of the Unit 3 Big Idea: **How did social and economic factors, technology, and people promote change in Canada?**

- What disagreements existed over Canada's role in the British Empire?

- What circumstances led to the creation of the Royal Canadian Navy?

- What political factors, events, and people led to Canada's involvement in the First World War?

- How can I compare different points of view regarding Canada's role in the Boer War?

Thinking About Literacy

Forming Conclusions

As you read this chapter, make notes of facts—either in your own words or as quotes—in the "I read" column. Include page numbers so you can find the information again quickly.

Write what you think the fact means or says about Canada's involvement in the world in the "I think" column. This is your opinion. You will complete the "Therefore" section at the end of this chapter.

I read	I think
Therefore	

Canada's Role in the British Empire

After Canada's Confederation in 1867, responsibility for its defence and foreign relations remained with Britain. This arrangement allowed the Canadian government to concentrate on expanding the population and boosting the economy. At the time, Britain was the strongest military power in the world. The British Navy could protect Canada from foreign threats. Canadians believed that being part of the British Empire would secure their future.

Canada and the British Empire

In the late 1800s, the cost of building warships began to rise steeply. Germany was Britain's strongest rival, and it began to build a new navy of steam-powered ships with newer and better technology. Britain began to lean on the **dominions** for help in its struggle to keep up with Germany. In a series of colonial conferences, Britain issued heavy demands of support from Empire countries:

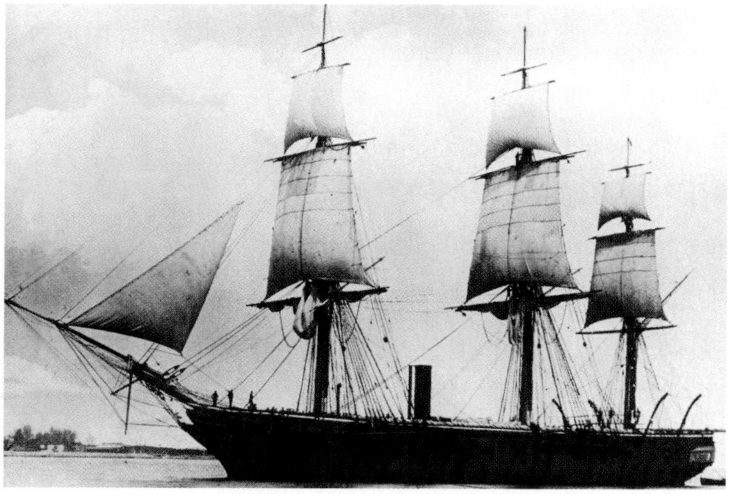

- supply troops, when requested, to fight in wars under British command to defend the British Empire
- maintain naval vessels for their own defence, but place them under British command in times of war
- send money to Britain to help with the increased costs of defending the Empire

In what ways did Canada benefit from its alliance with the British Empire?

WORDS MATTER

dominions independent countries that had been British colonies

Early steam-powered warships still sometimes hoisted sails to supplement the steam engines.

Canadian Attitudes Toward Defending the Empire

As before, political issues at this time split Canadians along language lines. The issue of Canada's role in the Empire was no exception.

English-Canadian Attitudes

The majority of English-speaking Canadians were of British origin. They felt that Canada had a duty to help Britain defend the Empire. In 1897, Queen Victoria celebrated her diamond jubilee—she had been queen for 60 years. English Canadians across the nation held parties to celebrate the event and to promote the unity of the Empire. Prime Minister Laurier travelled to London, England, to join the celebrations. At a dinner there, he told an audience

> *If a day were ever to come when England was in danger, let the bugle sound, let the fires be lit on the hills… whatever we can do shall be done by the colonies to help her.*

In 1899, Britain became involved in a war in southern Africa. Laurier's promise would be put to the test. You will read more about this later.

French-Canadian Attitudes

French-speaking Canadians were generally opposed to Canada's involvement in British conflicts. Britain, they argued, was not their homeland. Why should they fight to defend it? They were even less keen to defend France—Britain's ally against Germany. There had been almost no immigration from France since the British Conquest of Québec in 1760. French Canadians had no close ties to France. Most would be prepared to fight to defend Canada, but not Britain or France.

Checkpoint
The first sentence in this paragraph is a fact. The second is an opinion. With a partner, decide why. Add the information to your organizer.

On Dominion Day, 1897, residents of Fredericton, N.B., celebrated Queen Victoria's Jubilee with a bicycle parade.

Canadians at the National Acadia Day festival. Many French Canadians celebrate their Francophone identity.

The Imperial Federation Debate

In the 1890s, a new idea called Imperial Federation began to emerge. Its best-known supporter was Joseph Chamberlain, a British politician. Supporters of Imperial Federation believed that the dominions should build navies of their own that could be placed under British control in times of war. These ships could be sent anywhere in the world to defend the interests of the Empire and to protect the Empire's trade routes. Do you think Chamberlain's idea was fair?

Support for Imperial Federation

The *Manitoba Free Press* published a speech by George Grant, a Presbyterian minister and writer from Nova Scotia. He believed that Imperial Federation was an opportunity for Canada.

> *Imperial Federation... may be defined as a union between [Britain] and Canada that would give to Canada not only full management of its own affairs, but a fair share in the management and responsibilities of common affairs. As British citizens, ought we to ask for more? As Canadians... ought we to be satisfied with less?*
>
> *Mark it well, an independent Canada is out of the question. The days of small nations are over forever... Break up the British Empire, and what prospect is there of a worthy place in history for [Canada]? We have to choose between [being a strong member of the Empire], or a position somewhat like that of a South American Republic. Take your choice.*

Opposition to Imperial Federation

Imperial Federation meant that Britain would be in command of the Empire's navy. Many Canadians were unhappy with this idea. What point of view is expressed in this article in the *Toronto Evening News*?

> *The only point upon which the English, French, German, American, and native Canadian residents of the Dominion can unite is a common love for this their adopted country. This cannot take place while [Britain] rules our destinies and claims all the glory and absorbs the devotion of our people... We all respect the British flag, but [French-Canadians] can never love it, nor sing its praises, nor struggle for its greatness and supremacy as they could and would for a flag of their own.*

George Munro Grant

This postage stamp shows the extent of the British Empire in 1898. What message does it convey about Imperial Federation—for or against? What evidence did you base your decision on?

Canada's role in the British Empire was a subject of much debate in the 1890s. There were strong opinions on the various issues, with little room for compromise. How would Laurier deal with these issues in the face of war? Canadians would soon find out.

THINKING It Over

1. a) Draw a picture to represent each of the following people—an English-Canadian of British origin; a French Canadian; Laurier; George Grant; the author of the *Toronto Evening News* article. b) Draw a thought bubble coming out of each person's head summarizing the person's position on the defence of the Empire.

2. You learned in Chapter 8 that Laurier liked to find compromises between opposing parties. Suppose Britain had asked the dominions to send troops to fight in a war in a foreign country. Predict a compromise that you think Laurier might have taken, trying to satisfy those in favour and those opposed to closer Empire ties. Be creative. Keep your prediction for later reference.

What Role Did Canada Play in the Boer War?

In 1899, Britain became involved in a war in southern Africa. Britain wanted to colonize land where the descendants of Dutch settlers had lived for more than 300 years. The Dutch settlers called themselves the Farmers—or Boers, in their language. Britain expected to win a quick victory. Instead, the conflict, which came to be known as the Boer War, lasted almost three years. The British won some easy victories at first, so the Boers started to use guerrilla tactics.

The Boers would ambush British troops, killing as many soldiers as they could, before retreating into the open plains of the area. British troops became frustrated with these tactics. They put pressure on the Boers by cutting off their supplies and food, burning farms, and placing Boer civilians in **concentration camps**.

A British War or an Imperial War?

From the start, the British believed that the Boer War was not just their own. Losing to the Boers might lead to a loss of all their colonies in southern Africa. Britain would then lose their ports at the tip of the African continent, from which they guarded trade routes between Britain and Australia, New Zealand, and many parts of Asia. The British believed that this was an **imperial** war. This means that it concerned the whole British Empire. Britain requested that the dominions send troops and military equipment to help in the conflict. How would you feel if England became involved in a war today and asked Canada to participate?

WORDS MATTER

concentration camps special prisons for civilians who are political prisoners or prisoners of war

imperial of concern to an entire empire

WEB LINK •••••••••••••••••••••••

For more information on the Boer War, visit our Web site.

War in this era often involved digging trenches, such as this one.

Canada's Attitude Toward the Boer War

The British asked Canada to send troops to southern Africa and place them under British command. Based on what you have already read in this chapter, how do you think different groups of Canadians felt about the British request?

Laurier realized that Québec would never support sending Canadian troops to the war. On the other hand, he knew that most of Ontario would abandon the Liberals if he kept Canada neutral. Laurier had to make an important decision.

Laurier's Compromise

Laurier personally believed that Canada should stay out of the war, but he adopted an ingenious compromise:

- Canadian troops would not be ordered to go and fight in the war.

- Canada would, however, pay for and equip volunteer forces to join the fight.

- These volunteer forces would fight together as a Canadian unit, but would fall under British command.

Laurier and Bourassa Disagree

Henri Bourassa was a politician and journalist from Québec. He and Wilfrid Laurier disagreed on whether Canada should participate in the war. Bourassa believed that sending Canadian troops would act as a **precedent** for all future British wars. He felt that this would be used as justification for Canadian involvement in such wars. Bourassa disagreed with Laurier's practice of seeking compromise on so many political issues. He observed

> Upon his arrival at the gates of Paradise, Mr. Laurier's first action will be to propose an 'honourable compromise' between God and Satan.

Bourassa began to write newspaper articles attacking Laurier's position on major issues. He became Laurier's chief opponent in Québec.

A Canadian soldier in the Boer War uniform of the period. What other Canadian uniform does it resemble?

Henri Bourassa (1868–1952) was a member of parliament and of the Québec Assembly. He founded the newspaper *Le Devoir* in 1910 and was its editor until 1932. It is still one of the leading French-language newspapers in Canada.

Bourassa did not believe in all political compromises. He felt that French Canadians had been given special protections in order to ensure their support for Confederation. Governments should not try to abandon those protections now.

Henri Bourassa

Bourassa encouraged Canada to distance itself politically from Britain, and he helped to increase French-Canadian nationalism—pride and love for their country. He felt that Canada should not get involved in the Boer War.

Bourassa's influence extended beyond the Boer War. He made it increasingly difficult for Laurier to achieve compromises. In 1917, the Conservative government wanted to introduce conscription—requiring men to enlist as soldiers to fight in the war. Most English-speaking Canadians were in favour of conscription; most French Canadians opposed it. Laurier was still the leader of the Liberals, though he was no longer prime minister. He wanted to find a compromise. However, he felt that Bourassa had made such a position impossible. If Laurier tried to find a compromise, the Liberals might lose all their support in Québec. Laurier eventually opposed conscription.

In your opinion, what sort of people make the best politicians? Is it the compromisers, who try to find the middle ground? Or, is it the people who take strong positions and refuse to waver from their beliefs?

THINKING It Over

1. What was Bourassa's position on asking French Canadians to make compromises? What events, people, or other factors do you think shaped his position? *k* *t*

2. How did Bourassa's position on conscription make things more difficult for Laurier? *t*

3. Do you think it is better for politicians to take strong and unyielding positions, or to look for compromises? Explain your reasons. *t* *a*

Canadian Contributions to the War

At first, the Canadian government sent 1000 troops to the Boer War. It later sent additional forces. In Chapter 5, you read about Donald Smith, Lord Strathcona, who was president of the Bank of Montréal and a backer of the CPR. He personally established and paid for a volunteer regiment from western Canada to fight in the Boer War. It was called Lord Strathcona's Horse regiment and it participated in some of the key battles of the campaign in southern Africa.

During READING

Checkpoint

Look for facts in this section for your chart. Do not forget to add what you think each fact will mean for Canada under the "I think" section.

Lord Strathcona's Horse regiment included many cowboys, western frontiersmen, and members of the NWMP. Why do you think a private citizen would finance a military regiment?

Private Walter White

The Indian Act of 1876 said that registered First Nations people were not eligible to join the military. First Nations men who volunteered for service were turned away. During the Boer War, John Brant-Sero, a Grand River Mohawk, travelled to southern Africa at his own expense. He tried to volunteer for the British forces, but was rejected because he was not a status Indian. However, First Nations bands could deregister from the Indian Act, and the Anderdon band of Wyandotte (Hurons), near Sarnia, Ontario, did so in 1881. Members of the Anderdon band were therefore eligible to join the military. Walter White, of this band, volunteered in 1899. He was killed at Paardeberg, southern Africa, in February 1900, aged 19.

This National Aboriginal Veterans Monument is located in Ottawa. What do you think the various elements of the monument symbolize?

Women and War

During the Northwest Rebellion of 1885, women served as nurses for the first time in Canadian military history. From 1899 to 1902, women nurses supported Canadian troops in the Boer War. They served as a permanent, but separate, part of the Royal Canadian Army Medical Corps.

A permanent Canadian Nursing Service was created in the military in 1901. In 1906, female nurses became part of Canada's Regular Forces. During the First World War, more than 2800 women served with the Royal Canadian Army Medical Corps on hospital ships, in overseas hospitals, and in field ambulance units in combat zones.

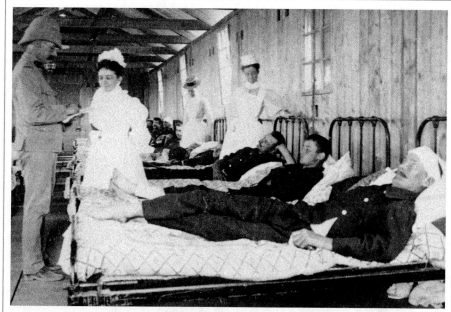

Why do you think women were permitted to serve as nurses during wartime when they were not encouraged to have careers during peacetime?

By the time the war ended in 1902, 7368 Canadian troops had served in South Africa. Twelve of the volunteers were women nurses who worked in military hospitals. They inspired hundreds of other women who later volunteered for such work in the First World War (1914–1918). Eighty-nine Canadians were killed in action, and another 130 died as a result of disease.

The British eventually won the Boer War. Canada had sent troops to fight in an Imperial struggle. When other Imperial disputes broke out, it was going to be more difficult for Canada to remain neutral. Despite what Laurier said on the matter, it set a precedent for Canada's policy in future wars.

THINKING It Over

1. How accurate was the prediction you made on page H 183 in the previous section of the chapter about what Laurier's compromise position would be if Britain called the dominions into a war? Explain.

2. What opinion do you think each of the following might have had about Canada's involvement in the Boer War? Discuss your ideas in a small group.
   a) Sir Wilfrid Laurier, b) Henri Bourassa, c) a nurse who volunteered for service in a field hospital, d) Lord Strathcona, and e) a British politician who is trying to get Canada to support the war.

3. In a mind map, organizer, or other visual representation, illustrate your own view of what Canada's position on sending troops to the Boer War should have been. Explain your position to a classmate.

4. At one time, matters such as race and gender were factors in whether a person was eligible to be a soldier. Make a list of criteria that you think should be factors in determining whether a person is suitable to be a soldier. Discuss your list with a classmate and explain the reasons for your choices.

Differing Views on War

The Canadians who volunteered to fight in the Boer War believed that they had a duty to aid their nation during wartime. So do most people who fight for their country.

A Trainee Soldier's View of War

A Canadian soldier described his horseback training in a letter to his father, in 1902.

> *Halifax, NS, January 7, 1902*
>
> *…we are having the most exciting time these days I have ever had in my life. Talk about a lacrosse or football match, why it is as tame as riding a broomstick—to what we are having now. We go down to the stables about 8:30 AM and saddle our chargers… and ready to move out of our stables at 9…*
>
> *It is great fun to be on the outer flank when we wheel. Of course the man on the inner flank just wheels his horse around on one point, but those who are on the outer part of the line must gallop like fury. I tell you it is great…*

A Doctor's View of the Boer War

In 1900, John McCrae was a 28-year-old lieutenant from Guelph, Ontario, who volunteered to go to the Boer War. He was a medical doctor and worked in the field hospitals assisting wounded soldiers. Once in Africa, he found that more troops were dying of disease than battle wounds. This frustrated McCrae. Here is how he described some of his experiences.

> *For absolute neglect and rotten administration, it is a model. I am ashamed of some members of my profession… Every day there are from 15 to 30 Tommies [British soldiers] dying from fever and dysentery. Every one that dies is sewn up in a blanket, and [one dollar is] taken out of the pay for the blanket. The soldier's game is not what it's cracked up to be.*

McCrae later became famous for his poem "In Flanders Fields," which is often read at Remembrance Day ceremonies.

What Do YOU Think?

1. For each extract, make a list of words to describe the emotions that the quotation stirs up in the reader. **k** **t**

2. Which of the lists do you think would best describe the feelings of most people in Canada at the end of the war? Explain. **t**

This painting depicts a battle in southern Africa in 1901. Which point of view do you think it represents? Explain.

Why Was the Royal Canadian Navy Created?

The disagreements over Canada's role in the Boer War marked the beginning of 15 years of military and political crises in Canada.

Europe Heads Toward War

In Europe, the threat of war grew during the early 1900s. Since the 1880s, European nations had been forming secret alliances. The Triple **Alliance** (1882) consisted of Germany, Italy, and Austria-Hungary. The Triple **Entente** (1907) included Great Britain, France, and Russia.

WORDS MATTER

alliance a union or agreement among groups working toward a common goal

entente an agreement to cooperate between opposing groups

dreadnoughts heavily armoured warships

European Alliances, 1914

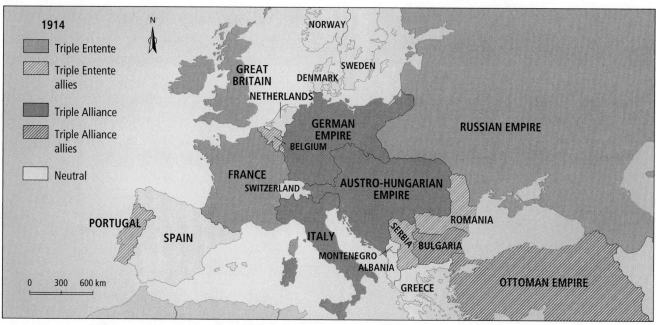

1914

Triple Entente

Triple Entente allies

Triple Alliance

Triple Alliance allies

Neutral

The division of Europe, showing the two major alliance systems

If a country belonging to one alliance system went to war with a country in the rival system, its allies would join in to help it. This meant that if a war broke out, it would be a major one as all six nations in the alliance systems would become involved.

The Dreadnoughts

If a war broke out between Britain and Germany, everyone expected that it would be a naval war. The ships of the opposing forces would go to sea, and huge naval battles would take place. When the war finally began in 1914, the reality was quite different. To get ready for this war, Britain and Germany began a program of building warships with much heavier armour than earlier vessels. These new ships were called **dreadnoughts**. This name came from the first British ship of this class to be built, the HMS Dreadnought. It entered service in 1906.

Asking the Dominions for Help

Britain wanted to have as many warships as possible under its command. In 1910, it sent a formal request to the dominions. To help defend the British Empire, the dominions were asked to

- build naval vessels and find crews for them

- place their ships under British command

- continue to pay for the maintenance of these vessels even though they were commanded by the British Navy

The British warship HMS Dreadnought. Such ships were very heavily armoured to protect them from enemy fire.

Canada's Response

In 1910, Laurier had been prime minister for 14 years. He had been through many crises in which English and French Canadians had taken opposing positions. He knew that Britain's request would cause new tensions among Canadians. How could Laurier create a solution that would satisfy both sides? Laurier thought about this for some time before responding to the British request. His government proposed the following

- Canada would create its own navy, to be called the Royal Canadian Navy.

- It would build and maintain warships for the defence of Canada.

- If Britain got involved in a war that involved Canada's interests, it would turn these warships over to Britain for the duration of the war.

- Only volunteers would crew on these vessels. No Canadian would be forced to fight under British command.

  From what you have already learned, do you think Laurier's compromise would satisfy both sides?

English Canadians

English Canadians held the same position they had supported during the Boer War crisis. Britain was Canada's closest ally, and Canada should provide whatever was needed, no strings attached.

During READING

Checkpoint
In your chart, list Laurier's compromises and attempted compromises in the "I read" section. Now write what you think each of these will mean for Canada's future in the "I Think" section. Go back and review the chapter to make sure you have them all.

French Canadians

French Canadians were shocked that Canada would even consider turning its warships over to the British, regardless of the war. Francophones wanted Canada to take a more independent position. They thought that Canada should not agree in advance to get involved in a war just because the British made the request.

Reaction to Laurier's Compromise

As you have seen, most English- and French-Canadians were uneasy about Laurier's compromise. Both sides of the debate were frustrated with Laurier for different reasons. Henri Bourassa began to organize opposition to the Liberals in Québec. In Ontario, the Conservatives gained more support.

The Royal Canadian Navy

The Naval Service Act of 1910 authorized the Canadian government to build warships. The first ones were to be bought from Britain, but the new ships were to be built in Canadian shipyards. A new college was established to train naval recruits. It was called the Royal Naval College of Canada, located in Halifax, Nova Scotia. **HMCS** *Rainbow* was stationed in Esquimalt, British Columbia. *HMCS Niobe* was stationed in Halifax.

The Royal Canadian Navy was not really an effective force at this time. It had too few ships. It was necessary to split the ships between east- and west-coast ports. Contrary to earlier predictions, the First World War never really developed into a full naval war. It was the Canadian army forces that made the most impact in Europe. Historians remember the creation of the navy more for the political divisions it encouraged than for any of its accomplishments.

WORDS MATTER

HMCS His/Her Majesty's Canadian Ship

WEB LINK ●∙∙∙∙∙∙∙∙∙∙∙∙∙∙∙

For more information on the history of the Royal Canadian Navy, visit our Web site.

Gunnery officers and men aboard cruiser HMCS Niobe, one of the navy's two ships

Canada's World Military Role

Then

In the 1890s, Canada's small population and limited economy meant that it did not have much international influence. As it could not afford the expensive steam-powered and steel-hulled warships necessary for naval battles, it did not have much of a military presence, either. Overall, Canada relied on Britain for its defence.

It was not until 1910 that the Royal Canadian Navy was founded. Even so, it was not very strong. When the First World War began in 1914, the Canadian navy had only two warships. That war was to be a turning point. Once war was declared, Canada began to produce war materials at a rapid rate. Almost 420 000 soldiers served overseas in the Canadian Expeditionary Force. When peace returned in 1918, about 60 000 Canadians had died in the war.

Would this poster convince you to join the army? Why or why not?

Now

Internationally, Canada is not regarded as a front rank military nation. The Canadian Forces employ about 60 000 men and women. Canada has recently participated in wars such as the Gulf War against Iraq (1991), and the Afghanistan War (started in 2001). Both of these wars were approved by the United Nations (UN).

Canada's best-known military role has been as UN peacekeepers. UN members send troops into war zones to help bring about peace and stability, and to protect civilians. The UN has recently stationed troops in Rwanda and in Bosnia and Herzegovina. Peacekeeping can be dangerous work, and Canadian soldiers have died while on duty.

Look at these two recruitment posters and decide on the main message of each one. Compare the aims of each poster.

THINKING It Over

1. Compare the positions of a) English Canadians and b) French Canadians about the creation of Canada's navy and the use of Canadian soldiers in the Boer War. How similar or different a position did each group take during these two military crises?

2. Compare Laurier's compromise position during each of these crises. How effective a politician do you think he was, based on what you know about these events?

How Canada Became Involved in the First World War

During READING

Checkpoint

Look at a modern map of Europe. Do you see Bosnia and Herzegovina and Serbia? Look at a map of the same area during the 1980s. What was the region called then? What does this tell you about this part of Europe?

WORDS MATTER

heir one who inherits

assassination murder of a leader for political purposes

ultimatum a final demand or set of terms, the rejection of which may lead to use of force

mobilization preparing the army for war

In June 1914, Archduke Franz Ferdinand and his wife, Duchess Sophie, were on a "goodwill" visit to Sarajevo, a city in the area of the Austro-Hungarian Empire, now called Bosnia and Herzegovina. Franz Ferdinand was **heir** to the throne of Austria-Hungary. They were riding in an open car when a teenage assassin suddenly came up to their car. He shot Franz Ferdinand and Sophie from point-blank range.

Serbia was another area of the Austro-Hungarian Empire. The assassin belonged to a secret Serbian nationalist group that wanted Austria-Hungary to give up control of Bosnia and Herzegovina.

Some political organizations use violence in the hope that the authority they are opposing will give in to their demands and thereby avoid further violence (remember the Fenians from Chapter 2). Instead of giving in, Austria-Hungary chose to take a strong stand against Serbia.

Within six weeks of the **assassination**, all the major countries of Europe were at war. So were Canada and the other countries of the British Empire. To understand all this, look at the chain of events of the summer of 1914 (see page H 195).

WEB LINK •••••••••••••••••••••

For more information on the causes of the First World War, visit our Web site.

Archduke Franz Ferdinand and Duchess Sophie moments before they were assassinated on June 28, 1914

June 28

- Franz Ferdinand and Sophie assassinated in Sarajevo.

July 6

- Kaiser Wilhelm II of Germany promises German support for Austria-Hungary in any military action in Serbia.

July 23

- Austria-Hungary delivers a list of demands to Serbia. It requires Serbia to get rid of all anti-Austrian army officers, teachers, and government workers; to allow Austrian officials to enter Serbia to investigate the shootings; and to co-operate fully with the Austrian inquiry. It is an **ultimatum**. It threatens severe consequences unless Serbia agrees to every demand. Serbia agrees to some of them.

July 25

- Russia begins a partial **mobilization** in case war breaks out.

July 28

- Austria-Hungary rejects Serbia's response to its ultimatum. It declares war against Serbia.

July 30

- Austria-Hungary and Germany demand that Russia stop mobilizing within 12 hours. Russia ignores the demand.

July 31

- Austria-Hungary adjusts its military plans to include the possibility of war against Russia.
- Britain asks France and Germany to guarantee that they will not invade Belgium, which is located between the two countries. France agrees, but Germany does not.

August 1

- Germany declares war on Russia.

August 2

- Germany demands that Belgium allow German troops free passage to France, if France and Germany go to war.

August 3

- Germany declares war on France.

August 4

- German troops invade Belgium and Luxembourg to mount an attack on France.
- Britain demands that German troops leave Belgium by midnight. Germany does not reply. Britain declares war on Germany.
- Canada is automatically at war on Britain's side.

Edith Anderson, born in 1890 on the Six Nations Grand River Reserve, cared for wounded soldiers in France.

TO THE WOMEN OF CANADA

1. You have read what the Germans have done in Belgium. Have you thought what they would do if they invaded this Country?

2. Do you realize that the safety of your home and children depends on our getting more men **NOW**?

3. Do you realize that the one word "GO" from you may send another man to fight for our King and Country?

4. When the War is over and someone asks your husband or your son what he did in the great War, is he to hang his head because you would not let him go?

WON'T YOU HELP AND SEND A MAN TO ENLIST TO-DAY?

Why do you think a war poster targeted women? How effectively does this poster communicate its message to its intended audience? Explain.

Canada Prepares for War

Throughout the summer of 1914, the likelihood of war in Europe increased. Canadians watched with interest and horror. Prime Minister Robert Borden firmly believed that Canadians should fight if war broke out. He felt that this would improve Canada's position in the world, and gain it international respect. Laurier, now Leader of the Opposition in the House of Commons, personally supported Canadian participation as long as only volunteer forces were sent to the war.

There were only 3000 troops in the regular army and about 60 000 militia, so Canada was hardly a strong power, but a Canadian Expeditionary Force was created. The minister of militia, Sam Hughes, invited volunteers to join the armed forces. It was hoped that 25 000 would come to the new military camp in Québec. Thirty-three thousand showed up. On October 3, the first troops sailed for Britain.

Among the volunteers for the war were almost 4000 First Nations men, some of whom were excellent sharpshooters who later received military medals for their accomplishments. The First Nations volunteers included one woman, Edith Anderson, a descendant of Mohawk leader Joseph Brant. Anderson served as a nurse.

The First World War did not turn out to be anything like what many of the volunteers had expected. They thought it would be a great adventure and that they would be home by Christmas. In fact, the war dragged on for more than four years and resulted in more than 60 000 Canadian deaths. The First World War was a result of conflicts between stubborn politicians and spoiled royals. What began as a local dispute quickly grew into an event that affected all of Europe and most of the world. Most Canadians strongly supported Canada's entry into the war. However, support for the war was much lower in Québec than elsewhere in Canada, as had been the case in previous military crises. In later history courses, you will learn how crucial the First World War was to the history of Canada.

Wartime Propaganda

Propaganda is a communication technique used to persuade people to believe a particular point of view. Propaganda can be particularly effective in wartime, when a nation feels threatened. In a war, all sides tend to use propaganda. It is an effective way to influence people by playing on their emotions and fears and by including only partial information. Look at the Canadian First World War poster in the margin for an excellent example of wartime propaganda.

Why did the assassination develop into a huge war? Historians have many opinions. Some historians say that Kaiser Wilhelm II, the Emperor of Germany, is the key villain. They say that his guarantee of support to Austria-Hungary on July 6, 1914, gave that country added confidence. If Wilhelm had suggested a calmer approach, Austria-Hungary might not have declared war, but worked out a compromise with Serbia.

Kaiser Wilhelm

Tsar Nicholas

Other historians see Wilhelm's role as more positive. Maybe Germany did not believe that a war would result from its guarantee. If Serbia saw that Austria-Hungary had Germany's support, maybe it would agree to the ultimatum. It was not Wilhelm's fault that events got out of hand and Russia mobilized its army.

There are also historians who see Tsar Nicholas II, Emperor of Russia, as the major villain. These historians say that Austria-Hungary expected nothing more than a small war in Serbia. All of a sudden, Nicholas was mobilizing his entire army to support the Slavic people of Serbia. Germany could not risk war with both countries at the same time. So, Germany tried to defeat France in the west before the Russian army was fully prepared to invade Germany from the east. Germany declared war on France, invaded Belgium, and the war began.

Opponents of this view say that Nicholas acted in a heroic manner, defending a people who were being oppressed by Austria-Hungary. These same people believe that Nicholas recognized that Austria-Hungary would defeat Serbia, but what then? Would Austria-Hungary march into other countries such as Bulgaria and Romania? If so, this would threaten Russia's security.

On a scale of one to ten (with one representing a villain and ten representing a hero), where would you place (a) Kaiser Wilhelm, and (b) Tsar Nicholas? Unsure? Why?

THINKING It Over

1. Pick three dates from the timeline on page H 195 that you think were most important in the development of a war that involved all of Europe. Draw a picture or write a short poem to describe each event you choose.

2. As a class, hold a "horseshoe debate" on the question, Was Canada right to participate in the First World War? For help in debating, see page S 11. Before the debate, write down your answer to the question and your reasons. After the debate, write down your answer. Did the debate change your response? Why or why not?

What You Will Need

- two decks of playing cards
  ace = 1
  face cards = 10
  other cards = their numerical value
- two pieces of blank paper
- two pencils

How to Play

A. Work with another person. It is 1910, and each of you is trying to match Laurier's achievement in creating the Royal Canadian Navy. To manage this task, you need

- money
- volunteers
- a balanced position between English and French opinions on the subject
- enough free space in shipyards to build the warships

B. Each player shuffles a deck of cards and places it in front of the other player. Each player uses a separate deck to play the game.

C. Each player deals the top four cards face up on the playing surface, and sorts them into suits, from left to right. (♣ ♦ ♥ ♠) If you have more than one card in a given suit, place them one above the other on the playing surface.

Suit	Represents	Winning Range
♣	Money. You need $100 m.	10 or any face card (each number = $10 m)
♦	Volunteers. You need 1000 volunteers.	10 or any face card (each number = 100 volunteers)
♥	English/French support. You need 70%+.	10 or any face card (each number = 7%)
♠	Shipyard capacity. You need 5 ships.	10 or any face card (each number = 1/2 a ship)

D. You are trying to have four groups of cards at the same time that fall into the winning ranges as shown in the chart. If you do not need a card, place it face down in a discard pile.

E. In turn, the players draw the top card off their deck. If it is in the winning range, they may keep it. If not, place it in a discard pile. Keep count of your turns on the piece of paper.

F. Conditions change over time. You may have control over something at one time but that can slip away from you because of surprise events. To simulate this, every tenth turn you must discard one "winning range" (face up) card before you draw from the deck.

G. Continue repeating steps E and F until the game is over. If a player's deck runs out, the opposing player shuffles the discard pile and places it face down.

How to Win

The game lasts until one player has assembled four winning range groups of cards. Both players check and verify the cards are correct.

THINKING It Over

1. Did the winner generally lead throughout the game, or start to move ahead in the final rounds?

2. How do you think that this game illustrates some of the difficulties Laurier faced in creating a Canadian navy? Explain.

3. What improvements would you make to the game to make it more accurate, or easier to play?

PUTTING IT ALL TOGETHER

In this chapter, you learned how international affairs affected Canada and promoted change. English-speaking and French-speaking Canadians often had different points of view on key issues. Prime Minister Laurier made compromises, such as sending 7000 volunteer troops to the Boer War and creating a military navy—this seemed to satisfy both sides.

The First World War erupted in 1914. Because of its past historical ties, Canada sided with Britain. More than 60 000 Canadians died in the battle. The war had a tremendous influence on the further development of Canada and its international reputation.

After READING

Forming Conclusions

In the "Therefore" section of the chart you started at the beginning of the chapter, write a conclusion based on the facts you have noted in the "I read" section and the opinions you have formed in the "I think" section.

I read	I think
Therefore	

THINKING It Through

1. Write two newspaper editorials that might have been written in 1899. 🄣 🄒 🄐

   a) The first editorial supports Canada's compromise solution over its participation in the Boer War.

   b) The second opposes it. (You can take the position adopted by Henri Bourassa that it was too pro-Empire, or the position of many English Canadians that it was not pro-Empire enough.)

   Each editorial should be about 150 words in length. It should contain:

   • a headline

   • a summary of key events that focused Canadian attention on southern Africa

   • a statement of opinion on Canadian participation in the Boer War

   • the reasons for this position (for example, the benefits for Canada of adopting this position)

2. Choose four terms from the Words Matter boxes, or other words that were unfamiliar to you before reading this chapter. For each word, create a visual that conveys the meaning of the term. Design a poster incorporating your visuals. 🄚 🄣 🄒 🄐

Back to the Big Idea

How did social and economic factors, technology, and people promote change in Canada?

You have examined some of the changes that affected Canada in this era. You have learned that waves of immigrants flooded into the country. You have seen how cities and the economy grew. You have read how people began to demand reform in everything from women's rights to labour laws. You have studied the debates over Canada's role in the British Empire. You have discovered some of the tensions that existed between English and French Canadians, and the attempts to resolve them. You have seen how Canada became involved in an overseas conflict and how this affected its political position in the world. Through all these events, you have seen how Aboriginal people were affected.

Now that you have finished this unit, use graphic organizers to review what you have learned. Write a point-form list of reasons to answer the question, **How did social and economic factors, technology, and people promote change in Canada?**

Show That You Know

Review what you have written to answer the Big Idea question on the previous page. Now imagine that you have been hired by the federal government to produce a documentary presentation about the social and economic factors, technology, and people that promoted change in Canada in the period from 1885 to 1914. A documentary is a film or broadcast production that presents a factual report rather than a fictional drama.

Step 1 Choose your medium

You can present your findings in any of the following forms—a computer slide show, a video presentation, a live dramatic presentation, or as the script and directions for a television program.

Tip: Skim through the chapters of Unit 3 to help you to identify subtopics that you can include.

Step 2 Identify your subtopics

Identify no more than four items that you will examine in your documentary, and limit your research to these items.

Tip: Review the following features of the Skills Tool Kit:

- Asking Questions (page S 8)
- Researching a Topic (page S 6)
- Using Primary and Secondary Sources (page S 4)

Make sure to complete steps 2–4 of The Inquiry/Research Process (page S 2).

Step 3 Research your topic

Use a variety of primary and secondary materials to find key information to include.

Step 4 Create your documentary

Take your research information and put it together in an organized manner. Present information about one subtopic at a time. Create an introduction and a conclusion for your documentary.

Tip: Test parts of your documentary on family or friends (not classmates) to make sure that it is clear and lively.

Step 5 Present your documentary

Clear communication is a vital part of presenting your findings. Make sure that you present your information in a creative and scholarly manner. Carefully review your documentary as you create each subtopic for Step 4 to make sure that it will hold your audience's interest.

GLOSSARY

act a piece of legislation passed by parliament

advocate to recommend or support by argument

alliance a union or agreement among groups working toward a common goal

assassination murder of a leader for political purposes

balance of trade the difference between a country's imports and exports

Canadiens Canadians of French descent

capitalists people who built and owned businesses

census an official count of the population including information such as occupation, gender, age, religion, and ethnic origin

colonial preference giving favoured treatment to colonial trade

concentration camps special prisons for civilians who are political prisoners or prisoners of war

Confederation the union of provinces and territories forming Canada

conference a meeting for discussion of information or ideas

conservative preferring what is safe and familiar rather than wanting change and risk

Corn Laws British laws that governed the import and export of grain; in Britain, cereal grains were called corn

cottage system the manufacture of goods made by many people working individually in their homes

country-born people of mixed British and First Nations ancestry

court martial military trial

Crown a symbolic term referring to the monarch of a country

dominions independent countries that had been British colonies

dreadnoughts heavily armoured warships

duties/tariffs taxes on imported goods

emigrate leave one's country to settle elsewhere

entente an agreement to cooperate between opposing groups

entrepreneurs people who start or organize businesses

equal representation each region has the same number of elected representatives

exploit to take advantage of someone or something for one's own benefit

expropriate legally take property from its owner

external trade trade with countries and colonies outside of British North America

factory system the manufacture of goods made by many people working together in a large building

federal relating to a system that has a central government as well as provincial or state governments

Fenians an Irish nationalist organization founded in the U.S. that encouraged revolutionary activity to overthrow British rule in Ireland

foreign investment money invested in companies in a country other than one's own

free trade trade without duties or tariffs

gold rush a mass movement to an area where gold has been discovered

guerrilla tactics fighting by means of ambush and surprise attacks

heir one who inherits

HMCS His/Her Majesty's Canadian Ship

homesteads lands turned over to settlers for the purpose of farming

House of Commons the house of parliament that is elected by voters and is based on representation by population

hypothesis an educated guess or theory that has not been proven

imperial of concern to an entire empire

incorporated formally organized as a community with its own local government

Indian the historic term for First Nations people. Though we now use the term First Nations, historic documents use "Indian"; the federal government still has a Department of Indian Affairs, as was assigned at Confederation

Indian status the term that identified people for recognition as Indians

industrialize develop industries, especially manufacturing industries

intercolonial trade trade among the BNA colonies

land speculators people who buy cheap property hoping its price will rise

Manifest Destiny the belief that the United States had a duty to take over all the land of North America

Métis people of mixed European and First Nations ancestry

mobilization preparing the army for war

movement a group of people with a common goal

multiculturalism many culturally distinct groups living within a society

navvies labourers; it is an abbreviation of the word "navigator" in the old-fashioned sense of a canal builder

nobility members of the highest class of society

panning for gold searching for gold by collecting, then washing gold-bearing gravel in a pan

pemmican dried meat, pounded and flavoured with fat and local berries

placers sandbanks containing minerals, in this case gold

political deadlock a situation where progress cannot be made because the parties involved do not agree

precedent something that has occurred that may be used as a reason for doing the same thing later

prejudice unfavourable feelings, opinions, or attitudes regarding a racial, religious, or national group

prohibition total abolition of the sale of alcohol

proportional representation a voting system in which a political party gets the same proportion of seats in government as the proportion of votes it received

prospectors people seeking valuable minerals, especially gold

provisional government a temporary government put in place until a permanent one is established

quarantine to keep people in isolation from others to prevent the spread of disease

racist intolerance of other races or the belief in the superiority of one race over another

reciprocity an exchange of privileges or favours as a basis for relations between two countries

referendum a vote by the citizens on a proposed government action

repealed abolished

representation by population the number of elected representatives is determined by the size of the population in the region represented

republic a system of government that has no monarchy; all the politicians are elected

reserves land set aside for exclusive use by First Nations people

riding the area represented by an elected official

Rupert's Land a vast area of land in northern and western Canada, owned by the HBC. The government of Canada purchased this land in 1869.

scrip a coupon that could be exchanged for land

Senate the house of parliament that is appointed by the prime minister and is based on equal representation for various regions

social gospel a movement that emphasized the application of Christian principles to social problems

staking a claim placing stakes around a chosen area of land and then registering ownership at the land office

stampeders people who rushed to gold strikes

tariffs/duties taxes on imported goods

temperance literally means moderation, but when used in relation to alcohol it meant to abstain

treason an act of betrayal or disloyalty to one's country or government

treaties legal documents outlining agreements between nations

ultimatum a final demand or set of terms, the rejection of which may lead to use of force

veins streaks of minerals in rock

wards of the state people who are under the care of the government; usually children or people who are unable to be responsible for themselves

INDEX